Economic Development
50 Years On
1958–2008

Edited by
Michael Mulreany

IPA
INSTITUTE OF PUBLIC
ADMINISTRATION

First published in 2009
by the
Institute of Public Administration
57–61 Lansdowne Road
Dublin 4
Ireland

www.ipa.ie

British Library Cataloguing in Publication Data
A catalogue record for this book is available from the British Library.

ISBN: 978-1-904541-81-3

Front cover photographs:
At the *Economic Development – 50 Years On* conference:
Top: Poet Thomas Kinsella with T. K. Whitaker
Bottom left: Historian and broadcaster John Bowman with T. K. Whitaker
Bottom right: T. K. Whitaker with Minister for Finance Brian Lenihan TD

Back cover photograph:
At the *Economic Development – 50 Years On* conference: (l–r) Tom Considine, Sean Cromien, Tomás Ó Cofaigh, T. K. Whitaker, Maurice Doyle, Paddy Mullarkey and David Doyle

Cover design by Alice Campbell, Dublin
Typeset by Computertype, Dublin
Printed in Ireland by ColourBooks Ltd, Dublin

Contents

Contributors

Frank Barry is Professor of International Business and Economic Development at Trinity College Dublin. He holds a PhD in Economics from Queen's University, Ontario, and is a specialist in the areas of international trade and foreign direct investment. Amongst his publications are an edited volume on *Understanding Ireland's Economic Growth* (Macmillan Press, 1999) and a co-authored book on *Multinational Firms in the World Economy* (Princeton University Press, 2004). His current research projects include 'Foreign Ownership of Irish Business under Protectionism' and 'Export Profits Tax Relief, 1956: Historical Origins of Ireland's Low Corporation-Tax Regime'.

John Bowman, PhD, is a broadcaster and historian. He is author of *De Valera and the Ulster Question, 1917–1973*. He presents current affairs and historical programmes on RTÉ radio and television.

Nick Crafts is Professor of Economic History at University of Warwick. Previous academic positions include London School of Economics, Oxford University and visiting appointments at UC Berkeley and Stanford. He was elected Fellow of the British Academy in 1992 and is a former Editor of the *Economic History Review* (1999–2004) and President of the Economic History Society (2004–7). Among his recent publications are: 'European Economic Growth, 1950–2005: An Overview' (Centre for Economic Policy Research); 'Recent European Economic Growth: Why Can't It Be Like the Golden Age?', *National Institute Economic Review* (2007); 'TFP Growth in British and German Manufacturing, 1950–1996', *Economic Journal*, with Terence C. Mills; *Interpreting Ireland's Economic Growth* (2005); background paper for UNIDO, *Industrial Development Report*.

David Doyle has been Secretary General at the Department of Finance since 1 July 2006. From 2001 to 2006, he was Second Secretary General in charge of the Sectoral Policy Division in the Department, where he was responsible for sectoral economic and social development across all activities of government; commercial state enterprises; public private partnerships and the spending dimension of the annual Budget. Prior to that, he held various positions in the Department in the Budget and Economic, Banking, Finance and International, and Sectoral Policy Divisions. Before joining the Department, he worked in the Department of Education and in Texaco. He is a graduate of UCD where he studied Economics, History and Education.

Ronan Fanning, PhD (Cantab), MRIA is Professor Emeritus of Modern History at University College Dublin. His major publications are *The Irish Department of Finance 1922–58* (1978) and *Independent Ireland* (1983); he has also published widely on British–Irish relations. He is joint editor of *Documents on Irish Foreign Policy*, the sixth volume (1939–41) of which was published in November 2008, and of the multi-volume *Dictionary of Irish Biography* (2009). His latest book, co-authored with Michael Lillis, is *The Lives of Eliza Lynch: Scandal and Courage* (Gill and Macmillan, 2009).

Garret FitzGerald obtained a BA (1946) and a PhD (1968) from University College Dublin and also graduated from King's Inns, Dublin, and was called to the Bar. Having worked in Aer Lingus for several years, he began a new career in 1958 as an economic consultant and academic, lecturing in Economics and in the Affairs of the European Economic Community (EEC) at UCD. He was elected as the first Chairman of the Irish Council of the European Movement. He was elected to Seanad Éireann in 1965, and to the Dáil in 1969. In 1978, he was appointed Minister for Foreign Affairs; in 1975, he led the first Irish presidency of the European Council of Ministers; in 1977, he was unanimously elected as leader of Fine Gael; in 1985, he successfully negotiated the Anglo-Irish Agreement with British Prime Minister Margaret Thatcher. He was twice elected as Taoiseach – in 1981 for nine months and in 1983 for four-and-a-half years. In 1987, he resigned as leader of the Fine Gael party, and in 1992 retired from the Dáil. Dr FitzGerald is currently Chancellor of the National University of Ireland, elected in November 1997, upon the resignation of Dr T. K. Whitaker. He continues to be involved in a number of private companies as director, in several consultancies, in lecturing and in journalism; he was the Ireland correspondent for the BBC, the *Economist* and the *Financial Times* and continues to write a weekly column in the *Irish Times*. He is the author of books on a range of political and economic issues. In 1991, he published his autobiography, *All in a Life*.

Tom Garvin BA, MA (NUI), PhD (Georgia), is Professor Emeritus of Politics at University College Dublin; Alumnus, Wilson Centre, Washington, DD; and Fulbright scholar. He is also a member of the Royal Irish Academy. Among his publications are: *1922–The Birth of Irish Democracy* and *Preventing the Future: Why was Ireland So Poor for So Long?*

Paul Hare has been Professor of Economics at Heriot-Watt University, Edinburgh, since 1985. He founded the Centre for Economic Reform and Transformation (CERT), an internationally respected research centre on the transition economies, in 1990. He has worked extensively on many of the transition economies, mostly on microeconomic issues such as privatisation, industrial restructuring and trade policy. This work has been supported by a mix of research grants from the UK and EU, and assignments from international financial institutions such as the World Bank and the IMF. Recent publications include a paper on North Korea and a contribution to a UNDP report on Macedonia. Professor Hare is currently working on institutions and development in the framework of a five-year research programme (2005–2010) on 'Improving Institutions for Pro-Poor Growth', based at the University of Manchester, funded by the UK's Department for International Development.

Brian Lenihan was first elected to the Dáil in 1996 in a by-election in the constituency of Dublin West, caused by the death of his father. He was re-elected in 1997 and 2002, topping the poll on each occasion. He was educated at Belvedere College Dublin, Trinity College Dublin (Foundation Scholar, First Class Hons BA Mod) and Cambridge University (First Class Hons LLB), and King's Inns. He lectured in Law at Trinity College 1984–96. He was called to the bar in 1984 and made senior counsel in 1997. From 2002 to 2007, he was Minister of State, with responsibility for children, at the Departments of Health and Children; Justice, Equality and Law Reform; and Education and Science. Prior to that, he was Chairperson of the All-Party Oireachtas Committee on the Constitution.

Michael Mulreany is Assistant Director General with responsibility for Education and Research at the Institute of Public Administration. He holds MA and PhD degrees in economics from University College Dublin. He has published widely on issues including public sector efficiency, cost benefit analysis, the EU, taxation and regulation. In 2004 he was instrumental in establishing the Whitaker School of Government and Management at the Institute of Public Administration.

Frances Ruane has been Director of the Economic and Social Research Institute since 2006. Her previous position was as Associate Professor in the Department of Economics at Trinity College Dublin, where she also held the posts of Director of the Policy Institute and Director of the MSc programme in Economic Policy

Studies. Earlier, she held positions in the Industrial Development Authority, the Central Bank of Ireland and Queen's University, Kingston, Ontario. Following her undergraduate studies in Economics, Politics and Statistics at University College Dublin, Frances Ruane studied at Nuffield College and was awarded the degrees of B.Phil. and D.Phil. from the University of Oxford. She is a member of the Royal Irish Academy, the Council of the Statistical and Social Inquiry Society of Ireland, the Council of Economic and Social Studies, and the editorial boards of the *Journal of International and Economic Policy* and the *International Review of Economics and Finance*. She is a member of the Higher Education Authority, the Health Research Board and the Council of Economic Advisers to the First Minister of Scotland. She has published extensively, especially in the fields of international economic and industrial development. Her current research interests centre on structural change induced by changing trade regimes and on exploring enterprise heterogeneity.

T. K. Whitaker entered the civil service in 1934. He was assigned to the Department of Finance in 1938 and became Secretary to the Department in 1956 at the age of 39. In 1969, he became Governor of the Central Bank of Ireland. He subsequently became Chancellor of the National University of Ireland, in 1976. He was a member of Seanad Éireann between 1977 and 1982 and a member of the Council of State between 1991 and 1998. He has served as president and chairman of a wide range of national bodies including the Commission of Inquiry into the Penal System (1984–5) and the Constitution Review Group (1995–6). He has been a board member both of Guinness and Bank of Ireland. Dr Whitaker was the main author of *Economic Development*, published in 1958. He is also author of *Financing by Credit Creation* (1947), *Interests* (1983) and *Protection on Free Trade – The Final Battle* (2006).

Foreword

The publication of *Economic Development* marked a turning point in our economic fortunes, and its author – Dr Ken Whitaker – is rightly credited with redirecting the course of Irish economic history. In September 2008, politicians, academics and others gathered to celebrate the fiftieth anniversary of its publication. I would like to thank the conference speakers and participants, as well as the Institute of Public Administration, for recognising the importance of this anniversary by organising the conference.

In recent years, we have witnessed in Ireland significant developments across a broad range of areas, notably in the social, economic, environmental and cross-border spheres. We now have living standards that are among the best in the world. These are developments that could have only been aspired to at the time of the publication of *Economic Development*. While the dramatic improvement in our economic fortunes over the last number of decades reflects many inter-related factors, the decision to abandon protectionism and to pursue a strategy of export-led growth was clearly the most important. Without trade liberalisation and the associated outward orientation of industrial policy, subsequent policy initiatives in other areas would have had a limited impact on living standards. Membership of the European Union, in particular, was a key factor in our global integration, and the benefits have been immense. Ireland joined the euro at its inception and this is providing great stability in the current exceptionally turbulent times.

It goes without saying that our successful journey and transformation over the years do not mean that the economy is immune to cyclical influences. But in today's very challenging economic environment many of the lessons of the past are still relevant. Maintaining the public finances on a sustainable path, investing for the future and pursuing competitiveness-enhancing wage developments were crucial, among other things, in our successful transition, and these policies remain key as we cope with, and ultimately emerge from, the current difficulties we face. We must also continue to embrace the global economy, but also to position ourselves so that we can respond to long-term structural changes that are occurring. In terms of the public finances, we will need to reconcile the various trade-offs that exist between the desirability for more public services, for relatively low levels of taxation and for appropriate levels of public indebtedness – our past experience clearly demonstrates that sustainable public finances are a prerequisite for continued economic and social prosperity.

When this conference took place last September, our economy was already facing very strong headwinds. These difficulties have intensified dramatically in the period since then. Activity has gone into reverse in most of our export markets, primarily as a result of severe global financial market disruption. Our cost competitiveness, which had already deteriorated significantly in recent years, has been further eroded by exchange-rate movements. The correction in the new-house-building sector has spread to other sectors of the domestic economy, with adverse implications for the labour market. We are now facing a significant contraction of domestic income levels. But our experience of past difficulties will stand to us. The recent Budget provides a roadmap for restoring the public finances to sustainability, while also providing measures to help underpin our banking system.

I am confident that the current challenges will be surmounted. Just over half a century ago, *Economic Development* charted the way forward, emphasising the need to embrace trade and investment and the importance of taking a long-term strategic view. These are as relevant today as they were then and it is worth reading the contributions and reflections in the rest of this publication in that light.

David Doyle
Secretary General
Department of Finance
May 2009

Acknowledgements

This book is the outcome of concerted effort. At the heart of this effort are the authors. Not to be overlooked are the staff who helped organise the conference on which the book is based.

In producing this volume, Patricia Ryan and Emma Culleton epitomised efficiency in providing the final text, and Emer Ryan, Eileen Kelly and Carolyn Gormley seamlessly progressed the production of the finished book. The IPA Library successfully responded to each request for relevant information.

I wish to express my gratitude to David Doyle, the Secretary General of the Department of Finance, to Jim O'Brien, Second Secretary General, and to other members of the Department's staff who were supportive at various stages.

Finally I wish to acknowledge the contribution of Ken Whitaker with whom it has been a privilege to work.

Michael Mulreany

1

Grey Book – Golden Jubilee
An Introduction to *Economic Development*

Michael Mulreany

In his essay on T. K. Whitaker, published in the centenary essays of the National University of Ireland (2008), Ronan Fanning recounted the words of a candidate taking the BA examination in history in University College Dublin in 1999:

> 'The person choosing to read a long survey of Irish history, for example from 1600 to the present day, is letting him or herself in for a long tale of misery and hardship. Cromwell, the Famine, emigration, independence but seemingly little improvement in the country. Then, suddenly, towards the end of our hypothetical book, our reader comes across a chapter with a title such as "New Beginnings" or "Turning the Tide".… The Messiah, in the shape of T.K. Whittaker (sic) has arrived.…'

This assessment by the anonymous and time-pressed student captures the historical importance of Whitaker and the key work, *Economic Development*, with which he is inextricably linked. Professional historians, reasoning more coolly, come to much the same conclusion. Murphy (1975) viewed *Economic Development* as a 'new departure'. Foster, in his history of modern Ireland (1988) argued that *Economic Development* was a 'watershed', a word also used by Ferriter (2006). And in 2007, Foster judged Whitaker to be 'the most brilliant and influential civil servant of his generation'. These opinions, of course, are shared not only among historians but among economists, sociologists, political scientists, public administrators and policy analysts – in itself a unique watershed in Irish opinion: few, if any, dissenting.

1

Post-War Economic Growth in Europe

The half-century that separates us from the publication of *Economic Development* clouds our view. We should bear in mind that the 1950s saw a major resurgence in Western European economies due, variously, to abundant and cheap labour, inexpensive technology and a recovery of optimism among investors. Labour was plentiful and cheap because of the inexorable long-term drift of people from agriculture, and the availability, at least in the short term, of workers from Eastern and Southern Europe. Cheap technology, which boosted productivity, was available from a generously supportive USA, which had opened up a 'technology gap' between itself and Western Europe. Optimism among investors flowed from the development of the new international post-war economic order and the steadily growing confidence that Keynesian demand management could harness the business cycle.

These factors, allied with improved communications, cheap and secure energy supplies, the need to repair wartime destruction and some $13 billion of US grants under the Marshall Plan, yielded unprecedented high rates of growth. Maddison (1987) has calculated that average compound rates of growth in GDP between 1950 and 1973 were 5.9 per cent in Germany, 5.1 per cent in France and 3.0 per cent in the UK. Eichengreen (2007) notes that Western Europe grew more than twice as fast from 1950 to 1973 as it did over the whole of the nineteenth and early twentieth century.

Olsen (1982) has argued that there were other positive factors of an institutional nature at play: war had destroyed, in the defeated nations, traditional rigid economic structures and vested interests and replaced them with new structures conducive to economic growth. This argument helps explain, for example, how co-determination between labour and management in Germany contributed to the Wirtschaftswunder; but as Eichengreen (2007) contends, it is inconsistent with the actual record of institutional continuity in the form of France's farm lobby and Germany's unions. Whatever the balance of truth between these latter institutional arguments, what is clear is that there was unprecedented growth in Western Europe in the 1950s.

The Irish Economy in the 1950s

Things were very different in the Irish economy during the 1950s. Table 1 lays out the disappointing facts of economic life. In 1958, the year when *Economic Development* was published, GNP was around £600m, the equivalent of over €15,900m in 2008 terms. Ireland's GNP figure for 2008 was €154bn, almost ten times the equivalent 1958 figure. Clearly the economic landscape was dramatically different fifty years ago.

Table 1: *Expenditure on Gross National Product at Current and Constant Market Prices*

Category	1953	1954	1955	1956	1957	1958	1959	1960	1961	1962
Personal expenditure on consumer goods and services	383.3	390.7	421.1	422.4	431.1	456.9	465.5	495.5	526.9	566
Net expenditure by public authorities on current goods and services	61.9	63.1	64.7	68.7	67.7	70.7	74.1	78.3	82.5	91
Gross domestic physical capital formation	87.4	80.4	101.2	82.6	72.7	71.9	104.8	98.4	107.4	130
Net Expenditure by the rest of the world	-7.0	-5.5	-35.5	-14.4	+9.2	-1.0	-8.7	-0.8	+1.2	-13
Gross national product at current market prices	525.6	528.7	551.5	559.3	580.7	598.5	635.7	671.4	718.0	774
Gross national product at constant market prices. Base 1953=100	100.0	101.1	102.9	101.9	102.9	99.9	104.4	110.3	115.6	118.5

Source: National Income and Expenditure 1962

Table 2: *Percentage Distribution of National Income by Sectors of Origin*

Sector	1953	1954	1955	1956	1957	1958	1959	1960	1961	1962
						per cent				
Agriculture	29.1	27.0	28.2	25.7	27.4	24.9	25.4	24.3	23.6	22.5
Industry	26.2	27.4	26.8	27.6	26.0	27.1	27.4	28.2	29.0	30.0
Distribution, transport and communications	15.0	15.4	15.2	15.5	15.0	15.3	15.5	15.7	16.0	16.3
Other domestic	17.4	17.8	18.1	19.2	19.2	20.2	20.1	20.2	20.0	20.2
Public administration and defence	5.7	5.6	5.5	5.8	5.6	5.7	5.4	5.4	5.3	5.3
Emigrants' remittances	2.5	2.5	2.4	2.4	2.5	2.5	2.4	2.4	2.3	2.0
Other foreign income	4.1	4.3	3.8	3.8	4.2	4.2	3.8	3.8	3.8	3.7
Total national income	100	100	100	100	100	100	100	100	100	100

Source: National Income and Expenditure 1962

The national gloom, which *Economic Development* helped to pierce, is understandable when one considers that, as shown in Table 1, using constant 1953 prices, there was a year-on-year decline in GNP between 1955 and 1956, and also that the GNP in 1958 was less than in 1953.

Table 2 also helps to evoke the times by illustrating the relative importance of agriculture and reminding us how emigrants' remittances featured, albeit at around 2.5 per cent, as a separately designated sector of GNP.

The reasons for Ireland's poor growth performance were many. The industrial base was small and ill-prepared to accept either excess labour from agriculture or technology transfer from the US. Within industry, the size of enterprise was small and ill-equipped to capture economies of scale. The dominant export market was the UK, which was among the slowest growing of the major European economies. The reliance of manufacturing industry on imports meant that any growth of industry risked causing short-term balance of payments problems. The greatest handicap was self-inflicted – a form of economic nationalism, really economic isolationism, which protected native industry behind import tariffs and discouraged inward foreign investment. Yes, it was true that the new state in the 1920s did not have the industrial base to supply basic necessities such as shoes, clothing and furniture and that, under protectionist policies, the volume of production had increased almost three times. However, it was clear by the mid-1950s that inward-looking policies were failing to provide an adequate standard of living. This perceived failure of existing economic policies was in itself a powerful impetus towards change.

Little wonder, therefore, that *Economic Development* identified a 'mood of despondency', and 'sense of anxiety' and declared the need to 'buttress confidence' and 'avert economic decadence'. Peppered throughout the document are numerous reminders of how underdeveloped Ireland was – just 60,000 pupils in secondary schools, of whom 24,000 were from the four counties Dublin, Cork, Limerick and Waterford (page 115); 82.5 per cent of industrial establishments employed fewer than 50 persons (page 152); cheese exports of only £20,370 (page 86); agricultural soils so deficient in phosphate that cattle showed clinical symptoms of aphosphorosis (page 64). In a telling passage, Whitaker (page 5) wrote:

After 35 years of native government people are asking whether we can achieve an acceptable degree of economic progress. The common talk amongst parents in the towns, as in rural Ireland, is of their children having to emigrate as soon as their education is completed in order to be sure of a reasonable livelihood.

Economic Development – **Key Features**

In a minute to the Minister of Finance, dated 12 December 1957, Whitaker formally described the programme that he and his colleagues had been working on since May of that year. It would consist of three elements: an outline of the state of the economy, indications of specific forms of productive developments and a statement of the principles to be followed.

The early chapters outline the state of the economy; for example Chapter 2 presents the dreary particulars: average income per head in Ireland was half that of Denmark and Britain, a third of that in Canada and a fifth of that in the US. Unemployment, not allowing for underemployment, was 9.2 per cent in 1957, even with 40,000 people emigrating: an emigration rate of 13.4 per 1,000, the highest in Western Europe. To complete the dismal picture, savings were low, private investment inadequate and productivity poor; there was insufficient training in management, and taxes were relatively high.

The specific forms of productive development considered by *Economic Development* are interwoven with the outline of sectors of the economy – agriculture, fisheries and forestry, industry and tourism. Some of the recommendations seem quirkily specific, due of course to the underdevelopment of the economy, the limited range of options available and the fact that we are looking back from a more sophisticated economy at a remove of half a century. Hence we read recommendations about the development possibilities for shooting estates, sea-angling, motels, biscuits and sweets, whiskey and gin, electricity and steel, turf and fertiliser, fishmeal plants, chocolate crumb, smoked and jellied eel and carrageen. We relive debates of the time regarding the relative merits of the Irish Shorthorn and Friesian cow and of the Irish Large White and Landrace pig – an evocation of an era of cattle treks from Munster through Connacht to Leinster, and pig smuggling from Northern Ireland – all conveyed in a model of clear administrative writing.

What makes *Economic Development* of true historical significance are the principles it enunciates against a background of inward-looking economic policies and traditional agricultural policies. Hence, for example, its emphasis on grassland and profitable export prospects for livestock contrasted with the traditional importance of tillage. Most importantly, *Economic Development* looked beyond protectionism (page 160) as follows:

> further industrial development must be largely on the basis of production for export markets and freer trade in Europe must be faced in due course, we can no longer rely on extensive tariff or quota protection.... A readiness to welcome foreign capital is a necessary complement to efforts to secure foreign participation in industrial development.

Economic Development was explicit in emphasising the importance of productive investment but was clear that, in addition to economic and technological factors, growth depended on a range of social, psychological and political factors. It underlined the role of education, skills, research and the application of scientific advances; the encouragement of initiative and the will to work; efficiency in organisation and management; the reduction of restrictive practices; and the need to gain the co-operation of trade unions.

Of course it is not a flawless document. Some lines of argument – for example, 'The easing of incomes in Ireland will however be a matter of raising farm incomes through increased output at lower unit costs' (page 27) – were undermined by the actual trend of growth toward industry, tourism and services more generally. It is easy to understand how agriculture was seen as a source of immediate gain; nonetheless, it is surprising to a modern reader to find that one-third of the chapters are directly devoted to agriculture – this rises to almost half the chapters if one includes forestry, fishing, turf, fertiliser, and industries based on agriculture. It is hard to understand how *Economic Development* could claim that there was virtual satisfaction of social investment needs in housing, schools and hospitals, over wide areas of the state. While acknowledging the importance of education, this was overly focused on agricultural education. The introduction of 'free education', with its positive impact on growth, came eight years later. The need for better organisation and increased productivity in the public service, a mandatory reflex in recent economic plans, gets little attention and is dealt with as a way to help stabilise and reduce taxation; a somewhat ironic oversight given that *Economic Development* itself was a model of organisation and productivity in the public service.

But to dwell on these points is to miss the key issue, which is that *Economic Development* redirected economic debate and policy toward achieving efficiency, competing in foreign markets and attracting foreign capital. Ireland first applied for membership of the EEC in 1961, three years after the publication of *Economic Development*; eventual membership in 1973, combined with the policy template of export orientation and openness to foreign capital advocated in *Economic Development*, paved the way to unprecedented growth levels in subsequent decades.

The immediate impact of the policies advocated by *Economic Development* was more subdued, reflecting the limited policy levers and resources available at the time. *Economic Development* had only one macroeconomic target and it was rather coy about it, due both to shortages of information and lack of input–output analysis of the Irish economy. It stated (page 125),

Between 1949 and 1956 the volume of gross national product increased at an annual rate of about 1%. It is not possible to say with any degree of certainty what effect the proposals made in this study would have in accelerating this rate of increase. However ... there is good reason to believe that, if the proposals were adopted, the rate of increase in the volume of gross national product, could, in time be doubled.

Table 3, which includes the Central Statistics Office revisions of the figures presented in Table 1, shows that GNP growth at around 4 per cent per annum exceeded that alluded to in *Economic Development*. A resurgence of growth in the European economy ensured that *Economic Development*, and the first *Programme for Economic Expansion* which flowed from it, had the good fortune to be buoyed along by the international tide.

Economic Development and the *Programme for Economic Expansion*

Whitaker and his colleagues began work in May 1957 on what was to become *Economic Development* in what was, in effect, a self-catalysed public sector initiative. The team that worked on *Economic Development* included three officials, Charlie Murray, Maurice Doyle and Tomás Ó Cofaigh, each of whom was to follow Whitaker in becoming Secretary General of the Department of Finance and Governor of the Central Bank. Whitaker constantly, as in his contribution to this volume, acknowledges the input of the full team which also included Maurice Horgan, Dónal Ó Loinsigh, Seámus O Ciosáin, Jim Dolan and Brendan Menton.

Whitaker informed the Minister for Finance, at first orally, and then by a minute, mentioned above, dated 12 December 1957, which was circulated for information of the Government. The sequence of events that unfolded can be followed in Fanning's authoritative history of the Department of Finance (1978). The government decided that other departments should assist the work and, by May 1958, a first draft was ready. The draft was sent, on foot of a government decision, to departments and state-sponsored bodies for urgent examination, and an amended draft was submitted by the Minister for Finance to government in July. In May and June, the draft had been read and favourably commented upon by staff at the World Bank, albeit working in an informal capacity. By late July, the government had commenced the process of drafting a White Paper based on *Economic Development*. The *Programme for Economic Expansion* was duly published as a White Paper on 12 November, and *Economic Development*, the seminal work from which it derived, was published on 22 November and, unusually for the Irish public service, was explicitly associated with T. K. Whitaker. It became colloquially known as the 'Grey Book' though Whitaker felt it was light green – a colour purist might prefer to call it light beige, sand or, appropriately, champagne.

Table 3: *Expenditure on Gross National Product at Current and Constant Market Prices*

Category	1958	1959	1960	1961	1962	1963	1964	1965
					£ million			
Personal expenditure on consumer goods and services	459.3	467.2	497.8	523.5	562.8	599.4	672.8	715
Net expenditure by public authorities on current goods and services	70.7	74.1	78.4	84.0	91.8	100.0	120.0	130
Gross domestic physical capital formation	72.1	104.9	99.9	116.4	139.1	159.0	190.4	215
Exports of goods and services	172.6	179.9	200.9	235.2	236.5	263.1	296.4	306
less Imports of goods and services	−206.0	−220.2	−235.6	−270.5	−287.0	−322.4	−367.7	−395
Net factor income from abroad	32.4	31.6	33.9	36.5	37.1	37.2	39.9	47
Gross national product at current market prices	601.1	637.5	675.3	725.1	780.3	836.3	951.8	1018
Gross national product at constant market prices	100.0	104.2	109.8	114.9	118.4	123.4	128.9	132.1

Source: National Income and Expenditure 1965

The White Paper, a much smaller document at fifty pages compared to the 250 pages of its progenitor, is clearly based on *Economic Development* but differs in certain respects. For example, it clearly sets a 2 per cent target for growth of GNP for the period of 1959–1964, and retains a more important role for tillage in relation to grassland and cattle than that envisaged by *Economic Development*. It also sidesteps politically awkward suggestions in *Economic Development* such as the need to site industry near the larger centres of population.

McCarthy (1990) showed how both *Economic Development* and the *Programme for Economic Expansion* emerged from a debate about economic policy continuing from the late 1940s. Strands of the debate can be found in Ireland's programme for the allocation of Marshall aid, in the advice of consultants from the US and in policy statements by political parties, particularly as enunciated by Costello, MacBride and Lemass. Lemass, indeed, expressed an interest in Italian economic planning, as Whitaker did in French economic planning. Lemass also, it must be acknowledged, as early as the late 1920s held views favourable to free trade. *Economic Development* must, therefore, be seen in the context of varied well-springs of economic thinking.

Against this background, however, *Economic Development* continues to stand out, while other contributions have receded. It was the seminal growth-oriented document arising out of reasoned analysis from the centre of Ireland's political and administrative system. In a way that seems startling today, it involved senior public servants seizing a measure of initiative and testing the limits of administrative authority. It would be barely conceivable today that a group of senior public servants would work on a major work of analysis and policy advice without the prior sanction, or indeed clear knowledge, of the relevant ministers. This is somewhat understandable, however, when one bears in mind the role of the Department of Finance at that time as 'general staff' to the Government (Public Services Organisation Review Group 1969).

It stands out also for its clear-eyed analysis of the difficulties Ireland faced; it does not shirk from declaring that 'the national candle cannot be burned at both ends'; it saw that 'research and efficiency go hand in hand' and, tellingly, that 'the real shortage is of ideas'. It understood that setting reasonably attainable national targets is an aspect of good leadership – possibly the earliest reference to leadership in Irish official literature. And it identified, in particular, the need to enlist and enthuse the young. It made politically difficult recommendations such as the move from tillage to grassland and the need to site industry close to major centres of population, and it signalled a break with the past when, for example, it stated (pp. 5–6) 'the greatest fault lies in pursuing a policy after it has proved to be unsuitable or ineffective'. It reiterated the importance of productive investment and pointed the way to outward-looking economic policies. In essence, it changed the way Ireland approached and made policy.

Celebrating Fifty Years of *Economic Development*

This volume contains a number of essays to celebrate fifty years of *Economic Development* – the golden jubilee of the Grey Book! It draws together distinguished national and international contributors providing a range of perspectives. From the Department of Finance, we include a foreword from David Doyle, Secretary General of the Department – the role occupied by Whitaker in 1958 – and Opening Comments from the Minister for Finance delivered at the IPA Conference in 2008 to mark the anniversary of *Economic Development*.

The articles that follow were prepared for the conference. In 'Looking Back to 1958', T. K. Whitaker reviews the background to *Economic Development* and the first *Programme for Economic Expansion*. Against the background of the current recession, he comments, as pertinently now as in 1958, 'it is only if we are educated, skilled and enterprising enough to produce goods and services commanding a high margin of gross profit or 'added value' that we can expect high and rising living standards'.

The three articles that follow give a range of historical perspectives. Professor Ronan Fanning of University College Dublin examines the political context, both nationally and internationally, from which *Economic Development* emerged. Professor Tom Garvin, also of UCD, looks at the post-war period 1945–61 through the lens of the national newspapers, a major repository of public commentary and opinion which helps capture the spirit of the times. Former Taoiseach and prolific author, Dr Garret FitzGerald, adds to our understanding of the historical contexts of *Economic Development* in his comments on Ireland's economic recovery in the 1950s.

The remaining articles have a more decidedly economic flavour. Professor Nick Crafts of the London School of Economics and the University of Warwick looks at Ireland's 'Celtic Tiger' growth in international and historical perspective. Professor Paul Hare from Heriot-Watt University continues the international perspective by drawing lessons from growth and development experiences around the world and traces some of the implications for Ireland. Professor Frank Barry of Trinity College Dublin looks at debates in Ireland on protectionism and free trade and at some theoretical underpinning of Whitaker's position. To round off proceedings, Professor Frances Ruane of the Economic and Social Research Institute examines some resonances for current economic policy-making from *Economic Development* – a fitting tribute to the authority and attention it still commands.

Historian John Bowman, who chaired the conference, brings together material from the questions and answers sessions, capturing the responses to a range of interesting queries.

The volume concludes with a facsimile reproduction of *Economic Development*. This allows the interested reader to follow the analysis from the outline of the economy, through the principles put forward both to address defects and to realise opportunities, to the suggested forms of productive investment.

This publication adds to the Institute of Public Administration's long association with T. K. Whitaker. In 1956, the year of his appointment as Secretary of the Department of Finance, the Institute published, in its journal *Administration*, Whitaker's paper, 'Capital Formation, Saving and Economic Progress', which he had read to the Social and Statistical Inquiry Society of Ireland in May of that year. In 1983, the IPA published *Interests*, a collection of his articles. In 2004, the Institute brought its education and research activities together under the title the Whitaker School of Government and Management. Most recently, in 2006, the IPA published both his *Protection or Free Trade: The Final Battle,* an important record of the policy debates on free trade, and *Retrospect 2006–1916*, a personal retrospective. It is indeed appropriate that we now publish this book to commemorate fifty years of *Economic Development –* back in 1957, the then Director of the IPA, Tom Barrington, discussed with Whitaker the possibility that the IPA would publish it; but that was before the Government took the bold decision to publish the study, thereby affirming its status as one of the key documents in the evolution of modern Ireland.

References

Economic Development (1958), Dublin: Stationery Office

Eichengreen, B, (2007), *The European Economy since 1945: Coordinated capitalism and beyond*, Princeton: Princeton University Press

Fanning, R., (1978) *The Irish Department of Finance 1922–58*, Dublin: Institute of Public Administration

Fanning, R., (2008), 'T. K. Whitaker, 1976–96' in T. Dunne (ed.), *The National University of Ireland: Centenary Essays*, Dublin: University College Dublin Press

Ferriter, D., (2006), *What If? – Alternative Views of Twentieth Century Ireland*, Dublin: Gill and Macmillan.

FitzGerald, G., (1968), *Planning in Ireland*, Dublin: Institute of Public Administration and London: Political and Economic Planning

Foster, R. F., (1988), *Modern Ireland 1600–1972*, London: Allen Lane

Foster, R. F. (2007), *Luck and the Irish: A Brief History of Change c. 1970–2000*, London: Allen Lane

Lyons, F. S. L., (1971), *Ireland since the Famine,* London: Weidenfeld and Nicolson

Maddison, A. (1987), 'Growth and Slowdown in Advanced Capitalist Economies: Techniques of Quantitative Assessment', *Journal of Economic Literature*, pp. 649–98

McCarthy, J. F., (1990), *Planning Ireland's Future: The Legacy of T. K. Whitaker*, Dublin: The Glendale Press

Murphy J. A., (1975), *Ireland in the Twentieth Century*, Dublin: Gill and Macmillan

National Income and Expenditure, various years, Dublin: Stationery Office

Olsen, M., (1982), *The Rise and Decline of Nations: Economic Growth, Stagflation and Social Rigidities*, New Haven: Yale University Press

Public Services Organisation Review Group (1969), *Report of Public Services Organisation Review Group* (Devlin Report), Dublin: Stationery Office

Whitaker, T. K., (1956), 'Capital Formation, Saving and Economic Progress', *Administration*, Vol. 4, No. 2, pp. 13–40

Whitaker, T. K. (1983), *Interests*, Dublin: Institute of Public Administration

Whitaker, T. K. (2006), *Protection or Free Trade: The Final Battle*, Dublin: Institute of Public Administration

Whitaker, T. K. (2006), *Retrospect 2006–1916*, Dublin: Institute of Public Administration

2

Opening Comments

Brian Lenihan, TD, Minister for Finance

Ladies and gentlemen, it is indeed our great privilege to be gathered here today with Dr Ken Whitaker on the occasion of the fiftieth anniversary of the publication of his seminal document, *Economic Development*. For you, Dr Whitaker, there must be an enormous sense of achievement and fulfilment in having your vision for the economic development of this nation enacted during your working life and in living in your venerable retirement to see the fruits of your far-sighted work which, without question, laid the foundations for the extraordinary advances that this country has made in the last fifteen years.

Along the way, there have been setbacks, mistakes, vicissitudes: we are going through difficult times at the moment – and all advice is welcome. But the work we are celebrating here this morning redirected the course of our history and set us on the path to becoming the successful, sophisticated economy we are today. I am very pleased that my Department and the IPA have organised this conference to mark this important anniversary and I am sure that you will have very valuable discussions during the day.

On my appointment as Minister for Finance, I decided I should read Professor Ronan Fanning's history of the Department. I was aware, of course, of the enormous impact of Dr Whitaker's document on our economic development but what struck me on reading Dr Fanning's history was the seismic shift in policy and indeed in culture that was brought about by the publication of *Economic Development* in 1958.

I have been rereading the document recently and I have to say, amidst all the economic analysis that is being produced now on a daily – if not hourly – basis, Dr Whitaker's wisdom shines through. And even though our economy has come a long way since 1958, *Economic Development* remains highly relevant as a vision for our future.

I would like to draw on some of the lessons learned from Dr Whitaker's work which continue to be pertinent in the more challenging economic environment in which we now find ourselves.

This audience will be aware of the context in which *Economic Development* was published: Ireland was inward-looking, predominantly agrarian, mostly subsistent, living standards roughly half those of our nearest neighbour. Our abject failure to create employment opportunities is reflected in the stark statistical fact that between 1926 and the first census undertaken after the publication of *Economic Development*, total employment actually declined by 14 per cent. Our people were our most important export. As Dr Whitaker said in his document:

> The common talk amongst parents in the towns, as in rural Ireland, is of their children having to emigrate as soon as their education is complete in order to be sure of a reasonable livelihood.

We have long since opened up our economy and we lead the field in Europe in terms of attracting foreign investment. But we still need to pursue export-led growth. The construction industry cannot be the main driver of growth in our economy. That day is gone: we have had our construction boom and now we have moved on to a different phase in our economic development.

That is not to say that there will not be a viable, successful construction sector: I have no doubt that there will, but it will not be the main driver of our economic growth.

Embracing the global economy has undoubtedly been the most important building block for improvements in living standards in Ireland, and today Ireland is one of the most open economies in the world. Our exports are increasingly concentrated in knowledge-intensive sectors of manufacturing and services, where our comparative advantage lies.

Ireland's experience of abandoning protectionism and embracing free trade has important lessons to this day. For instance, it is fair to say that protectionist sentiment has increased in parts of the developed world on foot of heightened uncertainty associated with outsourcing labour-intensive production activities to China, India and other emerging economies. In Ireland, however, we have learned the hard way that living standards are best enhanced by importing those goods and services which we are inefficient at producing, and concentrating our production efforts on those goods and services we are most efficient at producing. In this regard, the recent protectionist sentiment that has been voiced elsewhere has not become evident to any great extent in Ireland, and this is a positive development.

But we also recognise that in a global economy competitiveness pressures will intensify in the future. And here again, Dr Whitaker's work contains lessons for us today: in the introduction to *Economic Development*, he said,

It would be a policy of despair to accept that our costs of production must permanently be higher than those in other European countries.

He also warned:

If we do not expand production on a competitive basis, we shall fail to provide the basis necessary for the economic independence and material progress of the community.

Our competitiveness has played an important part in our economic growth over the last fifteen years. But we have lost that edge in recent times and we need again to heed the warnings of Dr Whitaker.

Further sustained improvements in our living standards will be contingent upon our ability continually to re-position the economy in the production and export of knowledge-intensive goods and services. We also recognise that the costs and benefits of globalisation are different across sectors – those in higher value-added sectors have the most to gain, with those in lower value-added sectors standing to gain the least. This is why the Government's programme of investment in deepening the skills pool, promoting life-long learning and in enhancing the stock of physical infrastructure is so important.

After the initial economic expansion of the 1960s the next key watershed was our entry to the Common Market, as it was then called, in 1973. Membership enabled us to diversify our trade pattern, to develop investment links with other European countries and to reduce our overall economic dependence on the UK business cycle. Today, about two-fifths of our merchandise exports are destined for the continental EU market. And while the UK is still an important export market its relative importance has declined, with just one-fifth of our merchandise exports currently destined for that market.

Of course, the Union has changed over time with perhaps the most important development being the completion of the Single European Market in 1993. This has given us unrestricted access to a very large market – today there are around 500 million people in the EU. The Single Market has also been a key driving force behind the large inflows of foreign direct investment into the EU during the 1990s, as US firms in particular sought access to this market. As I said already, Ireland, with its relatively low cost, highly skilled labour force benefited disproportionately from these flows.

The introduction of a common currency in January 1999 brought a further reduction of trade costs within the area; again a major benefit for a trading nation such as Ireland. And I must say, I am very concerned about our recent rejection of the Lisbon Treaty and what that says about our attitude as a nation to the European ideal. We have benefited enormously from Europe and our future economic success depends greatly on maintaining our position in the Union.

A constant theme in Dr Whitaker's document is the importance of productive investment. Much of our infrastructural development has been financed by EU structural funds but as a relatively high-income economy, we must now fund the bulk of investment in physical and human capital from our own resources. In the current environment in which tax revenue growth is actually declining, this raises important issues. Priority must be given to investment in those areas which generate the most significant returns, by which I mean those which most enhance the productive capacity of the economy and so contribute to future income and living-standard improvements. Once again, insights contained in *Economic Development* are relevant today. Dr Whitaker said,

> In the case of public investment, the term 'productive' cannot be limited to investments yielding an adequate return to the Exchequer. It extends also to investment which enlarges the national income by creating a flow of goods and services which are saleable without the aid of subsidies.

In recent years, we have been able to fund our significant capital expenditure programme from the very strong revenues that we have generated. This is no longer the case, and for the first time since 1995 we will be running a current budget deficit this year. The cyclical economic slowdown – both in its scale and in its composition – has had a major impact on tax revenue, with all tax heads being adversely affected. I am determined that public expenditure adjusts accordingly in order to restore international confidence in the Irish economy and in the public finances. This is the job that we in government are actively doing, and next month, I will present my Budget some seven weeks earlier than is normally the case. With resources less plentiful, the need to re-prioritise is essential given the changed circumstances we are in. The *Programme for Economic Expansion* which flowed from Dr Whitaker's work highlighted the need 'to obtain the utmost value for new outlay' and this remains the case today.

Obviously, constraining the growth in public expenditure will require expectations to adapt accordingly, and I hope that this can be achieved. If we can make difficult decisions together for the collective good of the country, then the consensus approach to policy formulation will stand the test of time. I welcome the conclusion of an agreement by the Social Partners earlier this week. And I hope that we can all work together to protect the huge strides we have made over the past decade or so, by acknowledging the changed economic and fiscal realities and setting out a realistic and deliverable way forward.

Dr Whitaker's leadership role within the civil service was an important element of the success of economic policy at that time. He realised the wealth of information that was available in government departments and requested free access to information, advice and assistance from other departments and state organisations. This enabled him to formulate a more complete picture of the problems as well as the opportunities facing the Irish economy at the time, and illustrates the importance he attached to the idea of evidence-based policy-making, something which all of us here would advocate.

It must also be acknowledged that because it was produced by a politically impartial civil service, the credibility of the analysis and of the resulting viewpoints contained in *Economic Development* were less subject to political dissent. Had the analysis been undertaken elsewhere, or if the impartiality of the civil service had been compromised in some manner, the integrity of the work could potentially have been compromised and the important measures delayed. This highlights the key role of an impartial civil service and, while we take this for granted here in Ireland, not every country is so lucky.

In conclusion, spare a thought for the political class. Opening up the economy at the time of the *Programme for Economic Expansion* involved politically difficult decisions. The downsizing of inefficient industries and the modernisation of agricultural production involved considerable employment losses at the time. In other words, because the situation could be seen as getting worse before it got better, implementing these policies demanded considerable political bravery. Great credit is rightly given to the politicians of the time, and, in particular, to Sean Lemass, for their vision and steadfast pursuit of a modernising agenda in our economy.

More than two decades later, Ray MacSharry and the then Government showed similar courage in bringing the public finances back under control and in taking the steps that produced the sophisticated and successful economy we have today.

In our budget in a month's time, the Government will produce its programme for economic recovery from the steep downturn we are experiencing at the moment. Much of the factors affecting us are outside our control, and the rapidity with which they have impacted on us has surprised.

There are tough decisions to be made. I believe that the people want us to protect the progress we have made because, unlike 1958, we all have too much to lose by not taking corrective action now.

Dr Whitaker, thank you for the inspiration you have given me in these challenging times and I wish you all well in your discussions today.

3

Looking Back to 1958

T. K. Whitaker

Golden Jubilee of *Economic Development*

Minister, I deeply appreciate your very kind and generous introduction to this
celebratory event. I want to thank the Good Lord for granting me the health of
mind and body which has enabled me to participate happily and gratefully in
this commemoration of the Golden Jubilee of the study called *Economic
Development* which promoted a basic change of policy – essentially, from
protectionism to free trade – which was proved to be of great national benefit.

I am very happy that two of the Finance colleagues who collaborated with
me in 1957/8 are still to the fore – Maurice Doyle and Tomás Ó Cofaigh. I
salute you and wish you well. Of the professional economists we consulted –
Professors Carter, Lynch and Ryan – the survivor, Louden Ryan, deserves
special recognition and thanks. He even came to the Department for a while to
help us on.

Regrettably, my principal collaborator, Charlie Murray, died early this year.
Others also have gone on *slí na fírinne*, remembered with affection and respect:
Maurice Horgan, Dónal Ó Loinsigh, Séamus Ó Ciosáin, Jim Dolan and Brendan
Menton.

We were a good team. Nobody had asked us to map out an escape route
from the utter despondency of the mid-1950s, plagued by emigration, unemployment, and virtual stagnation. We undertook this initiative of our own accord, on
top of our normal duties, welcoming it as an escape from the 'inverted
Micawberism' usually associated with the Department of Finance: waiting for
something to turn down! Indeed, we felt something of the Wordsworthian
enthusiasm that

Bliss it was in that dawn to be alive,
But to be young was very Heaven

All was not, of course, plain sailing from the 1960s on. There was a bleak passage in the 1980s, following extravagant public borrowings, before we emerged in the early 1990s into what Churchill liked to call 'the broad sunlit uplands'. Thanks to the IPA, the clash of interdepartmental argument, which preceded our move from Protection to Free Trade, has been put on record. It was this move that laid the basis for our remarkable progress, as a member of the European Economic Community, including the replacement of emigration by immigration and a significant rise in real incomes.

My warmest thanks to the Department of Finance and the IPA for their commemoration of a public service initiative which turned out well!

*

In this address, I try to outline both the lead-up, and the sequel, to the policy changes initiated by the study *Economic Development,* published fifty years ago and often called 'The Grey Book', though, to my eyes, the cover was green!

The 26-county Irish state, which achieved independence in 1922, was a frail entity, faced with a destructive civil war. It was predominantly agricultural and relatively poor, with average incomes less than one-half of those in Britain. The population of 3.25 million included a workforce of 1.25 million. Only one person was employed in industry for every eleven said to be 'engaged' in agriculture. 'Engaged', however, for most meant merely being unpaid relatives on farms too small to afford them full-time gainful employment. These so-called 'relatives assisting' formed a reservoir of hopeless, poverty-stricken men and women who filled the emigrant ships for decades.

The two main ruling parties of the period to the mid-1950s were joint inheritors of the Sinn Féin (self-sufficiency) idealism of a founding father, Arthur Griffith, himself a disciple of Friedrich List, the apostle of protection for infant industry. However, the prior attention of the earlier, 1922–32, administration had to be given to quelling a civil war, repairing the infrastructural damage consequent on many years of disturbed conditions, and confirming the financial soundness of the new state. A few moderate protective tariffs were imposed but only after careful inquiry.

The Electricity Supply Board and sugar-beet industry were established, reducing somewhat our dependence on imports. However, there was a gain of only 5,000 new jobs in transportable goods industries between 1926 and 1931. Emigration continued to lower the population.

The 1930s saw a much more active intervention. The advent to power of the new de Valera (Fianna Fáil) government in 1932 set the stage for a vigorous policy of protection and industrialisation. A financial dispute with Britain incited retaliatory recourse by both sides to tariffs and quotas. Internationally also, the trend of events was running against free trade and in favour of national protectionism. Irish policy was directed towards self-sufficiency rather than towards welcoming new industry from outside. There was concern that industry should be Irish-controlled, a policy reflected in the Control of Manufactures Acts and the setting-up of state-controlled monopolies in sugar and cement and a state-owned airline. In agriculture, too, self-sufficiency in wheat and sugar beet was encouraged in preference to beef and milk production.

Protection was granted rather freely and with little scientific assessment of what was needed in individual cases. From being an open trading area at the outset, the new state became one of the most protected, not by import duties alone but also by quantitative restrictions. The tariff wall continued rising until the later 1930s.

We should remind ourselves that protectionism was not an Irish aberration of the 1930s. The world at large was in the grip of depression: the prices of primary products had plummeted, the demand for goods had fallen catastrophically, and unemployment was severe and widespread. In 1931, the new government in Britain announced its intention of imposing a tariff – the first general British tariff since the 1850s – and of protecting British agriculture. Self-sufficiency through protection became a virtually universal aim. No less an economist than Keynes declared in Dublin, in 1933, that 'if I were an Irishman I should find much to attract me in the economic outlook of your present government towards self-sufficiency'.

The indiscriminate granting of protection did encourage a rapid development of low-technology industry, such as packaging, catering almost exclusively for the home market. By 1936, there were 101,000 people employed in transportable goods industries, nearly twice as many as a decade before.

Even during the 1930s there were signs that protected industries catering only for the home market were no solution to Ireland's employment problem. These industries had a high import requirement, which put strain on the external payments front. This proved to be one of the main constraints on development policy as long as agriculture was the main source of exports, and agricultural produce had to be consigned to the British market where prices were deliberately held at a low level and even access at times was not assured.

The Second World War and its scarcities postponed any widening of the Irish industrial base. Tariffs were largely suspended during the war, industrial output fell, net output in agriculture rose. After the war, as we entered the 1950s, exports of manufactured goods were still only 6 per cent of total exports, a long way short of the contribution of agriculture.

As supplies became more freely available in the post-war period, protective duties were gradually revived but with less conviction as to their efficacy as an instrument of development. The shortcomings of an uncritical protectionist policy were being recognised, particularly its cost and price effects and the inefficiency it induced. The chief protagonist of protection, Seán Lemass, had seen its shortcomings as wartime Minister for Supplies. Although his 1947 Industrial Efficiency and Prices Bill was never enacted, it was clear evidence of a more critical approach and can be seen as a precursor of the comprehensive drive for industrial modernisation and adaptation which he put into effect in the early 1960s when we first applied for membership of the EEC.

During most of the 1950s, the risk of excessive trade deficits was a serious policy constraint. Recurrent sterling crises brought pressure on Ireland and other sterling countries to curb imports and internal demand in order to avert a devaluation. Agricultural exports were still the predominant source of our foreign earnings and they were affected by unfavourable British pricing policies. It was not, indeed, until 1969 that industrial exports exceeded agricultural exports for the first time. Now both are dwarfed by external earnings from services.

The Public Capital Programme, the instrument by which economic expansion might have been sought in the 1950s, was rather ineffective as it was dominated by infrastructural and social, as distinct from more immediately productive, elements. New policy orientations were needed to bring private enterprise, native or foreign, into play on a bigger scale.

Despite the difficulties, the despondency and the poor economic performance of the earlier part of the 'fifties', the foundations of new policies for economic growth were being laid and the appropriate institutions established. Early in the decade, the Industrial Development Authority, Bórd Fáilte (to promote tourism), and Córas Tráchtála (to promote exports) had been set up. The industrial grants system, introduced in 1952, was extended in 1956. A 50 per cent tax rebate on export profits was introduced in that year by the Fine Gael Minister for Finance, Gerard Sweetman, who emphasised the need for 'a substantial increase in volume and efficiency of national production'. This was extended to 100 per cent in 1957 by a Fianna Fáil government.

Nevertheless, the mid-years of the 1950s plumbed the depths of hopelessness. One of the recurring balance-of-payments crises was overcome but only at the cost of stagnation, high unemployment and record emigration. The mood of despondency was palpable. Something had to be done or the achievement of national independence would prove to have been a futility. Various attempts were made to shine a beam forward in this dark night of the soul: they at least agreed on the need to devote more resources on an orderly basis to productive investment.

Here, with apologies, I have to join the story in person. As a young civil servant in the Department of Finance, I gained, by private study, a Master's degree in Economics from London University. I began drafting budget speeches in 1950. Shortly before being appointed Secretary to the Department, in May 1956, I read a paper to the Statistical and Social Inquiry Society which emphasised the need for more productive investment to help take us into an economic upswing. Later that year, a Capital Investment Advisory Committee was set up.

It became clear to me quickly, however, that a broader and deeper review was necessary, covering the whole field of economic activity. The basic policies of agricultural self-sufficiency and industrial protectionism needed critical reappraisal. This was indicated in the May 1957 Budget speech, in words I inserted referring to the need 'for a comprehensive review of our economic policy'. I had started quietly on this review, with the help of the colleagues named above, and had made substantial progress, before I wrote, towards the end of 1957, a minute to the Minister, Dr James Ryan, seeking his blessing. He sent this minute to the Government who endorsed his approval of the project, which was completed in May 1958, under the title 'Economic Development', and published in November of that year, together with a White Paper entitled *First Programme of Economic Expansion*, largely based upon it.

The publication of *Economic Development* was a break with the traditional privacy of the advice of civil servants to ministers. Some members of the Government would have preferred to maintain that privacy but more astute politicians – de Valera, Lemass and Ryan – saw the advantage of attributing a total reversal of policy to acceptance of the advice of independent civil servants. The Opposition mounted no attack, conscious perhaps that change was necessary and urgent.

That the new version of policy was called a 'programme' rather than a 'plan' reveals the contemporary fear and distrust of the Russian type of planned economy. We were aware, of course, of less objectionable precedents, such as French planning, The Vanoni Plan in Italy, and the Tennessee Valley Authority in the United States. The, for us, ominous background was the movement towards free trade in Europe, which Britain was likely to join – to Ireland's detriment unless we were ready to join too.

The First Programme reversed the direction of policy and gave a fillip to public confidence which, supported by buoyant world conditions, generated an outstanding economic performance. The boost to confidence may have been all the greater because it came from the most unlikely source, the Department of Finance, usually associated with the 'inverted Micawberism' mentioned earlier. An annual growth rate of 4 per cent brought GNP per capita from only 55 per cent of that in the UK in 1951 to 72 per cent by 1971. The change in traditional policy was fundamental. Not only, to simplify a little, did the *Programme*, recognising comparative advantage, put grass before grain, but, on the industrial side, it put export-oriented development, even if financed and directed by non-Irish entrepreneurs, before dependence on protected domestic enterprise affording only low 'added value'.

The *Programme's* rejection of the old-fashioned protectionism was explicit:

> It would be unrealistic, in the light of the probable emergence of a Free Trade Area, to rely on a policy of protection similar to that applied over the past 25 years or so … the only scope for substantial expansion lies in the production of goods for sale on export markets….

The European Economic Community had come into being as a common market for six nations in 1958. The wider Free Trade Area then mooted never came to pass. It had less interest for us because, unlike the EEC, it had no agricultural support element. Neither had the European Free Trade Area (EFTA) comprising Britain, the Nordic countries and Portugal. No attractive free-trade door being open to us, faith in free trade was in danger of being lost. At this critical time – and primarily for the eyes of Seán Lemass, as Taoiseach – a vigorous exchange of correspondence was conducted between the heads of the Departments of Finance, Industry and Commerce, Agriculture, and Foreign Affairs, in which Finance strongly maintained the free-trade case. Lemass remained a convert.[1]

From 1960 on, a research institute initially funded by the Ford Foundation (the ESRI) has provided independent comment and advice on policy. At the start of that decade, a thorough review of industrial efficiency was undertaken. Special loans, grants and tax incentives were provided to encourage firms to modernise and adapt to competitive trading conditions. Tariffs were even lowered unilaterally. Foreign firms were offered generous grants, on top of tax advantages, to set up here and export their output. When, in July 1961, Britain first applied to join the EEC, Ireland did so simultaneously but had to join the British on the sidelines when de Gaulle vetoed their application. A Free Trade Agreement was concluded with Britain at the end of 1965 and, when the British application to join the Six was renewed in May 1967, and again in 1969, after de Gaulle's resignation, Ireland reapplied also. Detailed negotiations were successfully completed in the 1970–1972 period, accession instruments were signed in January 1972, and Ireland, with strong public support in a referendum, became a member simultaneously with Britain on 1 January 1973. In retrospect,

---

[1] This correspondence was published in 2006 by the Institute of Public Administration under the title *Protection or Free Trade – The Final Battle.*

it can be said that de Gaulle did us a good turn in blocking our entry until we were much better prepared for membership.

We are now better educated, live much longer, are better housed and much better off than fifty years ago. In a population of 4.2 million, non-nationals account for 10 per cent and the numbers engaged in agriculture continue to fall. Nearly twice as many are at work as in the early 1970s. Most of those with a Leaving Certificate from secondary school go on to third level or higher, as against only one in seventeen when I left school – then it was pounds, not points, that secured entry to university. The standard of living, formerly well below that of Western Europe, is now amongst the highest – once the poorest, Ireland is now the second richest member of the EEC. Boys can expect to live eighteen years longer, and girls nearly five years longer still, than when I was young. As recently as 1960, the majority of the dwellings in the state had no running water. Now virtually none are without. The contribution of this alone to better hygiene, health and longevity must be significant.

Of course, not all is wine and roses! The less favourable developments include a higher incidence of crime and drug addiction, reflecting a weakening of the civilising influence of the Ten Commandments. Too many children are still dropping out of school too soon. There is also, I feel, a weaker sense of nationhood, less care for tradition, and insufficient concern for those in need.

Returning to economics, it is only if we are educated, skilled and enterprising enough to produce goods and services commanding a high margin of gross profit or 'added value' that we can expect high and rising living standards. Perverse financial policies in the 1970s, in defiance of oil price increases and in misguided pursuit of full employment, submerged us in foreign debt. The necessary retrenchment was painful. But return in the later 1980s to fiscal rectitude, combined with other favourable influences – including a rising level of education and skills, greater productivity, low corporate taxation, high inward investment, infrastructural improvements promoted by EEC Structural Funds, a fairer social partnership – ushered in an unparalleled economic upsurge in the 1900s – a fifty per cent rise on average in real incomes and a transformation of emigration into immigration, resulting in 50 per cent rise in population over the low point of fifty years ago.

The economy is now enduring a recession but the good policy advice of the Department of Finance will help to see us through to better times.

4

Economic Development:
The Political Context

Ronan Fanning

The primacy of international politics as the context for Irish economic policy is a commonplace. Today, buffeted by storms of global recession in the aftermath of the Irish people's rejection of the Lisbon Treaty, it is a commonplace of which we are all too keenly aware. Yet it is a commonplace that seems to have escaped many historians, economists and political scientists who have deplored the delay until 1958 of the national new departure inaugurated by the publication of *Economic Development*. The causes for this neglect of the international political context need not detain us: suffice it to say that the focus of such critics is sometimes as introverted and insular as the focus of those politicians and officials in earlier decades whom they so furiously denounce. Which is why I want to begin by reaffirming the primacy of the international dimension in explaining the tardiness of Irish economic development.

The global economic crisis inaugurated by the Wall Street crash of 1929 compounded the existing subordination of economic imperatives to the imperatives of Irish nationalism. 'Irish political economy,' observed Patrick Lynch in 1959, 'unfortunately, sometimes tends to be more political than economic' (Lynch, p. 129). He understated the case: from 1922 until at least 1948, Irish political economy was *always* more political than economic. The Treaty split and the civil war ensured that, in independent Ireland as under the Union, what most mattered was the continued conflict of opinion about the legitimacy of the British connection, not a national debate on the economic policies best suited to the new state. And the transition from the killing grounds of civil war to the more benign forum of the Oireachtas – accomplished once Fianna Fáil entered the Dáil in 1927 – left intact that first fact of political life.

For the most part, the international context was mediated through the suffocating micro-climate of the British–Irish relationship. In the short term, civil war made allies out of former enemies. The beleaguered pro-Treaty government of the infant state became beholden to the British government, to the Treasury, to the Bank of England and to the old Anglo–Irish financial community centred on the Bank of Ireland. All thoughts of economic independence, particularly those associated with the writings of Arthur Griffith and encapsulated in the words 'Sinn Féin', counted for nothing when cast in the balance against the fragility of the new state. The immediate result was to turn 'Griffith on his noble head' (Daniel). The economic priorities of the infant state were founded on the conventional wisdom of Whitehall: budgets must balance; borrowing – especially foreign borrowing – was bad; public expenditure must be pared to the bone, trade must be free; and the Irish currency must remain wedded to the British. But the pendulum swung back with a vengeance when Fianna Fáil came to power in 1932 and set about reaffirming the traditional assumptions of Irish economic nationalism: namely

> that the economic development of Ireland had been retarded by British misgovernment … that the economic development of Ireland depended on the policies adopted by the State that self-government would almost at once bring economic recovery and prosperity… that the future of the economy would be determined by what happens in Ireland. (Meenan, pp. 270–4)

This postponement of the introduction of the policies of economic nationalism embedded protectionism in a party political context, an effect compounded by Fianna Fáil's remaining in government until 1948. Then came the patriotic sanctification of protectionism in the Economic War of 1932–38. The British government was the first to resort to the imposition of protectionist tariffs (albeit to recoup Britain's losses on the land annuities); although the Irish government immediately retaliated in kind, it remains a moot point whether the notoriously cautious de Valera would have initiated a tariff war against Britain. But once the Economic War had begun, he saw no point in seeking financial or economic solutions to what he saw as a political problem; the key issue, he told his party's ard fheis, was 'whether the Irish nation is going to be free or not' (Moynihan, p. 227).

It was resolved only with the enactment of the 1937 Constitution opening the way for the Anglo–Irish agreements of April 1938, which ended the Economic War. But yet again economic objectives were subordinated to political imperatives; the defence agreement, whereby the British surrendered the ports retained under the Treaty and so fulfilled the necessary precondition for the exercise of Irish neutrality in the war already looming with Hitler's Germany, took priority over the financial and trade agreements.

Any prospect that the end of the Economic War might create conditions more conducive to economic development was shattered by the outbreak of the Second World War. A neutral and isolated island with only a tiny, embryonic merchant marine could never have escaped another, more intensive period of economic stagnation. Although stagnation was compounded by British measures of economic warfare, it remained politically cost-free when, as Tom Garvin has observed, 'self-sufficiency suddenly made sense, because of the extreme and unusual conditions of wartime' (Garvin, p. 38). Nor was there any significant improvement when the war ended. Irish neutrality was not forgotten or forgiven by the victorious powers. The retrospective economic price of neutrality was high. When it came to supplies of oil, fertilisers and other vital raw materials, Ireland languished at the end of the queue, her enduring post-war isolation well symbolised by the rejection of her initial application to join the United Nations.

In sum, then, the international political climate until 1948 militated against *any* prospect of economic development. So, too, did the domestic politics of anti-materialism rooted in the Irish-language revival and Irish Catholicism, the badges of identity common to both sides in the civil war. This found most notorious expression in Eamon de Valera's St Patrick's Day broadcast of 1943 when he spoke of 'that Ireland which we dreamed of' as 'the home of a people who valued material wealth only as the basis of right living, of a people who were satisfied with frugal comfort and devoted their leisure to the things of the spirit'. The inhibiting effect of such visions on the national psyche was immense and enduring. Ten years later, during his penultimate term of office as Taoiseach, and in the course of a ringing reaffirmation of the merits of self-sufficiency born of economic nationalism, de Valera saw nothing incongruous in invoking Bishop Berkeley's *Queries*,

> which just over 200 years ago ... posed several questions about Ireland's economic development to which we in Fianna Fáil, since we first came into office in 1932, have endeavoured to provide the concrete answers. (Moynihan, pp. 466, 565)

But the anti-materialist impulse was not confined to Fianna Fáil. John A. Costello, in a major speech as Taoiseach in 1948, likewise attacked 'the dark forces of materialism', while another prominent Fine Gael spokesman, Michael Tierney, wrote of his hopes that the Second World 'might be the final stage in the rapid failure of a whole materialistic philosophy of life', leading to the destruction of the 'Anglo-Saxon world order' (Fanning, 1983B, pp. 16–17).

Throughout the 1920s and 1930s, at least, the anti-materialist perspectives of government ministers and of Catholic bishops were mutually reinforcing. This repressive and authoritarian alliance between the clerical and political elites offered scant opportunity for the bureaucratic elite to launch independent initiatives in the economic arena. That the bureaucracy had endured and survived two traumatic changes of political masters under revolutionary and neo-revolutionary circumstances within ten years, in 1922 and in 1932, hardened its instincts for stability and survival rather than nurturing a spirit of enterprise.

Nor did independent Ireland's academic economists make an impact on the political climate. Those in the premier universities, in Dublin and closest to the seat of government, were constrained in their criticisms of Fianna Fáil's economic policies: UCD by its identification with the Cumann na nGaedheal governments and Trinity by its reputation as a Protestant bastion of Anglo-Irish ascendancy. That said, the sum total of the academic economists' contribution before 1948 was lamentable. For the most part, their preference was for descriptive, historically focused economics rather than for prescriptive, policy-driven economics. The records of the Statistical and Social Inquiry Society of Ireland (the only forum where civil servants felt free to speak publicly on economic issues) in 1946–50 expose their eloquent silence; in March 1949, for example, when a Cambridge economist read the first paper on econometrics ever presented to the society, not a single university economist spoke in the ensuing discussion (Fanning, 1984, pp. 147–55).

Yet there were a few straws fluttering in a fitful breeze of change during the war years. The 1944 report of the Commission on Vocational Organisation, chaired by Bishop Michael Browne of Galway, which was 'the first sustained attempt by a commission since independence to suggest that normalcy was not enough' (Lee, p. 344), depicted civil servants as cowering timorously behind a barrier of official anonymity. Two months later, Bishop Dignan of Clonfert, then the government-appointed chairman of the National Health Insurance Society, published a pamphlet on social security attacking the gross inadequacies of the health services.

It was also in 1944 that Dr James Deeny was drafted as Chief Medical Adviser into the Department of Local Government and Public Health where he wielded the most vigorous of new brooms; in December 1946, there followed the first substantive change in the organisation of central government since the Ministers and Secretaries Act of 1924, with the creation of two new government departments – Health and Social Welfare.

It was also during the war that officials in the Department of Finance began to absorb Keynes's writings and to relate them to the Irish experience, a process accelerated by the publication of the Beveridge Report and the British White Paper on Employment Policy. Beveridge also influenced Seán Lemass who initiated a Cabinet Committee on Economic Planning in November 1942; although this was more a product of short-lived and exaggerated apprehensions about unemployment levels after war ended than a commitment to planning in the sense in which that term was used in the late 1950s, and although its procedures soon sank into the bog of the general work of government, it was another sign of gradually changing attitudes (Fanning, 1978, pp. 352–3, 357, 384–6). Yet, while there were obvious interactions between these stirrings in the political, bureaucratic and clerical elites, there is no evidence that any one group sought to give a clear lead to another. The late 1940s witnessed ferment rather than any steady evolution to the climacteric of the late 1950s, ferment that saw the birth, in 1946, of a new republican party with a left-wing social policy, Clann na Poblachta.

The year 1948 saw the first rumblings of a tectonic shift in the domestic political context when the election brought to power Ireland's first inter-party government and shattered the stasis consequent upon sixteen continuous years of Fianna Fáil government. Both the new Taoiseach, John A. Costello, and the Minister for External Affairs and leader of Clann na Poblachta, Seán MacBride, made grandiose claims that their Republic of Ireland Act of 1948 – which finally severed Ireland's last links with the Commonwealth and so swept away all vestiges of ambiguity about Irish sovereignty – had taken the gun out of politics. I prefer to suggest that the 1948 Act took the crutch out of Irish politics: the crutch of that obsession with the British connection upon which Irish ministers had leant so long for excuse and explanation when taxed with their indifference to economic development.

Why, then, did the gestation of the *First Programme for Economic Expansion* take another ten years? Perhaps because it was not easy for the long-term politically disabled to learn to pick their way without crutches across a terrain unknown to all and alien to many. Even the protagonists of future change found it heavy going. One striking example was Seán Lemass's initial opposition to the Industrial Development Authority (IDA), established in 1950, which he was only with difficulty dissuaded from abolishing when Fianna Fáil returned to power in 1951. Another was Ken Whitaker's memorandum in February 1949, denouncing the deleterious effects of the Marshall Plan upon financial policy and asking, 'whether a less generous gesture by the United States would not have contributed more to European recovery by forcing countries to face the realities of the situation' – 'under Stalin and Molotov?' scrawled an irate Minister for Finance, Patrick McGilligan, in response (Fanning, 1978, pp. 438–9). But a decade before the publication of *Economic Development,* Seán Lemass and Ken Whitaker were both hobbled by the same political fetters: the need to hasten slowly to avoid the antagonism of more powerful peers. Only when, as Taoiseach and as Secretary of the Department of Finance respectively, they had climbed to the top of their separate greasy poles, could they afford to give full rein to their more radical instincts.

Such episodes also reveal how the ferment of the late 1940s gave way to a certain floundering in the early 1950s. The politicisation of economics had its disadvantages, one of which was Fianna Fáil's initial determination to dispute that any good could come out of the economic initiatives launched by the inter-party government of 1948–51. If McGilligan's Dáil speech introducing the first capital budget in 1950 was the earliest 'explicit expression of Keynes in an Irish budget', then MacEntee's deflationary budget of 1952 was no less striking a monument to the strength of economic conservatism (Fanning, 1978, pp. 456–60, 482–4). Although the *Reports of the Commission on Emigration* of 1948–54 also failed to command cross-party support, they helped to shape a national consensus. If a proximate origin not only of *Economic Development* but of its favourable reception can be identified, it rests somewhere in the national crisis of self-confidence induced by the accelerated emigration revealed by the 1956 census.

By 1957–8, electoral politics had forced all parties to identify economic development as an imperative of government The economy had never been the key issue in an Irish election until the Republic of Ireland Act, in Costello's words, enabled 'the people to centre their energies on the economic problems which had to be met' *(Irish Times,* 15 November 1948). The politicians, wrote Professor Desmond Williams, my predecessor as Professor of Modern History at UCD, in 1953, 'have adopted "economics"; they affect an understanding of economic terminology and are courting the affections and interests of professional economists' *(The Statist,* 24 October 1953). The frequency of general elections dramatically increased the speed of this transition: three times in less than six years, between May 1951 and March 1957, economic issues were flogged to death at the polls. The effect was further enhanced by four changes of government in the nine years between 1948 and 1957. Increasingly, the significant debates on economic policy were taking place *within,* rather than *between,* the two major parties. The point was adroitly made by James Ryan when he quoted from four Budget statements made by four successive Ministers for Finance (McGilligan, MacEntee, Sweetman and himself) and defied his audience 'to say who said what. I say that to show that there is really not much between us' *(Dáil Debates,* 173, 1078). The protagonists in the Fianna Fáil debate were Lemass and MacEntee. Lemass won the day with his celebrated '100,000 Jobs Speech' to the party faithful in Clery's Ballroom in October 1955, which was enshrined in a special supplement to the *Irish Press* and in subsequent Fianna Fáil folklore as the moment when Seán Lemass announced Ireland's programme of economic development (McCarthy, p. 26). The aborted budgetary proposals of the Minister for Finance, Gerard Sweetman, to cut food subsidies provoked comparable tensions among Fine Gael ministers in 1957 (McCarthy, p. 34). It was Sweetman who, in May 1956, had promoted Whitaker to the secretaryship of Finance in breach of hitherto sacrosanct principles of seniority, and it was Sweetman who established the Capital Investment Advisory Committee and who initiated an Irish application for membership of the International Monetary Fund and of the World Bank, steps on the road to *Economic Development.*

Nor should we ignore the changing character of inter-departmental politics after 1948. The 1948–51 government saw the Department of External Affairs flexing its muscles for the first time in the area of economic policy; this was driven partly by the ministerial dynamism and prejudices of Seán MacBride and partly by the economic interests of some senior officials, notably Freddie Boland. Another new departure was the translation of Patrick Lynch from the Department of Finance to the Taoiseach's Department where he acted as economic adviser to John A. Costello and first straddled the intellectual chasm hitherto dividing the two departments. More significant was the comparable role as Costello's economic adviser played in 1954–57 by Charlie Murray, nominally a principal officer in the Taoiseach's Department and who later co-ordinated the material incorporated in *Economic Development.*

'We are all planners now,' wrote Murray in a memorandum in January 1957 which was overtaken by the split among Fine Gael ministers on budgetary policy on 25 January and by the consequent 1957 election. And Sweetman echoed many of Murray's arguments in a February speech to the Fine Gael ard fheis, notably the implications for Ireland of the emergence of EFTA and of the Common Market (NAI TD S 16066A). The election campaign threw the issue of economic planning into still sharper relief and, in the interregnum between the election and Fianna Fáil's return to power, Murray wrote a 17-page commentary on the economy under such headings as the balance of payments and external reserves; savings and investment; industrial production and employment; unemployment; the banks and interest rates; and prices and national income. He highlighted 'the problem raised by industrial protection' and pleaded 'for fresh thinking about our protective policy' and concluded by pointing to 'the consequences, for employment, emigration and national development, of an inadequate rise in real national income'. The survival of an annotated copy of Murray's memorandum in Ken Whitaker's personal papers shows how closely the two men were co-operating even before Fianna Fáil's return to office.

In the meantime, Whitaker, who had gone to Washington to explore the prospects of Ireland's joining the World Bank and who returned to Dublin just in time to vote in the election, had prepared a seminal and apocalyptic ten-page memorandum entitled 'The Irish Economy, 1957' and dated 21 March 1957 – Jim Ryan's first full day in office as Minister for Finance.

The principal economic problem of the Irish Government will continue to be the safeguarding of political independence by ensuring economic viability. Without a sound and progressive economy political independence would be a crumbling façade….

It is accepted on all sides that we have come to a critical and decisive point in our economic affairs. It is only too clear that the policies we have hitherto followed have not resulted in a viable economy. It is equally clear that we face economic decay and the collapse of our political independence if we elect to shelter permanently behind a protectionist blockade. For this would mean accepting that our costs must permanently be higher than those of other European countries, both in industry and in large sections of agriculture. That would be a *policy* of despair…. The effect of any *policy* which entailed relatively low living standards here would be to sustain and stimulate the outflow of emigrants and make it impossible to preserve the 26 Counties as an economic entity.

In a remarkable passage which was tantamount to fluttering a Union Jack under the nose of a Fianna Fáil bull, Whitaker even suggested that,

if we do not expand our production on a competitive basis, we shall have failed to provide the economic basis for the political independence and material progress of the community. Indeed, if we expect to fail, it would be better to make an immediate move towards reincorporation in the United Kingdom rather than to wait until our economic decadence became even more apparent.

For these reasons the importance of the next five to ten years for the economic and political future of Ireland cannot be over-stressed. Policy must be re-shaped without regard to past views or commitments.

The circumstances under which Fianna Fáil resumed power in March 1957 minimised the possibility that Whitaker's proposals would provoke dissent either within the Cabinet or within the Fianna Fáil party. That Lemass had dissuaded de Valera from reappointing the innately conservative MacEntee as Minister for Finance was crucial. The emollient yet shrewd and powerful Jim Ryan – long one of Lemass's closest colleagues – was, moreover, the ideal Minister for Finance to deflect any residual resentment in the party. Although Lemass had by then assumed the mantle of de Valera's heir apparent, two years were to elapse before he acquired the authority of Taoiseach and he still provoked mixed feelings among some of his Cabinet colleagues, ranging from the hostility of his rivals for the first place to the suspicion of rural ministers who distrusted his metropolitan ways. While the implementation of the *First Programme* has always been identified with Lemass, it was de Valera who formally presided over the public and dramatic reversal of Fianna Fáil's protectionist policies embodied in *Economic Development*. Brian Farrell has suggested that 'the continuing presence of de Valera may have provided Lemass with a convenient cloak of seeming changelessness under which new policies, concerns and choices could be exchanged for old' (Farrell, p. 96). Indeed, one might go further and question whether such a U-turn could have been so effortlessly accomplished *without* de Valera's endorsement.

The 1957 election was the watershed marking the emergence of a political consensus spanning the two major parties on the need for an economic new departure. The need to foster such bipartisanship explains why Ken Whitaker acquired such deservedly heroic stature by virtue of *Economic Development* being published over his name. 'Publication as an anonymous government publication would give it political aspects which we did not want,' Lemass explained ten years later. 'The association with the name of a non-political civil servant would help to get its acceptance over political boundaries…. It was a deliberate decision, part of our effort to get economic development away from party political tags' (McCarthy, p. 57). On 18 April 1957, the Fianna Fáil government duly decided to apply to join the IMF and in mid-September Jim Ryan, Ken Whitaker and J. J. McElligott (the Governor of the Central Bank) represented Ireland for the first time at an annual meeting of the World Bank.

Once Whitaker presented the Taoiseach's Department with his celebrated and starkly titled memorandum, 'Has Ireland a Future?', in December 1957, the momentum that led to the publication of *Economic Development* twelve months later became irresistible. Consensus remained critical because the larger historical significance of the publication and reception of *Economic Development* was largely psychological. Indeed, one of its most often quoted passages opens with the assertion that there was 'a sound *psychological* reason for having an integrated development…. After thirty-five years of native government people are asking whether we can achieve an acceptable degree of economic progress'. At this level, *Economic Development* ultimately succeeded because so many wanted it to succeed. People craved the beat of a different drum and if the tunes to which they now began marching were still patriotic – albeit from a new hymnal of economic patriotism – then so much the better.

References

Daniel, T. K. (1976), 'Griffith on his noble head: the determinants of Cumann na nGaedheal's economic policy, 1922–32', *Irish Economic and Social History,* no. 3, pp. 55–65

Fanning, R. (1978), *The Irish Department of Finance 1922–58*, Dublin: Institute of Public Administration

Fanning, R. (1983), *Independent Ireland*, Dublin: Educational Company of Ireland

Fanning, R. (1983B), 'The *Four-Leaved Shamrock': Electoral Politics and the National Imagination in Independent Ireland*, Dublin: University College Dublin

Fanning, R. (1984), 'Economists and governments: Ireland, 1922–52' in Murphy, A. (ed.), *Economists and the Irish Economy from the Eighteenth Century to the Present Day*, Dublin: Irish Academic Press, pp. 138–56

Garvin, T. (2004), *Preventing the Future: Why was Ireland So Poor for So Long?*, Dublin: Gill and Macmillan

Lee, J. (1979), 'Aspects of corporatist thought in Ireland: the Commission on Vocational Organisation, 1939–43' in Cosgrove, A. and McCartney, D. (eds), *Studies in Irish History presented to R. Dudley Edwards*, Dublin: University College Dublin

Lynch, P. (1969), 'The economics of independence: some unsettled questions of Irish economics' in Chubb, B. and Lynch, P., *Economic Development and Planning*, Dublin: Institute of Public Administration

McCarthy, J. F. (ed.) (1990), *Planning Ireland's Future: The Legacy of T. K. Whitaker*, Dublin: Glendale Press

Meenan, J. (1970), *The Irish Economy since 1922*, Liverpool: Liverpool University Press

Moynihan, M. (ed.) (1980), *Speeches and Statements by Eamon de Valera 1917–73*, Dublin: Gill and Macmillan

5

Dublin Opinions: Dublin Newspapers and the Crisis of the 1950s

Tom Garvin

Dublin Newspapers in the Post-War World

Dublin daily journalism, in the effective absence of radio and TV, was well served by three national newspapers during the era 1945–1961: the *Irish Press, Irish Times* and *Irish Independent*. While the *Irish Press* was obviously and explicitly the mouthpiece of the Fianna Fáil party's leadership and particularly an echo of Seán Lemass, already indicating his future dominance of the political system as early as 1948, theoretically the *Irish Times* and *Irish Independent* were non-partisan. In reality, the *Independent* tended to support Fine Gael and be critical of de Valera and his party. As late as the 1950s, Fianna Fáil and the *Irish Press* still were twitting it for its urging on of the executions of the leaders of Easter Week 1916, its support for the Treaty and the war against the anti-treatyites in 1922–23. As a middle-class newspaper that was more popular than its political ally, the Fine Gael party, the *Independent* had to moderate its ideological leanings and be respectful to Fianna Fáil opinion and leadership, a stance which the *Press* felt it need not reciprocate in the case of its attitudes to Fine Gael. The two 'party papers' had continual and entertaining slanging matches in the 1950s about their respective political histories.

The *Irish Times* was the heir to the unionist tradition in the Republic, and was the 'Protestant paper', sympathetic to the Ulster unionist case, unlike the other two papers which still stuck to an anti-partitionist orthodoxy. It was already in the process of transforming itself into a liberal nationalist paper, but had not quite got there yet. The *Irish Times* had a companion evening paper, the *Evening*

Mail, which sickened and died, and the *Press* group produced a set of Sunday and evening stable companions to the daily.

However, even in the 1950s, the *Irish Times* had clearly developed a loyalty to the Dublin-run state, and was beginning to develop cautiously a liberal line with regard to the Catholic Church, and social issues such as adoption, emigration and education. The *Independent* had by far the largest circulation, followed by the *Press*, while the *Times* circulation was tiny and confined mainly to middle-class Protestant Dublin. In parts of rural Ireland the paper had to be sold under plain wrapper, almost as though it were contraband.

The *Press* was later to shrink while the increasingly liberal *Times* was to grow considerably and lose its perceived status as a sectarian and anti-national sheet, but these developments lay far in the future back in the 1940s.

The *Independent* was also by far the richest paper. The *Press* group was the youngest of the three, the *Irish Press* dating from only 1931. It also was to be the only group to die in the late twentieth century. The other two groups had long pre-independence histories.

There was, and still is, a niche for a gadfly press in Dublin. Chief among these at the time were the *Bell*, founded by Seán Ó Faoláin; the *Leader*, a survivor from the pre-revolutionary period, having founded in 1900; the impoverished monthly national communist *Irish Democrat* of London; and the weekly *Standard*, a Catholic paper which exhibited a curious mixture of democratic liberalism, censoriousness, tolerance, anti-communism and respectful attitudes towards such quasi-fascist worthies as Franco and Salazar. In some ways, the *Standard* reflected most completely the confused and confusing ideological current of the Irish Catholicism of the time. The *Irish Catholic* reflected a more uncompromising and literal-minded fideism.

Farming and the Economic Crisis

One immediate and evident contrast between the three Dublin daily newspapers was their attitude to farmers and farming. Both the *Irish Times* and the *Irish Independent* assumed that the economic future of the Republic was agrarian, although some shift in this basic assumption was evident during the 1950s and particularly in the later years of that decade. Articles on agriculture, on 'scientific farming', on the reluctance of the young to go into farming, and on the need for agricultural education were commonplace in both papers. Both papers had large-farm readership; the old 1930s argument about the cow versus the plough had already been settled in the former's favour. In stark contrast, the *Irish Press*, on the other hand, was determinedly pro-industry, while remaining equally determinedly nostalgic about the small-farm past or ancestry of the bulk of its readers; at times, it ignored farming in favour of industry, machinery and vocational training. It virtually never discussed farming as a serious career choice. Behind the *Press* there lurked the strong views of Seán Lemass, who seems to have known little about farming and possibly cared less. He was continually accused of forgetting about farming in his plans for economic development.

Lemass tended to argue that urban and rural interests were not opposed, but complementary, but he argued that unless the system of land use was changed so as to generate more employment, and industries started up to absorb the rural surplus population, depression in the economy was likely to be endemic. In practice, he acted during his years in office as Minister for Industry and Commerce and later Taoiseach as though farming were a busted flush and the long-term stagnating effects of the Land Acts meant that farming would have to be bypassed by industrial development.

In January 1948, Lemass remarked in the pages of the *Irish Press* that Fianna Fáil was not a class party, but a 'workers' party'.[1] By this he seems to have meant a pretty inclusive and broad sense of the term 'worker', including in the term members of the nascent Irish national business class and management cohort. He saw the *Press* as the voice of an emergent cross-class patriotic alliance that transcended sectional petty interests. All three papers published articles on agriculture, but the *Independent* and the *Irish Times* were far more likely to publish reports and articles of interest to larger, more commercial farmers or to small farmers who wished to improve their productivity and their acreage, or learn to use 'scientific methods'. This is not to say that the two papers neglected industry, but rather to note that they did not quite share the *Press* view that industrialisation was a must and was the only real way out of the trap of agrarian stagnation that the course of Irish history had sprung on the entire country. Lemass wanted to bypass completely what he possibly saw as the morass of Irish agriculture.

In March 1948, the *Independent* carried an editorial commenting on an official report on the condition of Irish land. It had huge potential for pasture production, but much of it lay unused. The paper commented acidly,

> It was an old story that in the nineteenth century the farmer was discouraged from improvement by insecurity of tenure; in the twentieth century he has been equally discouraged by instability of agricultural policy.[2]

By way of illustration, in May 1949, the paper pointed out that the pig industry had fed the country in 1931 and had provided pig products and live pigs for

---

[1] *Irish Press*, 10 January 1948
[2] *Irish Independent*, 11 March 1949

export. According to the Indo, the Government had subsequently virtually regulated the pig industry to death.[3] But rural life was commonly seen as superior to urban life, even by some in Fianna Fáil. Agriculture was seen as so central that nearly all of Marshall Aid funds were to be sunk in it. The Fine Gael Taoiseach, John A. Costello, announced in June 1950 that the land was the main source of national wealth.

> They had in the land of Ireland a noble inheritance and it was their responsibility to ensure that not only was it cultivated and developed but that no effort was spared to improve its condition, increase its fertility and extend its limits. The land … was the main material source of their wealth. They must direct unrelenting energy towards reclaiming of land neglected under alien rule.[4]

The Minister for Agriculture announced in July 1950 that an agricultural college was to be set up. Because of the usual Irish infighting between vested interest, in this case the universities (particularly University College Dublin and University College Cork) and Catholic clerical interests, it ended up being delayed, finally opening as the Agricultural Institute, in 1957; it was to develop into a high-powered and very successful institution.[5]

The *Irish Times* commented in May 1950 that the Inter-Party Government had a strong agrarian bias, despite the fact that farmers used primitive methods and Irish food was very overpriced. Later in the year, it noted that much agricultural land was falling into waste.[6] Not many educational scholarships were offered to young people, and those that were offered were highly skewed toward agriculture and farming, despite the fact that student demand was very obviously biased towards off-farm skills and employments. The *Independent* commented in December 1951 that even the sons and daughters of farmers were not particularly interested in scholarships: 'It appears that young farmers will not apply for these scholarships unless they intend to become agricultural inspectors.'[7] In July 1951 the new Fianna Fáil Minister for Agriculture commented on the low educational attainments of Irish farmers:

> The farmers in the past paid very little attention to a boy who was going to occupy the farm. Immediately he was able to take a fork in his hand he was

---

[3] *Irish Independent*, 21 May 1949
[4] *Irish Independent*, 11 June 1950
[5] *Irish Independent*, 22 July 1950
[6] *Irish Times*, 18 May 1950, 26 September 1950
[7] *Irish Independent*, 11 December 1951

put out on the land. The money the farmer had saved was spent on the education of other members of the family and that was why they had not had the progress in agriculture that they should have had in this country – because the farmers were being denied the education to which they were entitled.[8]

In one of his rare references to farming, Lemass suggested in January 1952 that Irish agriculture was old-fashioned and disorganised. He seemed to think that eventually a Darwinian process of the elimination of the unfit would, in the long run, lead to a modern and efficient agricultural industry.[9] Later in the month the *Irish Times* wailed in respect of Irish agriculture, 'On almost every side of agricultural life there is the same melancholy story of decay: but there is no sign that the decline will be arrested.'[10]

In July 1953, the *Press* editorialised to the effect that all the efforts at industrialisation behind tariff and quote protection had just about managed to absorb the surplus population leaving the land for urban centres and non-agrarian work in Ireland. As agriculture mechanised, rural employment would shrink and rural productivity would grow, the Fianna Fáil paper asserted.[11] A now vicariously frightening letter was published in the *Irish Times* in September 1952, written by Esmonde W. Little, late of the veterinary branch of the Department of Agriculture, who wrote, 'During the last hundred years we have been living on our capital of phosphorus in the soil, which is now in a great many areas almost exhausted.' Other vital minerals were also disappearing. The cattle were starving amid apparent plenty. Poorer counties were the worse afflicted, particularly in the north and west of the country. Phosphate manures and special feeds were needed.[12]

In February 1953, the London *Economist*, as quoted in the *Irish Times*, commented on the apparently pathological repetitiveness of Irish politics, basically because of political paralysis in the face of certain obviously necessary decisions that needed to be taken but which were being avoided. Irish agricultural production had been stagnant for a century, it claimed, with some, but not much, exaggeration.[13] In February 1954, the Organisation for Economic Cooperation and Development (OECD) observed that Ireland's agricultural output had not yet recovered to the level of 1929.[14]

---

[8] *Irish Times*, 23 July 1951
[9] *Irish Times*, 8 January 1952
[10] *Irish Times*, 22 January 1952
[11] *Irish Press*, 29 July 1953
[12] *Irish Times*, 1 September 1952
[13] *Irish Times*, 10 February 1953
[14] *Irish Independent*, 13 February 1954

Almost exactly a year earlier, Cardinal D'Alton praised the virtues of rural life, supplying in advance an ironic counterpoint to the evidently critical state of agrarian Ireland:

> Those who laboured on the land were more closely in touch than others with nature in its various moods and could be more in touch with God, Whose providence was clearly discernible in the yearly round of seasons.[15]

A thoughtful editorial in the *Times* in July noted that skilled workers and professionals were emigrating, and were uninterested in leading the nation.

> [The power of the Big House] like its shattered stones passed into the hands of farmers and smallholders who are only now, slowly and warily, beginning to come together out of the barren isolation which they enjoyed for so long. With a static agricultural production and a dwindling supply of labour, one wonders how unmixed a blessing the Land Acts really were.[16]

The *Times* referred to Ireland, some months later, as a 'nation marking time'.[17] As early as May 1954, the *Independent* noted that industry was developing faster than was agriculture.[18] In June, it reported a big slump even in processed agricultural products.[19] The *Independent* also reported in the same month that agricultural scholarships were still not being taken up, but that the under-equipped vocational education system, in stark contrast, could not keep up with the surge in popular demand. Despite all these fairly obvious straws in the wind, the paper announced in an extraordinarily defensive editorial a few days later that industrial development in Ireland had actually 'reached its limit', and more money would have to be poured into agriculture.[20] In October, as though it had been speaking in the journalistic equivalent of tongues, the Indo headlined a 'Big Jump in Industry' and a 'Marked Industrial Expansion' of 8 per cent in 1953 as compared with 1952.[21] The paper seems to have been suffering from some kind of intellectual schizophrenia, or perhaps it was merely being an authentic Joycean Cave of Winds. Alternatively, the paper was merely echoing a national condition of indecisiveness. In March 1954, the *Press*, always more single-minded than the *Independent*, rebuked James Dillon, sometime Minister for Agriculture, for

---

[15] *Irish Times*, 16 February 1953
[16] *Irish Times*, 7 July 1954
[17] *Irish Times*, 1 October 1954
[18] *Irish Independent*, 14 May 1954
[19] *Irish Independent*, 15 June 1954
[20] *Irish Independent*, 25, 29 June 1954
[21] *Irish Independent*, 1 October 1954

his ridiculing the prospects for industrialisation in the Republic.[22] Dillon was an eloquent defender of the idea that Ireland's future lay in agriculture, and all other ideas were so much poppycock.

The *Press* gave what seems to be its measured diagnosis of the ills of Irish agriculture, in November 1954, suggesting that the Land Acts lay behind the pathologies of Irish agriculture. It concluded its piece by arguing that Irish agriculture would have to learn to compete with its rivals even though they were far more advanced.[23]

At almost the same time, Bishop Cornelius Lucey of Cork announced that it would be a mistake to raise the school leaving age from fourteen to fifteen or even older. It would have the very undesirable effect of making young men not want to be farmers.[24] Evidently these envisaged farmers would be of a very traditionalist kind. His argument was a variant on the old idea that people should not be educated beyond the station that fate or God had allocated to them. Despite this kind of thinking in some high places, a slow earthquake was under way; the OEEC, as outlined in the Indo, noted in a prominently publicised report in December 1954 that the country had experienced a 'striking increase' in industrial output:

> Ireland's longstanding urban unemployment, which was aggravated by the minor recession of 1952, has been reduced to more accustomed proportions by a striking increase of industrial production. But the unemployment figures do not measure the full extent to which the Irish economy is at present unable to absorb the natural increase of the population since one person out of three emigrates. Some countries, because of overpopulation, look upon emigration as being in itself beneficial, but in the case of Ireland where the density of population has the effect of removing people early in their working lives, [it] now constitutes a serious obstacle to the development of the economy.[25]

The report added that Ireland had much unrealised industrial potential, particularly in the making of specialised products using local material content.

In 1955, the Indo thought that things agricultural were looking up. In March, it announced a huge increase in cattle exports.[26] However, in October it published six articles on rural life that drew a rather pessimistic picture. In the first, it reported that there was no Irish tradition of peasant prosperity, there was a great

---

[22] *Irish Press*, 9 March 1954
[23] *Irish Press*, 27 November 1954
[24] *Irish Times*, 16 June 1954
[25] *Irish Independent*, 7 December 1954
[26] *Irish Independent*, 31 March 1955

wish for security, and, it claimed in a fascinating aside, there was a real fear of envy.[27]

Fianna Fáil scepticism about Irish agriculture was articulated by Sean Moylan in May 1955 in his off-the-cuff remark to the effect that 'many people who praise the dual purpose cow did not realise that in many herds we had a no-purpose cow if the profits had to be fed back in concentrates.'[28] The London conservative weekly, the *Spectator*, commented at some length in April 1956 that the Irish were actually much more prosperous nowadays than they once had been, even though Irish agriculture remained 'prehistoric'. Irish industry had developed respectably, and the semi-state bodies were a particularly big success.[29] In August 1956, the Catholic newspaper, the *Standard*, lined up with the mainstream press in lamenting the state of rural Ireland:

> Now the Irish, bitter and grumbling, leave Ireland to work in Britain because the farmyards are too muddy, the villages too depressing, local transport too bad, wages too low, food prices too high, houses too few, work too scarce – under the government they themselves elected freely, unhampered by any man, uninfluenced except by the common techniques which are the stock in trade of politicians everywhere – the mixture of promise and prejudices which by nature seems to succeed the highest ideas on all sides in the rigid and paralysing framework of the party system.[30]

Hibernia, then the organ of the Knights of Columbanus, ran a revealing piece a little later in the year, by Fr Michael O'Carroll, a well-known Holy Ghost Fathers priest. The census had just indicted a new wave of emigration, and O'Carroll voiced an echo of an old fear of race death:

> [In England, Irish emigrants] are well-paid, they enjoy amenities they cannot have at home, they have larger opportunities for self-improvement and self-advancement. They are not hopelessly held back by barriers thrown up around certain classes and groups.

Irish society was unattractive and young people simply wanted to escape from it.[31] The *Press* reported in November the opinion of a businessman (Joseph Griffin of the Irish Glass Bottle company) to the effect that Irish agricultural

[27] *Irish Independent*, 13 October 1955
[28] *Irish Press*, 12 May 1956
[29] *Spectator*, 20 April 1956
[30] *Standard*, 31 August 1956
[31] *Hibernia*, September 1956

production was only 50 per cent of its actual potential. An *Irish Times* editorial in September 1956 reported that Irish farmers needed scientific training, but the Agricultural Institute was delayed due to the operations of vested interests.[32] In November 1956, Martin Smyth wrote in the *Times* that many farmers were lazy and did the minimum of work on the land. Anticipating Raymond Crotty by a generation, he proposed a land tax that would be inversely related to productivity.

> As long as these men control a large proportion of Ireland's best land, and believe in this policy, they can effectively block the progress of the whole country, and this is exactly what they are doing at present.[33]

Cyril McShane responded a week later in a brilliantly argued and empirically informed piece, arguing that farm output varied widely, and a land tax was not politically feasible. The dual-purpose cow existed because meat was only a secondary product. On small farms, more cattle were reared than could ever be brought to maturity, so they had to be sold on to larger farms. These half-starved animals were the only ones the larger farmer could buy. Intensive feeding would be wasted on such animals, and they had to be got rid of at three or four years old. In such a market, efficient modern farming was pointless, was the devastating conclusion.[34] In March 1957, Martin Smyth pointed out that half of Irish farmers had no title deeds to their land and it was difficult to get credit against Irish landholdings, partly because of this legal lacuna.[35]

In September 1957, a Trinity College Dublin economist said that the chief weakness of Irish agriculture was its dominance by the store cattle trade to Britain. Bovine tuberculosis was also a menace even to that trade.[36] Jack Lynch, then Minister for Education, asserted in May 1958 that education had been seen for too long as irrelevant to farm life:

> For too long we had been inclined to divorce education from the practical things of life. For too long we held that the farmer needed no more than the ability to read and write. The successful farmer must be reasonably well-educated with a knowledge of a number of the sciences which underlie modern farming.[37]

---

[32] *Irish Times*, 18 September 1956
[33] *Irish Times*, 1 November 1956
[34] *Irish Times*, 8 November 1956
[35] *Irish Times*, 28 March 1957
[36] *Irish Independent*, 22 September 1957
[37] *Irish Press*, 11 February 1958

In May, 1958, Bishop Con Lucey announced that the disappearance of the Irish small farmer would be tragic.[38] Even as late as 1959, the *Independent* stuck to its agrarian guns despite all evidence, editorialising '…the land is, and must long remain, the chief source of livelihood for our people.'[39] James Dillon defended the farmer valiantly in July 1959, claiming that Irish farmers could double their output if incentives to do so existed. Between 1947 and 1957, they had produced the lion's share of exports and also tripled the value of their exports. He also revived the old plough versus the cow or farmer versus rancher division that had underlain the Fianna Fáil versus Fine Gael cleavage in the 1930s.

The *Irish Times* finally changed sides, specifically rejecting the view that agriculture was the necessary basis for Irish economic progress, in January 1959. There was a quiet acceptance of emigration and population decline in Ireland, the paper observed, the calculation being that if the population were smaller, there would be more to go around: fewer mouths to feed. This was erroneous, it claimed. The paper displayed a kind of despairing patriotism, at a time when things were actually taking a decisive turn for the better.

> Since agriculture, however our methods may be improved and modernised, can no longer be trusted to take up the slack, it is clear that those economists are right who contend that we must increase our industrial exports or consent to our doom as a dying nation.[40]

Eight months later, the paper editorialised against all the evidence that trade trends were still discouraging, but displayed slightly more gumption:

> If we as a nation are not, as one sometimes despairingly feels, obsessed with some kind of a death wish, we must no longer tolerate the fumbling attempts of ageing governments, feather-bedded industries and backward farmers to toy with our destiny.[41]

In September 1959, Bishop William Philbin pleaded for the rescue of the small family farm. Small farms should be made viable, he argued, and too many smallholders were selling up and leaving the country. 'This development was the most alarming kind of emigration.'[42] The *Independent* reported in October under

---

[38] *Irish Independent*, 7 May 1958; on clerical fears, see Tom Garvin, *Preventing the Future*, Dublin: Gill and Macmillan 2004, pp. 36–37
[39] *Irish Independent*, 20 May 1959
[40] *Irish Times*, 29 January 1959
[41] *Irish Times*, 7 October 1959
[42] *Irish Independent*, 26 September 1959

a characteristically schizoid banner headline, 'IN SEVEN YEARS 67,000 PEOPLE LEFT THE LAND. Industrial employment improves.' Between 1951 and 1958, the paper announced, agricultural employment decreased by 67,000, construction declined by 15,000 while manufacturing rose by 7,000 between 1951 and 1955, declined by 5,000 during 1955–57 and made a partial recovery of 2,000 during 1957–58.

In 1959, the *Standard* ran a 'lonely hearts' column, inviting spouse seekers who were devout Catholics to write in to the paper so that they might be put in touch with possible partners. Hundreds of letters poured in. Typical letters described farmers in their forties looking for suitable wives in their thirties, and women in their thirties looking for men in their forties, not necessarily farmers. One angry letter came from a man of forty-four, living on a farm where the parents, presumably in their late seventies, enjoyed the old-age pension and also handled all the cash in the family business:

> Why not take down the pensions of these people who hold on grimly to the farms until their sons and daughters are in their middle age, still mere servants to 'Daddy' and 'Mammy'? … A child of forty-four years old afraid to mention marriage to 'Daddy and Mammy', though not marriage shy.[43]

In May 1960, the *Independent* finally accepted openly for the first time that Ireland's industrial development would have to be given priority over agriculture in government policy and economic leadership. This was in reaction to an OEEC report on the Irish economy, and to the long self-evident, politically inconvenient but much ignored fact that a stagnant Irish agriculture was increasingly being outstripped by a newly dynamic Irish industrial arm.[44] The stagnation of Irish agriculture had often been met with a deafening silence by some Irish journalists, civil servants and academics.

The Slow Acceptance of Industrialisation

Back in 1948, the idea that Ireland would have become a successful exporting country, and that such success would mean far more than exporting cattle and food to a hungry industrialised Britain next door was only beginning to dawn on policy-makers, journalists and the general public. In January 1949, Daniel Morrissey, in Lemass's traditional ministerial seat, declared the economy to be

---

[43] *Standard,* 6 March 1959
[44] *Irish Independent,* 9 May 1960
[45] *Irish Independent,* 19 January 1949

in good shape, with no external debt: 'Our greatest need in relation to industry was the shortage of skilled technicians and trained executives.'[45] The new industrialists seem to have occasionally felt themselves to be unpopular and even under siege. The national communist paper, the *Irish Democrat*, spotted this weakness in the new and superficially successful Ireland of 1951, in an article by Flann Campbell.[46] The new bourgeois Ireland was on shaky psychological and material foundations:

> To the superficial observer Eire today may seem more prosperous than at any time since the Treaty [of 1922]. Wealth in its *nouveau riche* form may be seen in many Irish towns; and Dublin particularly with its smart restaurants, chromium plated pubs, shining American cars, and well-filled luxury shops shows all the signs of solid bourgeois affluence (so long as you keep to the main streets and middle-class residential areas). To watch the smartly tweeded farmers' wives at Leopardstown Races or to observe a well-to-do Dublin businessman eating steaks in Jury's Hotel [in Dame Street] is to realise how triumphantly the Catholic middle class has arrived in Eire.
>
> It has been a long and stony road from the few barren acres of bogland or the miserable huckster's shop which was usually all the native Irish could hope for in the eighteenth century down to the lush pastures of Meath or Guiney's emporiums in O'Connell Street which are so typical of the middle class today, but the Catholic bourgeoisie have completed the journey at last, and show every sign of complacency at their achievement.
>
> At first sight there seems solid economic basis for this new-found prosperity. Irish Farmers, by far the biggest group in the country, are making more money than ever before. For every £100 they got pre-war they now get between £250 and £300. Industrial production has risen about forty per cent since 1939, and more people are employed in manufacturing than at any other time in Irish history....

But in reality, Campbell argued, Irish farm productivity had scarcely changed, the gap between rich and poor was widening and 'the whole rickety structure of prices and luxury living for the middle class' was built on very shaky foundations.

The *Irish Press* echoed obediently the Seán Lemass line on Irish development; without quite saying so, it implied that the country should bypass small-farm agriculture and wager on the strong: big farming to some extent and,

---

[45] *Irish Independent,* 19 January 1949
[46] *Irish Democrat,* July 1951

in particular, industry, the new and growing skilled working class and the new capitalist entrepreneurs and managerial elites.

In March 1948, the deeply conservative new inter-party Minister for Finance, Patrick McGilligan, announced that there would be no transatlantic air service, as had been planned by Fianna Fáil at the instigation of Lemass. The five Lockheed Constellations, state-of-the-art airliners of the time, which had been bought with precious dollars were to be sold off to British Overseas Airways Corporation (BOAC) to be used to revive British transatlantic aviation.[47] BOAC could not believe its luck, as hard-earned or borrowed Irish dollars had enabled it to mount a serious post-war challenge to the American airlines on the Atlantic. Lockheed had located its European servicing at Shannon, and there were already Dutch customers, the *Irish Press* wailed in April. There was plenty of work for young Irish technicians, announced the American manager. The vocational schools of Ireland were well capable of training them, he claimed.[48] William McMullan, General President of the Irish Transport and General Workers' Union, bluntly accused the new government of being hostile to industrialisation. Lemass, in opposition in January 1949, called for a general 'bold industrial drive'.

> He said that his experience as Minister for Industry and Commerce had convinced him that industrial progress was largely a matter of morale, which was the product of confidence. If the whole spirit of the nation was vigorous and enterprising, we would make progress against any difficulties.
>
> In relation to industry, confidence could be created by the clear enunciation of a practical policy – a policy which public opinion accepted as practical and desirable – carried out vigorously and decisively. Those who undertook industrial development must have confidence that the Government was on their side. That did not mean merely assurance of support against external attack, or against difficulties inherent in our economic position. It meant also support against ill-informed or malicious hostility at home.[49]

He also commented that the general Irish lack of any real experience was a central problem, and that industrial leaders and workers should organise themselves more or less like an army. The trade unions must also be brought into the national campaign to industrialise, much as in Labour Britain at the time. In January 1949, the trade union movement demanded the nationalisation of the

---

[47] *Irish Press,* 12 March 1948
[48] *Irish Press,* 12 April 1948
[49] *Irish Press,* 14 January 1949

transport system, which duly came about, producing the fairest flower of Irish bureaucratic corporatism, Córas Iompair Éireann (CIÉ), the Irish Transport Company.[50]

In January also, Daniel Morrissey, the inter-party Minister for Industry and Commerce, promised 'never' to abolish tariffs as long as Ireland's infant industries needed them, to retain state control of any new industries and to build up technical knowledge in the country. There was, he lamented, far too little of it. American capital was to be welcomed, but only on a minority basis; there were too many examples of foreign capital's lack of concern for Irish national interest in the behaviour of their Irish branches.[51] His rather cautiously worded developmentalism does not seem to have been shared by his Fine Gael colleagues; in February, the Road Grant was cut, and road improvement schemes were curtailed, partly at the insistence of the railway interest. The *Irish Times* editorialised in January 1949 to the effect that it was the Marshall Plan that had accelerated the Irish Government's change in policy from all-round protectionism to greater emphasis on export-led growth.[52] However, Irish industry remained solidly protectionist, and the Government was vacillating.

In February, the Old Lady of Westmoreland Street returned to the fray asking,

> How can the desire of this country's industrial organisers to free themselves from official controls be reconciled with their all but unanimous claims to protective tariffs or other state-sponsored privileges? How can recurrent demands for higher wages and shorter hours of work be made consistent with the need to bring down the market prices of life's necessities and the production costs of goods for export?[53]

In May 1949, William H. Taft of the American-led European Cooperation Administration told the Irish that the development of a healthy export trade was a priority for their country.[54] In opposition, De Valera obediently expressed in public his private doubts about the entire system of controls, tariffs and quota that his own party had built up over the previous two decades. He put this in the context of the American drive toward freeing up European trade, and his remarks were made not in Ireland, but at the European Consultative Assembly in Strasbourg.[55]

---

[50] *Irish Press,* 18 January and 5 February 1949
[51] *Irish Independent*, 13 January 1949
[52] *Irish Times,* 14 January 1949
[53] *Irish Times,* 14 February 1949
[54] *Irish Times,* 3 May 1949
[55] *Irish Press,* 3 September 1949

However, an understandable fear of damaging the protected industries and of a possible deindustrialisation surfaced occasionally. William Norton and Frank Aiken of Labour and Fianna Fáil respectively voiced their unease in September 1949, opposing the idea of a European customs union as being premature for the Irish economy.[56] Norton, a post office worker and trade union leader, was a convinced industrialiser and protectionist, whereas Aiken, an IRA veteran leader from South Armagh, was a team player who followed the industrialising line that was pushed by Lemass and blessed by De Valera. In December 1949, the *Irish Times* argued that Marshall Aid would dry up by 1952 and the vital supply of dollars would vanish. Emigrants' remittances, American tourists and exports to the western hemisphere would be the only sources of the precious currency, so important for the nascent recovery of the still-ruined European continent.[57]

Having shelved the transatlantic route as a waste of time, in 1949, the inter-party Government proceeded in 1950 to close down the CIÉ heavy engineering project that the Fianna Fáil government had instigated, another brainchild of Lemass. The *Press* headlined the decision: BASIS OF GREAT PRIMARY INDUSTRY LOST.[58] Lemass reported some months later:

> CIE fitters had tears in their eyes, at the sight of the finest machinery in the world going to loss. Must we always be satisfied with assembling here parts from Britain? Were we not going to get on to the manufacturing process some time?[59]

In March 1950, Morrissey commented that in 1926 there had been 102,000 workers in industry and services in the state, and by 1949 there were 200,000 in industry alone. The real increase was probably 2.5 times, he said, but it was still too small as a proportion of the total workforce. The new Industrial Development Authority (IDA) was to plan future industrialisation.[60] There was some vague sense in the papers of the potential of this new agency, which was to prove so central to Irish development over the ensuing decades. However, even Lemass took time to grasp its enormous importance to the future of the country; he distrusted its Fine Gael provenance. John Leydon, Lemass's right-hand man since 1932 and a senior civil servant of the time, was also originally somewhat uneasy about the idea, and influenced Lemass in his initial hostility. The man who seems to have really understood its significance was its godfather, Daniel

---

[56] *Irish Times,* 3 September 1949
[57] *Irish Times,* 10 December 1949
[58] *Irish Press,* 16 January 1950
[59] *Irish Press,* 31 May 1950
[60] *Irish Times,* 10 March 1950

Morrissey of Fine Gael; he pointed out that there was very little information about Irish industry available even to industrialists themselves, and the first job of the IDA would be to collect such information and make it available. Lemass changed his tune when he returned to government in 1951.[61]

The Bill setting up the IDA was actually denounced by some representatives of business interests meeting under the auspices of the Federation of Irish Industry. They objected in particular to the power it was proposed to give the new body to examine witnesses in a quasi-judicial manner, enforceable by fines of up to £50 in an era when £7 was seen by even communists as a decent weekly working wage. Rightly, the industrial leaders claimed that the powers of semi-judicial compulsory inquiry the Government proposed to give to the IDA were unconstitutional. Later it turned out that these powers were unnecessary, as the benefits of co-operating with the IDA became obvious, and industry queued up voluntarily to co-operate with it and get advice, information and grants. Industrial relations were poor. Workers were wary of employers, and both sets were wary of the Government. The *Irish Times* was quite sympathetic to the workers' traditional distrust of the establishment, whether it was the state, the bosses or even the union leaders. The following year, the paper commented:

> No objective-minded person can deny that the Irish working-class suspicion is well founded. Every attempt that is made to improve their living standards is met with hostility. One has merely to think of such socially beneficial legislation as the Social Security Bill or the Mother and Child scheme to realise this.

Back in office for more than a year in late 1952, Lemass remarked that the country was indeed running down its external assets and that they would be all gone in five or six years. Then, he predicted quite correctly, there would be a crisis. However, the Government under Fianna Fáil would be ready for it, he announced. It was increasing investment in cement, sugar, shipping and electrical plant. Half of this capital was being provided from private sources.[62] He admitted that he foresaw Irish agriculture eventually being rationalised by the weaker farmers being squeezed out of the workforce in favour of the strong more efficient ones.[63]

In early 1952, the *Irish Times* feared a reversion to protectionism and self-sufficiency, arguing that the country would have to brave the risks of modern

---

[61] Brian Farrell, *Sean Lemass,* Dublin: Gill and Macmillan, 1991, pp. 82–83
[62] *Irish Press*, 8 November 1952
[63] *Irish Times*, 8 January 1952

international trade if it were to escape poverty.[64] A few weeks later, a prominent unionist politician, J. E. Warnock, argued that Eire was an economic basket case, for no better reason than a perverse politics.[65] In an uncharacteristic piece of support for industry, the Indo editorialised in its praise in March 1952.[66]

Shortly afterwards, the *Irish Times* ran an interesting little survey of informed opinion about the country's economic problems, quizzing a leader of the Irish Housewives' Association, a farmer, a senior electricity supply official, a businessman, a drapers' representative, a well-known trade unionist and a representative of the service and professional associations. The usual suspects were cited. Irish economic sluggishness could be attributed to many factors, in particular retail price maintenance, too much protectionism, too many middle men parasitic on the economy, poor marketing of agricultural produce, high taxes, restrictive practices, unfair apprenticeship systems, too much government interference, price controls, international tensions, external circumstances beyond the country's control, unions forcing up costs, a small tax base and industrialists influencing politics in their own interest.[67]

In April 1952, the *Times* headlined 'HARSHEST BUDGET WE EVER FACED'. The editorial, entitled *'Dies Irae'* (Day of Wrath), pointed out that Marshall Aid was gone and only one in sixteen workers paid income tax.[68] The Stacey May report on the Irish economy, written by American experts, observed anti-materialist ideology for an authoritarian and heavy-handed governmental style, according to a quite accurate *Irish Times* story in November 1952. The report commented that Ireland's potential productive capability was enormous, and almost completely untapped.[69]

In June 1953, Lemass was positively gung-ho about Irish developmental prospects; he spoke about investment in infrastructure: electricity generation, land improvement, housing, health and education. All were needed to produce a higher level of economic activity, he said.[70] Repeatedly he gave the public ideological pep talks, in an almost single-handed attempt to change the psychology of the people from one that encouraged passivity to one that encouraged energy and optimism. In June 1953, he observed that development was essential. The country was going to get state-aided infrastructure in the form of new electricity generating plants, land improvement, housing, health and

[64] *Irish Times,* 19 January 1952
[65] *Irish Times,* 6 February 1952
[66] *Irish Independent,* 10 March 1952
[67] *Irish Times,* 9 and 12 February 1952
[68] *Irish Times,* 3 April 1952
[69] *Irish Times,* 21 and 22 November 1952
[70] *Irish Press*, 27 June 1953

education, all of which were needed to produce higher levels of economic activity.[71]

More soberly, an *Irish Press* editorial noted a month later that industrial development since 1932 had only just about absorbed the surplus labour, leaving agriculture as agriculture mechanised and increased production while shrinking employment.[72] Arguably, even this was a very rose-tinted view of Irish economic achievements. In August 1953 Lemass predicted a 'great period of national development and economic expansion'.[73] Despite all the bad news, something was indeed changing in an almost underground way in the Republic of Ireland. In October 1953, Aknefton, the political correspondent of the *Irish Times,* wrote:

> [The business pages of newspapers] reflect the state of growth of Irish industry and latterly have shown, beyond all doubt, a development which is new in so far as this country is concerned – the emergence into full prominence of a managerial class as the leaders of Irish trade, industry and commerce.

However, Irish industry was still intellectually backward, and Irish managers continued to be reluctant to discuss innovative changes with their workers before initiating changes.[74]

The *Irish Independent* relieved itself of the extraordinary opinion in June 1954 that Irish industry had developed to its absolute limit and therefore future investment should be in agriculture.[75] The cacophony and intellectual disunity was apparently endless: in July 1954, Norton lamented the lack of technical skills necessary for the new industrial venues.[76] Erskine Childers, often an acute observer, remarked in September that the greater productivity required a change of attitude on the part of three-quarters of the population, changes in the educational system and a campaign of instilling confidence in the future, dispelling the pervasive Irish sense of hopelessness:

> The changeover from production with minimum capital risk and maximum war scarcity plus protection, to intense production was the only way of increasing the income of the whole people. We are all agreed on that. The present system, Mr. Childers said, was more proof against the effects of world depression, but brought progress to a standstill.[77]

---

[71] Ibid.
[72] Ibid.
[73] *Irish Times,* 3 August 1953
[74] *Irish Times,* 10 October 1953
[75] *Irish Independent,* 29 June 1954
[76] *Irish Independent,* 23 July 1954
[77] *Irish Times,* 14 September 1954

The *Independent* commented in December 1954 on the beginnings of the French economic boom of the time, remarking that the country had moved away from the 'strangle' of protective tariffs.[78] There was a general, if rather confused, sense of new possibilities, although not yet a consensus as to what the general lines of economic and educational policy should be; nor did the will exist quite yet for a genuine new departure. People were evidently hunting around for new ideas. In July 1955, John O'Donovan, a well-known economist and a Fine Gael minister, opined that an adventurous minority of industrial concerns was already moving cautiously but bravely into the export markets.[79] Lemass outlined his own thinking more fully in October 1955, being once again in opposition. The *Press* headlined his speech and reported that his plan was to create 100,000 jobs in five years by means of state-led private enterprise strategies.

> In other words our view is that the Government must carry the main burden in the first instance, but must so arrange its programme that it can gradually fade out of the picture leaving private economic activity the main basis of national prosperity. It is clear that the scale of the public expenditure which will be required to bring national outlay to full employment within five years will be very considerable. Fianna Fáil reject the view, which is sometimes propagated in the press and elsewhere, that the sole object of Government policy should be to keep public expenditure at the lowest possible level.[80]

The second inter-party government, under its equivalent of Seán Lemass, Daniel Morrissey, defended its tentative attempts to attract foreign investment and get around the Control of Manufactures Acts of 1933–34; Morrissey was attempting to tiptoe around the protectionist mentality of some senior civil servants, in particular the implacable and legendry opposition to free trade of J. C. B. McCarthy, the Secretary of the Department of Industry and Commerce, and many, but by now not all, of the manufacturers. In this he had the sympathetic hearing of Gerard Sweetman, who had a background in economics and who listened also to Whitaker, Lynch and others. Morrissey, in November 1955 in the Dáil, defended his rather timid, but creative, new departure:

> There was apprehension among urban people at the recent statements the Minister had made with a view to attracting outside firms to produce here. Home industry should not merely get preference but should get whatever measure of protection that it required. While giving the fullest protection,

---

[78] *Irish Independent,* 15 December 1954
[79] *Irish Times*, 13 July 1985
[80] *Irish Press*, 12 October 1951

they might, however, be sure that merely because a firm was Irish it did not mean that it could become a monopoly sheltered completely from competition. There were some firms in this country who protested vehemently, not only against competition from foreign firms, but from Irish firms as well.[81]

He went on to remark, rather alarmingly, that Britain and Northern Ireland were attracting plenty of American investment, while the Republic was not; in effect, even though there were ways of getting around the acts by setting up shell companies and other devices of that sort, the fancy-free Americans merely took one look at the apparent hostility to capital in the Republic and went elsewhere.

Government-imposed price controls, survivals of wartime, were another turn-off. There was a general air of entrepreneurial frustration in the country, despite Lemass's boosterism. In the same month, Joseph Griffin, a well-known Dublin businessman, published a well-publicised paper on the significance of the price structure in the economy of the country. He had an early version of Cathal Guiomard's 'designer economy' in mind. He argued that Irish economic success, such as it was, occurred despite, rather than because of, the economic and political framework in which it had to operate. There was an 'atmosphere of frustration' in Ireland. The Irish had an 'underdeveloped country and the potential for an expanding economy and population'. He added, 'Only an ideal was lacking'. The usual lamentation was recited. Agriculture was underdeveloped and achieved only 50 per cent of its potential. Manufacturing potential was unexplored and unexamined. Industry was sluggish, and in services, education and culture progress was slow and underdeveloped. 'Frustration and cynicism are apparent in all walks of life and at all levels of society,' he said. Price controls depressed economic activity; in Britain and America the price structure was closer to the ideal.[82]

In January, Norton was in the United States, a putatively leftist Irish workers' leader voluntarily wooing American investment. He expressed willingness to offer tax concessions to foreign investors in the country; and the old protectionist psychology, together with the classic republican distrust of foreign capital and 'big business' was slowly but visibly fading away.[83] In February 1956, Costello urged encouragement of foreign investment, but only for export industries, a proposition that Lemass was to echo quite faithfully a year later.[84] The economic crash of 1956 was now on its way and the population was shrinking as emigration

[81] *Irish Press*, 3 November 1955
[82] *Irish Press*, 16 November 1955
[83] *Irish Times*, 10, 13 and 17 January 1956
[84] *Irish Press*, 8 February 1956

reached record levels and even the middle classes were leaving to a country where their children would have some kind of future. The *Press* headlined in June, 'ISSUE NOW SURVIVAL'.[85] A few weeks later, it announced, 'Emigration of Professional Groups Deplored'.[86]

There was now a slowly growing consensus between all the political leaders that something would have to be done, involving foreign investment, serious cultural change and educational development. In October 1956, the *Irish Times* editorialised to the effect that a national economic development plan should have been put together 'thirty years ago'. However, there was actually no mention of education in an otherwise progressive piece; hindsight wisdom tells us that this was part of a general pattern that was characteristic of the decade: education could expand only through private effort and by stealth.[87] In the 1950s, this is almost exactly what happened. In December, the *Times* announced that 1956 had been 'one of the worst years which this state has experienced'.[88]

Common Europe was coming, and was seen more clearly than it was in Britain, still mourning its dying empire. The long Irish love affair with Europe was beginning. In February 1957, the manager of Gateaux Ltd expressed the view that Ireland could not afford to stay out of the coming Common Market. People who had been protected for generations in their industries and who had never exported anything were getting 'too loudmouthed' about this issue.[89]

Fianna Fáil swept back into power in March 1957. In April, it was reported that Hungarian refugees were going back to the communist tyranny in Hungary, horrified as they were by Irish poverty. As the Irish joke of the time had it, the wolf was at the door, howling to get out.[90] In May, Lemass growled again at the pessimists: 'Those who are still pulling long faces and making gloomy forecasts about the future, will look just as foolish, when the future arrives, as the Jeremiahs of the past.'[91] He then announced that the once-sacred Control of Manufactures Acts were to be amended. In a silent tribute to the power of vested interests in post-war Ireland, an incredible twelve years after the end of the Second World War, he announced that wartime price controls were to be finally abolished on the grounds that they were obsolete and were a major deterrent to outside investment.

James Ryan, a senior Fianna Fáil figure, admitted that price control abolition had been opposed by many elements in the party, presumably for electoral

---

85 *Irish Press*, 6 June 1956
86 *Irish Press*, 18 June 1956
87 *Irish Times*, 2 October 1956
88 *Irish Times*, 14 December 1956
89 *Irish Press*, 22 February 1957
90 *Irish Times*, 24 April 1957
91 *Irish Press*, 27 May 1957

purposes; they could be represented quite easily as protecting the poor against the depredations of the rich.[92] John Conroy, President of the Irish Transport and General Workers' Union, ratified this action theoretically in what seems to have been a co-ordinated move, arguing noisily that controls just didn't work.[93] As usual, a progressive step had been blocked for years by what amounted to a conspiracy between backbenchers, employers and unions against the public interest. In August, Lemass claimed that foreign firms were beginning to wake up to the productive potential of Ireland.[94] He began to emphasise a new theme in 1957, that of efficiency in production, and an end to traditional Irish make-do and half-trained sloppiness.[95]

On 14 November 1957, in the symbolic wake of *Sputnik One*, Seán MacEntee warned industrialists that they should prepare for free trade and that all tariffs would be abolished in fifteen years.[96] A few weeks later, almost as if on cue (and possibly actually *on* cue), the OECD recommended that the Irish go in for more private and less public productive investment while being more supportive of business. Government should also afford the maximum scope to make profits and boost production. Secondly, public funds should be directed less at social investment. Dependence on the British market for meat and dairy product sales should be lessened by active search for other foreign markets.[97] In January 1958, the Federation of Irish Manufacturers announced that it would appoint a committee to examine the position of Irish industry under a free trade regime.[98] In February, an expert commented in the *Irish Press* that Irish industrialists were very reluctant to hire technicians. Jack Lynch, the new Minister for Education, commented that Irish people were far too prone to see no connection between education and the capacity to earn a living. Farmers, he observed, were particularly likely to have a disregard for education and training.[99] The President of the Federation of Irish Industry pointed out that Irish output of technically trained people per head of population was one-quarter of Britain's, one-tenth of America's and one-eighteenth that of the Soviet Union.[100]

In March 1958, Lemass said that whatever free trade regime emerged from the negotiations going on in Europe, the Irish would have to get used to the idea

[92] Ibid.
[93] *Irish Press*, 31 May 1957
[94] *Irish Times*, 22 August 1957
[95] *Irish Press*, 23 October 1957. See also, *Irish Press*, 25 September 1957
[96] *Irish Press*, 15 November 1957
[97] *Irish Press*, 23 December 1957
[98] *Irish Press*, 15 January 1958
[99] *Irish Press*, 11 February 1958
[100] *Irish Press*, 14 February 1958

of working in an internationalised economy where 'protection would no longer be the main instrument of industrial policy.'[101]

Whitaker's *Economic Development* was saying what a very large proportion of the population wanted to hear from government: that a new departure was overdue; in his case, the people were hearing it from a source they trusted. In a sense, the politicians were forced to hide behind the civil servants. The newspaper had gradually converged on a similar position regardless of their traditional allegiances, ideological crotchets or, in the cases of the *Irish Times* and *Irish Independent*, their deep-rooted commitment to agrarianism.

There was a general sense of change occurring and being inevitable and the overwhelming necessity of cultural change in particular to cope with the economic shifts that were about to happen. Joseph Griffin said with an air of new hope in November 1958, with reference to Whitaker's team and their White Paper outlining a four-year plan for economic expansion,

> We in Ireland are beginning – only beginning – to throw off the pall of gloom that has been darkening our days, confusing our minds and our policies, and distracting our intelligence and our energies. I sense it in many walks of life…. The doctrine of our poverty in material resources continues to plague and debilitate our people like a dark and brooding medieval superstition. Our educational system has not done enough to dispel it. It is not merely among workers or small farmers or the little people of the country that this doctrine survives, but among the educated in business and commerce, in industry and agriculture, in public administration and, alas, in our educational institutions. This doctrine of poverty destroys hope and where there is no hope there is no courage. Instead there is a sort of counter superstition. This myth of our [inevitable] poverty must at all costs be destroyed.[102]

In July 1959, the Taoiseach, Seán Lemass, with exquisite timing, announced:

> We have now the element of an accepted national economic policy. The fact that organisations representative of every economic interest accepted and supported the Government's economic programme is a splendid beginning.[103]

The economy began to grow in 1957–58, and by 1959 it was becoming obvious that a benign syndrome of economic improvement and growing public optimism was occurring. In late 1959, the *Irish Press* trumpeted, 'NEW PHASE FOR

---

[101] *Irish Independent*, 24 March 1958
[102] *Irish Press*, 12 November 1958
[103] *Irish Press*, 13 July 1959, direct speech restored

INDUSTRY. Well into Era of Bigger Projects'.[104] On 30 October, the paper boasted in a front-page headline, 'ECONOMY IS EXPANDING'. In November, it expanded on this by headlining the Lemass speech at the Fianna Fáil Ard-Fheis: 'PATRIOTISM THE MOTIVE POWER'.[105] The *Irish Times* editorialised in November that Irish industry's resistance to free trade was now finally fading. However, the paper also emphasised that such resistance would have been very determined in 1949, and would very likely have been successful; protection would itself have been politically protected ten years earlier. A senior industrial leader admitted that protection had gone on for far too long and had been applied far too widely. It had also overshadowed the very real achievements of modern Irish industry. Government and industry were, hand in hand, finding new markets for Irish products, he announced.[106]

The Third Report of the Capital Advisory Committee under Leydon reported at the same time and listed three serious weaknesses: poor education, a lack of enterprise, and a tendency to substitute subsidies for effort. Most capital investment was in effect redistributive and only very partly productive: 'standards of consumption are pushed up toward the British level, but real income per head is little more then half that in Britain; private savings are low.'[107] In January 1960, Lemass declared it to be a critical year. The Irish would have to learn new markets and become internationally competitive.

> In industry in particular, we have just about reached the limits of development based on present home market possibilities alone. The policy of high industrial protection on which we relied for industrial expansion heretofore has now nearly spent itself. It is no longer very effective as a stimulus to industrial growth. It may indeed become something of a handicap, to the extent that it may operate to preserve inefficient or obsolete production methods, or shelter restrictive labour practices, or other high-cost factors, which could not survive in more competitive conditions … we cannot remain in business, much less expand, if our production costs remain out of line with the rest of the world.[108]

D. A. Hegarty of Dublin Port and Docks Board made a similar point at about the same time. The Irish were far too insular. Irish management techniques were utterly obsolete and self-defeating. Employer/worker relationships, the training

---

[104] *Irish Press*, 23 September 1959
[105] *Irish Press*, 30 October and 11 November 1959
[106] *Irish Times*, 7 November 1959
[107] *Irish Independent*, 26 November 1958
[108] *Irish Independent*, 15 January 1960

of managers and work-study were non-existent or extremely primitive. Europe had developed a 'new industrial thinking' and this had resulted in an 'unparalleled prosperity'.[109] There was a general sense that Ireland's problems were psychological and cultural rather then material or structural. An inherited sense of second-rate status reinforced a strong tendency to be content with mediocre performance. Things were, however, changing: Britain was no longer a great power, Europe was on the way with American encouragement, and by 1960 Ireland was indeed waking up from what so many *contemporary* commentators saw as being a very long sleep.

---

[109] *Irish Independent*, 28 January 1960

6

Ireland's Economic Recovery in the 1950s

Garret FitzGerald

For some amongst us of mature age this is an occasion to bask in the reflected glory of Ken Whitaker: I am happy to be one of this small band and I am absolutely delighted to have this opportunity to salute a man, whom I have known since, fifty-five years ago, I was elected to the Council of the Statistical and Social Inquiry Society of Ireland, of which he had for some years previously been a member. Then a few years later I was privileged to participate with him and a small number of other public servants and economists in an informal Economics group that used to meet monthly in the Central Bank.

Then, in 1961, he asked me whether, during a first visit to the EC Commission in Brussels – on that occasion as an economic journalist – I might sound out and report back privately to him on possible Commission reactions to an Irish application for full membership of the Community – rather than mere Association with the EC, which is all that until then had been contemplated. Moreover, around the same time as, three months later, Seán Lemass announced in the Dáil our application for membership (in a speech so obscurely worded that neither of the two opposition leaders at first understood that we were applying for full membership rather than Associate), I also worked with him on the establishment of the Committee on Industrial Organisation to prepare Irish industry for free trade.

Concluding this brief personal note of reminiscence, when in 1964 I decided to enter politics, it was to him – my hero then as now! – that I first communicated my decision – which provoked a response from him to the effect that he was sure this was a mistake, as by doing this I would lose all the influence I had acquired as an economic journalist! He clearly did not think that I would have much influence as a politician!

However, I should like to use my time here to speak about what I see as having been the genesis of the *First Programme for Economic Expansion* – the occasion, on 25 May 1956 (just ten days or so before his appointment by his Minister, Gerard Sweetman, as Secretary of the Department of Finance at the age of 39), when Ken Whitaker read a seminal – indeed I would say revolutionary paper in Irish economic terms – to the Statistical and Social Inquiry Society of Ireland.

I want to quote several passages from that remarkable paper, because, as you will see, they remain eerily relevant to our situation today, half a century later. I am afraid that what this tells is that, whilst politicians can learn from their mistakes (at least from their really big mistakes!) in many cases memories of these do not survive even for a generation thereafter – for these mistakes are then repeated a mere ten or twenty years later, as we have seen happen twice, in 1977–81, and again at the start of the present century.

Fifty years ago, on overbuilding of dwellings, Ken Whitaker had this to say:

[Between] 1949 and 1954 dwellings alone formed as high a proportion of gross domestic capital formation as agriculture, mining, manufacturing and other construction combined.
[Exactly the same was again the case by 2005, when €21bn out of €43bn total investment was being invested in dwellings.]

He then went on to say that:

Rates of pay which are out of line with the international value of the products of home labour at the existing rate of exchange may be a serious obstacle to the attainment of full employment.
[Which is precisely where we find ourselves today, with wage levels inflated to a level that has once again made it impossible for us to compete successfully with our European partners. Within the past seven years this has inevitably led to a slowing of goods exports that has cost us the loss of one-quarter of our share of the world market for goods].

In that paper of fifty-two years ago, Ken Whitaker also pointed out the damage done to our economy because:

In three out of the seven years (1948–1954) (and doubtless also in 1955) the increase in national consumption exceeded the increase in national income, leading to the prevalence of inflationary conditions.

[Once again, in four of our seven most recent years (2000–2007), and also in 2008, the increase in national consumption exceeded the increase in national income].

He then went on to add that:

There must be some sacrifice of current welfare and consumption if there is to be any economic development in the future.

Which is precisely the lesson that we once again, in late 2008, have to draw from having so unwisely repeated during the years of this current decade the mistakes of the early 1950s and of the late 1970s, thus leaving our economy badly placed to cope with the combined impact of the bursting of our housing bubble plus the oil price hikes and the global credit crunch.

In this seminal paper, which contained the key elements of what was to become two years later the *First Programme for Economic Expansion*, he also made a most courageous onslaught on what was then our quarter-century-old system of industrial protection – which until that time had been a political hot potato that neither politicians nor civil servants had been willing to confront.

De Valera, you should remember, the apostle of the self-defeating doctrine of self-sufficiency, was then still the opposition leader – and would within twelve months become Taoiseach again, for the last time.

What Ken Whitaker said bluntly in that paper was that:

Prolonged protection, sheltering high domestic costs or inferior quality, blocks both the incentive and the capacity to expand production for export markets. Modification of protection, improvements in industrial organisation, and a closer gearing of pay to productivity, are necessary....

I recall that in the discussion that followed the paper, John Leydon, the very recently retired Secretary of the Department of Industry and Commerce, responded very critically to this part of Ken Whitaker's paper – a response that, however, is not reflected in the account of his remarks that he must have submitted to the Society's journal after the announcement of Ken Whitaker's appointment as Secretary of Finance just ten days after his address to the Statistical Society. Historians must – and do – beware of historical records that may have been retrospectively adjusted!

Finally I would like to add one footnote on the emergence of the *First Programme for Economic Expansion* itself, just two-and-a-half years after it had been presaged by that seminal address.

On 12 November 1958, the Government published its own Economic Programme, which incorporated much, but by no means all, of the proposals that Ken Whitaker had submitted six months earlier. (I have often wondered who exactly wrote that considerably revised and somewhat watered-down version of his proposals – surely not Ken Whitaker himself?)

However that may be, it was courageous and I believe wise of that Government to have authorised the publication ten days later of the text of the proposals that Ken Whitaker had submitted to them. Although this opened up the possibility of criticism of their rejection of some of his proposals, what it certainly did was to de-politicise the Programme, making it easier for the Opposition (in which the man who had appointed Ken Whitaker Secretary of the Department of Finance, Gerard Sweetman, continued to play a key role) to accept it. It was neither debated in the Dáil nor criticised by the Opposition, and thus secured the Government against its Programme being treated as a purely party political document. That helped to launch the economic recovery that brought our state its first, pre-EU, burst of economic growth.

7

The Celtic Tiger in Historical and International Perspective

Nicholas Crafts

Introduction

When *Economic Development* was published in 1958, there was good reason to worry about both Ireland's economic performance and its economic prospects. While most western European countries were enjoying rapid economic growth, Ireland was falling well behind the leaders. With an industrial-relations structure based on strong but decentralised collective bargaining, Ireland was not in a position to follow the corporatist path to rapid catch-up growth based on wage restraint in return for high investment, which prevailed in much of Europe. As a small, inefficient, and still quite agricultural economy on the periphery, there were good reasons to fear the consequences of moves to free trade within Europe.

Fast forward to 2007 and Ireland had overtaken all European economies except Norway in terms of real GNP per person and had just emerged from the Celtic Tiger period of economic growth. This phase had seen Ireland take off into a growth trajectory predicated on taking up the opportunities of globalisation and the ICT era. Between 1987 and 2007, under the auspices of social partnership, real GDP per person grew at 5.6 per cent per year, comparable with the fast-growth economies of east Asia and far ahead of any other European country.

This paper seeks to place these contrasting experiences firmly in the context of the post-war European experience of economic growth. Obviously, it is important to understand how the tortoise achieved metamorphosis into the hare but it is also instructive explicitly to consider why Ireland underperformed relative to its European peer group during the Golden Age and then outperformed in the late twentieth century. This will allow some reflections on the diagnosis and remedy set out in *Economic Development*, informed also by ideas taken from modern growth economics.

Irish Growth in the European Golden Age

The years 1950 to 1973 are conventionally known as the Golden Age of European economic growth. It is important to recognise that this was throughout a period of growth failure for Ireland. By 1973, Ireland had sunk to the bottom of the west European league in terms of the level of real GDP per person, below even Greece and Portugal. Table 1, in which the countries are ranked according to the level of real GDP per person in 1950 and which shows a strong inverse correlation between initial income and subsequent growth, gives a sense of the magnitude of the growth shortfall. Comparison with Austria and Italy suggests that growth of real GDP per person at 5 per cent per year rather than 3 per cent per year was par for the course and that the income level of 1973 might have been at least 50 per cent higher.

Table 1: *Levels and Rate of Growth of Real GDP/Person in Golden Age Europe ($1990GK and % per year)*

	GDP/Person, 1950	GDP/Person, 1973	Growth Rate 1950–73
Switzerland	9,064	18,204	3.08
Denmark	6,943	13,945	3.08
UK	6,939	12,025	2.42
Sweden	6,739	12,494	3.06
Netherlands	5,971	13,081	3.45
Belgium	5,462	12,170	3.54
Norway	5,430	11,324	3.24
France	5,271	13,114	4.04
West Germany	4,281	13,153	5.02
Finland	4,253	11,085	4.25
Austria	3,706	11,235	4.94
Italy	3,502	10,634	4.95
Ireland	3,453	6,867	3.03
Spain	2,189	7,661	5.60
Portugal	2,086	7,063	5.45
Greece	1,915	7,655	6.21

Note: levels are measured in constant prices at purchasing power parity in 1990 Geary-Khamis dollars.
Source: Maddison (2003)

A further insight into this disappointing growth performance can be obtained using growth accounting to examine the sources of Irish labour productivity growth, a technique that is particularly useful for benchmarking comparisons across countries. Table 2 reports results from an exercise of this kind carried out by Bosworth and Collins (2003). Compared with other relatively low-income economies of the time, Ireland in the 1960s had a shortfall in each of the sources of labour productivity growth, but education does not make much difference. Weaknesses in investment and, especially, total factor productivity (TFP) growth are highlighted as the key problems.[1]

Table 2: *Contributions to Labour Productivity Growth, 1960–1970*
(% per year)

	Capital-Deepening	Human-Capital-Deepening	Total Factor Productivity	Labour Productivity
Switzerland	1.40	0.40	1.37	3.17
Denmark	2.15	0.13	1.25	3.53
UK	1.45	0.17	1.24	2.86
Sweden	1.34	0.19	2.40	3.93
Netherlands	1.43	0.74	0.89	3.06
Belgium	1.36	0.42	2.33	4.11
Norway	1.18	0.48	1.80	3.46
France	2.02	0.29	2.62	4.93
West Germany	2.10	0.23	2.03	4.36
Finland	1.66	0.37	2.64	4.67
Austria	2.39	0.18	2.90	5.47
Italy	2.39	0.36	3.50	6.25
Ireland	1.78	0.22	2.21	4.21
Spain	2.45	0.38	3.73	6.56
Portugal	2.05	0.35	3.99	6.39
Greece	3.63	0.26	4.45	8.34

Note: Estimates based on the standard neoclassical growth accounting formula with imposed capital share of 0.35 in all cases; capital-deepening reflects the contribution of investment, human-capital-deepening denotes the contribution of improved educational attainment of the labour force, and total factor productivity captures the contribution of improvements in efficiency and technology.
Source: Database constructed for Bosworth and Collins (2003) kindly provided by the authors.

Table 3 reports that Ireland in 1960 had a low level of TFP by European standards. This appears to have been primarily a result of inefficiency rather than

---

[1] An alternative accounting exercise based on a growth-regression technique points even more strongly in this direction, see Crafts and Toniolo (1996) Table 1.14.

lack of access to appropriate technology and, moreover, Ireland shows up as inefficient relative to its peer group. Tables 2 and 3 taken together suggest that 1960s Ireland was rather slow to address its efficiency gap.

Table 3: *Decomposition of 1960 TFP Level into Efficiency and Technology Components (USA = 1.00)*

	TFP	*Efficiency*	*Technology*
Switzerland	1.05	1.00	1.05
Denmark	0.69	0.68	1.01
UK	0.85	0.89	0.95
Sweden	0.73	0.72	1.01
Netherlands	0.77	0.74	1.04
Belgium	0.65	0.64	1.01
Norway	0.54	0.63	0.86
France	0.72	0.71	1.01
Finland	0.62	0.60	1.04
Austria	0.60	0.64	0.94
Italy	0.67	0.71	0.94
Ireland	0.51	0.55	0.93
Spain	0.64	0.74	0.86
Portugal	0.57	0.66	0.87
Greece	0.49	0.57	0.86

Note: TFP = Efficiency*Technology
Source: Jerzmanowski (2007)

Modern growth economics based on the key concept of endogenous innovation would predict that inferior TFP performance would be a consequence of incentive structures, perhaps with regard to high direct taxation or inadequate competition, that were less conducive to innovation and cost reduction than elsewhere (Aghion and Howitt, 2006). This suggests that supply-side policies left something to be desired and the most plausible culprit is excessive protectionism, given that Ireland was slow to embrace trade liberalisation and had effective protection levels that were very high compared with its trading partners until the mid-1960s (Barry, 2008). It is less obvious that Ireland was exposed to unduly high direct taxation given that direct tax revenues were only about 12 per cent of GDP.

The diagnosis that T. K. Whitaker offered in 1958 in *Economic Development* was very much along these lines. He noted that Irish infant industry policies had failed, stressed that lower Irish tariffs would increase efficiency and productivity, and argued for the abolition of controls on foreign ownership of Irish industry. He also prioritised a reduction on income and profits taxes as a key requirement. Whitaker emphasised that productive investment was too low but his analysis was distinctly not based on the 'capital fundamentalism' that was fashionable among economists at the time. Rather, he argued that the dynamic might be found from faster TFP growth which would feed back to investment.[2] This is a stance of which Aghion and Howitt would approve.

Fully exploiting the potential for catch-up growth also depended on raising investment and the rate of capital deepening. Here, it is important to note an omission in the analysis of *Economic Development* that is highlighted by comparison with high-growth European countries. Eichengreen (2006) argues that, in these economies, state corporatism underwrote a co-operative equilibrium between capital and labour that delivered high investment in return for wage restraint.[3] This was clearly not a path followed by Ireland with its tradition of strong but decentralised collective bargaining (Crouch, 1993).

Whatever the merits of Whitaker's analysis, Ireland's growth performance continued to disappoint throughout the Golden Age. Trade liberalisation began, corporate tax reforms were introduced and inward technology transfer was encouraged with the new pro-FDI policy stance consolidated by the establishment of the Industrial Development Agency, in 1969. But growth regressions performed for the Crafts and Toniolo (2008) survey paper suggest that, if anything, Golden-Age Irish underperformance was slightly worse after 1960 than before.

The Transition to the Celtic Tiger

Economic Development clearly pointed the way in that it argued that Ireland must seize the opportunities arising from trade liberalisation, and foreign industrialists coming to Ireland would be a vital source of technology transfer. A recent econometric study concluded that income per person in Ireland in 2000 was 25.9 per cent higher than if economic integration had remained at its 1950s level (Badinger, 2005). Moreover, as everyone recognises, export-platform foreign direct investment (FDI) was central to transition to fast growth. Ireland became extremely successful in attracting FDI, and low corporate taxation was the most important reason for this (Gropp and Kostial, 2000). Beyond this, Ireland

---

[2] Whitaker did not use this terminology but it is clear that the things that he points to as releasing the dynamic would show up in a larger Solow residual: 'A dynamic has to be found and it is not necessarily increased capital investment, though this may be called for to support a higher rate of development once it is set in motion … there are other conditions of economic progress no less important … a raising of the general level of education, health and skill, the loosening of restrictive practices, whether of employers or employees, the practical encouragement of initiative and enterprise, the adoption of improved methods, techniques and principles of organisation and management both in agriculture and industry, and a greater readiness to apply scientific advances.' (Ireland, Department of Finance, 1958, p. 7)

[3] In an Aghion and Howitt-type growth model, incentive structures that raise the investment rate also have an indirect positive effect on TFP growth.

developed a sophisticated policy framework to select projects for financial support, and made complementary investments in education and infrastructure (Buckley and Ruane, 2006).

Table 4 reports estimates of the stock of American FDI per person. These show that in 1968, just before the establishment of the Industrial Development Agency, Ireland was on a par with EU countries generally but well below the UK. In 1986, on the eve of the growth take-off, Ireland had almost twice as much US FDI per person as the UK, and almost six times that in other EU countries. By the end of the Celtic Tiger period, the ratios were three times and almost nine times, respectively.

Table 4: *Inward US FDI Stock/Person ($)*

	Ireland	*UK*	*Rest of EU-15*
1968	42.9	120.2	39.6
1986	1,241.2	628.4	212.6
1995	2,212.5	1,819.9	601.3
2003	14,134.3	4,536.8	1,616.6

Note: measured at historic cost
Source: US, Bureau of Economic Analysis

FDI increasingly clustered in high-tech sectors associated, for example, with information technology and pharmaceuticals, and a quite new revealed comparative emerged based on these foreign-owned industries rather than specialisation based on Ireland's strengths in agriculture, food processing and so on, which is what *Economic Development* envisaged. This is important because trade liberalisation might reasonably have been seen as risky for a small peripheral economy with industry centralising in the European core, and divergence rather than convergence of incomes can result when economies of scale based on agglomeration dominate location decision at intermediate levels of trade costs (Krugman and Venables, 1990). In the event, tax advantages were enough to outweigh market-access considerations in key sectors with high-productivity growth, and to overcome the dangers of which new economic geography warns (Barry, 1996), and regression analysis suggests that the penalty of distance from the centre for European income levels halved in the second half of the twentieth century (Crafts and Toniolo, 2008).

There was, however, more than this to preparing for the Celtic Tiger. The Social Partnership inaugurated in 1987 delivered wage restraint in return for tax cuts and, in some ways reminiscent of the Eichengreen hypothesis, the advent of centralised wage bargaining promoted investment (Baccaro and Simoni, 2007). Ireland's late conversion to a social contract implied the absence of the corporatist legacy of high taxation and strict regulation common elsewhere in

1980s Europe. Enhanced investment in human capital was also apparent – the contribution of human capital deepening to labour productivity growth almost doubled to 0.38 percentage points per year in 1970–1990 (Bosworth and Collins, 2003) – and this was central to a lower equilibrium level of unemployment (Bergin and Kearney, 2004).

In sum, these developments implied that unemployment could fall dramatically from the 1987 rate of 17.5 per cent. Together with the responsiveness of migration flows to faster growth, these developments ensured that Ireland had an elastic labour supply and paved the way for rapid employment growth during the Celtic Tiger period. This implies that catch-up growth would be much less vulnerable to diminishing returns to capital accumulation than would normally be expected (Barry, 2002). The implication of this analysis is that the labour market matters to the growth process and that malfunctioning of the labour market had been a constraint on Irish growth, something which was not really appreciated when *Economic Development* was written in 1958.

The Celtic Tiger from an International Perspective

This idiosyncratic transition path meant that Irish growth during the Celtic Tiger period exhibited a number of special features that made it rather unusual compared with its western European peer group. An implication of this is that comparisons of Irish performance need to be carefully handled. It should also be recognised that while the sui-generis nature of Celtic Tiger growth does reflect the success of the supply-side policies that Ireland implemented, it also means that Ireland is not really a role model for others to follow.

It is generally agreed that recent Irish growth is better measured on a GNP – rather than GDP – basis because this leaves out the huge flow of repatriated profits of multinational companies which are inflated by transfer pricing encouraged by the generous corporate tax regime (Cassidy, 2004).[4] Ireland is a very trade-oriented economy with exports equal to 101 per cent of GNP in 2003 and those exports have been concentrated in products whose prices have been falling. The merchandise terms of external trade fell by about 10 per cent between 1987 and 2003, which means that real national income grew more slowly than real GNP by about 1 per cent per year (Crafts, 2005). This does not detract from the fact that Celtic-Tiger growth was remarkable but it does mean that the usual basis for international comparisons, namely, real GDP per person, exaggerates growth of Irish real national income per person by about 1.5 percentage points per year.

---

[4] Accordingly, Tables 5 to 7 use GNP rather than GDP for Ireland.

As was reported in Table 4, Ireland attracted a disproportionate amount of FDI. A very important corollary was that Ireland built up a much bigger ICT-production industry, the sector which experienced phenomenal technological progress and productivity growth at this time. Not surprisingly, TFP growth in this sector dominated in the latter part of the Celtic-Tiger period but it is also the case that TFP growth in the rest of the Irish economy was not particularly impressive, although inefficiency levels did fall quite sharply through the mid-1990s.[5] On the other hand, employment growth was quite spectacular by European standards, averaging 3.2 per cent per year during 1987 to 2003, compared with population growth of 0.7 per cent per year, and this was a major reason for rapid per-capita economic growth.

In 1987, Ireland was still at the bottom of the western European income-levels league table. Over the next sixteen years, growth of real GNP per person averaged just over 5.5 per cent per year, as Table 5 reports. This growth rate would have been highly respectable during the Golden Age, was easily the highest in Europe in this period, and was more than twice that achieved in the other low-income European economies.

Table 5: *Levels and Rate of Growth of Real GDP/Person during the Celtic Tiger Period ($1990GK and % per year)*

	GDP/Person, 1987	*GDP/Person, 2003*	*Growth Rate 1987–2003*
Switzerland	19,792	22,267	0.75
Norway	18,164	25,871	2.24
Denmark	18,023	23,080	1.56
Sweden	16,949	21,462	1.49
France	16,553	21,417	1.63
Germany	16,010	19,071	1.27
Netherlands	15,639	22,237	2.22
Belgium	15,541	21,206	1.96
UK	15,393	21,415	2.09
Finland	15,382	20,849	1.92
Austria	15,313	21,141	2.04
Italy	14,946	19,091	1.55
Spain	10,520	16,169	2.72
Greece	9,375	13,696	2.40
Portugal	9,185	13,904	2.63
Ireland	8,809	20,792	5.53

Notes: Germany is for 1989 to 2003, Ireland is GNP/Person.
Source: GGDC (2008).

---

[5] The estimates in Jerzmanowski (2007), on a similar basis to those reported above in Table 3, show Irish efficiency at 0.61 in 1985 and 0.76 in 1995.

The sources of this exceptional growth performance and the special features of Irish growth can be quantified using growth accounting. Table 6 shows the standard breakdown for labour productivity growth. Here there are two points to note with regard to comparisons with other European countries. First, while Ireland's labour productivity growth was the highest in Europe in this period, it was not nearly as far ahead of the pack as was real GDP per person. Second, TFP growth was the highest in Europe and accounted for about three-quarters of labour productivity growth, whereas the contributions of physical and human capital per worker were below the European median.

Table 6: *Contributions to Labour Productivity Growth, 1990–2003*
(% per year)

	Capital-Deepening	*Human-Capital-Deepening*	*Total Factor Productivity*	*Labour Productivity*
Switzerland	0.60	0.08	−0.23	0.45
Norway	0.31	0.21	1.81	2.33
Denmark	0.72	0.19	0.95	1.86
Sweden	0.73	0.44	1.16	2.33
France	0.58	0.27	0.13	0.98
Germany	0.76	0.17	0.60	1.53
Netherlands	0.26	0.28	0.07	0.61
Belgium	0.76	0.25	0.26	1.27
UK	0.91	0.41	0.74	2.06
Finland	0.49	0.31	1.49	2.29
Austria	0.86	0.27	0.37	1.50
Italy	0.60	0.38	0.14	1.12
Spain	0.63	0.37	−0.37	0.63
Greece	0.61	0.35	1.25	2.21
Portugal	1.13	0.47	−0.31	1.29
Ireland	0.49	0.26	2.24	2.99
Singapore	1.76	0.85	0.90	3.51
South Korea	2.40	0.50	0.91	3.81
Taiwan	2.67	0.40	1.69	4.76

Note: Ireland adjusted to GNP basis.
Source: Update of database constructed for Bosworth and Collins (2003) kindly provided by authors.

Table 7 accounts for the sources of output growth rather than productivity growth. Again, two points of comparison with the European peer group are worth highlighting. First, the exceptional contribution made by employment growth stands out. Only in Spain, where labour-market reform also played a significant role, is there a remotely similar contribution from labour inputs. Second, unlike Spain, Ireland succeeded in combining a very strong contribution from employment growth with a high rate of labour productivity growth, based on strong TFP growth.

Table 7: *Contributions to Real GDP Growth, 1990–2003 (% per year)*

	Due to Capital	Due to Labour	Total Factor Productivity	Real GDP Growth
Switzerland	0.75	0.35	−0.23	0.87
Norway	0.62	0.78	1.81	3.21
Denmark	0.78	0.29	0.95	2.02
Sweden	0.57	0.15	1.16	1.88
France	0.84	0.75	0.13	1.72
Germany	0.77	0.18	0.60	1.55
Netherlands	1.19	1.01	0.07	2.27
Belgium	0.96	0.63	0.26	1.85
UK	0.99	0.57	0.74	2.30
Finland	0.33	0.02	1.49	1.84
Austria	1.05	0.63	0.37	2.05
Italy	0.70	0.57	0.14	1.41
Spain	1.33	1.66	−0.37	2.62
Greece	0.79	0.69	1.25	2.73
Portugal	1.45	1.06	−0.31	2.20
Ireland	1.75	2.45	2.24	6.44
Singapore	2.62	2.45	0.90	5.97
South Korea	3.08	1.75	0.91	5.74
Taiwan	3.22	1.43	1.69	6.34

Notes: Ireland adjusted to GNP basis; contribution of human capital included in labour.
Source: Update of database constructed for Bosworth and Collins (2003) kindly provided by authors.

Tables 6 and 7 also allow comparison of the Celtic Tiger with the Asian Tigers. There is a strong similarity in terms of the contribution from labour inputs growth. But, in other respects, the differences are striking. Ireland has much superior TFP growth but has a much weaker contribution from capital inputs growth than the Asian Tigers, which have been renowned for their formidable shares of GDP devoted to investment, whereas the Irish investment rate over these years averaged just under 20 per cent of GDP.

Finally, Table 8 quantifies the role of TFP growth in the ICT production sector. It is immediately apparent that Ireland was truly exceptional in this regard.[6] Even compared with Finland, the ICT production sector was very big in Ireland in this period, and it is clear that TFP growth was dominated by ICT production in Ireland to a much greater extent than elsewhere. This has two important implications which are quite unusual, namely that TFP growth was principally delivered by the technology transfer of multinational companies and

---

[6] The estimates in Table 8 are in terms of GDP and are therefore distorted by the transfer-pricing issue discussed earlier. This clearly affects the detail but not the general thrust of the discussion.

that a large part of the benefits of this TFP growth accrued to foreigners as it fed into lower prices for the exports which comprised the vast majority of the sector's sales.

Table 8: *Decomposition of TFP Growth (% per year)*

	Finland	Ireland	EU	USA
1990–1995				
TFP Growth	1.23	2.96	1.12	0.61
From ICT production	0.16	1.17	0.14	0.25
Other	1.07	1.79	0.98	0.36
Memo Item				
ICT Domar Weight	2.61	11.73	1.50	2.63
1995–2001				
TFP Growth	2.67	3.61	0.46	0.80
From ICT Production	0.69	3.62	0.27	0.44
Other	1.98	−0.01	0.19	0.36
Memo Item				
ICT Domar Weight	8.26	22.56	2.07	2.96

Notes: ICT Domar Weight is gross output of ICT/GDP (%); EU excludes Belgium, Greece and Luxembourg in 1990–95 and excludes Luxembourg in 1995–2001
Sources: van Ark et al. (2003) and Timmer and van Ark (2005).

Ireland's growth during the Celtic-Tiger period was exceptional. It was driven by FDI and a very elastic labour supply. This reflected the good policy framework that had been assembled over the previous thirty years and the much greater openness this entailed. However, the implications of openness for growth depend on the specialisation that results and the productivity growth potential in the exportables sector. In this, Ireland was blessed with good luck in terms of the remarkable technological progress which transpired in ICT production. And other countries may not have the same scope for employment to expand in response to improved supply-side policy. So, while Ireland's growth record has lessons for other countries and students of endogenous-growth economics, there is a strong sui-generis flavour about the Celtic Tiger.

Economic Development Revisited

Economic Development had several important messages which subsequent history has shown to be absolutely right. The basic insight was that if the opportunities of openness were seized, independence would be vindicated in economic terms. The central vision was optimistic and rather like that of modern growth economics – establish appropriate incentive structures and faster growth would ensue. The suggestion that the dynamic might come from TFP growth rather than requiring a massive investment rate was prescient. And the arguments in favour of low corporate taxation and FDI as a key mode of technology transfer pointed to the path to the Celtic Tiger that Ireland followed.

Clearly, there was much that Whitaker could not foresee in 1958. The transformation of Irish exports, the way in which the potential disadvantages of peripherality were overcome, and the magnitude of the eventual boost to the growth rate must all have been pleasant surprises. Moreover, the analysis in *Economic Development* did not really encompass the social-partnership and labour-supply issues that were central to the rapid employment growth that was eventually such a distinctive feature of the Celtic Tiger.

The Celtic Tiger was, of course, predicated on globalisation. It is in this context, rather than the trade-restrictive and capital-immobile mid-twentieth century, that independence could really pay off. In 1958, it must have seemed that independence had done nothing for Irish economic development. Fifty years later, as Whitaker hoped, that view has clearly been refuted. After all, the key policy instrument that underpinned the transition to fast growth, a low corporate tax rate to attract FDI, was an option that would not have been available under British rule.

References

Aghion, P. and Howitt, P. (2006), 'Appropriate Growth Policy: A Unifying Framework', *Journal of the European Economic Association*, no. 4, pp. 269–314

Baccaro, L. and Simoni, M. (2007), 'Centralized Wage Bargaining and the "Celtic Tiger" Phenomenon', *Industrial Relations*, no. 46, pp. 426–69

Badinger, H. (2005), 'Growth Effects of Economic Integration: Evidence from the EU Member States', *Review of World Economics*, no. 141, pp. 50–78

Barry, F. (1996), 'Peripherality in Economic Geography and Modern Growth Theory: Evidence from Ireland's Adjustment to Free Trade', *The World Economy*, no. 19, pp. 345–65.

Barry, F. (2002), 'The Celtic Tiger Era: Delayed Convergence or Regional Boom?', *ESRI Quarterly Economic Commentary*, pp. 84–91

Barry, F. (2008), 'Politics, Institutions and Postwar Economic Growth in Ireland', *CESifo Forum*, vol. 9, no. 1, pp. 23–34

Bergin, A. and Kearney, I. (2004), 'Human Capital, the Labour Market and Productivity Growth in Ireland', ESRI Working Paper No. 158

Bosworth, B. P. and Collins, S. M. (2003), 'The Empirics of Growth: An Update', *Brookings Papers on Economic Activity*, no. 2, pp. 113–206

Buckley, P. and Ruane, F. (2006), 'Foreign Direct Investment in Ireland: Policy Implications for Emerging Economies', *The World Economy*, no. 29, pp. 1611–28

Cassidy, M. (2004), 'Productivity in Ireland: Trends and Issues', *Central Bank of Ireland Quarterly Bulletin*, Spring, pp. 83–105

Crafts, N. (2005), 'Interpreting Ireland's Economic Growth', background paper for UNIDO, *Industrial Development Report*

Crafts, N. and Toniolo, G. (1996), 'Postwar Growth: An Overview', in Crafts, N. and Toniolo, G. (eds), *Economic Growth in Europe Since 1945*, Cambridge: Cambridge University Press, pp. 1–37

Crafts, N. and Toniolo, G. (2008), 'European Economic Growth, 1950–2005: An Overview', CEPR Discussion Paper No. 6863

Crouch, C. (1993), *Industrial Relations and European State Traditions*, Oxford: Clarendon Press

Department of Finance (1958), *Economic Development*, Dublin: Stationery Office

Eichengreen, B. (2006), *The European Economy Since 1945*, Princeton: Princeton University Press

Groningen Growth and Development Centre (2008), *Total Economy Database*

Gropp, R. and Kostial, K. (2000), 'The Disappearing Tax Base: Is FDI Eroding Corporate Income Taxes?', IMF Working Paper No. 00/173

Jerzmanowski, M. (2007), 'Total Factor Productivity Differences: Appropriate Technology vs. Efficiency', *European Economic Review*, no. 51, pp. 2080–2110

Krugman, P. and Venables, A. J. (1990), 'Integration and the Competitiveness of Peripheral Industry', in J. de Macedo and C. Bliss (eds), *Unity and Diversity Within the European Economy*, Cambridge: Cambridge University Press

Maddison, A. (2003), *The World Economy: Historical Statistics*, Paris: OECD

Timmer, M. and van Ark, B. (2005), 'Does Information and Communication Technology Drive EU–US Productivity Growth Differentials?', *Oxford Economic Papers*, no. 57, pp. 693–716

van Ark, B., Melka, J., Mulder, N., Timmer, M. and Ypma, G. (2003), 'ICT Investments and Growth Accounts for the European Union', Goningen Growth and Development Centre Research Memorandum GD–56

8

Growth and Development – Lessons and Surprises

Paul G. Hare

Introduction

The Irish economy was performing poorly in the 1950s, lagging even somewhat behind the slowly advancing UK economy, which itself was then falling further behind the United States and also the major European economies that were recovering rapidly from the ravages of the Second World War. Ireland had high unemployment accompanied by significant emigration, so the population was continuing a slow decline while the economy expanded at best slowly, rarely more than 1 per cent per annum. Living standards stagnated and severe poverty was widespread, while the economic infrastructure remained generally quite underdeveloped.

This was clearly not at all a favourable backdrop to what became one of the economic miracles of the post-war period, the transformation of Ireland's economy from a sleepy backwater on the edge of Europe to one of the most prosperous economies in the European Union, a transformation that took place over just a few decades. Figure 1 shows just where the Irish economy now stands in relation to other European countries. Thus, in terms of its per-capita GDP, Ireland is now one of the better-off countries in Europe. Ireland's per-capita GDP in 2008 was estimated by Eurostat to be about 143 per cent of the EU-27 average, compared to the UK at 114 per cent of the EU-27 average.

It was not always so. The following graph (Figure 2) shows how Ireland's GDP per capita has evolved since 1970, relative to Greece, the UK, the US and to the EU-15. The near-horizontal line hovering around 100 for the whole period,

Figure 1: *GDP Per Capita in 2008 (as percentage of EU-27)*

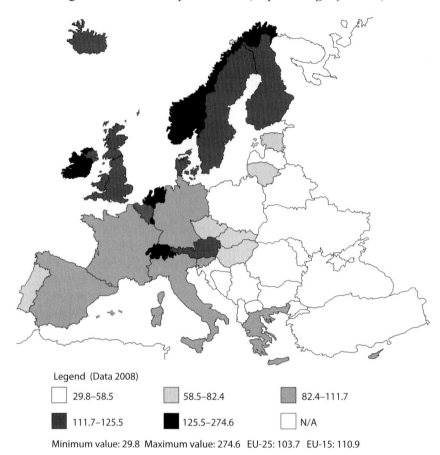

Legend (Data 2008)

☐	29.8–58.5	☐	58.5–82.4	■	82.4–111.7
■	111.7–125.5	■	125.5–274.6	☐	N/A

Minimum value: 29.8 Maximum value: 274.6 EU-25: 103.7 EU-15: 110.9

Source: Eurostat Database

representing the EU-15, does not mean that the EU-15 has not enjoyed economic growth in real terms, but merely that the region has consistently grown at about the average rate of the OECD as a whole, as has the UK. The two really interesting stories that can be pulled out of the graph concern Greece and Ireland. The former (shown by the light grey line) began in 1970 with a GDP per head a little over 80 per cent of the OECD average, gained ground for about a decade, coming up to 90 per cent of the OECD average, then from 1980 or so, fell back for about two decades, dropping to little over 70 per cent of the OECD average GDP per head by the year 2000. During the present decade, Greece's relative position has recovered again, but it is still only slightly ahead of where it stood back in 1970. Ireland, by contrast, has advanced dramatically, as shown by the broken black line in the chart. From a starting point well below Greece, Ireland's relative position advanced steadily up to the late 1980s, then more rapidly, overtaking the UK in the late 1990s and significantly catching up with the United States in the last decade.

Figure 2: *Ireland's GDP Per Capita in International Comparison*

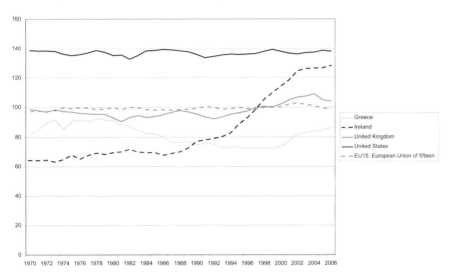

Note: For each year, the lines on the chart show GDP per capita for each country relative to the OECD average, which is fixed at 100 throughout.
Source: OECD Statistical Database

This extreme constant in growth experience as between Greece and Ireland since 1970 raises some intriguing questions, notably: (a) What factors helped Ireland to perform so well compared to Greece? (b) Were these factors temporary ones, and will they continue to drive Ireland's growth in the future? (c) Is the Irish growth experience sui generis, or are there aspects of it that can be drawn out to form a specific 'Irish economic model' that would be capable of generalisation to other contexts, other countries. This paper shall not be able to give complete answers to these questions, but by reviewing much of the recent growth experience around the world it shall at least make a start.

It is considered by many in Ireland that the 1958 publication of *Economic Development* (Whitaker, 1958), marked the beginning of the country's remarkable economic take-off. At the time, this cannot have seemed very likely, though Whitaker's well-argued report does appear to have lifted Ireland's political and media elites out of the vicious circle of negativity and despondency in which they mostly seemed to be trapped back then. Yet it did so not by advancing dramatic projections of future rapid economic growth in Ireland, for it was quite modest in that regard. It suggested quite tentatively that with 'better policies' Ireland might manage to raise its real GDP growth rate from perhaps 1 per cent to 2 per cent per annum. To achieve this, the report proposed numerous practical steps that could be taken, and offered some simple but extremely important observations on what was thought necessary to make an economy grow – such as more investment, more productive investment, and an end to Ireland's entrenched protectionism, points we return to later. To the extent that the report succeeded, therefore, it probably did so through the quality of its analysis, based on sound knowledge of the Irish economy and society of the 1950s. The careful analysis helped to change the climate of opinion about where the Irish economy was going and where it could go, helped to make a new and more dynamic direction seem believable, and by making it believable helped to make it happen. As ever, economic performance has a great deal to do with beliefs and expectations, and the confidence that these can engender both among politicians and among business leaders.

Growth and Development – The Wider Context

We now stand back from Ireland, in order to study the wider context of growth and development around the world. In doing so, we refer to the transition economies since 1990, China since the late 1970s, India since the 1980s, various economies that have experienced 'growth spurts' (e.g. Brazil), and a few other economies doing well over a long period (e.g. Botswana). In addition, for instructive contrast, we also pay attention to a number of failing economies (e.g. North Korea, Zimbabwe, Bolivia). This section will be fairly descriptive, while the next seeks to peer behind the veil of individual country 'stories' to highlight some of the more generic factors that influence growth rates and economic performance; accordingly, the next section is somewhat more analytical, though as far as possible the aim will be to explain issues in non-technical terms.

Accordingly, I start with some remarks about the transition economies of Central and Eastern Europe and the Former Soviet Union (the FSU). This region operated under highly centralised economic planning – albeit with a variety of reforms seeking to make the economies function more flexibly – until the collapse of communist regimes in 1989 (Central and Eastern Europe) and 1991 (FSU), after which nearly all the new governments declared their intention to build market-type economies as rapidly as they could. By the late 1970s, partly as a result of that decade's oil price crises (1973, 1979), and even more so in the 1980s, the centrally planned economies had become quite moribund. They participated to a decreasing extent in the world economy, mostly traded poor-quality goods with each other, and at best grew slowly. Living standards did slowly improve in most countries, but they lagged increasingly – and with the advent of modern TV and telecommunications, ever more visibly – behind the levels of western Europe and the United States. Politically, the appetite for repression had waned, and Gorbachev's mid-1980s declaration that each socialist country was free to choose its own path of development, both economically and politically, opened the way to the momentous changes that soon followed, at first cautiously as countries tested the water, then more boldly and rapidly.

Transition to the market entailed a number of common elements, though naturally with some important differences of detail between countries. More unexpectedly (to economists, at any rate!) it also entailed a comprehensive reconfiguration of the region's political landscape. Not only did the Soviet Union split into fifteen successor states (comprising the three Baltic States plus the twelve members of the Commonwealth of Independent States, or CIS), but Yugoslavia also disintegrated into several states, starting a process still not finally settled. Then Czechoslovakia split into two states at the start of 1993: the Czech Republic and Slovakia. Mercifully, this last split was conducted entirely peacefully, but several CIS states engaged in war with each other (e.g. Armenia and Azerbaijan) or in civil conflict (such as Georgia, Tajikistan, Moldova, Russia), and the break-up of Yugoslavia was also accompanied by warfare among the region's ethnic groups until the Dayton Peace Accords were signed in 1995. Thus for many countries, transition started badly, to put it mildly.

Even when the fighting stopped, a major exercise in state building was called for, to establish the basic structures and institutions needed to operate a modern state in each new country. Given all this, and the disruption of long-established economic links when communism ended, it is perhaps not too surprising that the entire transition economy region experienced what is now – rather euphemistically – termed a 'post-communist recession'. In the luckier countries, such as Poland, this was short and not too deep; but in much of the CIS it lasted for several years and involved falls in real GDP (according to official measures) by 50 per cent and more. Thus for some countries, the end of communism heralded both political crisis and turmoil, and economic disaster, with widespread and substantial falls in general living standards.

Aside from dismantling the old economic system, building a market-type economy was generally considered to involve the following: (a) macroeconomic stabilisation; (b) price and trade liberalisation; (c) privatisation and restructuring; and (d) institutional development. Under central planning, shortages were endemic almost everywhere, and households accumulated savings and cash balances that they could not readily spend on desired goods and services. Consequently, when transition reforms began with the expected extensive price and trade liberalisation – the easiest and most 'natural' part of the standard reform package – it was feared that there would be a burst of inflation. Moreover, if imports of consumer goods were suddenly allowed, trade balances would come under threat. This is why macroeconomic stabilisation was at the forefront of the initial round of reforms, to help choke off these inflationary pressures, to restrain the ensuing wage increases in order to limit the possible wage-price spiral, and to manage foreign currency reserves and the trade balance.

As it turned out, in Hungary and the former Czechoslovakia, initial imbalances were not too severe, the burst of inflation was modest and short-lived, and only mild stabilisation was required. In Poland, inflationary pressures were serious by late 1989, with inflation rising to several hundred per cent, but the stabilisation and reforms introduced in 1990 (the Balcerowicz plan) rapidly brought the situation back under control. Elsewhere, initial imbalances were worse and macroeconomic policy far less competent, with the result that inflation for a time was almost out of control. The CIS countries, in particular, suffered from the additional problems of a major trade shock, in that trade that had formerly been within the old USSR suddenly became international trade – so trade balances that formerly didn't matter suddenly did, and several countries found themselves with large structural deficits. These countries also had to cope with the introduction of new currencies, since it was soon apparent that the IMF's initial advice to maintain a rouble zone across the region was not going to prove workable. Much of the region experienced inflation rates in excess of 1,000 per cent for a year or two (usually 1993 and/or 1994) before gradually regaining macroeconomic control.

It was well understood in the transition economies that retaining all business in public hands would not prove a good basis for a successful market-type economy, and this led to two directions of reform. First, privatise existing state-owned firms, as noted above; and second, create a better business environment to encourage new business formation. Among some academics and in some countries, the former policy – privatisation – was emphasised most strongly, to the extent that there were calls for 'immediate' or very rapid privatisation of virtually everything. This in turn led to privatisation by vouchers or other forms of near give-away, either to workers and managers (e.g. Russia, to a large extent) or to the general population (e.g. in the former Czechoslovakia). Elsewhere, countries such as Hungary followed a more even-handed approach, privatising more slowly and mostly through sales of shares while simultaneously improving general business conditions. By the mid-1990s, the results were becoming clear, with the private sector already accounting for at least half of economic output in most of the region, and of that half it turned out that a substantial fraction consisted of new firms that had not existed before 1990. Thus, building a private sector was not just about privatisation, as some had thought.

As a result of many inefficient investment decisions made under central planning, sometimes influenced by absurdities of the socialist pricing model (such as near-free energy, low freight charges, low or zero charges for land used by industry), all transition economies started life with a legacy of loss-making firms, amounting to half the industrial production capacity in certain countries. While in normal economies, failing firms are closing and new ones opening all the time, closures or restructuring on this scale were well outside most countries' experience. Hence it was no surprise that in many countries, especially in the CIS and in south-eastern Europe, governments tended to protect these firms rather than face the political fallout from high unemployment. Much restructuring has been undertaken, some quite successful, but many of these inefficient firms still survive, wasting resources that, in my view, would by now be better spent on fostering new businesses.

The remaining element of the standard transition package, institutional reforms, was probably the element least well understood, and many countries neglected it for too long. In part, there was often a somewhat naive assumption that if a country ended central planning, markets would just spring up and operate 'normally'; and in part, one has to admit that some rather important institutional reforms are simply very boring, making it hard to gain law-makers' attention and commitment. In the latter, 'boring' category are such measures as reforms to introduce international accounting standards into an economy, or laws about competition policy and market behaviour. Laws about protecting property rights and private business contracts also proved problematic in many countries, not least because the importance of such protection was not widely understood. Moreover, protection is needed both against other private agents (who might try to cheat or defraud their business partners) and against the state itself (which might try to expropriate or unfairly tax a successful business). In countries with a long tradition of state control and centralisation, this last danger was not widely appreciated. We shall have more to say about institutions later in the paper.

Figure 3 sums up the growth experience since 1990 of a small selection of transition economies, showing clearly the post-communist recision and subsequent recovery. All the countries shown are growing fairly rapidly. Poland probably exhibits the best overall performance, while Russia and Kazakhstan both experienced longer recessions but are now growing faster than the other countries – other than Armenia, which is now growing very rapidly from a low base.

In terms of the sheer numbers of people being lifted out of poverty, China since the late 1970s and India since the 1980s are undoubtedly the world's leading success stories. And it must be conceded that we do not yet fully understand why, or what exactly changed in these two societies to engender their apparent take-off into sustained growth at a rapid rate. Of course, theories abound, but neither economy quite fits some of the theories about growth we discuss later. For the moment, we simply sum up their performance in Figure 4,

Figure 3: *Growth in Selected Transition Economies, 1990–2006*

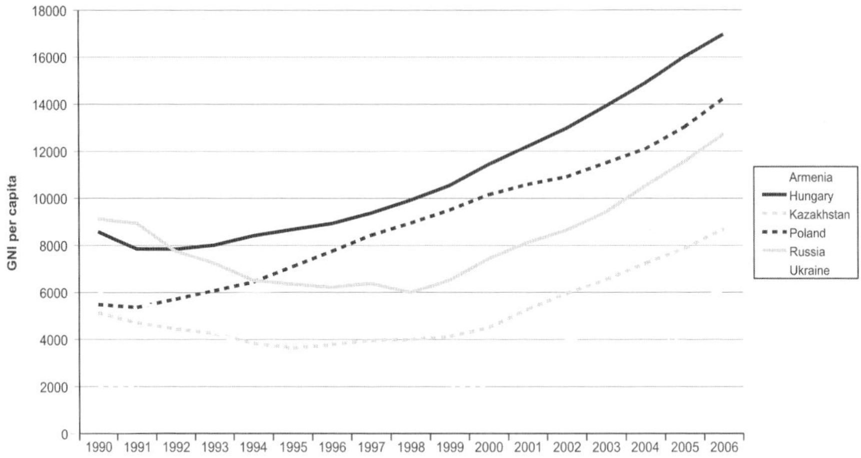

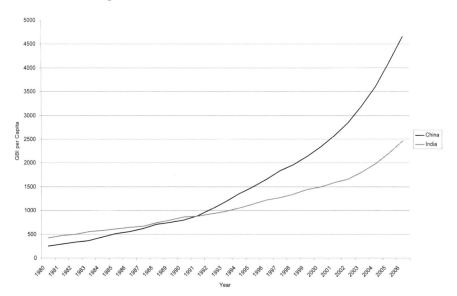

Note: Vertical axis is measured in current dollars, in PPP terms.
Source: World Bank Development Indicators, 2008

Figure 4: *Growth in China and India since 1980*

Note: Vertical axis is measured in current dollars, in PPP terms.
Source: World Bank Development Indicators, 2008

showing their growth since 1980. China's average income was judged to be below that of India back in 1980, but China soon overtook and now has almost double India's income per capita. However, India's growth has been gradually accelerating.

Elsewhere in the world, a few developing countries have sustained high economic growth for periods of several decades, typically based on valuable resources (e.g. Botswana, with diamonds) or strong export earnings (e.g. Mauritius, exports of textiles), and many others have enjoyed spells of growth that have not been sustained for long. On the other hand, many countries rich in natural resources have done very badly. Countries such as Angola and Nigeria come to mind, where far too much of the oil wealth seems to have been stolen or otherwise misused by corrupt governments. Collier (2007) also emphasises that poor countries that are landlocked tend to perform badly, especially if their neighbours are also poor or engaged in civil strife. However, being landlocked is not per se a bad thing, as Switzerland and Austria readily confirm; but these countries possess good infrastructure, governments relatively free from corruption, and excellent access to wealthy neighbouring markets for their exports. These factors all prove very helpful.

To conclude this section, we remark on three spectacularly failing economies, namely North Korea, Zimbabwe and Bolivia. North Korea is especially interesting as, if anything, its per-capita income after the Korean War (ended in 1953) was probably slightly above that of the South. Since then, although there was some growth into the 1970s, several decades of socialist planning have left the country impoverished, with a severe famine at the end of the 1990s and running into the present decade (Haggard and Noland, 2007). The country was not helped by the 1991 disintegration of its major trade partner, the former Soviet Union, into fifteen separate countries: trade collapsed, but instead of adjusting by seeking new markets, North Korea became economically increasingly isolated, with little engagement with the world economy (Hare, 2007). Acemoglu et al. (2005) estimated that by the year 2000, North Korea's per-capita income was only about $1,000, while that in South Korea was just over $16,000; moreover, incomes in the North were stagnating, while those in the South continued to advance. Thus a massive and ever-increasing difference has opened up between the average income levels in North and South Korea, the North remaining extremely poor. No doubt there are many reasons for this gap, but it is hard not to see it as a consequence of the fundamental difference in economic system between the two parts of the Korean peninsula, in other words a consequence of institutions.

Zimbabwe is an economy that was once held up as an example of sound economic management and steady economic progress in Africa. After the Republic of South Africa, it was the strongest economy in sub-Saharan Africa and it performed quite well for the first decade or so after independence in 1979–80, with real GDP growth averaging around 4.5 per cent per annum. Since 1990, there was increasing pressure on the country's white farmers to transfer their land to black Zimbabweans. Initially, this was to be on the basis of land purchases, with some funding from the British government to help buy out 'willing' farmers. But few white farmers were willing and little land was actually transferred. Finally, in 2000, the Mugabe government sought to amend Zimbabwe's constitution, essentially to legalise the expropriation of most of the country's white farmers without compensation. When put to a referendum, this new constitution was rejected by the people of Zimbabwe, whereupon Mugabe's 'War Veterans' and other like-minded people were encouraged to start a campaign of direct action to take over the white farms. This campaign became extremely violent, and most white farmers were evicted, their farms being taken over by leading Zanu PF (the ruling political party) officials and political leaders, War Veterans, and the like. Most of the new 'owners' had little or no knowledge of or interest in farming, with the result that Zimbabwe's valuable agricultural exports collapsed, and even the local food supply became more precarious as production continued to fall. Moreover, the widespread violence in the country quickly destroyed another of Zimbabwe's important foreign currency earners, namely the tourism industry.

Since 2000, it is estimated that Zimbabwe's GDP has fallen by over 40 per cent, with many businesses closing down and unemployment very high. Many people – probably 2–3 million by now out of a total population of 13.3 million – have simply crossed the border into South Africa to find work, and many others must operate in the informal economy in order to survive. Meanwhile, falling tax revenues led to rising government deficits and a gradual loss of macroeconomic control. The result is the world's only country currently experiencing severe hyperinflation, with complete monetary collapse surely only months away. Thus the last decade of economic management in Zimbabwe demonstrates just how easy it is to destroy a successful economy – by abusing property rights, by failing to manage the balance of payments and the government finances, and by fostering a climate of violence and intimidation across the country. The country's decline has nothing to do with western imperialism or UN economic sanctions (which in any case only apply to the country's top leaders) as Mugabe claims; rather, it has been entirely self-inflicted. On a brighter note, it is worth adding here that once Zimbabwe is ready to adopt sounder policies, economic recovery should not prove too difficult, and so the country's future prospects are not as dire as present circumstances might seem to imply. Coorey et al. (2007) argue, for instance, that with a strong fiscal consolidation and strict monetary discipline, output can largely recover in just one to two years, with inflation falling rapidly.

Our last failing country, Bolivia, is a different sort of failure, since it is neither socialist like North Korea, nor a former success story like Zimbabwe. Bolivia, however, is the only country on the South American continent where living standards have barely advanced since 1950. Almost everywhere else, living standards have at least doubled since then. Yet in many respects Bolivia is not so different from some of the neighbouring countries, with the same inequality of land-holding, the property rights of the rich moderately well protected (as much through their links with political elites as through formal legal processes), and political life dominated by wealthy oligarchs (at least until the recent election of populist President Evo Morales in December 2005). Several factors can be adduced to explain Bolivia's poor performance. First, the country is landlocked and relatively isolated, with quite limited participation in foreign trade; second, Bolivia invests rather little of its GDP in developing production, in recent years usually not much more than 10 per cent of GDP; third, Bolivian political life has been unusually unstable, with several military coups and many short-lived governments; last, among Bolivians there appears to be at best a very limited willingness to trust business partners, which makes many business transactions either expensive or, even worse, impossible. Taken together, these factors have given rise to an unfavourable business environment and sustained weak economic performance.

Requirements for Successful Development[1]

After this highly selective survey of growth experience around the world, we now draw out and analyse some of the principal factors found to be important in facilitating or promoting economic growth. To begin, experience around the world shows that few countries grow for long unless they ensure sound macroeconomic conditions. In practice, this is a multi-dimensional requirement, including low inflation, manageable budget and external deficits, and credibly manageable levels of debt. As usual, it is very hard to attach precise numbers to these factors, not least because the inter-relations between them are influenced by the dynamics of growth in a given economy.

Thus, if an economy is growing very slowly, say 1–2 per cent per annum in real terms, and has a general government budget deficit of 5 per cent of GDP (i.e., this is the deficit based on fully consolidated public-sector accounts), with an accumulated public debt of, say, 60 per cent of GDP, then the debt of the public sector is growing much faster than GDP, ensuring that aggregate public-sector debt is a rising share of GDP. Servicing such debt then accounts for ever-rising shares of public spending, and becomes increasingly unmanageable. Conversely,

---

[1] Some of this section draws heavily on Hare (2008).

in a country with the same government deficit and initial debt, but growing much faster, say at 10 per cent per annum, the debt grows more slowly than GDP, so declines gradually as a share of GDP. In this case, debt is not getting out of control.

Much the same sort of argument applies to a country's external accounts. Here the issue has to do with the inter-connections between a trade deficit, the growth in external debt, and the two factors that can help to reduce the debt or make it more manageable, namely export growth and capital inflows, including foreign direct investment (FDI). A large external debt can be managed in a country with fast-growing GDP and/or fast-growing exports, while the same debt in a country whose GDP and exports were stagnant or growing only slowly could prove catastrophic.

Inflation, too, is considered bad for growth, but the arguments as to when this is likely to be the case, and why, are quite complex and need careful examination. Two extreme cases stand out. First, sustained inflation at high rates, such as well over 100 per cent per annum, is harmful because it renders any contracts expressed in monetary terms extremely risky and makes any long-term business agreements difficult to sustain. Savings depreciate rapidly and debts are also eroded rapidly in real terms, since most contracts are expressed in nominal monetary terms, unadjusted for inflation in the general price level. At seriously high rates of inflation this shades into the extremes of hyper-inflation (conventionally defined as inflation faster than 50 per cent per month), usually reflecting the near complete breakdown of monetary discipline and control. No country has found sustained high inflation consistent with positive GDP growth. Second, rapid and unpredictably variable inflation is damaging even when the average inflation rate is much lower than the above case. Thus, if inflation is just 20 per cent per annum, but fluctuates apparently randomly between 5 per cent and 45 per cent, say, this is a nightmare for anyone planning a long-term business contract. It is hard to predict either the costs or the revenues associated, for example, with a new investment, and the likelihood is that such investment will simply not then take place.

The very real problems highlighted here make clear why macroeconomic stability is important for sustained economic growth, but they do not amount to a firm prescription regarding the exact conditions required to achieve such stability. The EU's Maastricht conditions for entering the European Monetary Union (EU), taken together with the policies of the European Central Bank (ECB) for the Eurozone, provide one set of guidelines for macroeconomic stability. These conditions state that a country's public debt should not exceed 60 per cent of its GDP, and that the government deficit should not exceed 3 per cent of GDP; and the ECB sets Eurozone interest rates to achieve, over the medium term, an inflation rate of, at most, 2 per cent per annum. The UK government has a similar set of fiscal and monetary indicators as its policy framework, though the numerical targets differ somewhat from the EU's; they, too, are interpreted 'flexibly'.

From the point of view of market confidence and policy credibility, it is probably not a bad idea to build macroeconomic policy around specific targets like this, but I am not aware of anything in economic theory that might guide us to any particular numbers. Moreover, there is the further practical point that governments running up against the constraints set by whatever framework they claim to be operating tend to find ways of 'evading' them: targets are redefined, time periods over which some target is to be achieved are 'adjusted', and so on (see Buiter and Grafe, 2003). In the end, the only effective form of public accountability in regard to the basic parameters of macroeconomic policy is the next general election, and the threat of being ejected from office.

Investment, too, is generally found to be essential for growth. More concretely, moderate to high rates of investment (i.e., typically in excess of 20 per cent of GDP), allocated efficiently and credibly funded (from a mix of domestic and external savings), are very important. Let us now explore this notion more carefully. It is clear that high rates of investment are not sufficient for growth, since there are plenty of examples around the world of countries investing a lot and failing to grow. The 1980s, the last decade of the former Soviet Union, provides one of the more striking examples of this, since investment certainly occurred at respectable rates, mostly above 20 per cent of estimated GDP, while the economy experienced very weak growth for the whole decade. Thus, investment not only has to be undertaken, but on average it must be efficient and productive.

A simple equation from elementary growth theory for a closed economy, focusing on the supply side of the economy, makes this point very forcefully. The equation is:

$$g = s/v \qquad\qquad (1)$$

where g is the rate of growth of real GDP, s is the savings ratio, and v is the (incremental) capital-output ratio of the economy concerned (see Solow, 1970). In a more complex model, additional factors such as depreciation of the existing capital stock, foreign trade and FDI, and sometimes the effects of technological change might also influence the growth rate, but we return to that later. For now, we remain with (1). Consider three examples:

(a) Suppose $s = 0.4$ and $v = 4$. This means that the country saves and invests 40 per cent of its GDP, and four units of new capital are needed to generate an addition flow of one unit per period of additional income. With these parameters, (1) implies that $g = 0.1$, or 10 per cent per annum. Something like this fits China quite well, I would suggest, with its very high savings ratio and moderate investment efficiency.

(b) Next, suppose $s = 0.25$ and $v = 3$. Then $g = 0.083$, or 8.3 per cent per annum. This fits quite a number of rapidly growing countries, possibly including Kazakhstan and Russia (though Russia has not been growing quite so rapidly). The aggregate savings (and hence investment) ratio is lower than that for China, while the assumed average efficiency of investment is somewhat higher than China's (i.e. v is lower).

(c) Last, suppose $s = 0.12$ and $v = 6$. Then $g = 0.02$, or 2 per cent per annum. A country in this situation is investing rather little, just 12 per cent of GDP, and is doing so very inefficiently, each unit of investment adding very little to GDP, since six additional units of capital are needed to produce a flow of one unit of additional income. The result is very slow growth, as can be found in many of the poorer developing countries.

To sum up, then, equation (1) implies that to grow at a respectable annual rate, such as more than 5 per cent per annum, an economy needs some combination of a relatively high savings ratio, s, and a relatively low capital-output ratio, v. Although originally developed for a closed economy, (1) remains valid for the open economy case, too. Hence, in thinking about the savings (and investment) ratio, we need to have in mind not just savings by the domestic economic agents – firms, households, government – but also external savings that are invested in the economy concerned. The latter takes various forms, the most common being foreign portfolio investment and foreign direct investment (FDI). Sometimes countries claim that they are 'too poor to save' and that their development, therefore, will rely largely on inflows of FDI. In practice, this approach is unworkable, since virtually everywhere most investment is financed largely from domestic savings. Hence domestic banks and financial markets need, above all, to mobilise and to allocate domestic savings efficiently as a major element in the process of stimulating sustained economic growth.

So much for the savings/investment aspect of (1). Now consider the capital-output ratio, v. To put it simply, and I hope sufficiently clearly, a low value for v means that a unit of investment generates substantial additional output on a continuing basis. This is what we mean by stating that investment needs to be productive. Most investment resources should be devoted to building factories, shops, offices and the like, associated with profit-seeking and mostly private businesses. In addition, much investment in infrastructure such as airports, port facilities, road and rail networks, public utilities, and so on is clearly productive in the same sense, provided that it doesn't take the form of 'white elephants' – e.g. building a road going 'nowhere', or a new port where there is no demand for its services. If v is high, meaning that on average investment is not very productive, then either there are general problems in the economy holding down the returns to private-sector investment (e.g. excessive corruption, regulatory barriers, etc.), or the mix of selected projects is heavily weighted towards unproductive activities like building presidential palaces and other such monuments, or perhaps to constructing large defence facilities. It is worth adding here that precisely these points about the roles of savings, investment, and investment efficiency can be found in the pages of *Economic Development* (Whitaker, 1958).

Besides the need for a sound macroeconomic environment and a high rate of productive investment, sustained growth is also assisted by a good business environment, by efforts to improve labour force quality, and by openness to the world economy. The notion of a good business environment can be considered in terms of the basic conditions for doing business, as in the World Bank's annual *Doing Business* surveys (see World Bank, 2008), or in terms of outcomes. The basic conditions include such things as how long it takes to set up a business, whether credit is readily available, how much corruption new businesses can expect to encounter, how frequently firms are 'inspected' by various public authorities, how they deal with exports and imports, and so on. Thus the conditions are very much about assessing how business-friendly the given country appears to be, and to that extent the various published indicators are both interesting and useful. In the last two surveys, Ireland has come out close to the top of the list: specifically, the country currently stands in eighth place out of the 178 countries included in these surveys of business conditions. However, the various indicators are far from the full story, since what really matters for growth is not so much these background conditions per se, but rather how they translate into rates of new business formation, business closures and firm growth. In other words, what really count are the business outcomes; here, too, Ireland's record in recent decades looks quite strong.

An often-neglected aspect of the growth process has to do with improving labour force quality.

In the early stages of growth, economies are often able to draw labour out of relatively low-productivity agriculture into higher-productivity industry, and later services. This process can give the impression that labour supply is not a problem, that it is unlikely to place a constraint on future growth. But most modern production (including modern business and financial services) is actually quite demanding in terms of the required labour force skills, so most countries cannot expect to sustain growth for long on the back of transferring unskilled labour out of agriculture (this labour is not, of course, really unskilled, but farming skills and knowledge do not readily transfer to other sectors). Hence, the successful countries around the world learn quite early in their growth processes that improvements in education are vital for continued growth. Moreover, this is not just about imparting basic literacy and numeracy across the entire working population, but also involves higher-level knowledge and skills of the sort needed in the upper levels of the civil service, in management, in research and development. In that context, the UN's Millennium Development Goals, the second of which is to achieve universal primary education by 2015, are insufficient to get poor countries on track for sustained economic growth. This point was acknowledged in the report of the UK's Commission on Africa, which placed great emphasis on reviving and strengthening Africa's universities (Commission, 2005). Unfortunately, little progress has yet been achieved towards this goal, but I think the issue is nevertheless a very important one.

Turning to engagement with the world economy, we generally expect exports as a share of GDP to be lower in large, already diversified economies than in small economies with a comparatively narrow domestic production base. To a large extent, this high export share in smaller economies is what enables consumption to be diversified even in a very specialised economy, since export earnings are used to pay for the required very diverse imports. It is not uncommon to find, in a small economy, that exports exceed GDP, while in a large one they may be only 20–30 per cent of GDP; in Ireland, for example, exports in 2006 amounted to about 80 per cent of GDP in market prices, the sort of high ratio one would expect in a small country – but this success represented a massive change from the protectionism that characterised the 1950s. Further, in recent decades, virtually all the most successful growth experience has been export-led. Thus, deliberate and extensive engagement with the world economy has generally proved to be an effective development strategy, and has done more to lift people out of poverty than any amount of development assistance (as emphasised in WTO, 2008; see also Wolf, 2004).

Integration in the world economy involves a mix of elements: (a) Trade in goods; (b) Trade in services; (c) Income flows: profits, dividends, remittances; (d) Aid and other external support (grants and loans); (e) Capital flows – FDI; (f) Capital flows – financial (short term and long term); and (g) Flows of people: inward and outward migration. We consider each element in turn.

Countries usually start by liberalising trade in goods and services, then later liberalise the capital account – this was the path followed by many of the transition economies, for instance, as well as several other recent success stories. It is important to rationalise, simplify, and lower the general level of tariffs on imports, as well as to reduce and simplify non-tariff barriers, an ongoing process that has been encouraged by the GATT, and since 1995 by the World Trade Organization. Then export promotion is also normally essential, since liberalising imports without actively fostering exports can prove self-defeating as several countries around the world have found to their cost (e.g. in recent years, several countries in Africa; see Ackah and Morrissey, 2005; and Iyoha, 2005).

It is not necessary to dwell here on the next two items, income flows and aid, except to remark that in Ireland's case, flows from the EU have played an important role in financing developments in the country's infrastructure. As regards capital flows, however, early capital account liberalisation was, for a time, strongly encouraged by the IMF and other international institutions, though experience of numerous financial crises in the past decade or so affecting a wide range of countries (most recently the late 1990s crisis that hit Russia and some other CIS countries very hard), together with the current turbulence in world financial markets, have led to considerable backtracking from this 'standard' position. In any event, the liberalisation of capital flows commonly starts by encouraging FDI, which has been linked to privatisation programmes in many countries. In the Irish case, there was not much privatisation to be done, and most FDI has therefore been associated with wholly new ventures.

Migration flows generally depend on economic opportunities at home and abroad, as well as on the immigration policies of potential partner countries and/or on the porosity of their borders. A bad economic situation at home, such as sluggish economic growth accompanied by high and rising rates of unemployment, often stimulates out-migration, especially if an accessible neighbouring country offers attractive job opportunities. This was the situation for Ireland at least until the late 1960s, with Irish emigrants moving to the UK and to the United States in large numbers. Albanians moving to work in Greece, or Armenians moving to work in Russia are other commonplace examples of this phenomenon, but there are many more. Migration is sometimes politically problematic, though for the sending country it does frequently offer several benefits: (i) domestic labour market problems are eased; (ii) the migrant workers frequently send some of their income back home (remittances), and for some countries this is a major source of foreign currency; and (iii) migrant workers often acquire skills and knowledge which, when they return home, eventually benefit their home economy. The last of these effects is what Ireland has been experiencing in the past two decades or so, as the country's rapid growth has stimulated substantial inward migration.

The last 'growth factor' that we consider in this section is one that has become relatively 'popular' in the recent literature on growth and development, namely institutions. Institutions are relatively stable social arrangements, often embodying various kinds of norms, customs and conventions (see North, 2005). In the economic domain they frequently possess a number of special characteristics such as influencing the behaviour of economic agents, embodying shared expectations, and assuming the form of a 'repeated game'. The last point is especially important, and means that economic agents (buyers and sellers in the simplest cases) do not think of their business transaction as being 'one off'. Instead, they expect to be engaged in a whole series of similar transactions, and this then provides incentives for them to follow the rules, operate fairly, and so on. In this sense, the 'rules of the game' can often turn out to be self-reinforcing, a useful characteristic (this can be true even without the help of a 'state' to enforce compliance, as Greif, 2006, and Dixit, 2004, have shown in various examples of informal trading networks).

Institutions, which can be either informal or formal, operate at different levels and in different contexts. At the most basic level can be found the social norms and customs that govern most everyday behaviour, whether explicitly economic or not. Next are the various resources and assets of a society, and the rights, powers and responsibilities associated with each of them. Last, we find the specific organisations that embody the institutional arrangements of the given society/economy. These include individual firms (which can be either formal or informal), households (mostly informal and customary, but usually with some formal legal underpinnings, e.g. marriage law, family law, inheritance law, etc.), business associations, economic departments and agencies of the government, the courts, and the military establishment (see Acemoglu and Robinson, 2006). From an economic standpoint, institutions are needed to provide for three key functions, namely the protection of property rights (both from other private agents and from the state itself) (on the rule of law, see Dam, 2007); supporting transactions (e.g. contract law, improve information flows, accommodate risk, etc.); and facilitating co-operation and co-ordination, especially where these are beneficial for society but would not likely result from the unrestrained market mechanism (see Bardhan, 2005).

My own interest in institutions arose from my study of the centrally planned economies, and more recently the economies in transition, as they have been re-designated. As noted above, institutional reforms are a major element of the now standard 'transition reform package'. However, decades of central planning not only left the former communist countries with the 'wrong' institutions; it also left behind a legacy of uneconomic production in two important senses: (i) much production was poorly located or in branches of production where the economy concerned had little chance of producing competitively, so transition began with this massive structural problem; and (ii) each economy contained amazingly few enterprises, most of which were far too large – the size structure of firms was completely different from what one observes in any 'normal' market economy, with hardly any small and medium-sized firms to be found. Hence the process of institution building in these economies was accompanied by rapid structural change that, naturally, placed great strain on the emerging, more or less democratic, political structures.

In the context of efforts to open up and diversify an economy, and to support its growth, well-designed institutions can help in several significant ways, including:

- Provision of market information, especially about new export opportunities (e.g. embassies could do this); in surprisingly many countries, the provision of basic market information is amazingly poor.
- Improvement of flows of technical knowledge and the ability to use it (through higher education, R&D activities – both public and private, manpower training).
- Facilitation of easy entry and exit of firms to and from the market, and support of restructuring efforts for those established firms that have a viable future.
- Development, planning, and upgrade of infrastructure (e.g. transport links, port and airport facilities, border crossings, telecoms, energy supplies, factory and office space, etc.).
- Provision of credit and other financial services, through a competently regulated banking system and financial markets.
- Creation of a simple, clear regulatory framework, with stable rules, covering such matters as competition policy, health and safety aspects of production, regulation of technical standards and product quality, service standards and customer guarantees, etc.
- Provision of a simple, clear, stable tax system, ideally with low tax rates for business.

In the last two points, simplicity and clarity were emphasised, reflecting my view that, especially in smaller and less prosperous countries, it makes economic sense to adopt policy frameworks that are administratively manageable and less susceptible to corruption and lobbying than more complex frameworks can be. Sometimes this will imply the adoption of simple policies that may not, in a formal economic sense, be strictly efficient or optimal in an ideal world. My point, however, is that the world is not particularly 'ideal', and we often have to make practical accommodations to that reality.

In any economy, naturally, institutional conditions and how effectively particular institutions function are influenced by the prevailing political configuration. Specifically, there are major issues to do with the credibility of the state. For instance, how do we know whether a successful firm will not be taken over by the state? Or whether a failing firm will not be protected unfairly because of its political connections? Or whether a regulator will be allowed to perform its tasks without state interference? Or whether banks will be directed to issue credit to firms 'officially favoured'? Unfortunately, none of these examples is remote from reality, as numerous cases of all of them can be highlighted around the world, including in some of the more developed countries. Also, and quite damagingly in economic terms, the prevalence of such phenomena encourages entrepreneurs to direct their efforts to seeking state favours rather than towards improving their market position. These issues of 'state behaviour' are likely to assume greater importance – and hence pose a greater danger – both in small countries where politicians and top business leaders are likely to be, perhaps, too closely connected; and in countries where the state accounts for a high fraction of GDP, since in such countries the state is already predisposed to be quite interventionist.

While it is by now well understood that 'institutions matter' for growth, it should not be assumed that countries just need to set up the 'right' institutions in order to succeed. For while we know what economic functions the institutions need to provide, it cannot be said with confidence that one or other institutional design is clearly superior to others, not least because much depends in practice on the cultural and social context of the country concerned. Moreover, some countries have done well with surprisingly informal institutions. China is the most striking recent example, with much quasi-private economic activity springing up since the late 1970s, unsupported until very recently by any formal, legally protected private property rights. One can only explain this by suggesting that, after the political turmoil of the Cultural Revolution, most Chinese were ready to get on with their lives with little or no state interference, and this included in the economic sphere. Informally, people believed that their business activity would be protected, and that the state would not interfere, and practice rapidly confirmed this tacit understanding.

For a time, too, the mix of policies and institutions represented by the 'Washington Consensus' was recommended to many countries around the world as a virtually guaranteed recipe for successful growth (see Williamson, 2004). While most of its ten main recommendations actually made good economic sense and stood the test of time, they did not turn out to be sufficient for growth. This was, I believe, largely because the recommendations were country-independent, and hence failed to take account of specific features of individual countries – institutional, political, cultural, etc. – that make particular policies and institutional reforms work more or less well. The same point is made even more forcibly in Clark (2007, esp. Chatper 8), who argues that in most respects Medieval England in the period 1200–1500 came close to satisfying all of the Washington Consensus conditions, indeed in some instances far better than our modern economies do, yet there was no steady technological advance and no growth in per-capita incomes. Real per-capita incomes in England, it seems, were essentially the same in AD1600 as they had been in AD1000. The industrial revolution and the accompanying economic take-off did not commence in England until well into the eighteenth century, and elsewhere it came even later.

To sum up this section, we have argued that the following factors are generally important for a country's ability to grow and prosper: a sound macroeconomic framework; high rates of productive investment; a good business environment; an adequate supply of high-quality workers; openness to the world economy; and good economic institutions. Much of what I have argued above about these factors is supported by a very comprehensive recent study of growth experience around the world, namely CGD (2008). This study was commissioned by the World Bank and sponsored by four governments (UK, Sweden, Netherlands and Australia) and a private foundation. It is extremely thorough and carefully argued, and, aside from the topics discussed here, it also favours a pragmatic, experimental approach to institutional reforms and the design of economic policy. I would strongly agree, albeit with the caveat that neither institutions nor policies should 'chop and change' too frequently: new ideas need time to bed down before we can be sure whether or not they are going to work, and excessively frequent change can itself undermine the credibility of major policy-making institutions.

Last, the reader may have noticed that I have said nothing about the importance of natural resources for economic growth. This was no accident, quite simply because the weight of evidence shows that possession of abundant natural resources is, on average, bad for growth, as several carefully conducted multi-country econometric studies have demonstrated (e.g. see Sachs and Warner, 1999). One can also point to several post-war success stories such as Japan, Hong Kong, Singapore and the Republic of Korea where growth has been exceptionally successful from a very limited natural resource base. In contrast, resource-rich countries like Angola and Nigeria, which should by now be very prosperous, still languish in serious and widespread poverty, much of the resource wealth, unfortunately, having been siphoned off into elite bank accounts. Some countries stand out from this pattern. Thus, Norway has managed its oil and gas wealth well, and so far there is every indication that – despite some quite serious corruption – Kazakhstan is doing so. But more often, natural resource wealth elicits rent-seeking behaviour and fosters corruption, undermining the integrity and honesty of often quite weak governments. Given this general picture, Ireland perhaps did well to be poor in natural resources!

Policies to Support Growth

Having identified a range of factors found to be important for sustained economic growth, we next consider how government economic policy can help to foster and support growth. In doing so, we need to be aware of a number of practical considerations:

- Implementing policies to meet all of the identified conditions will not usually prove sufficient to deliver growth, as a range of additional cultural, social and political factors often complicate the picture; and we simply do not know enough about the causes of growth to guarantee results.

- We do, however, as noted above, know quite a lot about how to ruin an economy; so whatever we advise or implement in a given country, it is vital to avoid the really bad mistakes likely to yield such an outcome.

- It is probably unwise to try to implement everything at once, as most countries would simply be unable to absorb significant change in too many areas simultaneously, and so results would almost certainly fall short of expectations.

- This point is supported by the arguments of Rodrik (2007), who suggests that in many countries it would be possible to identify one or two factors that are the principal 'blockages' impeding growth and development; initial reforms and policies should then focus on removing these blockages; other needed reforms can come later.

- That said, there are probably some countries where very wide-ranging reforms are indeed needed before sustained growth has much of a chance; if reforms are not implemented all at once, this suggests that getting growth going could take a long time. I suspect that this is the reality in several of the world's poorer countries – a couple of decades of gradual reforms might be needed before growth is suddenly able to get going. This poses an enormous challenge, not least politically, since elites might be tempted to enrich themselves sooner rather than later, instead of devoting their efforts to the painstaking process of putting in place the conditions for their country's growth. Politicians might just be too impatient, or too dishonest.

- Last, implicitly in this discussion I am assuming that countries – or their people – actually wish to grow economically. This might not always be so. Some countries might be entirely content with their traditional way of life, and if that is sustainable with limited engagement with the world economy there is surely no reason why it should not continue indefinitely. Some countries, of course, seek both higher living standards and the preservation of traditional cultures, religious practices, customs and the like – it remains an open question whether this is always possible. Hence, in what follows I focus on cases where countries do seek higher living standards in the sense understood across the developed world, without dwelling on these cultural contradictions.

Making and implementing practical economic policy is usually a good deal more complicated and multidimensional a task than economists are inclined to suppose. In some instances, such as in much of *macroeconomic policy*, our formal analysis yields policy advice that usually takes a very simple form, such as to fix certain tax rates, to aim for a particular public spending target, or to set the base interest rate in the monetary system, without fully appreciating that how and how well such measures work depends quite subtly on wider features of the policy-making environment. In other areas, such as *privatisation policy* – a particular interest of mine given my research on the economies in transition – economic theory has surprisingly little to say except to concur that firms are likely to perform better in private hands than under state control. But even that observation by itself does not take us very far, not least as it turns out to be not always correct. Then there is the important area of *trade policy*, where economic theory is well developed and favours zero or low and uniform tariffs, preferably unaccompanied by distorting and inefficient non-tariff barriers (NTBs). However, practical trade policy is vastly more complex than this and spills over into many other areas of economic (and indeed, political) life. Rather than attempt a comprehensive account of economic policy, for which I have no space, I shall therefore focus here on these three areas since they are more than sufficient to enable me to draw out some useful lessons.

Macroeconomic policy
Broadly speaking, the stance of macroeconomic policy is determined by a very small number of key parameters: the level of government demand for goods and services (such as the 'demand' for teachers, health-care workers, and the current costs of public capital projects, etc.), G; total tax collection from all sources (commodities, individuals, firms, assets), T; social transfers (e.g. unemployment pay, disability allowances, state pensions, etc.), S; the total public sector (or, to use IMF terminology, general government) debt, D; and the servicing costs of that debt, d. For macroeconomic balance, we need the current public-sector deficit, $b = G + S + d - T$, to lie within acceptable limits. There is no point in running an economy with large surpluses (corresponding to negative b), for then the government can make everyone better off by raising G or S, or by reducing T, or some combination of these, and would presumably choose to do so. Equally, it is dangerous as we saw above to run an economy for long with a large deficit because that feeds into higher debt and future servicing costs. Hence b normally needs to be small in magnitude as a percentage of GDP, perhaps in the range: – $3\% < b/GDP < 3\%$, though as ever, it is hard to justify specific numbers without knowing more about the country context.

So much for the fiscal aspects of macroeconomic policy. The monetary side concerns interest rates, inflation, and possibly the exchange rate (depending on the prevailing exchange-rate regime). In an elementary one-period model, it is easy to think of fiscal and monetary policy as independent aspects of policy, but in a more realistic multi-period setting this is clearly not the case. For the government deficit is financed both by issuing securities, both short-term and long-term, and by printing (high-powered) money. Thus, managing fiscal policy entails financial market operations that in turn influence monetary conditions, inflation and the like; and conversely. For this reason, the idea that monetary policy can ever really be 'independent' of fiscal policy and the government is somewhat mythical. However, it does make sense, I think, to give the monetary authority operational independence in terms of setting the base interest rate, as is done in the UK (Bank of England) and as is also done across the Eurozone (European Central Bank).

This framework for macroeconomic policy-making leaves a great deal of scope for making important choices about the composition of government spending (G), the level and structure of taxation (T) and hence the amounts and types of redistribution (S) needed to meet government objectives. These are all fundamentally political decisions. Despite this, not many countries around the world consistently manage their macroeconomic policy terribly well, and it is worth making a few points here to help understand why this should be the case:

- There is a natural asymmetry over cutting or increasing G, since the former is invariably politically contentious, while the latter enables a government to please all its various constituencies. A similar point (with signs reversed) can also be made about T. Hence, in a democracy, it is not surprising to find, on average, that governments run deficits rather than surpluses.
- This tendency is exacerbated by the reluctance – perhaps for electoral reasons – to look far enough ahead to see the consequences of persistent deficits in terms of future inflation and slower growth. Now and again, countries are lucky enough to have a strong government with a big enough majority to enable it to take some tough decisions (e.g. the UK under Margaret Thatcher), or they are forced to do so by economic crises (e.g. Russia and other CIS countries after 1998). But more often countries drift, because in the short-term it is politically easier (e.g. Hungary).
- One way for governments to commit themselves to 'sound' macroeconomic policy is to set up institutions that bind them in various ways. Examples are laws requiring deficits to be kept below certain limits (as the United States has attempted), and attempts to make the operation of monetary policy independent of the government (as referred to above). Nice ideas, but they are severely tested when conditions become difficult, which can occur all too easily as a result of unexpected economic shocks or simply misjudgments/mistakes about government revenues or spending in a given period. It is, in practice, too easy for governments to set aside their supposed commitments when they see the need, and most governments do so to some extent.

- At a deeper level, and leaving aside its extensive technical and administrative requirements which lie way beyond the scope of this paper, what makes macroeconomic policy work – in the relatively few countries where it really does – is a mix of conditions to do with public expectations and confidence, and the constitution of the state. To put it simply, policy works because, and to the extent that, the general population expects it to. People need to know that they can vote out of office a government that is perceived to perform too poorly, and that when voted out, the government will indeed go (remarkably, and most impressively, most transition economies have met this condition well, though in a few CIS states elections have been heavily manipulated). People also need some assurance that the government will not itself act illegally, and that it will respect its own courts when found to be at fault, thereby supporting the 'rule of law'. Rather few countries fully meet this condition, and some do so only as the end result of what has sometimes been a pretty terrible history (e.g. the UK with its Civil War in the seventeenth century). In small countries, it can be extremely hard to achieve the required degree of judicial independence and authority, and at times it can therefore assist policy credibility for some top-level judicial functions to be 'outsourced' to a jurisdiction with a stronger reputation. Interestingly, this sort of practice was not uncommon in medieval times among the numerous small German principalities, so it is not a particularly new idea.

Privatisation policy (including economic regulation)
Mostly we accept that the private sector is superior to the state when it comes to organising business activity because of its more focused incentives (seeking higher profits), greater efficiency, better management, and so on. The 1980s and 1990s experience of privatisation in the UK generally confirmed this view, albeit with two caveats: (a) the UK government realised that the general competitive environment within which firms operated also mattered a great deal; and (b) the government realised that public utilities needed not only competition, where that was possible, but also regulation to ensure that important social objectives were achieved at an acceptable cost. Since the 1980s there has been a great deal of privatisation in many countries, experience that is reviewed extensively in Megginson and Netter (2001).

Particularly interesting in this regard has been the experience of the transition economies since 1990 or so. At the start, practically all firms in these economies were state owned, and so in almost all countries (except outliers like Belarus and Turkmenistan) comprehensive privatisation came onto the policy agenda immediately, in addition to encouraging wholly new firms to start up. It was understood that getting established business out of state hands was an essential part of building a well-functioning market economy. The question was, how to do it. As noted above, economic analysis provided at best only limited guidance, so there was much learning 'on the job', and no doubt many mistakes along the way. By the year 2000, most production in all the transition economies took place in the private sector, representing a truly amazing pace of privatisation during the previous decade.

Issues to be settled included: what to privatise; what methods of privatisation to use; who the new owners should be; how state-owned assets should be valued; whether there should be any restitution to former owners; how privatisation should be financed; what administrative structures should be set up to manage the privatisation process; how to deal with firms considered 'strategically important'; how to deal with firms that most likely had no economic future; and how to regulate firms such as public utilities once they were privatised. For the sake of brevity, I limit discussion to a few key observations:

- Generally, it was considered that all firms should be privatised, though a few countries maintained lists of firms they considered strategically important, which were not to be privatised early or at all. To outsiders, these lists seemed like fairly motley collections of firms, with no obvious economic rationale for their selection. Unfortunately, this was the case largely because membership of a list was nearly always the result of lobbying by firms wanting to enjoy continued state protection, not a particularly desirable criterion.

- How to privatise was often highly controversial. It quickly became clear, after some early experimentation in Poland, that the UK's approach to privatisation was completely unworkable in Eastern Europe. With so many firms to privatise in each country within a very short time-scale, it was quite out of the question to sell each one on the basis of separate Acts of Parliament as had been done in the UK. Moreover, the transition economy banking systems could not have coped either, at least until the late 1990s. Instead of such a case-by-case approach, all transition economies passed general enabling legislation to facilitate privatisation, and then established various forms of privatisation agency or state asset management agency to oversee the process of privatisation. This was certainly the right approach, although it did open up opportunities for corruption in countries where the ensuing implementation lacked transparency and proper accountability.

- Regarding the methods of privatisation, countries opted for sale to single buyers or consortia; voucher schemes that effectively gave away the firms, either to the general population, or predominantly to their management and workers; or mixed approaches. Few countries attempted to return assets to former owners, rightly in my view. Sales are attractive because they enable countries to bring in much-needed new capital, management expertise, technology, and often improved access to markets. On the other hand, given the poor state of domestic financial markets in the transition economies, and low stocks of personal savings, it was apparent that not many companies would end up being owned by the local population. Indeed, I have on several occasions advised countries that if they chose to privatise predominantly by selling companies, most new owners would be 'foreigners, crooks, or members of the former (communist) *nomenklatura*', since these would be the only groups with money – legitimate or otherwise. This need not prevent them from choosing this route, but it seemed better to proceed with some understanding of the likely outcomes. Overall, I would generally judge privatisation by sale to be superior to giveaways for the reasons noted above.

- Valuing the firms to be privatised in Central and Eastern Europe proved to be a complete nightmare, partly because of deficiencies of the prevailing socialist accounting systems, partly because the firms had never operated in a 'normal' market environment. Initially no one had any idea which firms would be capable of operating competitively and profitably, or which simply had no economic future. In this context, I have encountered instances where the valuations attached to the same firm by respected western accounting firms differed by a factor of three (or even more). Despite this problem, countries such as Hungary privatised a great deal by direct sale, and did so remarkably successfully. Other countries such as Russia 'sold' firms to management and workers (and to some extent to the wider population), assets being paid for using vouchers that people had obtained for only a nominal price. Moreover, the assets in these transactions were valued at their historic accounting cost. This is not necessarily a terrible idea in stable times, when selling perfectly viable firms; but it amounted to a giveaway in Russia, since these 'sales' took place just after a spell of inflation at over 1,000 per cent.

- The firms not being privatised, namely those that were to remain in the state sector for various reasons, received surprisingly little attention in the early 1990s. Eventually, though, it was realised that they needed to operate more commercially and to be better managed. Achieving this was not easy, not least because of a shortage of managers with worthwhile market-economy skills, especially in areas such as finance and marketing, which were largely absent from the profiles of socialist managers in the old system. Also, many firms needed substantial restructuring to modernise their production and make them viable in the new conditions. There was a lack of skills to accomplish this, too, and I was always sceptical of the ability of state agencies to do it, given how poorly they had run the firms in the past. Gradually, though, progress occurred, with only a few 'slow reformers' continuing to protect their old, inefficient firms from market pressures.

- During the 1990s, and in some countries more recently, most transition economies privatised all or part of their major public utilities. In doing so, they mostly learned from the models and mistakes of other countries, though in a few cases countries contemplated using privatisation models that were well beyond their likely administrative capacity to manage. Luckily, most such schemes were dropped or delayed. Accompanying these privatisations were calls to establish UK-style regulators to ensure that privatised utilities paid attention to their social obligations and set prices at 'politically acceptable' levels. The last phrase, however, reveals the problem, namely the unavoidable intrusion of politics. In the UK, utility regulators just about manage to hold on to their operational independence, and governments do not override their pronouncements (one suspects, of course, that some political lobbying goes on in the background) – so the regulators combine technical expertise and political credibility quite nicely, and are taken seriously as a consequence. There was no way this was going to happen in Eastern Europe, as politicians were simply not ready to hand over the necessary authority. Thus, early calls to establish regulators were a little naive and some of the new authorities worked quite badly. In the end, it was usually best to leave regulation within the relevant ministry, where the politics remained part of the landscape.

Trade policy

As we saw earlier, trade liberalisation is often thought of, in rather straight-forward terms, as a question of reducing and simplifying tariffs, and reducing or eliminating whatever non-tariff barriers (NTBs) might be in place. These are certainly important steps, but they are far from being the whole story. Part of the process, for many countries, is also to sign up to the most relevant Free Trade Area (FTA) or Customs Union (CU), the formal difference between these being that a CU has a common external tariff while an FTA does not. Thus NAFTA, the North American Free Trade Agreement, is an FTA involving Canada, the United States and Mexico, whereas the European Union forms a CU.

Many policy-makers and politicians appear to be convinced that by signing up to one or more of these agreements they are indeed liberalising trade, helping to make their countries more efficient and competitive. However, this is not always the case. Some countries join several agreements, which creates an administrative quagmire as each agreement has its own conditions and restrictions, including often quite complicated 'rules of origin'; some agreements, moreover, are restrictive precisely in those sectors where the given country might have enjoyed a competitive advantage; some agreements are the result of pressure from a dominant power; and some are agreements between countries that do not even trade much with each other, where benefits cannot be expected to be large.

Parts of Africa now have what some have termed a 'spaghetti bowl' of preferential trade agreements, so complex as to be largely unmanageable, and certainly not a good way to promote trade; quite the contrary, in fact, since the complexity combined with limited administrative capacity is an open invitation to corruption. A similar picture has been the case for some years among the countries of south-eastern Europe, all small and ideally highly trade-dependent countries. In that region, there were more than twenty bilateral trade agreements between the various countries and it has taken considerable international pressure to persuade them that a single free trade area would be simpler and more effective. Finally, the idea now seems to have been accepted and is gradually coming into effect. Even so, Bhagwati (2008) argues strongly that the growing network of free trade areas and other 'preferential' trading arrangements around the world is damaging for world trade and prosperity. It is not a step on the way to the free trade ideal, as some would argue, and is a trend to be resisted.

Aside from the above formal aspects of trade policy, the effective implementation of a liberal and supportive approach to international trade involves a number of other elements. These include the following:

- As noted earlier, active export promotion is an important component of an effective trade policy, and this is likely to include measures to market the country's merchandise exports and to support them with credit and export credit guarantees. With exportable services such as finance, insurance, consultancy, education, tourism and so on, vigorous marketing is also needed, but in these case the clients generally come to the country to receive the services (except for such items as distance-learning education, or internet sales of products).
- In addition, as Broadman (2005) argued for the economies in transition, supporting trade requires a wide variety of what he terms 'behind-the-border' reforms to complement the basic trade reforms themselves. One aspect of this is to strengthen the competitive environment through competition policy and the like, and to improve market flexibility both in terms of facilitating easy entry and exit of firms, and through enhancing labour market flexibility. Another aspect involves improving the trade-related infrastructure such as ports, transport links, telecommunications and IT services. Aside from this physical dimension, there is also the vital administrative dimension in the form of trade-related documentation, permits, technical standards and their enforcement, and trade-related health issues. While these procedures are important, it makes sense to keep their total burden as light as possible.

Lessons and Surprises

After this wide-ranging discussion of countries' diverse growth experience, the principal factors considered to foster sustained economic growth, and the ways in which well-designed policies can support the process, what have we learnt? And given the occasion of the present conference, marking the fiftieth anniversary of the report, *Economic Development*, what has Ireland to learn from our discussion? These are the issues on which we focus in this concluding section.

Lessons
Countries grow under diverse circumstances and subject to a wide range of domestic political arrangements and regional alliances. However, it is possible to elicit from all the diversity a few crucial economic factors that appear to be needed for sustainable growth to occur. These include:

- Sound macroeconomic policy
- High rates of fixed capital formation, invested productively
- A good business environment
- Efforts to improve labour force quality
- Openness to the world economy (especially for small economies)
- Good economic institutions, both formal and informal (notably to do with property rights and business contracts, with protection required both against other private-sector agents and against the state itself).

We also noted, though, that these conditions are not always sufficient for economic growth, since various social and cultural factors can all too easily get in the way of economic development, as can diverse elite groups who might pursue their own private interests at the expense of the wider nation.

Further, we saw that while successful growth cannot be guaranteed, failure can. In other words, we know all too well how to ruin an economy, and a few examples across the world are currently demonstrating that all too distressingly.

Surprises
One surprise is the fact that, for a country to grow successfully, the possession of significant natural resources is not necessarily very helpful since, on average, resource-rich countries are prone to extensive rent-seeking and corruption on the part of their political elites. Of course there are exceptions, such as Norway, but they are relatively few.

A second surprise has to do with the role of expectations and confidence in growth processes, as against the influence of formal institutions. The most striking instance of this is the case of China, referred to above. Growing quickly since the late 1970s, none of its success can be attributed to its wonderful system of formal property rights and commercial courts, since these institutions hardly existed until very recently and are still not fully developed. What worked for

China, I think, was simply the widespread belief that private economic activity (or 'quasi-private', as strictly private activity was not even legal at all at first) would indeed be protected by local political elites (the Communist Party), and that people would be allowed to earn high incomes without fear of arbitrary confiscation. Events have proven these beliefs to be correct, but all could so easily have turned out very differently.

The third surprise, at least for an economist like myself, has been the limited role for economic analysis in designing sound economic policies to promote growth. In many cases, such as in connection with trade policy, theory does provide some nice models that enable us to analyse various types of tariff policy, and it also gives rise to recommendations favouring free, or at least very liberal trade. So far, so good. But this is really only the starting point for concrete and practical trade policy, since, as we saw above, there are many detailed issues that need to be included in a properly developed policy. Often, to find a good policy, one has to proceed empirically and pragmatically, trying out different approaches to discover what works best in a given country environment. This can be quite a slow and messy business. Further, as regards privatisation, we saw that economic theory does argue that it is likely to be beneficial, but offers virtually no guidance beyond that relatively banal observation. Hence, as policy-makers in the transition economies rapidly discovered, the practicalities of implementing privatisation were complex and difficult, with many available approaches to be tried out in each country.

Implications for Ireland
Finally, I hesitate to say much about Ireland as it is not a country that I have studied in any depth, but let me offer a few brief closing remarks.

1. In terms of the 'lessons' listed above, it does seem that Ireland scores pretty well on most items, which is encouraging. True, there are doubts about the current stance of the country's macroeconomic policy, though I would see this more as short-term imbalances rather than as longer-term threats. Otherwise, the record of the last three decades is an impressive one.
2. In some respects, though, Ireland's economic institutions, especially where they concern issues of competition policy; selection of personnel for senior positions (e.g. in private business, the civil service, the universities); the awarding of government contracts; and so on, seem inherently quite vulnerable to corruption, special pleading, 'jobs for the boys', and other such undesirable distortions. 'Jobs for the boys' (and girls, too, naturally) is a widespread practice in many countries, and generally refers to the practice of securing jobs through personal connections and the like. If the boys (and girls) who actually get the jobs are sufficiently deserving and competent, then

the system need not be so bad (though it is never fair). But how does a country build up the 'ethos' that makes this happen and sustains it? In a small country like Ireland, where at elite level everyone knows everyone else, this is surely immensely difficult, though Ireland's record to date seems surprisingly good. To ensure both fairness and high standards, I would nevertheless favour extensive use of international panels of experts, along with a high degree of openness and transparency. To achieve this, Ireland still has some way to go.

3. Last, what made *Economic Development* such a success as a report? I would highlight three things. First, it was strong on detail and practical solutions, and understood well – at a time when the idea was not yet firmly established in economics circles – the critical importance of getting more investment and making it productive. Second, the report argued that Ireland should not continue to be protectionist, and that it should open up to the world economy. Third, and I suspect almost by accident, it managed to be optimistic about Ireland's economic prospects, replacing the doom-laden projections that were more prevalent prior to 1958. It helped the Irish people to believe in themselves and to believe that they could prosper, and so they did.

References

Acemoglu, D. and Robinson, J. A. (2006), *Economic Origins of Dictatorship and Democracy*, New York: Cambridge University Press

Acemoglu, D., Johnson, S., and Robinson, J. (2005), 'Institutions as the Fundamental Cause of Long-Run Growth', in Aghion, P. and Durlauf, S. (eds), *Handbook of Economic Growth, volume 1A*, Amsterdam: North Holland

Ackah, C. and Morrissey, O. (2005), 'Trade Policy and Performance in Sub-Saharan Africa since the 1980s', *Economic Research Working Paper No.78*, Tunis: African Development Bank

Alam, A., Casero, P. A., Khan, F. and Udomsaph, C. (2008), *Unleashing Prosperity: Productivity Growth in Eastern Europe and the Former Soviet Union*, Washington, DC: The World Bank

Bardhan, P. (2005), *Scarcity, Conflicts and Cooperation*, Cambridge, MA: MIT Press

Bhagwati, J. (2008), *Termites in the Trading System: How Preferential Agreements Undermine Free Trade*, Council on Foreign Relations, Oxford: Oxford University Press

Broadman, H. G. (ed.) (2005), *From Disintegration to Integration: Eastern Europe and the Former Soviet Union in International Trade*, Washington, DC: The World Bank

Buiter, W. and Grafe, C. (2003), 'Reforming EMU's Fiscal Policy Rules: Some Suggestions for Enhancing Fiscal Sustainability and Macroeconomic Stability in an Enlarged European Union', in Buti, M. (ed.), *Monetary and Fiscal Policies in EMU: Interactions and Coordination*, Cambridge: Cambridge University Press, pp. 92–145

CGD (2008), *The Growth Report: Strategies for Sustained Growth and Inclusive Development*, Report of the Commission on Growth and Development, Washington, DC: The World Bank

Clark, G. (2007), *A Farewell to Alms: A Brief Economic History of the World*, Princeton, NJ: Princeton University Press

Collier, P. (2007), *The Bottom Billion: Why the Poorest Countries are Failing and What Can Be Done about It*, Oxford: Oxford University Press

Commission (2005), *Our Common Interest: Report of the Commission for Africa*, London: Commission for Africa

Coorey, S., Clausen, J. R., Funke, N., Munoz, S., and Ould-Abdullah, B. (2007), 'Lessons from High Inflation Episodes for Stabilizing the Economy in Zimbabwe', *IMF Working Paper WP*/07/99, Washington, DC: International Monetary Fund

Dam, K. W. (2006), *The Law-Growth Nexus: The Rule of Law and Economic Development*, Washington, DC: The Brookings Institution

Dixit, A. K. (2004), *Lawlessness and Economics: Alternative Modes of Governance*, Princeton: Princeton University Press

Goldberg, Y., Branstetter, L., Goddard, J. G., and Kuriakose, S. (2008), *Globalization and Technology Absorption in Europe and Central Asia: The Role of Trade, FDI, and Cross-border Knowledge Flows*, World Bank Working Paper No. 150, Washington, DC: The World Bank

Government of Ireland (1958), *Programme for Economic Expansion*, Government of Ireland, Dublin: Stationery Office (often referred to informally as the *First Programme for Economic Expansion*)

Greif, A. (2006), *Institutions and the Path to the Modern Economy*, New York: Cambridge University Press

Haggard, S. and Noland, M. (2007), *Famine in North Korea: Markets, Aid, and Reform*, New York: Columbia University Press

Hare, P. G. (2008), 'Institutions and Diversification of the Economies in Transition: Policy Challenges', Paper for UNECE Conference in April 2008, Geneva: UNECE

Hare, P. G. (2007), 'Industrial Policy for North Korea', *International Journal of Korean Unification Studies*, vol. 16, no. 2, pp. 29–53

Iyoha, M. A. (2005), 'Enhancing Africa's Trade: From Marginalization to an Export-Led Approach to Development', Economic Research Working Paper No. 77, Tunis: African Development Bank

Megginson, W. L. and Netter, J. N. (2001), 'From State to Market: A Survey of Empirical Studies on Privatization', *Journal of Economic Literature*, vol. 39, no. 2, pp. 321–89

Mitra, P. (2008), *Innovation, Inclusion and Integration: From Transition to Convergence in Eastern Europe and the Former Soviet Union*, Washington, DC: The World Bank

North, D. (2005), *Understanding the Process of Economic Change*, Princeton, NJ: Princeton University Press

Plan (2007), *Transforming Ireland: A Better Quality of Life for All*, National Development Plan 2007–2013, Dublin: Stationery Office

Rodrik, D. (2007), *One Economics, Many Recipes: Globalization, Institutions and Economic Growth*, Princeton: Princeton University Press

Sachs, J. D. and Warner, A. M. (1999), 'The Big Rush, Natural Resource Booms and Growth', *Journal of Development Economics*, vol. 59, no. 1, pp. 43–76

Whitaker, T. K. (1958), *Economic Development*, Department of Finance, Dublin: Stationery Office

Williamson, J. (2004), 'The Washington Consensus as Prescription for Development', Lecture delivered to the World Bank, Washington, DC: Institute of International Economics

Wolf, M. (2004), *Why Globalization Works*, New Haven: Yale University Press

World Bank (2008), *Doing Business in 2008*, Washington, DC: The World Bank

WTO (2008), *World Trade Report 2008: Trade in a Globalizing World*, Geneva: WTO

9

Theoretical and Pragmatic Elements in the Civil Service Debates on Trade Liberalisation

Frank Barry

Introduction

The 1938 Anglo-Irish Trade Agreement, which ended the economic war with Britain, also marked the end of Fianna Fáil radicalism in the agricultural sphere. In her 1992 book, *Industrial Development and Irish National Identity 1922–39*, Mary Daly notes that it established a new equilibrium that balanced the forces of export-oriented agriculture and protected industry. What was it that shattered this equilibrium in the late 1950s and paved the way towards freer trade?[1]

Internal and external developments combined to ensure that the existing equilibrium could no longer prevail. The very poor performance of the Irish economy over the 1950s forced a reappraisal of the supposed benefits of protectionism. That the formation of the EEC and the imminent establishment of EFTA might on their own have caused such a reappraisal, even had performance been better, is suggested by concurrent developments in two other small protectionist economies on the outer periphery of Europe – Finland and Portugal. Portugal became a founder member of EFTA in 1960, while Finland, which needed to negotiate to be allowed to maintain its special relationship with

---

[1] The response of Irish agriculture to what appeared in the summer of 2008 to be an imminent WTO agreement illustrates that today's equilibrium is the reverse of that prevailing in 1938. Industry and services favour further liberalisation, while agriculture is now protectionist.

110

the Soviet Union, signed a free trade agreement with the new block in 1961. Ireland's path to trade liberalisation would prove to be more complicated.

The Rupturing of the Protectionist Equilibrium

Developments in Ireland in the 1950s
Protectionist Ireland missed out on the post-war European boom. Real per-annum growth over the 1950s averaged 2 per cent, compared to 5–6 per cent for Western Europe. Aggregate Irish employment declined each year over the decade and a massive 400,000 people emigrated, with 1.8 per cent of the population departing in the peak year, 1957. Conditions were particularly severe following the balance of payments crisis of 1955, which led to a severe fiscal contraction and two to three years of declining real GDP (depending on the data source employed).[2]

Conditions improved from 1958, assisted by the innovation of Export Profits Tax Relief (EPTR), which had been introduced in 1956 by the short-lived second coalition government of the time.[3] Industrial exports expanded strongly and new foreign firms started to trickle in, accounting apparently for all of the growth in manufacturing employment (which began to rise steadily from 1957).[4] One suspects that this is what T. K. Whitaker had in mind when he observed that Gerard Sweetman, the Fine Gael Finance Minister in 1956, was 'singularly unfortunate … in that his government was overthrown before the ideas which he implemented could bear fruit' (quoted in Fanning 1978, p. 511).[5]

De Tocqueville famously argued that revolutions occur when conditions are improving rather than when they are at their worst. Might this insight offer anything to our understanding of how protectionism began to lose the debate? Both Garret FitzGerald's analysis and that of Whitaker himself suggest that it might. The Department of Finance memo of December 1959, 'Reasons for Reducing Protection', noted that 'the current high level of industrial production,

---

[2] Honohan and Ó Gráda (1998) have shown that the balance of payments crisis was partly the result of a policy blunder, which saw the Irish authorities attempt to hold interest rates below UK levels.
[3] The original 50 per cent tax remission was increased to 100 per cent two years later. The Control of Manufactures Acts, which had sought to restrict foreign ownership, were also largely repealed in 1958, though the Acts had never been rigidly enforced (Daly, 1984).
[4] IDA (1973) provides a list of new foreign firms entering Ireland from the mid-1950s, while O'Hearn (1987) provides calculations of new foreign-firm employment. His estimates suggest a total of 1,700 jobs in new foreign firms in 1959, rising to more than 3,000 in 1960.
[5] Though Fanning mentions this in the context of the establishment of the Capital Investment Advisory Committee and the initiation of Ireland's application for membership of the IMF and the World Bank, it seems clear from Whitaker's own writings that he had EPTR in mind as well. Thus he writes, in Whitaker (1983, p. 9), that 'tax reliefs were introduced in that year (1956) by the Minister for Finance, Gerard Sweetman, who emphasised the need for 'a substantial increase in the volume and efficiency of national production''. The latter is a key theme in Whitaker's writings.

which shows no sign of slackening, would make the present an appropriate time to begin to lower tariffs'. FitzGerald (1968) contends, furthermore, that the improvement in the conditions of industry influenced the assessment of the Committee on Industrial Organisation, which had been set up in 1961 to report on industrial prospects under free trade conditions. 'Public opinion', he writes, 'was struck by the conclusion ... that there was a viable industrial base, with individual inefficient firms, rather than a series of industries incapable of withstanding competition.'

These discussions shed an interesting light on the burgeoning international literature on policy reform.[6] Reforms are often provoked by crises or by the perception of crisis, as in the case of the accession to power of Margaret Thatcher in the UK (though historian Arnold Toynbee's notion of 'challenge and response' should be borne in mind – all societies face challenges; success or failure lies in their capacity to respond). Why might a crisis be necessary for reforms to be implemented? Some analysts focus on interest-group realignments, where a sufficiently large deterioration may cause previous adversaries of reform to turn in favour. One influential analysis (Grossman and Helpman, 2001) posits that politicians balance a concern for aggregate social welfare with a desire to maintain the support of special-interest lobby groups. This may be overly mechanistic, however, in assuming that the policy options that maximise social welfare are known in advance. The 'force of ideas' argument – whereby intellectuals and opinion-makers need to convince politicians and the electorate that a major policy change is for the common good – can help overcome the influence of particular interest groups, as well as expanding knowledge of the mapping between policy choices and outcomes.

While a crisis might make the need for reform more apparent, it will not necessarily represent the circumstances most conducive to their adoption. High unemployment, balance of payments crises and slow growth are not generally conducive to trade liberalisation.[7] Trade liberalisation may even reduce welfare in the short run when labour markets are inflexible, slowing down the transfer of resources between declining and expanding industries.

De Tocqueville's insight is supported by the OECD's observation that fiscal expansion and a healthy budgetary situation tend to be associated with more structural reform, and difficult fiscal situations with less, in that anti-reform groups may need to be 'bought off'. This might explain why some of the main recommendations of *Economic Development* – for a significant reduction in

---

[6] See e.g. Hood (1990), Olofsgård (2003), Koromzay (2004) and OECD (2007).

[7] Irwin (1993) observes that 'long periods of macroeconomic stability provide an environment conducive to the adoption of liberal trade policies.'

taxation, and for public capital investment to be redirected from social to productive investment projects – were not in fact implemented.[8]

The Formation of the European Trading Blocks

When *Economic Development* and the Government White Paper, *Programme for Economic Expansion*, were written, there was a widespread presumption that a Western European Free Trade Area was in the offing, and the White Paper noted that

> It would be unrealistic, in the light of the probable emergence of a Free Trade Area to rely on a policy of protection similar to that applied over the last 25 years or so…. The rules of the Free Trade Area will require a gradual and systematic reduction in existing tariffs.[9]

These OEEC-sponsored negotiations broke down at the end of 1958, however, and Europe divided into the six-country EEC and what would become in 1960 the seven-country European Free Trade Association (EFTA).[10]

Concurrent developments in Portugal and Finland, two other small and highly protectionist economies, suggest that these developments, even in isolation, would have forced a reappraisal of Ireland's protectionist strategy.[11] Though Portugal under autocratic rule was resistant to the notion of European free trade, Salazar publicly recognised in 1957 that the creation of the Common Market disrupted the existing equilibrium ('broke the balance of trade') and the country had no choice but to respond when its single most important European trading partner, the UK, led the EFTA initiative. Portugal subsequently became one of the founding members of EFTA, though it managed to negotiate 'under-development concessions' comprising a long adjustment period.

Finland was also highly protectionist at the time, and its room for manoeuvre was constrained by the Soviet Union, with which it had signed a Trade Agreement in 1947 where each granted the other Most Favoured Nation (MFN) status. The formation of EFTA required a Finnish response as well, however, as both of its major trading partners – Sweden and the UK – were founder members,

---

[8] Bew and Patterson (1982) suggest that the expansion in social investment represented a Fianna Fáil strategy to recapture its working class constituency in the aftermath of the election losses of the 1950s.

[9] *Programme for Economic Expansion*, 1958, pp. 37–8

[10] Initial EFTA membership included the UK, Sweden, Norway, Denmark, Portugal, Austria and Switzerland.

[11] On the Portuguese and Finnish cases respectively, see Andresen-Leitão (2001) and Paavonen (2001). For a comparative analysis of the movement towards trade liberalisation in Ireland, Portugal and Finland, see Barry and Weir (2007).

though no deal with EFTA could be allowed to threaten its bilateral relations with the Soviet Union. Though EFTA members initially baulked at these concessions, they were eventually accepted and the FINN-EFTA free trade agreement was signed in 1961.

For Ireland, these same external developments meant that standing still was not an option. The first decision to be faced was whether to seek to join EFTA. This is the background context to the civil service debates discussed in the next section. Ireland's industrial preferences in the British market would be eroded by the formation of EFTA, whether Ireland joined or not. EFTA membership would have entailed reducing industrial protection and exposing the domestic market to further competition. Whitaker believed that this would be beneficial and would improve Irish industrial export prospects both in Britain and in the rest of EFTA. Industry and Commerce argued that it would be catastrophic. Irish agriculture had little to gain from EFTA as the agreement did not cover agricultural trade.

The debates covered here ceased before Britain's intention to seek EEC membership was announced in 1961, which triggered a concurrent Irish application. When these were rejected, the Irish decision – for reasons to be discussed below – was to pursue enhanced trade liberalisation with the UK rather than with the entire EFTA group. The comprehensive Anglo-Irish Free Trade Agreement of 1965, which was to be fully implemented by 1975, signalled the final victory over Irish industrial protectionism.

The Civil Service Debates on Trade Liberalisation

The civil service debates on trade liberalisation with which this paper is concerned took place between October 1959 and January 1960 and largely pitched the Department of Finance (in the person of T. K. Whitaker) against the Department of Industry and Commerce (in the person of J. C. B. McCarthy), with occasional interventions from Agriculture, Foreign Affairs, the Department of the Taoiseach and others.[12] They have been cited in many historical studies and have been drawn together and published by T. K. Whitaker in 2006 under the title *Protection or Free Trade – The Final Battle*. As Whitaker explains, this 'semi-official' correspondence (the term refers to an exchange of letters between officials posing questions or arguments) was intended especially for the eyes of

---

[12] Whitaker (1974) describes the period 1959 to 1961 as '… a "crunch" period in the move to free trade. Despite recognition of its probable inevitability, free trade, naturally enough, was not universally welcome and the original impetus towards it ran the risk of running into the sands of frustrated isolation.'

the new Taoiseach, Seán Lemass, who had assumed office only a few months previously, in June 1959. The memos – from all sides – are models of clarity and succinctness.

The debate opens on the question of Ireland's position on EFTA membership, with the presumption being that the concessionary terms obtained by Portugal would be available to Ireland also. Industry and Commerce is dramatically pessimistic. The Department had suggested earlier that as many as 100,000 of the 150,000 or so manufacturing jobs of that time could be lost if trade were liberalised across all of Western Europe.[13] 'These conclusions', it states, 'are broadly valid also' with respect to EFTA membership. Depending on the precise nature of the terms to be agreed with Portugal, Industry and Commerce suggests that between 20 and 40 per cent of manufacturing employment could be threatened. In this, the department is clearly equating *competition* with *ruin*. It warns furthermore that as Britain comprised over 50 per cent of the EFTA economy, and since Ireland already had almost complete duty-free access to the British market, there would be little prospect of gains to offset the influx of goods from both the UK and other EFTA member states – the more so since the other EFTA members had 'somewhat similar economies' to Ireland.

A note to Whitaker from Maurice Moynihan, Secretary of the Department of the Taoiseach, appears to accept this reasoning. In his response, Whitaker disputes the extent of liberalisation that the Portuguese terms would entail. Far more significantly, however, he argues that the discipline of progressive tariff reduction would increase efficiency and reduce costs, thereby enhancing prospects for increased exports not just to EFTA but to other countries as well. Presciently, he adds that EFTA membership would encourage further export-oriented foreign direct investment inflows to Ireland.[14] This position is repeated in his comments on the Department of Industry and Commerce memo entitled 'Ireland and the Outer Seven', which states that 'the conclusion in the memorandum that there appears to be little case for contemplating joining EFTA is unwarranted'. Association with EFTA is clearly seen by Whitaker as a means to force a reduction in protection, which would promote greater efficiency and reduce costs.

---

[13] This is strongly reminiscent of the IFA reaction to what appeared to be a likely WTO deal in the summer of 2008; see Matthews (2008).

[14] Would this have compensated for Ireland's loss of preferential access to the UK market which the formation of EFTA entailed? A similar question was addressed later by McAleese (1975) in his analysis of the consequences for Ireland of joint Irish and UK accession to the EU. McAleese estimated that, for manufactured exports, the benefits of improved access to the six original EU member states would be wiped out by the loss of preferential access to the UK, but that the FDI effect of the former was likely to be much stronger than the FDI effect of the latter, as proved subsequently – of course – to be the case.

He notes that a separate summary is being prepared within Finance of the arguments in favour of tariff reduction even apart from free trade developments in Europe, though his internal Finance memo to Charley Murray (who would follow him later as Secretary of the department) proposes that Finance set out the case for 'a progressive lowering of our protective tariffs in the context of a free trade area which includes Britain – and this irrespective of any improvements in our agricultural relations with Britain', that is, essentially to set out the case for EFTA membership.

In response to a memo from the Department of Agriculture which argues that EFTA membership would probably require Britain to extend equivalent agricultural access to other EFTA member states and that Irish interests would therefore be best served by seeking a Free Trade Area arrangement with Britain alone, however, Whitaker writes to Jack Nagle, Secretary of the Department of Agriculture, signifying his agreement with this general thesis.[15] This triggers an increased emphasis on the 'pure' case for trade liberalisation, as distinct from the argument that liberalisation might be used as a bargaining chip to extract concessions from others. Industry and Commerce, however, continues to adhere to the latter view.

On 14 December 1959, Finance issued its memo on 'Reasons for Reducing Protection'. The argument is that:

- The inadequacy of protectionism as a remedy for the problems of unemployment and emigration had become obvious. Manufacturing employment barely increased over the 1950s. The only hope for further job creation was for Irish industry to enlarge its sales on export markets, which required an improvement in quality and a reduction in unit costs.
- Action was becoming more urgent as competition in export markets would grow as other European countries achieved greater specialisation, higher output and lower costs through tariff reductions and freer trade.
- As long as protection was maintained, there would be no compulsion to increase quality and efficiency.
- High costs in protected industries were being transmitted to other sectors. This reduced competitiveness more generally, and the consequent lowering of living standards vis-à-vis Britain encouraged emigration.
- While the non-competitiveness of many Irish industrial products was related to the smallness of the home market and the lack of opportunities for

---

[15] Nagle, interestingly, writes that 'it is difficult to see why Britain should want this country to join the EFTA (as) she would be bringing additional competition for her exporters into a market where at present they are predominant' (i.e. that they have preferential access to the Irish market). Political historian Maurice Fitzgerald (2001, footnote 15) has subsequently unearthed evidence that the UK was antagonistic to the notion of Irish membership, at least in the early stages of EFTA.

economies of scale and specialisation, the risk of exposure to competition from larger units in other countries tended to be exaggerated. In many industries, smaller-scale firms could be equally efficient and a broader market would provide opportunities for smaller enterprises to specialise in distinctive goods.

- A progressive lowering of tariffs was necessary for economic progress, regardless of what was happening in the outside world.

Before turning to analyse these arguments from the perspective of current international trade theory, we should note the final pragmatic policy advice:

> Increasing competition on the home market would be a much more general and effective spur to improvements in efficiency than special aids and incentives to which only the progressive undertakings would respond.

This point is again emphasised in later correspondence, as for example in a letter to Industry and Commerce dated 31 December 1959, when Whitaker writes that 'an externally-applied discipline would arouse less opposition, appear less discriminatory and be more effective than a system operated at the discretion of the domestic administration'. This seems designed to combat the discretionary powers of the Department of Industry and Commerce, and perhaps also the interventionist instincts of Lemass himself.[16]

How do these arguments stand up in the light of the body of international trade theory as it stands today? The conventional trade theory of the 1950s would have been based on the theory of comparative advantage and the assumption of constant returns to scale. These elements imply that trade will take place primarily between countries that are very different from each other (in terms of factor endowments of land, labour, capital, education etc.) and will be of the *inter-industry* type (where countries will export the output of some industries and import the output of a different set of industries).

In fact, however, most global trade takes place between countries that are relatively similar to each other in their factor endowments, while much if not most trade is *intra-industry* (entailing the exchange of different varieties of the same product) rather than *inter-industry* in nature. These observations led to the emergence in the 1980s of what has come to be known as 'new trade theory', which is based on a recognition of the pervasiveness of scale economies and imperfect competition.[17]

---

[16] Industry and Commerce had responded to the original memo pointing to the need to be able 'speedily to reverse engines as and when experience dictated'.

[17] See e.g. Helpman and Krugman (1985).

Paul Krugman (2002) writes that, as late as 1984,

> the observation that increasing returns could be a reason for trade between seemingly similar countries was by no means a well-understood proposition: certainly it was never covered in most textbooks or courses, undergraduate or graduate. The idea that trade might reflect an overlay of increasing-returns specialization on comparative advantage was not there at all…. Many trade theorists still regarded the main possible contribution of scale economies to the story as being a tendency for large countries to export scale-sensitive goods…. To the extent that welfare analysis was carried out, it focused on the concern that small countries might lose out because of their scale disadvantages.

It is apparent that *Reasons for Reducing Protection*, however, anticipated some of the main elements of the new trade theory perspective. Liberalisation, by expanding the size of the market, would allow Irish firms to exploit economies of scale in particular industries, and even smaller Irish enterprises could prosper by specialising in distinctive varieties. This latter point was reinforced in a letter to Whitaker by M. D. McCarthy, Director of the Central Statistics Office, former Professor of Mathematical Physics at University College Cork, and later President of UCC. In a passage that Whitaker later includes verbatim in a letter to Industry and Commerce, the CSO Director noted that liberalisation will require abandoning certain *product lines* which have become unprofitable and moving into profitable lines, 'and the test of profitability in this connection is the ability to sell in export markets'.

The quality of the civil service correspondence is further demonstrated by a comment on the Finance memo offered by Con Cremin, Secretary of the Department of External Affairs. Cremin proposes *as a theoretical possibility* that 'as long as the existing freedom of outward movement (of labour) prevails, the possibility exists that a setback in industrial production for whatever cause (including the reduction and removal of protection) will result not in higher productivity and greater competitiveness but in an outflow of redundant manpower.' We know today – from Paul Krugman's pioneering work in the field of 'new economic geography' – that this is indeed a theoretical possibility.

Krugman (2002) explains the argument, in typical reader-friendly fashion, as follows:

> It is obvious – in retrospect – that something special happens when factor mobility interacts with increasing returns. Suppose that there are strong advantages to concentration of factors – where these advantages may take the form of true external economies, but may also be due to 'linkage' effects

arising from the effect of concentration on the size of markets and the availability of inputs. And suppose also that some factors are more mobile than others. Then factor mobility will tend to increase differences among regions rather than reducing them, and instead of substituting for regional specialization will promote it. Start with an exceptional concentration of nerds in the vicinity of Stanford University; the resulting industry specialization will attract more nerds, reinforcing the nerd-friendliness of the local environment, and you end up with Silicon Valley. Similar processes lead to concentrations of ambitious people in London, beautiful people in Hollywood, and so on; and more broadly, they lead most of the population of sparsely populated North America to live in a few densely populated metropolitan corridors.

This was the danger to which Cremin alludes, and which Nagle, Secretary of the Department of Agriculture, expresses as well.[18] Whitaker's response is that he sees no convincing argument, on practical or theoretical grounds, for the opposite thesis, namely that the maintenance of a policy of high protection will raise employment and living standards and reduce emigration.

What of the practical import of these arguments? The analysis in Barry (1996) suggests that Ireland may have lost some of its indigenous increasing-returns industries over the adjustment to free trade (what we might call the 'Krugman-Cremin' hypothesis). Ireland's protectionist economy would have been too small, however, to allow minimum efficient scale to be attained in these sectors, which would have been characterised as well by X-inefficiencies and rent-seeking, so that the benefit derived from their presence initially would never have been as strong as in the theoretical models. Furthermore, they were more than replaced by the arrival of foreign-owned firms in increasing-returns sectors.[19] And, of course, comparative advantage ensured strong productivity growth in indigenous non-increasing-returns industries (the 'comparative advantage' logic on which increasing-returns specialisation is overlaid, as in Krugman's 2002 explanation).

---

[18] Nagle refers to an interesting article by O'Mahony (1959), which criticises *Economic Development* for failing to address the difficulties of enhancing competitiveness when Irish wages are largely determined by UK levels. What are required, according to O'Mahony, are very high standards of education and training and large general tax reductions. Surprisingly he makes no mention of Export Profits Tax Relief, which Garret FitzGerald in an article in the same issue of *Studies* identifies as the main stimulus to the growth of exports over the previous few years.

[19] Gao (1999) shows that foreign direct investment will substantially reduce the possibility that trade liberalisation will accentuate income differences between core and periphery.

Concluding Comments

Political decisions are made by politicians, who are always mindful of the need to bring their own political constituencies and the general electorate along with them. Political considerations explain why some of the key recommendations of *Economic Development* were not implemented. Such considerations also came into play when the unilateral across-the-board tariff cuts that Whitaker had recommended in the civil service debates were finally implemented in 1963 and 1964. By that time, the overriding diplomatic goal had become the need to ensure that any subsequent application for EEC membership would be successful. Policy-makers realised that any repeat of the attempt to negotiate for under-developed status in the OEEC talks would generate opposition within the ECC. The tariff cuts, and the later signing of the comprehensive Anglo-Irish Free Trade Agreement of 1965, were designed to undercut such opposition and to expedite ultimate EEC entry.

References

Andresen-Leitão, N. (2001), 'Portugal's European Integration Policy, 1947–72', *Journal of European Integration History* (Special Issue on Peripheral Countries and the Integration of Europe), vol. 7, no. 1, pp. 25–35

Barry, F. (1996), 'Peripherality in Economic Geography and Modern Growth Theory: Evidence from Ireland's Adjustment to Free Trade', *World Economy*, vol. 19, no. 3, pp. 345–65

Barry, F., and Weir, S. (2007), 'The Politics and Process of Trade Liberalisation in Finland, Portugal and Ireland', presentation made to research workshop on Post-War Convergence in the European Periphery, Department of Social Science History, University of Helsinki, 27–28 September 2007

Bew, P. and Patterson, H. (1982), *Seán Lemass and the Making of Modern Ireland 1945–66*, Dublin: Gill and Macmillan

Daly, M. (1984), 'An Irish Ireland for Business?: The Control of Manufactures Acts, 1932 and 1934', *Irish Historical Studies*

Daly, M. (1992), *Industrial Development and Irish National Identity, 1922–39,* Syracuse, NY: Syracuse University Press

Fanning, R. (1978), *The Irish Department of Finance 1922–58*, Dublin: Institute of Public Administration

FitzGerald, G. (1959), 'Mr. Whitaker and Industry', *Studies*, no. XLVIII, pp. 138–50

FitzGerald, G. (1968), *Planning in Ireland*, Dublin: Institute of Public Administration

Fitzgerald, M. (2001), 'Ireland's Relations With the EEC: From the Treaties of Rome to Membership', *Journal of European Integration History*, vol. 7, no. 1, pp. 11–24

Gao, T. (1999), 'Economic Geography and Vertical Multinational Production', *Journal of International Economics*, vol. 48, no. 2, pp. 301–20

Grossman, G. and Helpman, E. (2001), *Special Interest Group Politics*, Cambridge, MA: MIT Press.

Helpman, E. and Krugman, P. (1985), *Market Structure and Foreign Trade*, Cambridge, MA: MIT Press

Honohan, P. and Ó Gráda, C. (1998), 'The Irish Macroeconomic Crisis of 1955–56: How Much Was Due to Monetary Policy?', *Irish Economic and Social History*

Hood, C. (1990), *Explaining Economic Policy Reversals*, Buckingham: Open University Press

IDA (1973), *Ireland: Industrial Handbook*, Dublin: Industrial Development Authority

Irwin, D. A. (1993), 'Multilateral and Bilateral Trade Policies in the World Trading System: An Historical Perspective', in de Melo, J. and Panagariya, A. (eds.), *New Dimensions in Regional Integration*, Cambridge: Cambridge University Press

Koromzay, V. (2004), 'Some Reflections on the Political Economy of Reform', unpublished, OECD

Krugman, P. (2002), 'Was it all in Ohlin?', in Findlay, R., Jonung, L. and Lundahl, M. (eds.), *Bertil Ohlin: A Centennial Celebration (1899–1999)*. Cambridge: MIT Press

Matthews, A. (2008), 'IFA's Scare Campaign Damages Ireland Inc.', *Irish Times*, Saturday 26 July

McAleese, D. (1975), 'Ireland in the Enlarged EEC: Economic Consequences and Prospects', in Vaizey, J. (ed.), *Economic Sovereignty and Regional Policy: A Symposium on Regional Problems in Britain and Ireland*, Dublin: Gill and Macmillan

Murphy, G. (2003), *Economic Realignment and the Politics of EEC Entry: Ireland 1948–72*, Bethesda, MD: Academica

OECD (2007), 'What Shapes the Implementation of Structural Reform?', Chapter 7 in *Going For Growth*

O'Hearn, D. (1987), 'Estimates of New Foreign Manufacturing Employment in Ireland, 1956–72', *Economic and Social Review*, vol. 18, no. 3, pp. 173–88

Olofsgård, A. (2003), 'The Political Economy of Reform: Institutional Change as a Tool for Political Credibility', background paper prepared for the 2005 World Bank *World Development Report*

O'Mahony, D. (1959), 'Economic Expansion in Ireland', *Studies*, no. XLVIII, pp. 129–37.

Paavonen, T. (2001), 'From Isolation to the Core: Finland's Position towards European Integration, 1960–95', *Journal of European Integration History*, (special issue on Peripheral Countries and the Integration of Europe), vol. 7, no. 1, pp. 53–75

Whitaker, T. K. (1974), 'From Protection to Free Trade: The Irish Experience', reprinted in Whitaker, T. K. (1983), *Interests*, Dublin: Institute of Public Administration

Whitaker, T. K. (1983), 'Ireland's Development Experience', in Whitaker, T. K. (1983), *Interests*, Dublin: Institute of Public Administration

Whitaker, T. K. (2006), *Protection or Free Trade: The Final Battle*, Dublin: Institute of Public Administration

10

Resonances from *Economic Development* for Current Economic Policy-making

Frances Ruane[1]

Introduction[2]

On 25 November 1958, an article in the *Irish Times* stated that the publication of *Economic Development* was 'a unique event, because for the first time, an Irish Government has revealed in full detail the view put to it on the whole range of economic policies by its principal adviser, the Secretary of the Department of Finance'. The (unnamed) journalist went on to note that in its *Programme for Economic Expansion*, published ahead of *Economic Development*, the Government had endorsed most of its content, and, in particular, the suggestion of allocating more state investment to support productive enterprise. He further noted that the new productive investment would be superimposed on top of the existing socially oriented programmes – in other words, there was no plan for a

[1] The views expressed in this paper are my own. All the data used in Section 2 come from the ESRI databank. I am grateful to Thomas Conefrey for assistance with compiling the data series in Section 2, and for comments on early drafts of the paper. I am very grateful to John FitzGerald and Ken Whitaker for invaluable discussions during the course of writing this paper. The usual disclaimer applies.
[2] This paper was written in early September 2008, when it was already recognised that the Irish economy was in recession. However, it was completed before Ireland entered a period of severe financial crisis (linked to the global crisis that began in the USA as the problems of the sub-prime mortgages developed) and an exceptionally rapid decline in tax revenues.

major reallocation of existing public resources. The article also recognised that the plan was not perfect, but it was optimistic that any criticisms it might attract would be aimed at making it a better plan. The journalist's tone is one that is empathetic to a country recognising its problems and planning to deal with them.

The publication of *Economic Development* came at a time when Ireland was suffering continuously high levels of emigration and unemployment – the twin signals of economic failure – while the rest of Europe was booming. Growth rates were very low or even negative. Balance of payments deficits were high and rising – reflecting in part the decline in Ireland's trade balance. Crucial messages running through the document were that policy needed to promote economic growth as the way to address unemployment and emigration, and that economic growth required structural change.

The process whereby economic policy changes direction is a complex one, and while there are moments, such as the publication of *Economic Development*, where this change is clearly recognised, the reality is that the seeds of change long predated that publication. Then, as now, policy change is about process rather than about the public document that discusses the need for change and what it will involve. What was exceptional in the mid-1950s was that a group of civil servants and carefully selected others put into the public domain their considered view of the real problems that faced the Irish economy and identified the changes they thought were required. Allowing the publication of a separate document reflected a new maturity on the part of the political system, indicating that politicians had confidence in the ability of the civil servants to produce an independent and competent analysis of the Irish economy. It also recognised that political decision-making could not ignore economic realities.

While the basic analysis in *Economic Development* was sound, it had an inherently static approach (reflecting economic theory of the time), and consequently their conclusion that agriculture and food-based industries would be the route to faster growth turned out to be wide of the mark.[3] It is also not clear whether the implications of Keynesian economics for Irish macro policy were fully understood.[4] Nonetheless, as we would all recognise today, there were three crucial elements in that analysis which were absolutely correct:

---

[3] The basic logic of the economic understanding was that improvements in technology in agriculture would increase its output and hence its purchasing power. This would stimulate further demand for goods and services, leading to additional employment in industry and services but no increase in agricultural employment. In effect, employment generation would be in manufacturing and tourism. This led to the conclusion that: 'In general, however, it would seem that attention should be concentrated primarily on raising the efficiency and volume of production in agriculture and in industries based on agriculture.' Chapter 2, Para 32.

[4] Several economists have visited this issue, including Patrick Honohan and Cormac Ó Gráda.

- An appreciation of the potential benefits of opening up the Irish economy to trade and foreign direct investment, and conversely the serious damage that would be done to the Irish economy by continuing the 25-year-old policy of combining high levels of protection with a prohibition on foreign direct investment;
- Tentative evidence of the usefulness of Keynesian economics to inform the role of the state in smoothing economic cycles; and
- A recognition of the significant challenge faced by the public service, with scarce resources, trying to plan and deliver policies that would support the restructuring necessary to generate higher levels of economic growth.

The French have a saying – *plus ça change, plus c'est la même chose* – an expression which quickly comes to mind in looking at Ireland in 2008, some fifty years later. Now, as then, we are still dealing with these same three elements.[5]

- Openness is an issue today in terms of the challenges and potential generated by globalisation (a word that did not even exist in 1958). This openness means a continual restructuring of our economy into higher value-added products and services and constant pressures for innovation. It also means increasing internationalisation of domestic production, if we are to remain globally competitive.
- We are now faced again with managing economic cycles with limited independent monetary policy instruments, with a growing budget deficit, with current fiscal policy constrained both by EU rules and by having adopted what has been described as an 'accounting' rather than 'economic' approach to handling large fiscal surpluses in recent years.[6]
- We are also faced with determining how best to allocate a tighter capital budget, under the National Development Programme, which is intended to enhance current and future growth rates. This requires now, as it did in the 1950s, a stronger culture of planning and evaluation than we have managed to achieve in many of the intervening fifty years.[7]

---

[5] *Economic Development* states that we are at '…a critical and decisive point in our economic affairs' – an expression that would not go amiss in 2008.

[6] In effect, the Keynesian counter-cyclical policy message has been forgotten over recent years, as policy has been pro-cyclical, driven by the idea that 'when you have it, spend it'.

[7] Whatever about the criticisms that can be made about Irish economic policy over the period, in terms of its general direction, it has been positive overall, though weaker on the Keynesian dimension. The benefits of this are very apparent when one comes to compare the successes of economic and social policies with the failures of spatial policy.

This paper explores some potential resonances for policy-making in Ireland in 2008 by examining the links between the approach to economic policy-making in *Economic Development* and those underpinning the *National Development Plan 2007–2013: Transforming Ireland* and NESC Paper No. 117: *The Irish Economy in the 21st Century.*

In the second section, we look at three sets of economic indicators that highlight how we have progressed since the 1950s. These indicators help to place the current challenges in perspective. In the third section we look briefly at how the policy process has changed over the five decades since 1958, while in the fourth section we look at some of the possible lessons from *Economic Development* for the short to medium term.

What has Changed in the Past Fifty Years?

In this section we look at three sets of economic variables and how they have changed over the half century since *Economic Development* was published:

1. The state of the economy (in terms of the labour market, economic structure, per-capita growth and foreign debt);
2. The state of the public finances (in terms of national debt and interest payments); and
3. The openness of the economy (in terms of what net trade contributes to growth).

Labour market – unemployment and emigration
The scale of unemployment and emigration were the two most tangible indicators of economic failure in the 1950s. High levels of unemployment meant that many young people emigrated and emigration itself set a cap on the size of the unemployment rate. The unemployment rate in 1958 was just under 6 per cent and in that year net emigration was almost 60,000.[8] Leaving emigration aside, the unemployment rate understates the extent of the unemployment problem, as there was massive underemployment at the time in agriculture.[9]

Two features are striking in Figure 1. Firstly, the cyclical pattern of unemployment over the fifty years (low (high) during periods of relatively high (low) growth) is evident, particularly in the earlier years of this decade. Secondly, the upward trend in unemployment from the late 1970s through the 1980s and

---

[8] Had those 60,000 not emigrated, the unemployment rate – making the conservative estimate that 50 per cent of them would have been in the labour force – would have been around 8 per cent.
[9] The underemployment was implicitly recognised in *Economic Development,* which saw output growth potential in agriculture if it modernised, but no employment growth potential.

into the 1990s is very clear. The early 1990s was described at the time as having 'jobless growth' as the reduction in unemployment trailed the growth in output.[10] However, as Ireland regained international competitiveness, the results predicted by the early ESRI *Medium-Term Reviews* were found to hold – unemployment rates fell rapidly and increasing numbers entered the labour force.[11]

Figure 1: *Unemployment Rates, 1951–2009*[12]

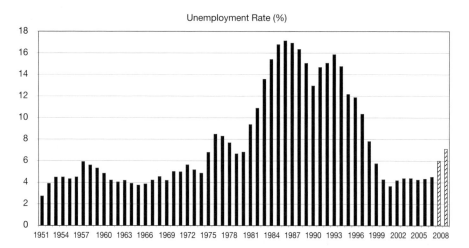

Given the openness of the Irish labour market, the unemployment figures have to be looked at in the context of net emigration, as shown in Figure 2. While unemployment fell in the years following the publication of *Economic Development*, net emigration remained relatively high, and it was 1972 before the switch occurred between net emigration and net immigration. Net immigration peaked at 20,000 in the mid-1970s, seeming to confirm Ireland's potential sustainability as an economic region in the face of increasingly open labour markets.[13] The sensitivity of migrant flows to conditions in the Irish and UK markets became apparent again in the mid-1980s as net emigration rose quickly, peaking at over 40,000 in 1989. Ireland experienced levels of net immigration in recent years that were not just unprecedented historically but, in

[10] See Guiomard (1994).

[11] The source of the addition to the labour force was increased female participation and returned migrants.

[12] The estimates for unemployment for 2008 and 2009 come from the ESRI *Quarterly Economic Commentary,* Summer 2008.

[13] Most of the immigrants were returning emigrants from the 1960s with their families.

Figure 2: *Net Migration 1955–2009*[14]

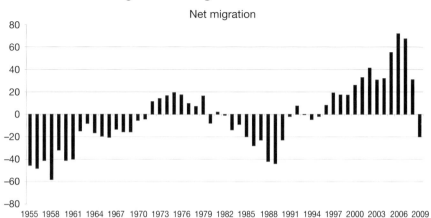

Net migration

terms of scale, were unprecedented internationally. The recent drop in immigration and the likely switch to net emigration in 2009 are clear evidence of both the mobility of labour in changing economic circumstances and the globalisation of labour.

High (low) rates of unemployment and out(in)-migration indicate an economy where the labour market is not generating jobs. We now turn to look at jobs and their sectoral allocation over the period since 1961.

Changing economic structure and growth

Figure 3 allows us to look at both employment change and the change in economic structure since 1961. We look at four broad sectors – agriculture, industry, market services and non-market services.[15] The hope expressed in *Economic Development* was that industrial employment would grow significantly, supported by the growth in agricultural output but not employment. Marketed services featured very modestly in *Economic Development*, with tourism being the only traded service meriting attention.

The most striking feature of Figure 3 is that employment has almost doubled since 1961, and that most of this change occurred since 1991.[16] Such an increase was unthinkable in 1991, let alone 1961, and suggests that inappropriate policies had stood in the way of economic and employment growth.[17]

---

[14] The estimates for migration in 2008 and 2009 come from the ESRI *Quarterly Economic Commentary*, Summer 2008.

[15] Non-market services are primarily government services that are provided outside the market system.

[16] The population grew by 25 per cent in 1961–91 and 20 per cent in 1991–2006.

[17] This issue has been a topic of much research in Ireland – see, for example, Barry (1999) and Honohan and Walsh (2002).

Figure 3: *Sectoral Growth and Composition of Employment, 1961–2007 (various years)*

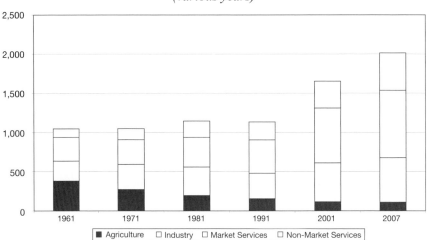

Linking back to the unemployment and migration data in Figures 1 and 2, we see that between 1961 and 1971 there was almost no change in employment numbers but considerable reallocation across sectors – in effect, the numbers released from agriculture were just about being absorbed in the other three sectors, with the largest share moving into industry. In the 1971–81 decade, during which Ireland entered the EU, total employment grew by 9 per cent. Despite the huge boost to Irish agriculture under the Common Agricultural Policy, the share of agriculture in employment continued to decline, while the share of non-market services rose very considerably. In the decade 1981–91, aggregate employment fell slightly, with non-market services holding their share while employment transferred out of both agriculture and industry into marketed services. The decade 1991–2001 saw total employment grow at a remarkable rate of just under 50 per cent – from 1.1 million to 1.6 million. Industrial employment grew in numbers but not in share while there was substantial growth in both types of services. In the period since 2001, the most striking change has been the increase in non-market services employment by almost 40 per cent (to 476,000). Employment in market services increased by 23 per cent to almost 860,000 as the combination of domestic growth for services and the international tradability of services led to a significant expansion in this sector.

Figure 4 shows the growth in GNP and in per-capita GNP since 1958. Three features of this figure merit comment. First, it is clear that we have had cyclical growth patterns over the past fifty years – if we learn anything from the past, we must surely learn that growth rates are not constant and we should expect variation across years.

Second, we see that on either side of the disastrous 1980s, we had relatively high growth. The growth in the latter half of the 1990s was clearly 'off-scale', and in part reflected the growth that should have come earlier had we not incurred the economic mistakes of the late 1970s and early 1980s.

Figure 4: *Growth in GNP and GNP Per Capita*

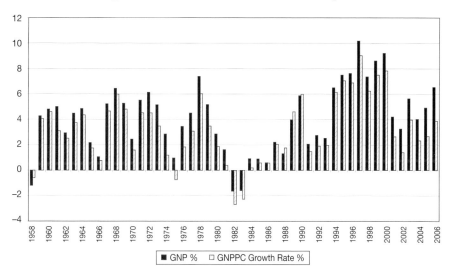

Third, the differences in the GNP growth rate and the GNP growth rate per capita are quite striking – the latter is what really matters from a welfare/quality of life point of view. Except for the period known for 'jobless growth', GNP rose faster than GNP per capita.[18] The growing gap between the two reflects the growth in population over the recent period and is also consistent with more slowly rising productivity. Clearly the growth rates for 2008 and 2009 will represent a significant change on what we have experienced in the period up to 2008.

Foreign debt

A recurrent theme throughout *Economic Development* was the level of foreign government debt and the extent to which it was a drain on domestic resources. Figure 5 shows government foreign debt interest payments as a percentage of tax revenue and of GDP. While debt service was an expressed concern in *Economic Development*, looking at the period since 1960, we see that debt service costs relative to GDP were quite low at that time and remained so until the mid-1970s. The ratio rose rapidly after that period, reflecting the scale of

---

[18] See Guiomard (1995).

borrowing, the high rates of interest and low rates of GDP growth. The effect of rising GDP and access to low interest rates in relation to monetary union saw the ratio fall dramatically from 1995, so that it now accounts for little more than half of 1 per cent of GDP.[19] However, this indicator is no longer important since we entered the Euro Area.

Figure 5: *Government Foreign Debt Interest Payment to Tax Revenue and GDP, 1960–2005*

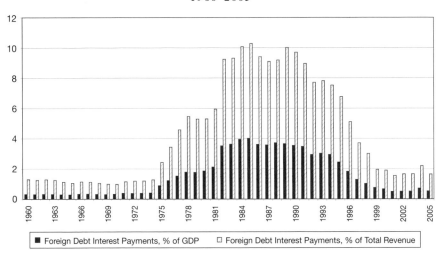

From a government perspective, what matters is its capacity to pay the interest and so we look at the foreign interest payments relative to tax revenue. We can see that in the period from 1982 to 1995, foreign interest payments were over 6 per cent of tax revenue and as high at 10 per cent in three of those years. Today's ratio is rising very rapidly but is still far less than those high rates. What is worth noting, however, is how quickly the ratio rose in the 1970s and fell in the 1990s. The latter fall was driven strongly by the strength of exchequer associated with rapid economic growth. This change is reflected in Figure 6, which covers the period since 1975 only.

While interest payments continued to increase right throughout the 1980s, the Exchequer Borrowing Requirement was in fact falling, and it, together with the General Government Deficit, was actually negative for many years in the past decade. This pattern set its own challenges for government in that, with large-scale infrastructural and other deficits, it was under severe pressure to relax the budgetary and efficiency constraints that a tighter fiscal environment would have created.

---

[19] It should be noted, however, that private debt has risen dramatically in the past decade.

Figure 6: *Exchequer Borrowing Requirement and General Government Deficit*

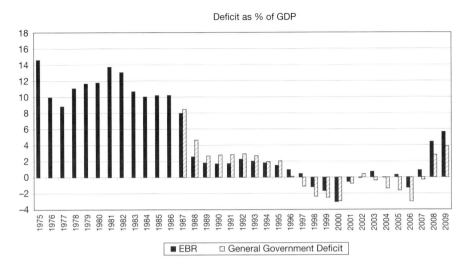

Deficit as % of GDP

Trade and growth

It is well known that Ireland now has one of the most open economies in the world, as measured in terms of its ratio of traded goods/services to GDP/GNP.[20] The openness is a product of our pro-trade policy (going back to the 1960s and advocated strongly in *Economic Development*), the scale of our domestic market (whose relatively small size does not allow economies of scale in production without sales into international markets), and the large share of Irish business that is foreign-owned. In effect, our engagement with international markets has contributed very positively to recent economic growth, and as a country, Ireland benefits very significantly from the further integration of Europe brought about by the addition of new members states and the reduction in cross-border barriers to economic activity under the Single Market Programme.

Figure 7 decomposes growth into domestic and external sources. The pattern shows that if we ignore foreign markets and the need to be competitive, we do so at our peril. We now see that the growth driven by internal factors only cannot be sustained, and for us to grow at our (supply-driven) potential over the coming decade, we need to ensure that the contribution to growth from external factors remains positive.[21] A further message from this figure is that external trade

---

[20] Ireland ranked first place in terms of the AT Kearney Globalisation Index for several years since 2000.

[21] This is a recurrent message in the ESRI's *Medium-Term Reviews*.

growth is highly volatile – an unavoidable consequence of being engaged in the global economy. This consequence was recognised with stunning bluntness in *Economic Development.*[22]

Figure 7: *Internal/External Sources Contributing to Growth, 1962–2006*

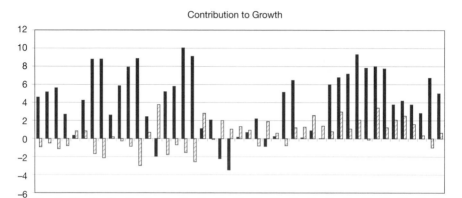

These seven charts show that while we have made extraordinary progress since 1958, the path of development has been very uneven. While external factors contributed strongly to the unevenness, the way in which we have exercised policy has also contributed to the uneven growth pattern. To illustrate the cost of adopting pro- rather than counter-cyclical policies, just think how different Ireland would look if it had grown at the average rate of the whole period.[23] Might it have been possible with a better policy process to have avoided the infrastructure and fiscal crises, the mismanagement of the health system, the unstructured growth of higher education and the very costly labour market disruptions?

Policy Process

In this section, we explore some elements of the policy process from *Economic Development* and relate them to the current process of economic policy-making in Ireland.

---

[22] *Economic Development* states this very succinctly: 'Our imports and exports can fluctuate in an embarrassing way.' Chapter 4, Para 19.

[23] This is a very useful thought experiment for any economy, and particularly Ireland, given the striking contrasts between the 1980s and 1990s.

As noted above, the separation of the government's programme from the analysis of the economy by civil servants and other specialists was a major event for Ireland. In a sense, the publication of *Economic Development* recognised, perhaps for the first time in Ireland, the technical requirements for sound economic management. It would appear that prior to 1958 economic policy had been driven strongly by political ideology, involving little input from economics expertise per se, and the civil service role was simply to administer the policies associated with that ideology.[24] Discussion of the reason for the change at that time is beyond the scope of this paper. However, it is important to recognise that the publication of civil service documents of this type and scale was not the norm in Ireland or elsewhere at the time.[25] In effect, while the government's perspective and policies were reflected in its *Programme for Economic Expansion*, it was prepared to put into the public domain the independent analysis of Ireland's problems and opportunities by a group of what some might call 'technocrats'. This might be seen as an early example of transparency in national policy-making anywhere.

As a document, *Economic Development* subscribed to the principle of being as evidence-based[26] as possible and acknowledged some outside influences.[27] Subsequent history would suggest that the strong support by T. K. Whitaker and his department for the establishment of the Economic and Social Research Institute (ESRI) reflected an acknowledgement that the amount of evidence available to inform policy-making was limited.[28] In essence, there were three elements to *Economic Development*:

1. The first element was a thorough analysis of the Irish economy, at an aggregate and a sectoral level, in terms of deficiencies and the principles that needed to be invoked to correct them.

---

[24] The ideology was characterised by a protectionist trade policy and policies to conserve the positions of key vested-interest groups, with no real appreciation of the damage these policies were doing to the country's economy.

[25] While there were expert documents produced on specific issues – such as emigration and banking – there were no expert documents produced on the system as a whole. The importance of the systemic approach to policy is that is demonstrates publicly the need for trade-offs in policy choices.

[26] Chapter 1 states that: 'The mind needs the support of facts and figures', an approach supported by the Chair of the Group and by the inclusion of the Head of the Central Statistics Office as a member.

[27] Frank Barry discusses this issue in his paper above. The full influences are not acknowledged in the document – the Introduction mentioned just two individuals: Sir Alec Cairncross and Bishop Philbin of Raphoe. This is in stark contrast with NESC Paper 117, which includes several pages of academic references and agency reports.

[28] T. K. Whitaker played an exceptionally active role in persuading the Ford Foundation to provide the initial funding for the ESRI, while R. C. Geary played a pivotal role in attracting leading international researchers to come to the Institute since there was a dearth of empirical economists in Ireland at the time.

2. The second element was the focus on Ireland's potential: What exactly could be achieved if the right policies were in place? By how much could growth increase so that we would catch up with our European neighbours? What is perhaps not fully appreciated is that the importance of competitiveness as an essential prerequisite for realising this potential was recognised in 1958.[29]

3. The third element was the use of a ten-year perspective in framing policy, combined with the identification of the national capital programme as the key policy instrument. In context we must recognise that this was a long timeframe for a country that was then less than forty years old. We should note that it was closer to a perspective rather than a rigid plan, reflecting an awareness of the large external influences over which Ireland would have no control.[30] Again, this provided evidence of Ireland's growing maturity and the imminent shedding of protectionist policies.

If we were to look today at a parallel for the policy process implicit in the preparation of *Economic Development*, we would find the three elements in different places:

1. Increasingly the current view of the economy, how it works and, in particular, the link between the economy and society, is now encapsulated in documents produced by the National Economic and Social Council (NESC). Its most recent document, NESC Paper No. 117: *The Irish Economy in the 21st Century*, is informed by a range of influences, and some or all of these are duly acknowledged in the bibliography. This represents a big change compared with 1958. The 'technocratic view' in *Economic Development* has been replaced by a 'consensual view' agreed by the social partners, informed by the NESC Secretariat drawing on a range of policy documents produced by and for government departments and agencies. The link between NESC, Social Partnership and the Department of An Taoiseach also means that the role of the Department of Finance in this context seems to be quite different from what it was in 1958. It is not evident how significant a role the Department of An Taoiseach, *qua* department, played in the production of *Economic Development*.

2. In terms of looking at Ireland's potential, the ESRI's *Medium-Term Review (MTR),* based on a two/three year cycle, is the main instrument for exploring, within a global context, what is possible if we manage the economy well and

---

[29] For example, *Economic Development* states: 'If we do not expand production on a competitive basis, we shall fail to provide the basis necessary for the economic independence and material progress of the community.'

[30] It also recognised an ambiguity towards economic planning at the time, as Eastern European communism was seen as being 'plan-centric' in its approach.

continue to be competitive. The global context is now more complex and the modelling is much more complex, but the overlap between the issues explored in key chapters of *Economic Development* and in a typical *MTR* is very striking, e.g., competitiveness, growing productivity, public-sector efficiency, control of public-sector pay.

3. In terms of the ten-year perspective, this is now much more developed than it was and has been implemented through our sequence of *National Development Plans* since 1989. These plans are produced in a more 'bottom-up' way than the Whitaker plan in 1958, with departments providing inputs, and other institutions and agencies, including the ESRI, assisting the Department of Finance in drawing together a coherent plan.[31] Furthermore, today's plans have substantial resources attached to them, in contrast with the 1958 plan, which relied totally on the funds available in annual budgets for implementation. They also incorporate a more structured multi-annual approach.

By international standards, it could be said that Irish economic policy-making is exceptionally mature in the extent to which it takes a long-term view – something that can be linked back to *Economic Development.* In effect, long-term economic development issues, and even the policies put in place, tend to run above politics in Ireland. Indeed, taking politics out of serious economic crises was central to the 'Irish Inc' approach adopted in solving the disastrous problems of the mid–late 1980s.[32] Arguably we are currently back in such a position today.

The preparation of large-scale planning documents means that the annual budget is less important to the direction of policy now than it was in the 1980s. Indeed, arguably its main role is to manage economic cycles, which (from a Keynesian perspective) means reducing public expenditure during a boom period, and vice versa during a recession. The importance of planning in the Irish policy process means that we take it for granted that the current NDP should be rationally based and should run beyond the life of the present government, lest these longer-term policy perspectives be eroded by the 'political business cycle'.[33] That said, there would be widespread agreement that the scale though not the general direction of the current plan was not independent of the political

---

[31] An interesting issue for economic historians is how we came to abandon the approach adopted in the *First, Second* and *Third Programmes for Economic Expansion* in the early 1970s, only returning to such planning-type documents under the requirements of the EU structural funds in the late 1980s.

[32] In effect, the Tallaght Strategy allowed Ireland to re-engage in rational policy-making, without which the prosperity of the 1990s would not have occurred.

[33] This is required to avoid the 'damaging inconsistencies and conflicts' noted in *Economic Development.*

cycle. In a rational economic framework, the scale of the plan should match both the absorption capacity of the economy itself[34] and its ability to deliver that without undermining the structure of the economy. It should also take account of the capacity of the public-sector system to deliver the projects and programmes at the standards of evaluation and monitoring to which it has committed, while the precise roll-out of the plan would reflect the demand management context.[35]

A distinct difference between *Economic Development* and the current NESC and NDP documents is the dominant focus on sectors in *Economic Development* compared with a more 'market-focused' approach, in terms of both products and factor markets, in the NESC and NDP documents. In fact, the focus on joined-up thinking at this level has moved well beyond where it started in 1958, and there is now a greater appreciation that sectors contain heterogeneous enterprises that interact differently with the market, and that markets respond to relative price changes. Furthermore, while it may well not have been the case, reading *Economic Development* one has a sense of its authors not quite believing in markets, in terms of their resource allocation potential. Implicitly direct government intervention was seen as the driver of change. Indeed, one of the great changes in Ireland in the past couple of decades is a slowly growing awareness of the way markets operate – whether it is the market for university places (through the points system), for air travel or for housing. The sectoral focus in the current documents is on internationally traded services and on high-tech manufacturing, and the ways in which these connect with the markets for skilled labour and technology. By contrast, the sectoral discussion in *Economic Development* was dominated by agriculture,[36] where policy interventions were described at an extraordinary level of detail, while there was virtually no detail available on the manufacturing or service sectors.[37] There are lengthy discussions

---

[34] For example, the ability of the higher education system to expand its research output without reducing the quality of the undergraduate education system it offers, or the construction industry to provide infrastructure at cost levels that allow a real return on capital for the state.

[35] The commitment of the Department of Finance to high-quality evaluation and monitoring is set out in presentations by David Doyle (2004) and Jim O'Brien (2007) to annual conferences of the Irish Evaluation Network.

[36] The dominance of agriculture derives from the conclusion that: 'In general, however, it would seem that attention should be concentrated primarily on raising the efficiency and volume of production in agriculture and in industries based on agriculture.' The only real mention of services is in relation to tourism about which there is quite some discussion because of its perceived importance as a foreign exchange earner.

[37] The absence of discussion on manufacturing, which in the subsequent three decades was to become the major engine of economic growth, was in part caused by the absence of hard or soft data on the sector. The latter was to be rectified to some degree by the development of CSO data and the reports produced by the Committees for Industrial Organisation (CIOs) that were set up in the 1960s to explore how the industrial sector needed to prepare for free trade.

on capital availability in *Economic Development*, a focus that is almost entirely absent from recent documents, reflecting no doubt the integration of Ireland into global capital markets.

A striking similarity between *Economic Development* and the NESC/NDP documents is the importance all attach to competitiveness and the dangers of ignoring it. This is ultimately about recognising long-term economy-wide interests and setting these above short-term vested interests. To some, it might appear that Ireland discovered competitiveness as an issue only in the 1990s – as symbolised in the establishment of the National Competitiveness Council. However, this is not true, as *Economic Development* is full of statements pointing to its importance in 1958, starting with the statement: 'Our level of real incomes depends on our competitive efficiency'[38] in Chapter 1, and later stating: 'If we do not expand production on a competitive basis, we shall fail to provide the basis necessary for the economic independence and material progress of the community.' And, in a statement that is as relevant today as it was in 1958, we find in *Economic Development*:

Economic Expansion could be seriously hindered both by restrictive practices on the part of trade unions and by insistence on frequent and indiscriminate increases in wages and salaries exceeding any benefit from increases in productivity and causing a general rise in production costs.[39]

Lessons for the Short to Medium Term

Before looking at potential lessons from 1958 for today, let us focus briefly on the ways in which the economy is different from how it was in 1958.

Openness: While *Economic Development* stressed the importance of greater openness, the extent of openness today is much greater. This means that we get greater upswings from international growth but we also get correspondingly greater downswings.[40] Furthermore, the economy today is much more globally diversified – where in 1958 most trade and factor mobility was between Ireland and the UK, today our international relationships are much stronger with mainland Europe and with the USA. Clearly the extent of integration between Ireland and other EU countries is completely different now from what it was in 1958. Furthermore, the extent of integration of the two countries on the island of Ireland is obviously much greater now.

---

[38] See Chapter 1, Page 2.
[39] See Chapter 3, Para 14.
[40] We are extremely conscious of the latter today, having enjoyed the benefits of many years of upswing in the past two decades.

Growth engine: Whereas in 1958 the economy did not have a growth engine, we potentially have one today, centred on high-tech internationally traded manufacturing and services.[41] However, the growth engine is found mainly in foreign-owned enterprises, and, despite recent reports, we are still a considerable distance away from having large numbers of strong internationally trading indigenous businesses. We ignore at our peril our dependence on these foreign-owned enterprises, and the need to provide a competitive environment in which they can prosper. Of particular concern here, and similar to 1958, is the poor productivity performance in many parts of indigenous manufacturing, even in those enterprises that are exporting.[42]

Human capital: Ireland's level of human capital in the 1950s was very low and increasing slowly. This contrasted with the rest of Europe, where secondary education was the norm, and where larger proportions of the population were continuing on to post-secondary education. Today our participation levels are much higher at senior secondary and at tertiary levels but lag way behind our OECD comparator countries at the fourth (PhD/research) level – a level not even envisaged in *Economic Development*.

Role of the market: Whereas in 1958 there was no confidence in the role of markets to reorient development, there is, as noted above, much more recognition today that markets do work. Consumer and business people now see that: if airlines[43] and inter-city buses are deregulated, better service and lower prices result; if prices are uncompetitive, producers lose market share; if wage costs are too high, employment falls; if charges are levied on plastic bags, shoppers move to alternatives. That having been said, the lack of confidence in markets remains a weakness in Ireland, with a tendency to presume that government must intervene in some areas where the market can do the job much better. Furthermore, we need to address the failure of certain publicly provided services, such as urban buses, to provide a good service to Irish consumers.[44]

Public-sector efficiency: While there is some recognition in *Economic Development* of the need for increasing public-sector efficiency, there is greater

---

[41] To the extent that there was a growth engine in the 1950s, it was in the agricultural sector.

[42] Recent research on indigenous manufacturing shows a productivity performance that does not indicate potential for rapid output growth or for large increases in pay. See Gleeson and Ruane (2008).

[43] For example, while tourism was the only service sector that received attention in *Economic Development,* there was no mention of the cost of getting onto the island, which remained high until Ryanair entered the market in the late 1980s.

[44] This continues despite publications like *Better Regulation* and the advice of the OECD to the Irish government.

recognition of that need today, and very slowly growing recognition that, in a knowledge society, more specialised skills are needed within the civil and public service. While there is the commitment to increased efficiency in the public service, evidence of real reform remains to be seen.[45] There is considerable cost, in terms of economic growth, in having a public sector that is relatively costly and not properly resourced to deliver services efficiently. A further source of risk is the dependence on consultants for technical and specialist knowledge.

Growth potential: Whereas in 1958, there was little confidence that we could achieve a better equilibrium, with lower unemployment and no involuntary emigration, today we know that it is possible – and this should provide the confidence needed for taking the tough decisions necessary to deal with our current difficulties.

*

Reflecting on *Economic Development*, reviewing recent government publications on the economy, and bearing in mind the challenges faced by policy-makers in the present fiscal climate, several observations come to mind.

Competitiveness matters: Ireland's success in turning the economy around in the past came from growth through international trade and internationally mobile investment. The lesson, which *Economic Development* recognised in 1958 but which is periodically forgotten, is clear – Ireland cannot succeed if it is not globally competitive. No one, neither government, nor employers, nor trade unions, nor consumers can simply 'wish away' that economic reality – if they try to do this, history shows that the country loses. For example, *Economic Development* suggests that if the competitiveness level is lower than Europe, living standards must be lower. It goes on to recognise that lower living standards are acceptable only as part of a programme of national regeneration. This conclusion is as relevant in 2008 as it was in 1958 and in 1987. Anticipating the type of situation we currently face, Chapter 3, Paragraph 14 notes that:

> The success of any policy of economic development will depend on the effective and continuous cooperation of the trade unions in promoting increased productivity and in avoiding increases in wages and salaries which would injure export prospects.

So the message for today is clear – Ireland must win back its competitiveness, and that means starting with a pay policy that does not raise public-sector costs

---

[45] See OECD (2008).

and does not reduce private-sector employment. In today's climate, this may mean a review of the current levels of public-sector pay and whether they impede economic recovery and longer-term prosperity.

Economic cycles happen: Economic cycles are a fact of life – they happen again and again and we must continuously plan with this in mind. Our experience, from time to time, of long periods of sustained growth in our major markets, such as in the 1990s, should not cause us to forget this. Government needs to operate counter-cyclical policies and thus be ready for a downturn – it should not be taken by surprise when the inevitable happens. Strong global competitiveness means that the impact of a downturn can be moderated, but this is not the situation Irish business faces in 2008, where the economy has lost international competitiveness in recent years, and recent policies have been pro-cyclical.

Thus, in today's difficult climate, flexibility is needed on both sides of the table in the business sector – employers and senior managers must recognise that ability-to-pay constraints apply just as much – and arguably much more – to their salaries and bonuses as they do to those of their lower-paid employees. If financial viability is to be assured, flexibility in the face of a recession should cover all dimensions of a company's operations: numbers of employees at all levels up to the highest management levels, remuneration rates for employers/employees, work practices at all levels, returns to the owners of the companies, and so on. Inevitably this means greater efforts in monitoring resources and managing staff than in a boom period. The greater the flexibility, the more likely a private-sector company and its employees are to weather the recession and recover when it is over.

The situation in the public sector is somewhat similar to that section of the private sector that is protected from market competition.[46] There is no market threat to generate pressure for flexibility. So if revenues are down in the public sector, what happens? Historically, if wages continue to increase rather than stay constant or fall, and if work practices are slow to change, the only flexibility that government has as an employer is to reduce output, that is, reduce the scale of programmes it supports or reduce the quality of services it provides directly to the public, with the latter linked to not replacing those who leave (retire from) the sector. This is clearly a much lower degree of flexibility than that found in the globally trading private sector, and it calls us to question the ability of the public sector to manage a strong economic downturn such as we have in 2008/9. It raises the question of whether it is possible to continue with a situation where

---

[46] The protection may be through past or current regulation or through the absence of an active competition policy in the past.

some individuals (i.e., those in the public sector and the private sector who face no global competition) suffer much less than those in sectors facing global competition when the international economy is in recession. In the absence of downward pay adjustments in the public sector and the protected private sector, the potential recipients/consumers of the services of these sectors will suffer.

Finally, it is worth noting that while we have benefited very considerably from being part of the Euro Area, one consequence of this is that it restricts our use of monetary instruments.[47] It points to the importance of getting fiscal and incomes policies right, and of using such monetary controls as we have effectively. Indeed, *Economic Development* provides some very pertinent advice in this regard – concluding a discussion on banking, it notes:

> … the exercise of financial responsibility may require unpopular measures of restriction as often as it admits of liberality and expansion.[48]

So the message for today is that we would do well to recognise the power of economic cycles, and act accordingly. This means recognising the cost of operating pro-cyclical policies in recent years and planning our way out of this present situation in a long-term systematic way – revising decisions and re-prioritising as needed. In essence, the development plans we have in place set out a general direction and if this direction is correct, the cycle does not change the direction but merely the pace of development. However, if the plans contain elements that do not stand up to scrutiny on closer inspection, then the present downturn provides an opportunity to revisit these elements with a more critical mindset.

Adaptability is essential. The ability of people to adapt quickly to changing situations is vital to competitiveness and ultimately to economic prosperity. Indeed, the first paragraph of *Economic Development* says all that is needed: 'Readiness to adapt to changing conditions is a sine qua non' for economic success. The extent of the change envisaged in *Economic Development* was great – but it was not expected to be as unrelenting as the changes we experience today.

While talk of change is easy, the reality is much more difficult, especially in large complex organisations, whether in the public or the private sector. Today, we have to accept that we are in a world that is ever-changing from an economic perspective, fuelled by the globalisation process, by technology change, by

---

[47] This is nothing new historically and rather similar to the situation in 1958 when we were parity-linked to £sterling.
[48] See Chapter 3, Para 18.

environmental concerns, and so on. Organisations that have no market driver for adaptability face particular challenges in handling change. For example, what does it mean to 'be ready to adapt' in the public sector, and how is the commitment to adaptability achieved?

In the private sector, if the market generates large profits in a boom and losses in a recession, the government needs to recognise that it should not try to protect enterprises in difficulty unless there are specific reasons to do this that go beyond the enterprise itself.[49] In the Irish context, this means that, very regrettably for some employees, it is unwise for the government to intervene if some construction and property development companies are forced to close. If small companies in the private sector do not adapt to change in a recession, they simply fail and they fail quickly. If large companies do not adapt, they lose market share and profitability, and may ultimately fail. This has implications for employers and employees in any company – in a dynamic world they have a shared interest in that nothing is certain except that to survive they must be competitive and innovative.[50] Putting it bluntly, the restrictive practices of employers and employees are rapidly self-defeating in a dynamic open economy environment – whereas in a closed market, the speed of decline is much slower and those practices are less immediately costly.

So the message for today in those parts of the economy where there are no market pressures on individuals for change is that there are huge pressures on managers to deliver on that change. In the public sector, the modest proposals in the recent OECD (2008) report should be seen as a starting point and nothing more. This discussion links to the final issue to be addressed.

Leadership: There is much talk today of the need for leadership in Ireland to deal with the present challenges. Following years of Celtic-Tiger hype, there is a need now to counteract the rapid shift to despondency. Such despondency was rampant in the 1950s, though at that time the situation was much worse, with many families living at bare subsistence levels. This contrasts with the situation today where we have just come through almost two decades where we enjoyed a virtuous circle of growth, reinforced by increased labour supply (through increased numbers of school-leavers, women re-entering the workforce and immigrants). This has generated a larger domestic market, creating incentives

---

[49] The interventions of many governments across the world in the current banking crisis come to mind.

[50] The paper by Sir Alex Cairncross quoted in Chapter 1 of *Economic Development*, states that 'the nerve centre of the whole forward movement may lie, not in finance, but in entrepreneurial capacity'. This was really quite different from the thinking of the time in Ireland, namely, that capital constraints were the greatest problem, but more akin to what we recognise today in terms of the need for entrepreneurship and innovation.

for entrepreneurs to invest and, in consequence, generate increased employment and living standards. While there are still issues related to equality, we have clear evidence to show that deprivation and absolute poverty have declined very substantially since the mid-1990s.[51]

Central to good and sustained leadership is realism – a time to face up to issues squarely, in contrast to recent years when the benefits of exceptionally high growth rates allowed us to take easier routes.[52] The following are some possible actions where benefits could be realised, with any significant increase in public spending:

- Facing down the inefficiencies in public-sector monopolies and the powers of vested interests (including the professional groups);
- Narrowing the gap between the rhetoric about the quality of our education system at every level and its reality;
- Putting into operation the commitment to efficiency in the delivery of public-sector programmes and projects;
- Facing up to the challenges of implementing regulatory regimes that will better serve national interests;
- Dealing with the implications of potentially large increases in population and the cultural diversity that will accompany them.

Leadership in the present situation is about ultimately dealing with some major challenges that have lain in the shadows for too long. The loss in competitiveness is to the fore, as is public-sector reform. Reform is a slow process and, to keep the public finances on target, it may be time to question what has previously been seen as unquestionable, namely that public-sector salaries should be adjusted to take account of the government's 'inability to pay', so that the pain of adjustment to the present global and national problems should be shared across the economy. This would foster social partnership and contribute to Ireland's regaining economic competitiveness.[53]

We are, in the words of *Economic Development* at '…a critical and decisive point in our economic affairs', and then, as now, as in 1987, both the private and public sectors need to take the longer view and make those decisions that will leave us in good stead as international markets pick up. The advantage of taking

---

[51] This is set out in some detail in *The Best of Times? The Social Impact of the Celtic Tiger*, edited by ESRI researchers and published by the IPA in 2007.

[52] The availability of extraordinary levels of growth in tax revenues was a real problem when the country at large seemed to have adopted an operational philosophy of 'buying its way' out of every tough problem.

[53] Concerns that such wage adjustments would be to the benefit of profits does not arise in the case of the public sector.

the large overview is that inconsistencies are avoided – but to do this trade-offs need to be recognised, something that is not ever easy in a political context.

References

Barry, F. (ed.) (1999), *Understanding Ireland's Economic Growth*, London: Macmillan Press

Department of Finance (2007), *National Development Plan, 2007–2013*, Dublin: Stationery Office

Department of Finance (1958), *Economic Development,* Dublin: Stationery Office

Department of Finance (1958), *Programme for Economic Expansion*, Dublin: Stationery Office

Department of the Taoiseach (2004), *White Paper on Regulating Better*, Dublin: Stationery Office

Doyle, D. (2004), 'Keynote Address', Presentation to Conference on Culture of Evaluation – Exploring the Irish Experience of Evaluation, Irish Evaluation Network, Dublin City University, 24 September 2004, accessed at http://www.dcu.ie/education_studies/ien/iendata/David%20Doyle%20 Keynote%20Speaker.ppt

Economic and Social Research Institute, *Medium-Term Review*, Dublin: Economic and Social Research Institute, spring 2008 and various years

Economic and Social Research Institute (2008), *Quarterly Economic Commentary,* summer, Dublin: Economic and Social Research Institute

Fahey, T., Russell, H. and Whelan, C. (eds), *Best of Times? The Social Impact of the Celtic Tiger*, Dublin: Institute of Public Administration

Foreign Policy, various years. *AT Kearney/Foreign Policy Globalisation Index*, accessed at http://www.atkearney.com

Gleeson, A. M. and Ruane, F. P. (2008), 'Exporting and Productivity Growth: Micro Evidence from a Small Open Economy', Paper delivered to the European Trade Study Group Conference, Warsaw, September 2008, accessed at http://www.etsg.org/ETSG2008/Papers/Gleeson.pdf

Guiomard, C. (1995), *The Irish Disease and How to Cure it: Common Sense Economics for a Competitive World*, Dublin: Oak Tree Press

Honohan, P. and Ó Gráda, C. (1998), 'The Irish Macroeconomic Crisis of 1955–56: How Much Was Due to Monetary Policy?', *Irish Economic and Social History*, vol. 24, pp. 52–80

Honohan, P. and Walsh, B. M. (2002), 'Catching up with the Hare', *Brookings Papers on Economic Activity*, no. 1

Irish Times, The (1958), 'Economic Expansion – The White Paper and the Economic Study', 25 November

National Economic and Social Council (2008), *The Irish Economy in the Early 21st Century*, Dublin: National Economic and Social Council

O'Brien, J. (2007), 'Value for Money and Evaluation in the Public Sector', Presentation to the Relationship of Evaluation to Emerging Approaches to Quality Assurance in Organisations, Irish Evaluation Network, Ballsbridge, Dublin, 19 January 2007, accessed at http://www.dcu.ie/ education_studies/ ien/ien_presentations/Jim%20O'Brien.pdf

OECD (2008), 'Ireland: Towards an Integrated Public Service', OECD: *Public Management Reviews*

Questions and Answers:
First Session

Panel: T. K. Whitaker, Garret FitzGerald, Tom Garvin, Ronan Fanning

Chair: John Bowman

Chair: Who was responsible for writing the *First Programme for Economic Expansion*?

T. K. Whitaker: Charlie Murray was mainly responsible.

Chair: In general, who opposed the publication of *Economic Development*? Or was anyone against it being published under your name?

T. K. Whitaker: The traditionalist ministers like Sean McEntee. But also, as I mentioned, the three supreme politicians – De Valera, Lemass and Jim Ryan – were in favour of it for the very good reason that it enabled them to reverse totally the policy that they had and attribute it to civil service advice. The amazing thing is, as far as I can recall, no debate in the Dáil, no opposition motion about the application or the effects of the document.

Chair: That was also, of course, a product of the fact that Gerard Sweetman had been Finance Minister in the 1954–57 coalition government.

T. K. Whitaker: Oh yes, yes.

Chair: The pessimism – as Tom Garvin is bringing out – of the 1950s
                is manifest. *Is Ireland dying?* was the title of one book; and
                there was an editorial in *The Irish Times* as to whether,
                demographically, we weren't going to vanish.

T. K. Whitaker: It was a period of the deepest gloom. I remember it so well, and
                any light that was shone in that dark time was very welcome.

G. FitzGerald: Emigration was such that – I was at Aer Lingus at the time –
                and both the British and Irish economies were in trouble and I
                had to lay on extra flights every single day in March 1957 for
                the Irish in Britain who lost their jobs to get to Shannon to go
                to America on flights especially put on by the Belgian and
                French airlines who normally didn't route their North American
                flights through Shannon. It was the first really large-scale
                emigration to the US since 1929.

Finola Kennedy: When you look back to the foundation of the state and you look,
                for instance, at Tom Garvin's book, there is a very, very
                interesting point – actually it was Dermot Keogh in a review of
                Tom's book – raised in regard to the lack of study of the
                conservatism of the banking system and the extraordinary
                degree to which, then, we were a creditor country and yet we
                had very substantial assets. The debates were beginning in the
                Dáil about what was to be done with these, and we had a
                banking commission. And when Dev was in opposition in the
                late 1920s, he was always making charges about these financial
                conservatives, but when he got into power and set up a banking
                commission, he put many very conservative people on it. So
                that when it reported – apart from some of the minority reports
                I got from Alfred O'Rahilly which were dismissed – the
                Economist in London said the composition of the Banking
                Commission had been equivalent to a packed jury. So that he
                really never took any kind of grip or put any *smacht* [discipline]
                on the Irish banks who were at that stage funnelling the savings
                of these poor farmers into British government securities. And
                now, many years later, we have the exact mirror image of banks
                which got completely out of control in lashing out credit, and
                we have no external assets; we have no reserves worth talking

about held by the Central Bank. They have been going down all the time. The excuse is we are part of the Euro so we don't need external reserves and the balance of payments is an irrelevance, which of course it's not, because we must export to pay for our imports. So that's really been the question, which, John, you have now elicited from me, which I wasn't going to open my mouth about, as to what would the people on the platform do – or is my question worth asking? – the contrast between then and now and that the failure on both occasions to really … notwithstanding what you will be very familiar with – the section of the 1937 constitution that the overriding guiding rule for the creation of credit is the welfare of the Irish people, a much-ignored item in *Bunreacht na hÉireann*?

Chair: Garret.

G. FitzGerald: It's a good question. I hadn't reflected on the contrast between the 1930s and today and how it's all gone so wrong. But we're part of a global economy, an open economy, and deregulation has been the big thing for many years past. Let the capitalist system work its marvellous healing everywhere – and we went along with that. And it wouldn't have been easy for us, I think, to perhaps buck that trend. But now governments have started nationalising banks again. That used to be the hope of the extreme left in Ireland but the extreme left policy is now being implemented by Mr Bush in America, so it's a very changed world; and I'm afraid we're not very well placed to deal with the consequences of this present situation, for the reasons I've given: the unnoticed deterioration in our competitiveness in the last six years, which, I hope, we'll begin to face up to for the first time.

T. K. Whitaker: One of the disadvantages of prolonged survival is that your hearing begins to fade.... So if anyone wants to ask a specific question, and I hear it, I'll give an answer.

Chair: Ken, I'm sure, on occasion, you find that very useful. Tom.

T. Garvin: Well, if I was a necromancer, I could resurrect the soul of one of these very conservative bankers from 1950 or thereabout. He would say: 'I would be a lunatic to put money into Irish farming', for example. First of all, if you tried to foreclose on a farm if the farmer didn't pay his debts, you would be shot by his neighbours, if not by the farmer himself. And secondly the farm often could not be sold because of a kind of folk custom entail – entail meaning you have a life interest in your farm but the farm must be passed on to one of your sons, and commonly even a particular son is named, usually the eldest one. This passed out of Irish law in 1853 but a version of it was enforced by Irish farmers up until about a generation ago – possibly still is, I don't know – but it meant that farmland couldn't be sold, and I think that's one of the basic problems: that there wasn't all that much to invest in, in Ireland.

Ruairí Quinn: During the period from 1952 to '53 when you were beginning to look at the failure of protectionism and the need to export abroad, and running parallel, as I understand, economically, the history of what was clearly the decline of sterling as an international reserve currency, did the question ever arise in the privacy of your conversations about the necessity to break the link with sterling so as to price Irish goods at a more competitive export price at one level and, in effect, to raise an effective economic cost of importation without putting in tariffs? Was that ever an item of discussion or given serious consideration?

T. K. Whitaker: I think the short answer would have to be negative to your question about serious questioning of the link with sterling. I think there was always a great fear of the psychological effects of such a thing as evidence of a deteriorating economy, and so my answer is, no, it wasn't very seriously considered at any time.

Chair: And did Seán MacBride – I know he was Foreign Minister, but he liked to think he was also Finance Minister – did he not nibble away at this agenda? And how seriously, or otherwise, was he treated in the Department of Finance?

T. K. Whitaker: Otherwise! [laughter]

Eoin O'Brien: I suppose I come to this debate as somebody who works with and advocates on behalf of that section of Irish society that has been left behind by the very dramatic economic growth that we're speaking about here. And I just wanted to make a very brief comment, which is this: I think on celebrating the contribution of Ken Whitaker to Irish economic development we have a choice, which is – whether we reflect on and learn from the substantive lessons of *Economic Development* or whether we actually embrace the spirit of Ken Whitaker in developing those innovative ideas at the time. And, for me, that's a very important distinction which we need to reflect on. If we do the first, then I think we follow the path Frances Ruane very eloquently outlined in the *Irish Times* last week, which is we look at things like export-orientated growth; we look at putting the economy first and getting the economy right before we start to try and address some of the structural inequalities in Irish society. And though, I think if we were to do that, you would see the economy beginning to stabilise in a number of years, the difficulty would be that many of these people who have been left behind over the last fifteen years will continue to be left behind because we won't have addressed that crucial problem.

I think if we embrace the second of those options, the spirit of T. K. Whitaker, somebody who challenged the prevailing consensus of his time and tried to find new and innovative ways to do something, which we have been talking about for about a decade but we haven't yet succeeded in doing, which is finding a mechanism for developing Irish society, which advances not only economic development but also social development at the same time – adequately integrating these two things. So I would much prefer to see us actually looking at how can we look at what T. K. Whitaker said in his own comments this morning – 'Develop a more critical approach' was the phrase he used, to the prevailing economic consensus – and find new policy solutions to address those kinds of things.

R. Fanning: I just want to try and answer Finola Kennedy's question. I think the answer is political again. Once de Valera comes into power in 1932, the change he is interested in is political change: it's changing the connection with Britain; it's rewriting the constitution; it's abolishing the Treaty; and in all other respects he wants to go 'steady as she goes'. There is a very interesting conversation he has a couple of days after he comes into office, with McElligott and the other heads of the government departments, and the end of that conversation he says to them, 'That's fine.' They explain to him how the system of government works, the chains of command and all the rest of it. He just more or less says, 'Carry on', and I think that's also one of the reasons why he put someone so intensely conservative in financial matters as Sean McEntee in Finance, and why he left him there for so long – because he didn't want to have, to put it crudely, he didn't want to fight with the Brits about anything else. And I think it relates to what Ken was saying also – the psychological shock there would have been. And I think the third point is that the membership – when it comes to the membership of the Banking Commission – that that would have come in the first instance … those names would have come out of the Department of Finance. So obviously they're going to name their former secretary, Joe Brennan, who becomes chairman – and the names come from McEntee, so of course it's a recipe for conservatism. But I think the fundamental answer was that de Valera was not interested in change and he wasn't interested in anything which was likely to deflect him from his central objective which was political, and until – as I tried to explain in my own paper – until that happens, nothing else can happen.

G. FitzGerald: We wasted several decades fussing about the symbolism of monarchy. That's what they were about up until 1949. We ignored the fact that the real problem for Ireland was our total dependence on the British economy, which as late as the early 1960s we exported 80 per cent of our goods to. It's true that we couldn't break that link unless we had access to other markets. We were stuck in that situation but we were distracted from that reality, and the interesting thing is that our extreme nationalists never woke up to that. So when at last the opportunity came to break out, because of the possibility of access to other markets – remember that Britain was the slowest-growing economy in Europe from the 1890s until 1980, and I fear it might become so again because of its overdependence on the financial sector and the consequence of where they stand today, but that's another day's work – and it was only when the EU became a possibility that people like Lemass and Ken Whitaker woke up to it then, to break out from that: we could, in fact, if we got the opportunity of exporting to the dynamic – as it was then –

continent of Europe and broke out from under Britain that we had a chance at real independence, independence in foreign policy, the capacity to run our own policy, to negotiate our own arrangement with the French, for example, follow our interests with France – literally whichever country shared our view on a particular issue. And that was a huge achievement; but interestingly the extreme nationalists – the Sinn Féiners and the extreme left – never woke up to this fact, and their policies continued to be anti-EU, which was the one thing that gave us our independence and gave us our break from Britain. So, you know, the lack of any real understanding of the appalling impact of economic dependence on the slowest-growing economy in Europe right since the end of the nineteenth century – slowness in realising that and the distraction of this business about whether or not you called it a republic or whether the king signs documents – that was very damaging to us. But of course we couldn't do much until the UK ... with the possibility of the EU, it all opened up, and Sean Lemass and Whitaker landed us into that and gave us independence which we are at the moment in danger of losing. We could now be pushed back under Britain again. Anybody who has read – but nobody can have read it, I think, or very few – the speech by Giscard d'Estaing at the *Daily Telegraph* conference on 9 September, which proposed special status for Britain, giving up many of its roles in the EU, and suggests that some other countries might do the same – a most pointed reference to us ... that people like him are very happy to see Britain becoming semi-detached and us pushed back into the British orbit, losing our independence after forty years, and that's what the issue of the Lisbon Treaty is about if and when we face up to it. That's a long answer to a different question...

Chair: Ken, you emphasised the importance of James Ryan being in Finance when *Economic Development* was brought forward. Was that really a case of *not* Sean McEntee? Do you believe that if Sean McEntee was there that there would have been a real difficulty in getting this through, or do you think Lemass would have carried it? What is your read on that?

T. K. Whitaker: It would have been much harder to get it through but it would have been done nevertheless, I think; and some members of the government like Sean Lemass would undoubtedly have taken it up.

Chair: So would you then disagree with what Ronan was saying about Brian Farrell's point that Lemass enjoyed the cover for the heresy and 180-degree U-turn; that Lemass enjoyed de Valera's cover, that it was an asset to him? But was that cover necessary to make the U-turn or would he have delivered anyway?

T. K. Whitaker: It was necessary. I mean, de Valera was interested only in politics, as Garret was saying, and had this idyllic view of a rustic economy and, in fact, so much so that when I brought the first visitors from the International Monetary Fund to see him in 1952, he treated them to another version of that famous St Patrick's Day speech, and, when we came out into the corridor, the head of the delegation said to me, 'A strange man, your prime minister'. But in some way he had the good sense to leave economic affairs to Lemass and to trust him in that respect.

Chair: And wasn't there an occasion when you were visiting Sean Lemass in hospital and he asked you to bring some books to him? Would you like to share that story?

T. K. Whitaker: I forget the detail…

Chair: The economic textbooks because now that Lemass had spare time … de Valera had other reading plans for him?

T. K. Whitaker: He had been laid up for a few months and he had sent a message to me, would I suggest a few books he might read. And I thought of much more general books – classics of English literature – but the message came back that he wanted books on economics, so I prescribed a few. But to what effect I don't really know.

R. Fanning: If I could just pick up on a point that Garret made about the EU – I think I didn't speak about that today because we really stopped in 1957, but I think it's an immediate and very important spin-off of the building of the bipartisan consensus that I was trying to explain; because the extraordinary thing that T. K. and Lemass achieved at the time of the first application is that, to all intents and purposes, the debate about whether Ireland should go into Europe is over now – we don't join until 1972 – but the debate is effectively over as early as that, and that I think flowed directly out of the consensualist approach I was trying to explain.

T. Garvin: I don't think we should forget that Lemass was a free trader and he was a free trader as a very young man. In 1929, he wrote a position paper for Fianna Fáil – then, of course, in opposition, and about to come into government a few years later – in which he prophesied a future European Union as proposed by one of the prime ministers of France during the 1920s – Aristide Briand – and he said, 'I am a philosophical free trader in effect', he says. However, we live in a continent which instead of having one customs unit, as it had in 1914, in effect it now has twenty-three and we're going to have to be the twenty-fourth because we have no other choice but to protect our back against the other protected countries' economies of that time; so he has always looked forward to some kind of a European America. In fact, he looked at the USA in that document as a very, very rich country that owes its wealth and its dynamism to the enormous size of its market. In Europe, we can only rival that if we all get together in one great country union. Now, I don't think he thought he would have to wait thirty years for the customs union – which he did, of course, but a few things like Adolf Hitler and World War II … a few difficulties like that kind of got in the way; but, eventually, I think he was quite prepared for free trade. He just was opportunistic about when he thought it could be brought in and when protection could also be dismantled. He also was … I think, politically – he had political difficulties with people who benefited from protectionism and who had a fair amount of political clout and could slow it up or stop it happening for some years in the 1950s.

Sean Aylward: I first wanted to say a word of praise for the wider contribution to Irish societal development by Ken Whitaker, and I would like to recall the seminal work he did on the Commission on the Penal System, which was published in 1985, and I think I was a direct beneficiary of his work in that regard in my own earlier career. The question I would like to put to Ken is about the extraordinary shape of his career with the Department of

Finance. I wondered how did you become secretary so young and wondered why did you leave it so early in 1969? And also, finally, congratulations on this day and this celebration. Thank you.

T. K. Whitaker: Thanks, Sean. I'll answer your first question. Why did I leave it so early? I had spent thirteen years as secretary of the department, and by then the government had decided that seven years was enough to endure for many senior civil servants, and so thirteen was almost twice the then normal tenure of office. And secondly, even when I had finished in the Central Bank, I spent quite a long time in the public service, so I emerged into what turned out to be, in my experience, something that justifies the Japanese proverb that the evening is the best part of the day.

Questions and Answers:
Second Session

Panel: Nick Crafts, Paul Hare, Frank Barry, Frances Ruane

Chair: John Bowman

Chair: As a case study, do you think *Economic Development*, and the Irish experience since, is best understood as unique? Or are you looking for laws that are at work here and which could apply to other economies and political systems?

N. Crafts: I think it's a bit of each actually in the sense that I think, as Paul's talk has made clear, Ireland has done things which are generally sensible, which would follow from a subtle version of the good economic textbook. That said, it seems to me that if you said to another European country, could they emulate and imitate Ireland, the answer, in a way, is no. There is now a limit to the element of the sui generis to this, and I probably didn't say it very clearly but it's the subtext to the later part of the talk and, in particular, these new economic geography models do suggest that when you've got a sector that's flying away, you're basically blocking out the other guys. So if the Welsh came along twenty years later and tried to repeat the story, it'd be too late.

Chair: We're on the periphery here – I'll put it that way – and what is the periphery? If you're an American investor, you might look at Ireland and it's in the Atlantic and it's Anglophone and it doesn't look at all on the periphery: it's a springboard into Europe.

155

N. Crafts:	I think that's absolutely right and I probably should have said that explicitly. Ireland is within the EU. It's an excellent platform base for exporting to Europe and, relative to world market potential, Ireland is rather close.
Tom Healy:	Just two questions. One for Nick: it struck me that education didn't feature that much perhaps in our discussions today, except, of course, in your growth accounting equations you clearly identified the role of total factor productivity growth. The mediocre performance of the 1960s, contrasted with the 1990s and the present decade, suggests, I think, that the role of knowledge and knowledge-intensive sectors is quite crucial, and, I suppose, my first question really is: if we're talking about a mind-set change fifty years ago and today, are we still looking at investment in education inappropriately in government accounting as well as in national accounting as a consumption item rather than an investment item? Parallel to that – and I'll just park the other question for a little while – going back to 1958: that was, I suppose, two or three years before the term 'human capital' was coined by Shultz and Becker ... anybody in the audience remember what was the input of the education sector to *Economic Development*, from Marlborough Street and beyond, or were education and the economy two completely separate spheres at that time?
N. Crafts:	Let me answer about the education story, which I didn't dwell on in the talk. There is a bit more in the final version of the paper. A couple of things struck me on looking at the numbers: firstly, as you get past 1970, the human capital deepening contribution almost doubles compared with earlier; there is really quite a big change. And secondly, what struck me in looking at Irish policy was that there really were again what seemed to me some pretty smart moves aiming to create new forms of education, aiming to complement the FDI strategy. So certain branches of tertiary education expanding quite quickly without necessarily going to the full degree course and so on – those all seemed to me to be very pragmatic sensible ways of recognising that human capital is a very important comple-mentary factor of production to what was the thrust of policy. That seems to me that I probably should have said a bit more about that in the talk. I didn't mean to suggest that it played no part at all – far from it.

P. Hare: I don't think I have much to add to what Nick has already said on the role of education. I certainly think it is very important once any economy gets above the most basic elements of development. It does seem to me that Ireland moved very much in the right direction in that regard.

Chair: But, Frank, it is also true that, in the wake of *Economic Development*, and *Investment in Education* – and indeed there was a very important article in *Studies*, again signed by the secretary of the time, which I think was possibly the precedent.

F. Barry: Can I say something about that actually? I suppose it's Tom Garvin that should be answering this question as his most recent book is very much on how Ireland got the turnaround in the educational throughput together. But I just want to make two points. One is the OECD report, which is what John is referring to here, which is what Garvin points out – it made newspaper headlines when it came out, reporting that half the school-children were leaving schools at the age of 13, and in the language of policy reform – and the politics of policy reform – that created a sense of crisis. And we know that, within three years, Donogh O'Malley had introduced not just free second-level education but also free transport networks to make sure rural kids could still get to school, so that sense of creating crisis is important in the sense of policy reform literature. And the other point, as Nick says, about the Regional Technical Colleges – or Institutes of Technology, as they are now called – that they played an important role because our educational system co-evolved with our industrial development strategy through foreign direct investment. The original idea for the RTCs came from a senior civil servant who convinced the relevant minister that this was a way to go. I always think this is very important. We take our civil service for granted here. We take for granted that it's meritocratic, that it's well-functioning. I do a lot of work these days in African economies, and Paul, of course, in transitional economies, and this is not the norm: it's not the norm to have a well-functioning civil service that does their homework and comes up with very, very valuable ideas that ministers can choose to adopt or not. Your question about the role it played in *Economic Development*: I don't know the answer to that.

F. Ruane: It is certainly striking to me that it wasn't being discussed in *Economic Development*, and the contrast between Ireland 1958 and our other European neighbours was huge in terms of participation in second-level education, that that was a lagged effect which might well explain why the economic growth thing was delayed. The effect that Nick was talking about was delayed well into the 1980s. I think it's – well, I would have had a very strong sense and awareness from the late 1960s onwards that education spend was social spend; it wasn't economic spend until quite late on, despite the Martin O'Donoghue–Paddy Lynch argument which may have had some sway in certain circles. But as it was talked about, as it was conceived of, people were talking about it as equality of opportunity, getting it out there, but the notion that it was to be a sizable factor contributing, as was being suggested, to our economic growth concept – people thought, that might be all right in theory but are we sure it's going to happen? Then it finally did begin to happen and with very much a strong impact.

Chair: But it was Sean O'Connor's article in *Studies* which provided the heresy of a civil servant signing such an article. I remember the buzz. I'm not suggesting that all civil servants start writing ... Garret, you wanted to say something?

G. FitzGerald: Didn't play much of a role in the document but there is now a curious feature of Irish education: we now educate people to a qualitative level which is equivalent to Northern Europe and much better than Southern Europe in proportion to people ... one of the highest in Europe: 60 per cent secondary education. We have constantly been way ahead of Britain, which has the lowest education rate outside Turkey, the biggest dropout rate, a very low proportion to higher education; it's only catching up now. We're usually 25 per cent higher than Britain – how do we do this? We don't spend much money on it. We're spending a lot less than other countries. The reason is for a fact we've never allowed for – economists can't calculate it – motivation. The fact is the motivation of Irish parents wishing their children to be educated to get reasonable jobs rather than terrible jobs, and the very high activity rate of trade unions ensuring that teachers are better paid than in most other countries. For a long time only Germany paid more than what our teachers were paid. This has given us a high productivity. We're actually educating people to a high level and a high proportion at a third less cost than the rest of Europe. Education productivity is very high here but economists never build that in and, in fact, it's great that we're able to build on that. We're able to achieve so much because of this incalculable factor. Even with large classes, if people are motivated, they get a good result. Portugal has half our people in primary education and it is one of the most under-educated countries in Europe … and low quality of it. The quality of the educational system at every level is hugely important and it should feature larger at events like this.

Eoin Hand: In the archive of the World Bank, in the first section of the Ireland file, there is a letter from the Gresham Hotel, from the first mission of the World Bank to Ireland, from a gentleman, Mr Benjamin King, who says that he's met Mr Whitaker, and it's a bit patronising. Whitaker has given him a draft of his document, which he writes is not a bad analysis of the Irish situation. It has prompted me to think that, in a way, *Economic Development* – and I wonder what the speakers think – *Economic Development* represents a home-grown internalisation of what would subsequently be thought of as the Washington consensus or economic orthodoxy, and that, in a way, through thick and thin, through good times and bad times, we've always referred back to the *Economic Development* plan because it has that lasting value which would have been there even before the 1950s, and is there today, that these points that Nick brought out – the low taxation, all that stuff – that is very standard economic orthodoxy, and that's why it has lasting value, because he brought it into the mainstream of the way we thought about ourselves?

Chair: Paul, can I ask you and can I ask the panel the question that I asked Nick already: is this a case history to be thought of as unique and bespoke or is this something that is replicable in other economies? What are the lessons?

P. Hare: I think each country is unique. There are going to be some common factors you can pull out and apply elsewhere, but there is going to be some element of uniqueness too. That's, in a way – if I can just comment on the World Bank observation that was made just now – that's what, in a way, makes the World Bank's standard approaches to policy not too good. You do need individual adaptations to the individual circumstances of the country, and it's interesting these days that both the World Bank and the IMF talk a great deal about what they call 'country ownership of their policies', and what that's supposed to mean is that the countries themselves agree with them, effectively write their reports, and so on. But actually, if you read lots of the World Bank and IMF reports, which I do, they look surprisingly similar, and it's quite hard to believe that somebody sitting in Chad would have chosen the same words as somebody sitting in Paraguay, but that is the case when you read the reports – just a few little details are changed. One gets the impression that the idea of ownership – which I strongly agree with, but which unfortunately to a bit too much of an extent is still an ideology rather than a reality. And I would like to see, myself, much more care and differentiation in the way the World Bank and the IMF approach their member countries.

F. Ruane: One of the things that strikes me when you look at Ireland's approach to policy and that of a number of other countries – there are a couple of things that, I think, that, because the development policy came out of a view of totality of the economy, even though, if you like, the growth engine was wrong – that notion that things were connected, that notion of beginning to think like that. One of the things it did was it gave us a sort of portfolio approach to development. So, for example, even though we saw pharmaceuticals and electronics as being key areas for growth, it didn't rule out everything else. And, even when we went to those … if you take, for example, when we were going into the computer industry, we got in DELL and Gateway, and various people ... everyone knew some companies wouldn't survive – that was totally known at the time. But the notion was you took a risk, you took a balanced view. I remember looking at a study I did some years ago on the electronics sector, and comparing it with one sector or part of Japan, and we actually had almost every stage, and there were almost twelve stages of production in electronics, and we had representation in virtually every one of them. Nobody was sure where the money or the jobs were going to be. We were actually out there right across the board, and there was this island in this part of Japan with a very big population, much bigger than ourselves, specialising in one area of production. So, I think the portfolio effect that connected us between things … I think that is a recipe that does generalise to everybody else. I think where we were at that point in time – of Europe, of English-speaking, of American FDI, of electronics – there were a number of these that worked in our favour. So I don't think you could take that recipe – Alex Salmond in Scotland found it an attractive one, but there is now no way that, if he tried to copy it, that it would work at this juncture.

F. Barry: Well, another one of my favourite quotes, which I always use, comes from a recent paper of Garret's – I hate quoting you so much but you say it and it just encapsulates something so valuable from your experience as a politician – that democratic politicians are so circumscribed in their behaviour by the power of vested interest groups that in many ways it's amazing they are able to implement policies that are beneficial to social welfare. You put it in better terms, of course, than that. That makes you think: politicians – even if they want to make good decisions – how do they get around this block of vested interest groups? So, in many ways, what they need to do is exploit circumstances, whether external circumstances as I was talking about there – the onset of European free trade would have forced Ireland to think about where do we go from here, because the playing field has changed very extensively. They exploit those changed external circumstances and exploit changed internal circumstances. The crisis that we had here … but you probably all know historian Arnold Toynbee and his notion of challenge and response – that all societies face challenges but your success or failure resides in how you respond to them. And one of the important things that we see from *Economic Development* is the importance of having good policy advisers – who are not always listened to, but good-quality advisers in place. This is one of the benefits of having a meritocratic civil service … that it ensures that your policy advisers are disinterested to a large extent. And the other thing that Frances Ruane talked about: an extensive dialogue within Ireland – open, so that there was some transparency about the likely consequences of economic policy decisions.

Economic

Development

DUBLIN:
PUBLISHED BY THE STATIONERY OFFICE.

To be purchased from the
GOVERNMENT PUBLICATIONS SALE OFFICE, G.P.O. ARCADE, DUBLIN
or through any Bookseller.

Price seven shillings and sixpence.

(Pr. 4803.)

ECONOMIC DEVELOPMENT

This study of national development problems and opportunities was prepared by the Secretary of the Department of Finance, with the cooperation of others in, or connected with, the public service. The views and recommendations it contains were considered by the Government in the formulation of its recently-issued Programme for Economic Expansion. The study is being published to make available the information assembled and coordinated in it and to stimulate interest in the subject of national development.

The study was completed in May, 1958, but in some instances it has been found possible to take into account developments subsequent to that date.

Department of Finance,
November, 1958.

CONTENTS

APPENDICES

ECONOMIC DEVELOPMENT

CHAPTER 1

INTRODUCTION

1. How this study originated is shown in the documents reproduced as Appendix 1. It is well to reiterate here that the aim is not to draw up a detailed five or ten-year plan of national development. For a small country so exposed to the perpetual flux of world economic forces there would be little sense in trying to establish a rigid pattern of development. The aim is rather (a) to highlight the main deficiencies and potentialities of the economy and (b) to suggest the principles to be followed to correct the deficiencies and realise the opportunities, indicating a number of specific forms of productive development which appear to offer good long-term prospects. One must be prepared at all times for fluctuations and upsets. A readiness to adapt to changing conditions is a *sine qua non* of material progress. Nevertheless, one may reasonably hope to find some guiding principles which it would be advantageous to follow through thick and thin.

2. While planning in a rigid sense is not useful in our circumstances, there can be no doubt about the wisdom of looking ahead and trying to direct national policy along the most productive lines. A year is too restricted a frame of reference for policy decisions. Their effects overflow such arbitrary boundaries. It is, of course, necessary to seek Parliamentary approval year by year for financial policy as indicated in the annual budget. But this yearly process, if it is to be fully effective in contributing to national development, must be set in a much broader framework. An attempt should be made to secure a more general coordination of financial and economic policy with a view to the maximum progress being made in the years immediately ahead. Otherwise, unintended but damaging inconsistencies and conflicts can only too easily arise.

3. To think ahead the mind needs the support of facts and figures. The present position and the immediate prospects are the safest starting-point but as one ventures further into the future the estimates on which one must rely become more and more doubtful. This cannot be helped. One can only try to ensure that, here and now, the most competent estimates are made. In this study, care is taken to explain how any forecasts have been arrived at. No more can be done—their ultimate validity cannot be assured.

4. Apart from its obvious value in making policy more long-term and logical, forward thinking is particularly urgent and necessary for other reasons. It is apparent that we have come to a critical and decisive point in our economic affairs. The policies hitherto followed, though given a fair trial, have not resulted in a viable economy. We have power, transport facilities, public services, houses, hospitals and a general " infrastructure " on a scale which is reasonable by western European standards, yet large-scale emigration and unemployment still persist. The population is falling, the national income rising more slowly than in the rest of Europe. A great and sustained effort to increase production, employment and living standards is necessary to avert economic decadence.

5. The possibility of freer trade in Europe carries disquieting implications for some Irish industries and raises special problems of adaptation and adjustment. It necessitates also a re-appraisal of future industrial and agricultural prospects. It seems clear that, sooner or later, protection will have to go and the challenge of free trade be accepted. There is really no other choice for a country wishing to keep pace materially with the rest of Europe. It would be a policy of despair to accept that our costs of production must permanently be higher than those of other European countries, either in industry or in agriculture. Our level of real incomes depends on our competitive efficiency. If that must be lower than in the rest of Europe we should have to be content with relatively low living standards. With the alternative of emigration available we are unlikely, either as a community or as individuals, to accept such a situation for long unless it is seen as an essential part of a programme of national regeneration. The effect of any policy entailing relatively low living standards here for all time would be to sustain and stimulate the outflow of emigrants and in the end jeopardise our economic independence. Any little benefit obtained in terms of employment in protected non-competitive industries would be outweighed by losses through emigration and general economic impoverishment. If we do not expand production on a competitive basis, we shall fail to provide the basis necessary for the economic independence and material progress of the community. Even a spectacular increase in efficiency and output will still leave us for a long time at a relative disadvantage to Britain and many other countries in respect of real income per head of the population. Indeed, if we are to catch up at all, our annual rate of improvement must exceed theirs.

6. Our economic progress requires that more resources be devoted to productive purposes. But there is as yet no agreement on a systematic programme of development. There is need for urgent determination of the productive purposes to which resources should be applied and of

the unproductive, or relatively unproductive, activities which can, with the minimum social disadvantage, be curtailed to set free resources for productive development.

7. It is well to state that by " productive investment " in this study is meant investment yielding an adequate return to the national economy as a whole. Private investment is not normally undertaken unless there appears to be a fair prospect of financial success, that is, of the investment producing commodities saleable at competitive prices. In the case of public investment, the term " productive " cannot be limited to investments yielding an adequate direct return to the Exchequer. It extends also to investment which enlarges the national income by creating a flow of goods and services which are saleable without the aid of subsidies; for this will result indirectly in revenue to pay debt charges. Whether the first test is satisfied is easy to establish, but the second is often a matter of doubt. It is clear that, where neither test is satisfied and part, if not all, of the cost of servicing the capital must be met by a levy on the taxpayer, the investment results in a redistribution rather than an increase in national income. Progress in the building up of real national income depends on capital and labour being devoted to industrial and agricultural development, particularly for export, rather than to the provision of welfare services for home consumption. In an expanding economy, where real incomes are rising and the demand for goods and services is growing, opportunities for useful and continuing employment will arise automatically and, as has been shown in Germany since the war, a progressive improvement in social amenities will be possible without undue strain on the economy.

8. It should be added that there is no conflict between what are termed " socially desirable " and " economic " objectives. " Socially desirable " objectives will not be permanently realised merely by increasing " social " investment. The erection of houses, schools and hospitals—socially desirable in themselves—will, of course, provide employment but the employment ceases once the period of construction is over and the unemployed man is then left with an amenity which, if he remains unemployed, will contribute but little to his standard of living. Investment which is not productive may provide employment but it does so only for a time and at the cost of weakening the capacity of the economy as a whole to provide lasting and self-sustaining employment. For these reasons the emphasis must be on productive investment, though not, of course, to the exclusion of all social investment. The permanent increase in employment associated with an expansion of real national output is to be preferred to the purely temporary increase which is all that non-productive investment, entailing a mere redistribution of existing incomes, can bring about.

9. Without positive action by the Government, a slowing down

3

in housing and certain other forms of social investment will occur from now on because needs are virtually satisfied over wide areas of the State. This decline in building will cause a reduction in employment. The continuance of large-scale investment in housing or other forms of social building would not, however, be justified merely to create artificial employment opportunities. If the objective of an expanding economy is not to be jeopardised, the right course is to replace social investment by productive investment which will provide self-sustaining and permanent employment. This means that no time can be lost in devising a realistic long-term programme of productive investment.

10. In the context of a programme of economic development extending over five years or longer, it would be easier not only to avoid inconsistencies between individual decisions but also to secure acceptance of decisions which, presented in isolation, might arouse strong opposition. It would be more apparent to all sections of the community that certain adjustments of present policy were necessary and it would be less difficult to have efforts made and sacrifices borne if they were seen to be a necessary contribution to national welfare and were not in danger of being nullified by neglect or extravagance elsewhere.

11. A further reason for careful mapping of future economic policy is that we have no longer the surplus resources with which to meet deficits in external payments. Our wartime accumulation of sterling reserves has been run down. Our post-war dollar borrowings have been spent. But our balance of payments remains unstable. The present state of balance is exceptional—the year 1957 being the first year since 1946 in which a deficit was not recorded—and it is insecure. The equilibrium attained is at a depressed level of domestic economic activity and is due in part to the using up of stocks. A reduction in supplies of cattle, a fall in their export price, and rising money incomes and expenditure, due to wage and salary increases, are only some of the factors capable of disturbing this precarious balance and causing renewed loss of national capital. In fact, the import excess has been tending to increase since August, 1957. It is, therefore, of the greatest importance that policy be concentrated henceforth on the development of productive capacity, so as to sustain and strengthen our economic position and external purchasing power. To allow social services or non-productive forms of expenditure priority over productive projects would cause a misdirection of resources and increase the difficulties of development by raising our production costs, artificially stimulating our imports and putting us in deficit again with the rest of the world.

12. There is also a sound *psychological* reason for having an integrated development programme. The absence of such a programme tends to deepen the all-too-prevalent mood of despondency about the

country's future. A sense of anxiety is, indeed, justified. But it can too easily degenerate into feelings of frustration and despair. After 35 years of native government people are asking whether we can achieve an acceptable degree of economic progress. The common talk amongst parents in the towns, as in rural Ireland, is of their children having to emigrate as soon as their education is completed in order to be sure of a reasonable livelihood. To the children themselves and to many already in employment the jobs available at home look unattractive by comparison with those obtainable in such variety and so readily elsewhere. All this seems to be setting up a vicious circle—of increasing emigration, resulting in a smaller domestic market depleted of initiative and skill, and a reduced incentive, whether for Irishmen or foreigners, to undertake and organise the productive enterprises which alone can provide increased employment opportunities and higher living standards. There is, therefore, a real need at present to buttress confidence in the country's future and to stimulate the interest and enthusiasm of the young in particular. A general resurgence of will may be helped by setting up targets of national endeavour which appear to be reasonably attainable and mutually consistent. This is an aspect of good leadership. But there is nothing to be gained by setting up fanciful targets. Failure to reach such targets would merely produce disillusionment and renew the mood of national despondency. Realism also demands an awareness that, at present, and for a long time ahead, the material reward for work here may be less than that obtainable elsewhere but that there are many countervailing advantages in living in Ireland. No programme of development can be effective unless it generates increased effort, enterprise and saving on the part of a multitude of individuals. Its eventual success or failure will depend primarily on the individual reactions of the Irish people. If they have not the will to develop, even the best possible programme is useless.

13. A concerted and comprehensive programme aimed at a steady progress in material welfare, even though supported by the Churches and other leaders of opinion, could only be successful if the individual members of the community were realistic and patriotic enough to accept the standard of living produced by their own exertions here, even if it should continue for some time to be lower than the standard available abroad. Otherwise the possibility of economic progress scarcely exists.

14. For all these reasons the importance of the next five to ten years for the economic and political future of Ireland cannot be overstressed. Policies should be re-examined without regard to past views or commitments. It is desirable to remind ourselves that at all times in a nation's history decisions have to be taken; that there is no guarantee when they are taken that they will prove right; and that the greatest fault lies in pursuing a policy after it has proved to be unsuitable

or ineffective. What matters above all is to understand the present position and find the best and quickest ways of improving it.

15. This study is intended to help in the preparation of a programme of economic development. Information which may be useful in this connection is assembled for ease of reference. The general scheme of the work is, first, to outline the present economic position, concentrating on the main deficiencies and opportunities. Then, before making a closer analysis of the four main heads under which progress can obviously be achieved—agriculture, fisheries, industry and tourism—it is necessary to examine the extent to which resources may be expected to be available for development needs and the financial policy needed to assure the maximum rate of economic progress. No programme of development can be regarded as realistic which is not founded on a reasonable assessment of the resources likely to be available to finance it. The closer analysis of agriculture, fisheries, industry and tourism is intended to indicate the general lines of development which can most effectively be followed over the next five years or so. Some specific possibilities are also discussed but as illustrations only. The conclusions of the study are summarised in the final chapter.

16. It may, perhaps, be said here that problems of economic development are exercising the minds of statesmen, economists, scientists and administrators all over the world. It is clear that development can be accelerated by Government policy but how this can best be done is by no means obvious. It is reasonable to suppose that the solution must vary according to the. circumstances of individual countries. Economists have not so far developed any general theory of economic development. The present state of thought in the matter is summarised as follows by Professor A. K. Cairncross in a recent article*:

> " Economists would agree on the central importance in economic development of capital accumulation and technological progress, but they would not necessarily agree on the precise rôle played by either, for both are simultaneously causes and symptoms of development. Some are impressed by the barrier that illiteracy and ignorance interpose and would lay most stress on education as a means of securing the rapid spread of modern ideas. Some represent industrialisation as the key to development, and regard agricultural improvement as consequential; others would reverse the order of priority and emphasise the difficulty of expanding the market for industrial products so long as agricultural incomes are low and food relatively expensive. Sometimes it is the heavy industries alone that are picked on as the spearhead, or the machine tool industry is assigned a special rôle; sometimes the theory runs in terms of balanced growth and the simultaneous building up of a variety of industries, each generating income and providing, directly

* " Economic Development and the West "—*The Three Banks Review*, December, 1957.

6

or indirectly, a market for the others. There are differences also about the possibility of absorbing, without loss to agricultural output, large numbers of workers from the countryside. To some economists the existence of a vast rural surplus of man-power implies the need for a corresponding expansion in industrial capacity, financed, if need be, through drastic taxation; while, for others, the gains to be expected from taking up any slack in the economy are not very significant so long as the existing technological frontiers are not advanced."

17. Professor Cairncross later in the same article states, and most economists would agree, that "the nerve centre of the whole forward movement may lie, not in finance, but in entrepreneurial capacity." He points out that it is doubtful whether investment in public utilities and facilities in countries that lack other essentials of development will allow them to "take-off" (and Irish experience would seem to support this). There is, he says, "no guarantee that economic activity will automatically gear itself to the expanded transport, power and other services that have been brought into existence." He points out that "historically, the initial advance has rarely been the result of capital expenditure: it has far more commonly followed the expansion of markets, especially foreign markets, the discovery of new mineral resources, the introduction of new techniques involving only a moderate capital outlay, the arrival of foreign immigrants eager to make a place for themselves by a display of enterprise." The usual sequence of events is that a step forward is made in one sector of the economy and that this makes it easier for the rest of the economy to advance.

18. These observations are not without relevance to the problem of economic development in Ireland. A *dynamic* has to be found and released and it is not necessarily increased capital investment, though this may be called for to support a higher rate of development once it is set in motion. It would, indeed, be a mistake to think that a faster rate of increase in output is a matter simply of stepping up the volume of home investment. It is true that there is a close relationship between output per head and the amount of capital per head but there are other conditions of economic progress no less important than increased capitalisation. The first of these is the development of a better appreciation of the dependence of material progress on individual output. Others are a raising of the general level of education, health and skill, the loosening of restrictive practices, whether of employers or employees, the practical encouragement of initiative and enterprise, the adoption of improved methods, techniques and principles of organisation and management both in agriculture and industry, and a greater readiness to apply scientific advances. Attention to matters such as these may yield even greater increases in production than direct capitalisation in the form of new plant and machinery though this does not, of course, imply that increased capitalisation is not also required. It is

essential for sustained and balanced progress that an increase in productive capital should be supported not only by advances in education and technical training but also—though these are not short in Ireland—by the provision of basic utilities and amenities, including power supplies, good housing and transport services. Harmonious development calls also for suitable fiscal and monetary policies designed to increase the supply of savings and the incentive to invest in productive enterprises. As between countries, differences in climate, political institutions, educational and technical facilities, individual attitudes to work, trade union outlook and policy can be as important as differences in natural resources or in the volume of investment in causing divergent rates of development. Economic growth is, in fact, a complex process depending on social, psychological and political as well as economic and technical factors. In Ireland, the trend of population is an important factor inasmuch as dynamism and flexibility are rarely associated with a declining home population, whereas even a stable population would have good prospects of economic advance if its exports were competitive.

19. This study suggests that, given favourable public policies and private dispositions, a dynamic of progress awaits release in agriculture, fisheries, industry and tourism. It is hoped that it will be possible to set this force to work simultaneously in these major branches of the Irish economy. The opportunities of development may not be great enough to give all who are born in Ireland a standard of living they would accept—though there are advantages of living here not to be reckoned in money terms—but such as they are they should be exploited. It is not unreasonable to hope that sufficient advance can be made in the next decade not merely to consolidate our economic independence but to enable us to provide higher material standards for a rising population.

20. At the end of this introductory chapter it may be permissible for the Secretary of the Department of Finance to introduce a personal note. I wish to express my grateful recognition of the advice and comments received, on particular aspects of the study, from the Governor of the Central Bank, the Chairman of the Industrial Development Authority, and from colleagues in other Departments, including the Secretaries and other senior officers of the Departments of Industry and Commerce, Agriculture, Lands and Education. For more general criticism I am grateful to the Secretary of the Department of the Taoiseach, the Director of the Central Statistics Office and the professional economists on the Capital Investment Advisory Committee (Professor C. F. Carter, Mr. P. Lynch and Dr. W. J. L. Ryan). To Mr. C. H. Murray of the Department of the Taoiseach and to officers of my own Department (especially Messrs. M. F. Doyle, S. Ó Ciosáin, M. Horgan, D. Ó Loinsigh, J. Dolan, T. Ó Cobhthaigh and Dr. B.

Menton) I am indebted for preparing much of the groundwork. All this generous assistance made the task of co-ordination and synthesis much less difficult. I must personally accept the responsibility where I have not followed the advice received and it is necessary to say that no Department as such, nor any individual other than myself, is committed to the whole range of views and suggestions put forward.

21. In pressing on with this study, despite the claims of ordinary office work, it has been an inspiration to turn to the following words of the Bishop of Clonfert, Most Rev. Dr. Philbin : —

> " Our version of history has tended to make us think of freedom as an end in itself and of independent government—like marriage in a fairy story—as the solution of all ills. Freedom is useful in proportion to the use we make of it. We seem to have relaxed our patriotic energies just at the time when there was most need to mobilise them. Although our enterprise in purely spiritual fields has never been greater, we have shown little initiative or organisational ability in agriculture and industry and commerce. There is here the widest and most varied field for the play of the vital force that our religion contains."
>
> (*Studies,* Autumn, 1957).

This study is a contribution, in the spirit advocated by the Bishop of Clonfert, towards the working out of the national good in the economic sphere. It is hoped that, supplemented by productive ideas from other sources, it will help to dispel despondency about the country's future. We can afford our present standard of living, which is so much higher than most of the inhabitants of this world enjoy. Possibilities of improvement are there, if we wish to realise them. It would be well to shut the door on the past and to move forward, energetically, intelligently and with the will to succeed, but without expecting miracles of progress in a short time.

CHAPTER 2

ECONOMIC POSITION—GENERAL OUTLINE

1. It seems best to begin by taking a quick glance at the economy generally, with an eye particularly on the features most relevant to a study of potentialities of development. A more detailed study of agriculture and industry will be made later, with an analysis of specific possibilities, after the important question of the volume of development resources likely to be available has been examined.

I. ECONOMIC BACKGROUND

National Income

2. An introductory idea of our relative economic position is afforded by the assessment that, according to the generally accepted basis of comparison, the average income per head of the population is roughly one-half of that in Denmark and Britain, one-third of that in Canada and one-fifth of that in the United States; the figures for 1956, as derived from O.E.E.C. statistics, are: Ireland, $423; Denmark, $809; Britain, $909; Canada, $1,420; U.S.A., $2,067. An alternative assessment (by Colin Clark, 1950) in terms of " international units per head " (of similar purchasing power) put us in a similar position but with narrower differentials—Ireland 446, Denmark 670, United Kingdom 631, Canada 847, United States 1,053. Although international comparisons of this nature are subject to considerable qualifications, it is clear that per capita income in Ireland is relatively low. This is largely accounted for by the nature of the Irish economy, with an agricultural potential only partly realised and an industrial sector still in an under-developed state. These conditions are reflected in two major undesirable features, a high rate of emigration and a serious unemployment problem.

Emigration

3. What has been said about relative incomes suggests one reason why large numbers of Irish citizens should be attracted to Great Britain, Canada and the United States. Moreover, they are not unwelcome in these countries, many have relations there and there is no language difficulty. Emigration is not, of course, a recent phenomenon—it was an outstanding feature of the 19th century—but it has persisted since the establishment of the Irish State and has, in recent years, absorbed more than the natural increase in population. The annual rate of net emigration in 1951/56, viz. 13.4 per 1,000 average population, is about 60 per cent.

greater than the rate of the previous five years, more than twice the rate of the inter-war period and by far the highest rate amongst Western European countries. Some 40,000 persons are emigrating annually, mostly to the United Kingdom, attracted by more diverse and progressive employment opportunities, and by higher living standards.

4. While emigration has enabled both those who emigrate and those who remain at home to obtain a greater improvement in living standards than the national product would otherwise allow, it has deprived the economy of the stimulus of an expanding home market, and has, consequently, hampered industrial expansion and economic development.

Unemployment

5. Along with, or rather in spite of, a high rate of emigration Ireland has a higher rate of unemployment than most Western European countries. Unemployment has varied in the post-war years from 10.6% of the insured non-agricultural population in 1946 to 6.8% in 1955; the percentage figures for 1956 and 1957 were 7.7 and 9.2 respectively. In addition, despite the heavy emigration from rural areas, there is substantial under-employment on the land. The existence of under-employment on the land is an indication that agriculture can scarcely be expected to provide directly the additional employment necessary to stem the tide of emigration and that, for this purpose, the main reliance must be placed on increased employment in industry and services.

Production and standard of living

6. Between 1949 and 1956 the volume of gross national product increased by 8% as compared with 21% for Britain and 42% for O.E.E.C. countries generally. In agriculture, the volume of gross output rose by 9.9% over the same period or at an average rate of 1½% per annum as compared with a rate of 4% per annum for all O.E.E.C. countries. The increase in the volume of industrial output between 1949 and 1956 was 30% as compared with 62% for O.E.E.C. countries.

7. The relatively slow rise in Irish production and, therefore, in the capacity of the economy to provide higher standards for a stable or growing population has acted as a stimulus to emigration. Proximity to and ease of intercourse with Britain tend to set, at British levels, the *expected* standards for Irish wages and salaries, private consumption and services generally, irrespective of differences in natural resources and productivity. Output in Ireland does not suffice—and however much improved may never suffice—to support British standards but the ready availability of employment in Britain on attractive terms tends to

make labour unwilling to accept the inferior position. Not only are persons who cannot find employment in rural and urban areas leaving the country, but even employed persons are leaving their jobs for more highly-paid employment in Britain.

8. The question of the *acceptability* of living standards is, therefore, of critical importance. Both industry and agriculture must be made efficient and competitive or the living standards they provide will become even less acceptable and the emigration which for many years has siphoned off the whole of the natural increase in the population will continue unabated, if not, indeed, at a higher rate than before.

Agriculture

9. Agriculture (in which about 40% of the working population is engaged) accounted for £133 million or 28.9% of the national income in 1956, compared with 25.2% for industry, 14.1% for distribution and transport, 8.9% for public administration and defence and 16.7% for other domestic incomes. The number engaged in agriculture (including forestry and fishing) in 1956 was 445,000, compared with 186,000 in manufacturing industries and 292,000 in all industries (including building and construction 82,000).

10. The primary product of Irish agriculture is grass and the main activity of the farming community the production of grazing animals. Some 85% of the country's agricultural land is devoted to grass and the number of cattle supported by it stood at 4.5 million in 1957, including 1.2 million milch cows.

11. The emphasis on livestock production is a response to the demand of the British market for live animals to be fattened in Britain. Unlike dairy and crop products, cattle are produced and exported without State protection or subsidy. The grasslands, if improved, could carry bigger numbers of cattle and sheep without a commensurate increase in costs.

Fisheries

12. Notwithstanding our proximity to valuable fishing grounds the total value of sea fish (excluding salmon) returned as landed in 1957 was only £1 million. Of the quantity landed, about 41% was exported. Wholetime employment in fishing was provided for only 1,600. Consumption of fish per head of the population is one of the lowest in Europe and is less than half that in Britain. Apart from the potential home demand there are good possibilities of expanding the export trade to Britain and continental countries. The inadequate development of sea fishing is associated with its treatment, particularly along the west-

ern seaboard, as an adjunct of agriculture rather than as a separate industry. The policy of encouraging inshore fishing has resulted in the neglect of deep-sea fishing and insufficient investment in processing plant and equipment.

Manufacturing Industry

13. Ireland made a late start in the industrial field. The lack of an industrial tradition, managerial skill, adequate risk capital and native raw materials, with a heavily industrialised country as a close neighbour, made the new State's task of establishing industries particularly difficult. An extensive system of protective tariffs and quotas was needed to aid the infant industries and to overcome traditional consumer preferences, large scale advertising of British products and, in many cases, higher domestic costs of production. New employment for about 100,000 workers has been provided in protected industries and the volume of output of manufacturing industries has been trebled. Nevertheless the process of transition from a predominantly agricultural to a balanced economy is still far from complete and the pattern of industrial organisation is only developing. The percentage of the gross domestic product that comes from industry as a whole is only 28 as compared with a figure of over 40 for most O.E.E.C. countries. The percentage of those at work who were engaged in all industry in 1957 was 24.9 while the percentage engaged in manufacturing industry was no more than 16.1. Such industrial expansion as has been possible has not sufficed to absorb the surplus labour force.

14. It would not have been possible without protection to secure the establishment and development of many of the industries on the scale which has been achieved. The danger has always been apparent, however, that protection might impair the incentive to reduce costs and increase efficiency. This danger arises particularly where protection is granted shortly after an industry is started and the degree of protection conceded may be greater than the production costs attainable under efficient operating conditions would warrant. The responsibility of making periodic reviews of existing tariffs has been imposed on the Industrial Development Authority but so far, for various reasons, these reviews have been infrequent. Very few tariffs have been reduced; some have, indeed, been increased. A number of the protected industries have reduced production costs sufficiently to compete successfully in export markets but in many productivity remains considerably below the British level. This is partly a reflection of the problem of catering for a small home market which yet demands a considerable range of products.

15. Apart from questions of efficiency of plant, management and labour, one reason for relatively high production costs is that the home

market for many types of goods is too small to support industry on a scale which would enable goods to be produced at prices competitive with those of British and Continental products. To enlarge their scale of output manufacturers have been encouraged—by tax incentives, technical assistance and the specialist services of Córas Tráchtála, Teoranta—to develop and expand their exports.

16. It has been necessary to make the case in the preliminary negotiations with regard to the proposed European Free Trade Area that, if Ireland becomes a member of the Area, she should be dispensed from undertaking in full the obligations of membership until her economy has attained a satisfactory relationship with those of the more highly industrialised members. It is obviously essential not only that existing industries should become progressively more efficient but also that new industries should be competitive in export markets and capable of withstanding the challenge presented by the Free Trade Area.

Tourism

17. During the five years 1953-1957, gross earnings from tourism and travel have averaged £31½ million a year and the net income from this source, i.e., after deducting expenditure abroad by Irish tourists, is the largest item in the country's net invisible earnings, having averaged £19½ million per annum, or approximately one-third of total net invisible earnings. Dollar earnings could be substantially increased by the further development of the industry; at present approximately 20% of the annual income from tourism comes from American visitors to this country. Indeed, earnings generally—from Britain and the Continent as well as America—could be substantially increased. Tourism provides considerable employment, mainly in the transport, hotel and catering, and entertainment industries, but also for the many thousands who are engaged in meeting the needs of visitors by providing goods and services. There is an annual grant from public funds of up to £500,000 towards the publicity and other expenses of Bord Fáilte Éireann. Direct financial assistance to the industry is available by way of State-guaranteed loans for the provision of hotel accommodation and amenities and services at holiday resorts.

Pattern of External Trade

18. External trade is of particular importance in the Irish economy, imports and exports forming a high percentage of national income and expenditure. The external trade pattern possesses two well-defined characteristics. One is that, while imports come from a wide range of countries, exports are concentrated to a very large extent on one market, the United Kingdom. Exports to that country usually account for more than 80% of total exports, while about 50% of

imports come from other countries. The second characteristic is that Ireland has each year a substantial deficit in visible trade, merchandise exports paying for about 60% of imports. This is partly the result of the need of Irish industries for imported raw materials and equipment, and the demand for imported consumer goods. It also reflects the difficulty of expanding an export trade which consists, to some 75%, of agricultural products (including processed items). Almost all of these are exported to the United Kingdom, a country which itself gives very considerable encouragement to the development of its domestic agriculture and which has important external sources of supply other than Ireland.

19. While the present position has its advantages, it is desirable that efforts should be made in future development to expand the range of exports and widen their distribution. In 1956 there was a gratifying increase in exports to non-sterling O.E.E.C. countries, the total of £11.0 million being about double the figure for the previous year. The trade was almost maintained in 1957 despite a fall of £1.7 million in exports to France caused by measures taken by the French Government to ease balance of payments difficulties. Exports to Germany and Italy, in particular, showed further substantial increases in 1957. It is hoped that this represents a trend towards increasing diversity of exports and export markets.

Balance of Payments

20. Generally, it has been only in wartime, when imports were severely curtailed but exports of cattle and foodstuffs continued, that Ireland has had surpluses in her balance of payments and in this way built up external assets. During the inter-war years there was a slight tendency to run down those assets and from 1947 to 1956 balance of payments deficits more than offset the surpluses earned during the last war.

21. Visible exports in recent years have fallen short of imports by an amount of the order of £70 million a year—an average which conceals substantial fluctuations. The gap has to some extent been bridged by tourists' expenditure, income from Ireland's external assets, emigrants' remittances and other receipts but deficits in the balance of payments occurred, in varying amounts, in each of the years 1947 to 1956 inclusive. These deficits were financed by drawing on sterling accumulated as forced savings during the war and by incurring dollar (i.e., Marshall Aid) and other indebtedness.

22. A balance in external payments was, however, achieved in the financial year ended 31st March, 1957, and maintained in the following

15

year, largely as a result of increased exports of cattle. There was a surplus of about £9 million in the balance of payments in the calendar year 1957, the first surplus since 1946. The precarious and unsatisfactory nature of the present balance has already been referred to in Chapter 1, paragraph 11.

23. The economy must be protected from any undue loss of external resources, particularly from their wasteful use merely to support consumption in excess of current production. The aim should be not just to maintain a balance but to bring external payments into line at a higher level of employment and economic activity.

Savings and Investment

24. Apart from being relatively small in amount, the figures of current savings in Ireland show considerable variations from year to year. Their smallness is due to the moderate level of most individual incomes and to the fact that company profits constitute a smaller percentage of national income than in many other countries. Both as regards amount and variability savings are affected by external as well as internal influences. International insecurity and the growing consciousness of the progressive depreciation in the value of money are tending everywhere to disturb and discourage private saving. Collective provision, through social insurance and assistance, for personal contingencies such as unemployment, ill-health, widowhood and old age, has weakened former incentives to individual saving. Apart from this, savings appear to fluctuate not only with variations in the volume and distribution of *national* income but also in sympathy with savings trends in neighbouring countries.

25. The resources supplied by current savings for investment are, consequently, limited, so limited, indeed, that over the eight years 1949 to 1956 current savings fell short by £172 million—or 40%—of covering net domestic capital formation. This shortage was made good by external borrowing (Marshall Aid Loan), investment by externs, and disinvestment. It is only current savings that add to national capital. External borrowing and disinvestment must be subtracted from net domestic capital formation in order to arrive at the true rate of formation of *national* capital. This has been disappointingly low by comparison with other European countries and is one of the reasons why Ireland's rate of material progress has been much below the European average. To illustrate the disparity between capital formation in Ireland and the rest of Europe the following indices may be quoted:

16

	Gross domestic capital formation at constant market prices		Gross domestic *fixed* capital formation (excluding changes in stocks) at constant market prices		Gross national product at constant market prices	
	1949	1956	1949	1956	1949	1956
Ireland	100	94	100	122	100	108
Britain and the Six Counties ...	100	152	100	142	100	121
All O.E.E.C. countries ...	100	158	100	163	100	142

26. Private, as distinct from public, investment has so far been insufficient to establish a reasonable level of economic activity. The Government has undertaken a large-scale investment programme to complete housing and hospital building needs and to provide for electricity development (including rural electrification), turf production, agricultural development, afforestation, tourism, etc. It was of the nature of this investment, which has constituted over one-half of total gross fixed capital formation in recent years, that a great part of it should be mainly of a social rather than of a directly productive character. In the last five years only about one-third of investment by public authorities can be regarded as giving a direct financial return roughly commensurate with the cost of borrowing. The low level of current savings and the depletion of available external reserves make for difficulty in achieving the higher rate of directly productive investment, private and public, which is necessary if the rate of economic advance is to be accelerated.

II. PRINCIPAL DEFECTS AND POTENTIALITIES

27. The more detailed study which will be made later of the agricultural and industrial situation will bring out more clearly the principal defects in the present state of the economy and the principal means by which they might be remedied. The foregoing necessarily brief outline does, however, point to the following as the main anxieties:

(1) Since 1951 emigration has been proceeding at a rate which not merely neutralises the natural increase but actually causes a net drop in population, with depressing psychological and economic effects.

(2) The rate of increase in real national income is much lower than in Britain and in Europe generally, a fact which reinforces the tendency to emigrate.

(3) Savings are small and irregular and even the low rate of domestic capital formation in the past would not have been achieved but for the use of external reserves which are now greatly depleted.

17

(4) Domestic investment is not directed sufficiently towards immediately productive purposes. Private enterprise investment is
inadequate to maintain a high level of employment and
economic activity and public authority investment has hitherto
been predominantly social in character.

(5) In association with the foregoing are to be found relatively high
taxation and low productivity, insufficient training in management and supervision, excessive restrictionism and inadequate
technical knowledge.

28. On the other hand, the principal conditions of improvement
might be summarised as follows:

(1) The building up of national capital as a basis for the improvement of employment opportunities and living standards depends
(a) on the most productive use of savings and (b) on an increase
in savings.

(2) Saving and economic production should be encouraged. As
saving is largely a function of income, this means primarily
that enterprise and development of a *productive* character
should be stimulated so that real national income may be
enlarged.

(3) The raising of output in agriculture and industry should have
a much higher priority than at present in the allocation of
savings. The utmost use should be made of means of raising
output which are sparing of capital so as to make savings go
as far as possible and thus relieve the immediate sacrifice in
consumption.

29. In effect, this means that public and private development of
a productive character must be stimulated and organized so as largely
to replace the non-productive investment which bulks so largely at
present in *public* investment and, therefore, in national capital formation. This is not to say that it is a matter for the State or public bodies
alone to initiate or execute development projects. There are projects
that must be organized by such authorities and financed, in whole or
in part, from public funds. But it would be wrong to rely on public
investments being found which would be both productive and, at the
same time, adequate to sustain a high rate of economic progress. It
would, indeed, be impossible for Departments of State or other public
authorities to visualise more than a fraction of the future possibilities
of productive development. One would naturally expect the principal
source of new productive ideas, in a predominantly free enterprise
economy, to be the private sector, enlarged by imported enterprise,
organizational ability and technical competence, and the principal
function of the State to be that of stimulating such ideas and helping

18

to bring them to fruition by the provision, where necessary, of capital, fiscal incentives and other facilities.

30. To provide the capital necessary for productive development, whether public or private, the volume of current savings must be not merely maintained but increased. At the same time, the maximum amount of capital must be released for productive purposes by a reduction in non-productive and inadequately productive investment. The opportunity for this switch will occur in part automatically, in view of the inevitable decline in social investment according as needs are met, but it must be fully grasped and reinforced by a positive curtailment of non-productive capital outlay if real progress is to be made. As a result of the heavy public outlay in the past, an extensive social infrastructure has been provided. The serious economic harm caused by the unproductive use of scarce capital renders it imperative to concentrate in future on productive development. Otherwise, the ever-higher taxation necessary to finance rapidly increasing deadweight debt charges will make further inroads on incomes and savings, industry and trade will be deprived of both the capital and the incentive to pursue a vigorous programme of modernisation and expansion, the gap between living standards at home and elsewhere will be widened, and the attractions of emigration will be increased.

31. According as social investment declines, the problem will arise of finding employment of a productive nature to compensate for the inevitable reduction in employment in the construction of houses, hospitals, etc. It cannot, of course, be expected that productive schemes, whether private or public, will be such as to absorb *in each particular locality* the labour disemployed as a result of reductions in social capital outlay. Employment opportunities will disappear in some areas or occupations and re-appear in others. In this matter, the country as a whole must be regarded as an economic entity and policy must aim at a general improvement in economic and social conditions. The only feasible course is gradually to withdraw resources from non-productive works and make them available for productive investment, thus softening the impact of the inevitable adjustment in employment conditions in particular areas and occupations. The aim must be to maintain and, if possible, increase economic activity *as a whole* thus ensuring a progressive improvement in the real national product and therefore in permanent employment and the general standard of living.

32. Ireland has the significant advantages of political stability, a plentiful labour supply, ample power resources and an extensive transport system. The infrastructure is already there; it is physical output per head which is most in need of stimulation and development. There is no royal road to success in this matter. The complex conditions

19

ot economic progress have already been mentioned in Chapter 1, paragraph 18; they include better education, more efficient management and a greater will to work, as well as increased capitalisation. The various measures already adopted with a view to encouraging investment in Irish enterprise are summarised in Appendix 2. It will be necessary to consider whether these go far enough. It is, in any event, clear that, apart from capital, technical advice and assistance will be needed not alone to ensure generally that future investment will be fully productive but also in connection with specific proposals. It is expected that the World Bank, the O.E.E.C. and our Capital Investment Advisory Committee will advise on these topics.

33. In general, however, it would seem that attention should be concentrated primarily on raising the efficiency and volume of production in agriculture and in industries based on agriculture. Otherwise, there is little chance of avoiding economic stagnation and a continual loss in population. The measures already in force—extensive and costly though they are—have not succeeded in increasing agricultural output at a satisfactory rate or on a fully economic basis. The provision on a wider scale and the wholehearted acceptance by farmers of expert technical advice and assistance is needed. Means will have to be found to secure increased use of fertilisers, improvement of grasslands, more efficient and extensive use of home-grown feeding stuffs for conversion into export products, the reduction of costs and prices through increased yields and better marketing arrangements. It is necessary to re-examine existing measures of financial assistance in order to relate them more directly to increased and more efficient production. Separate chapters are devoted later to matters such as these.

34. At this point, it need only be emphasised that, if an increase in agricultural production at competitive prices were achieved, the purchasing power of the farming community would be greatly raised and their demand for goods and services stimulated. The effect of this in creating additional employment in industry and services is vitally important because the possibilities of absorbing labour in agriculture are limited. Indeed, the provision of lasting employment turns on the concurrent development of manufacturing industry (mainly for export) and of tertiary industries, particularly tourism. But all this can be set in motion by improvements in agriculture, where the immediate potentialities of increased production are very great.

CHAPTER 3

FINANCIAL AND MONETARY POLICY

1. Financial and monetary policy should help and stimulate development. In our circumstances this means that it should favour saving, encourage enterprise and discourage excessive consumption.

2. High taxation is one of the greatest impediments to economic progress because of its adverse effects on saving and on enterprise. Inequity may add to the disincentive effect of taxation but, broadly speaking, it is only income tax which has been criticised as inequitable in Ireland. The whole question of the taxation of incomes and profits is being examined at present by a special Commission. All that need be said here is that taxation (central and local government and extrabudgetary funds) is high, amounting in 1957 to some 27% of national income, and it is only by reducing it that inequities and other defects can be removed. Specific reliefs and " incentives " are a poor substitute for a general reduction in taxation and are apt to lend support to charges of inequity.

3. High taxation is necessitated by high expenditure and can be reduced only if expenditure is reduced or if taxable incomes are raised (e.g., by productive investment) and the cost of current services is at the same time held rigidly in check. To understand why taxation has been rising continuously it is necessary to analyse budgetary trends since, say, 1950. Unless we know what forces are pushing up expenditure—and check those forces—there is obviously no hope of bringing down or even stabilising the level of taxation.

4. Between 1950-51 and 1957-58 there has been a net increase of £49 million in current State expenditure. The main items responsible for this increase are:

	£ million
Service of Debt	15.70
Social Services	12.76
Remuneration	10.36
Health	4.75
Agricultural Price Supports	4.14
Roads	2.87
Pensions	2.12
Railways	2.11
Agricultural Grant	1.57
Education	1.00
Defence	0.69

21

The main offsetting reduction is Food Subsidies—£10.85 million. Full particulars of increases and reductions are given in Appendix 3.

5. It will be noted that the service of debt is the largest single item, accounting for 32% of the net increase. The growth in debt service charges is, in the main, the result of heavy capital outlay—a feature of which has been that, for the most part, it does not yield either a direct or an indirect return to the Exchequer sufficient to cover the cost of borrowing. The increase in social services is associated partly with the withdrawal of food subsidies and partly with the general rise in prices. The increase in remuneration is the direct effect of the extension to State-paid employees of the wage and salary increases which have occurred at such frequent intervals in outside employment.

6. Part of the net increase of £49 million in expenditure has been covered by increased non-tax revenue, which, of course, includes an increase in the return received from State assets and advances. Some £32 million had, however, to be raised from taxation, mainly under the following heads:

	£ million
Tobacco	8.98
Oils	7.78
Income tax, Surtax and Corporation Profits Tax	7.71
Beer	3.57
Road Tax	2.87
Motor Cars and Parts	0.78
Stamp Duties	0.35
Betting Duty	0.30
Entertainments Duty	0.25
Death Duties	0.23

There have been the following increases—amongst others—in taxation: a rise of 1/- in the standard rate of income tax, extensive increases in death duties on estates in ranges over £12,500 and net additional duties of 1/7¼d. per gallon on petrol, 5½d. a glass on spirits, 1/- on 20 cigarettes and 3d. a pint on beer. These heavy impositions, combined with the effect of increases in trading costs and margins, have brought taxation ever closer to the point of diminishing returns. The increase in incomes which would cause a natural buoyancy in revenue has been largely wanting. Indeed, the limit of taxable capacity has been reached in some directions and it is difficult to see any method by which additional revenue on a substantial scale could be raised without injurious effects on employment and on economic activity in general. A general purchase tax, for instance, would have an immediate reaction on sales of Irish products and would probably, in the end, have inflationary effects on wages and salaries and the cost of living. It is desirable that taxes on spending should bear most heavily on less essential imports as this helps to ensure the retention at home of as much as possible of the stimulating effect of capital formation on employment.

7. Unless our taxation is relatively light this country can scarcely hope to attract foreign capital, enterprise and organisational competence. Not alone does rising expenditure preclude a general reduction in the rates of taxation on incomes and profits but it presses steadily upwards the existing high level of taxation generally. It has already upset the traditionally advantageous relationship between this country and Britain as regards the incidence of taxation on individual incomes.

The following are outstanding differences:

(i) In Britain child allowance may, depending on the age of the child, be £100, £125 or £150 per child. In Ireland the allowance is £100 flat.

(ii) The maximum allowance for earned income is £1,550 in Britain as compared with £400 here.

(iii) The starting point for sur-tax liability is £2,000 in Britain as compared with £1,500 here.

(iv) Certain allowances, viz., child, housekeeper and dependent relative and, for a married man, the difference (£100) between the single and married personal allowance, are granted in Britain against sur-tax liability but not in Ireland.

These differences—despite the higher *standard* rate of tax in Britain —have the following results:

(1) a married man with children may be liable for less tax in Britain than in Ireland at all earned income levels up to £10,000, and

(2) in Britain a man with a wife and three children between 11 and 16 begins to pay sur-tax when he has over £2,475 a year, whereas here he becomes liable to sur-tax when he passes £1,500.

Finally, it may be remarked that for a married man with two children over 11 and not over 16 the Irish rates of income tax and sur-tax result in *higher taxation of earned income in the whole range £2,000 to £10,000 per annum than in Britain, the United States, Canada and Australia.*

8. The adverse influence of taxation on the disposition of wealthy foreigners to live here (and spend money, give employment, interest themselves in local development, etc.) is not confined to income taxation alone. It extends also to death duties. Legacy and succession duties were abolished in Britain in 1949. They apply on a scale rising to 10% here. Estate Duty rates were increased in 1951 to 53% on the

largest estates as compared with 60% to 80% in Britain. Formerly the Irish rates on estates exceeding £250,000 in value ranged from 36.4% to 41.6% and the narrowing of the differential has made a big difference in the attitude of many people towards living here. It should also be noted that Estate Duty rates are higher here than in the Six Counties on dutiable estates with valuations up to £4,000 and between £10,000 and £85,000. Representations have been made to the effect that the State may well lose substantial amounts of estate duties and sur-tax through emigration of wealthy residents if the present system continues. Hopes of reducing taxation are, however, being thwarted by the yearly increase in debt service and other charges. As a result, not only is the entry of foreign capital, enterprise and experience being discouraged but home industry and trade are being deprived, by high taxation, of the capital and incentive to pursue a vigorous programme of modernisation and expansion, a matter of particular concern because of the adjustments required by the prospects of freer trade in Europe.

9. Gross debt service already accounts for almost 20% of the total current expenditure of the Central Government, the various social services and subsidies for 30%, and pay and pensions for a similar amount. The whole of the expenditure of the Social Insurance Fund and most of the expenditure of local authorities is of a social character. In other words, the current budgets of the State and public authorities generally are much more concerned with redistributing the national income than with increasing it.

10. The way towards stabilisation and eventual reduction of taxation clearly lies:

(a) in moderating the growth in *debt service charges* by reducing the proportion of non-productive, and increasing the proportion of productive, projects in total public investment;

(b) in curbing the increase in *administrative charges*, i.e., increases in pay and pensions should be offset, in great part, by better organisation of the public services, increased productivity and other economies;

(c) in deferring further improvements in the *social services* until a steady growth in real national income is well established. If resources are being used to the maximum to provide productive employment and raise all-round living standards it is impossible to devote them at the same time to improvements in social welfare—the national candle cannot be burned at both ends;

(d) in keeping *subsidies* to a minimum, using them, even to promote production, only where their temporary support is clearly necessary to secure a significant and permanent increase in economic production. Subsidies, whether in the form of direct grants or of tax reliefs, have to be paid for by general charges on the community which are a deterrent to enterprise and economic progress. There is no sector of the economy strong enough not merely to advance itself but to carry another sector permanently on its back;

(e) in directing public expenditure as far as possible into productive channels and in taking advantage of every opportunity of effecting economies.

The positive objective of financial policy must be to arrive as quickly as possible at the point at which it will be possible to give the economy the tonic of a significant reduction, above all, in direct taxes on incomes, profits and savings. This should take precedence over any reduction in indirect taxes (particularly those which bear on less essential imports) and over any increase in expenditure which does not directly promote increased national output at competitive prices. Until unproductive outlay is reduced and resources are set free for productive enterprise by means of lower taxation we can hope for little in the way of economic progress.

11. The Irish economy cannot be insulated against outside economic and financial influences. It will have to reckon not only with freer trade in Europe but with the effects of variations in the level of British—and American—prosperity and employment. These variations may have a big impact on the volume of demand, and the prices paid, for Irish exports and in this and other ways, seriously affect Irish incomes and employment. There is very little we can do about this : prosperity, like peace, is indivisible and no one country, and certainly not a small one, can escape the consequences of a recession in the bigger economies. There are, however, two consolations: (1) we will share in any *improvement* in world prosperity because of its effect on the demand for meat and other exports and (2) the major economies will do their best to maintain a high and steady rate of material progress —their Governments are all committed to policies of full employment.

12. It is, of course, conditions in Britain that will affect us most. We have a vested interest in British prosperity. Even if we had not, we would have no right to criticise financial policies which are aimed at strengthening the British economy, even if at times we may regret the indirect influence of some policy measures (e.g. in the matter of interest rates) on financial conditions here. The maintenance, on the one hand, of the value and acceptability of sterling as an international medium of payment and, on the other, of the availability of ample domestic credit is of greater significance to us than the adverse effect

on productive development of high interest rates. This adverse effect can easily be exaggerated. Interest is generally not of great consequence in production costs and high interest rates have not prevented Germany, for instance, from achieving a vast expansion in production and prosperity. The upward trend over the past few years in interest rates is, in any case, a world-wide reflection of capital scarcity. The accentuation of this trend in Britain is due to special policy measures taken to protect sterling. This accentuated or artificial raising of interest rates is costly to Britain herself because of her enormous short-term liabilities in sterling and will not be maintained for longer than is necessary (*vide* the March, 1958, reduction of 1% in Bank of England Rate). Despite the freedom of movement of funds between the two areas and the overlapping of banks it has been possible to keep the deposit and lending rates of the Irish banks from rising to the same extent as in Britain. It must not be forgotten, however, that we have only limited scope for manoeuvre in the matter of interest rates. We can achieve no more than a temporary curbing of a trend, a temporary easing or deferment of its impact. Even if we were quite alone in the world, interest rates here would be high so long as savings are deficient in relation to the demand for capital.

13. If it is true, as is sometimes suggested (rather against the more recent evidence), that a limited degree of inflation is a necessary condition of economic progress in under-developed countries, we are not hampered, in this respect, by any constricting external forces. In fact, we have enjoyed what many would regard as excessive inflationary scope. Our currency policy, as determined by statute, is not the maintenance of the internal value of the Irish pound but the safeguarding of its parity with sterling. So far, sterling, to a greater extent than the dollar, deutschemark and certain other currencies, has been a depreciating currency. The statutory test has, therefore, not been a harsh one; our continuing to satisfy it depends on our not incurring excessive deficits in our balance of payments. Given the latitude by our currency arrangements of inflating as fast as Britain, the responsibility of not inflating faster, that is of avoiding dangerous deficits in our external payments, is all the heavier. Financial policy should be such as will maintain a high level of productive activity without jeopardising the exchange value of our currency. Prudence, indeed, demands that we should not confine our attention to the maintenance of parity with sterling; we should bear in mind the need to strengthen our competitive position in the markets of countries whose currencies may depreciate less than sterling.

14. Special reference must be made in this context to wages and salaries. The two to one ratio between average income per head in Britain and Ireland is due to our poorer natural resources and to such

factors as the higher proportion of small farmers with low average incomes in Ireland rather than to any general depression in Irish wages and salaries. In fact, in some trades, wage rates tend to be higher in Ireland than in England. Generally, however, because of smaller scale of output, lower productivity and less overtime working, *earnings* in Irish industry are lower than in England. Salaries, as a whole, are also below British standards. The raising of incomes in Ireland will primarily, however, be a matter of raising farm incomes through increased output at lower unit costs. The effect will be to increase the demand for the products of Irish industries and services. The opportunities for the expansion of industrial production and employment will not be fully realised unless labour costs per unit of output are low enough to make the price of the product competitive in world markets. To ensure competitive costs per unit of output it may be necessary to accept for a time lower wages rates than in Britain, however efficiently production may be organised or however modern the capital equipment may be. Economic expansion could be seriously hindered both by restrictive practices on the part of trade unions and by insistence on frequent and indiscriminate increases in wages and salaries exceeding any benefit from increases in productivity and causing a general rise in production costs. These are amongst the greatest inflationary forces and are a constant threat to the balance of payments. The rise in production costs tends to lessen export and employment prospects, while the rise in money incomes tends to cause increased expenditure on imports. The success of any policy of economic development will depend on the effective and continuous co-operation of the trade unions in promoting increased productivity and in avoiding increases in wages and salaries which would injure export prospects or dislocate the balance of payments. The unions should be concerned, not with the cost-of-living index, but with whether their members are sharing fairly, either through lower prices or through higher wages, in the improvement in *real* national income. The pamphlet, *Planning Full Employment*, issued by the Provisional United Trade Union Organisation is evidence of the Organisation's interest in the broader aspect of economic development and of its awareness that problems must be tackled in a realistic manner.

15. Credit may be an inflationary force and has, therefore, to be kept within proper bounds. But it has an important part to play in economic development. As to the rôle of the commercial banks:

(i) Their first obligation is to stay solvent. As they finance our trade and hold our " front line " external reserves, this means not only that their liabilities to depositors should be fully covered by earning assets but that their liquid reserves should be adequate in relation to deposits. Experience and expert opinion confirm that, in relation to deposits within Ireland, a net external assets ratio of 30% represents no more than a " minimum safe level " for the commercial banks as a whole. In practice, the ratio may vary for individual banks because, e.g., of variations in the proportion of their current to their deposit accounts.

(ii) The banks should use increases in their resources to expand their domestic advances and investments if there is an unsatisfied demand for credit for productive purposes, rather than to build up a global external reserve ratio *in excess* of 30%.* Interest-bearing balances with the Central Bank (see paragraph 16 (ii)) would rank as the equivalent of external reserves in assessing this ratio. On the other hand, if the ratio tends to fall below 30% a tightening of bank credit must be expected and must be accepted as a corrective to the balance of payments drain which is causing the fall in liquid assets. It must not be forgotten that fluctuations in our balance of payments can, as experience teaches, be both sudden and severe and that the reserves of the commercial banks are exposed to the first impact of such fluctuations.

(iii) While a 30% ratio is a minimum with banking organised as at present, there may be some scope for lowering the ratio and freeing additional resources for domestic development by the strengthening of banking organisation through bank amalgamations. Amalgamations should be facilitated by legislation as they would tend, in any event, towards lower bank lending rates as a result of the elimination of redundant branches and the reduction of overhead costs generally.

(iv) The commercial banks (and insurance companies) should join the State in providing long-term capital for industry through the Industrial Credit Company. In this respect a very commendable first step was taken by the banks this year.

(v) The commercial banks as a whole (rather than the State) should provide the capital required for private agricultural development, either through the Agricultural Credit Corporation or through their own branches. As custodians of the savings of farmers they are the natural source of credit for agriculture and by reason of their intimate local knowledge are in the best position to operate a flexible credit system.

(vi) The banks' aim should be to make credit available on the most liberal terms possible consistent with retaining the goodwill of depositors and preserving their own solvency.

16. In the field of central banking the desiderata may be listed as follows : —

* Fluctuations within, say, 27-33% might be regarded as normal and those outside that range as requiring corrective action.

28

(i) There should be the closest liaison between the Central Bank and the Minister for Finance so that by constant consultation and collaboration effect may be given to a financial policy favouring development to the utmost but avoiding any significant deficit in the balance of payments. If our external account were being kept in order but productive development were in danger of being frustrated by a shortage of capital from home sources, the Central Bank might consider it unnecessary to continue building up the " second-line " external reserves in the Legal Tender Note Fund, i.e., future increases in the note issue could be backed by Irish Government securities. It will be remembered, in this context, that Ireland's subscription to the International Monetary Fund gives her access, on favourable terms, to an overdraft facility of $60 million to meet temporary balance of payments difficulties.

(ii) It should be arranged that, for clearing purposes, the commercial banks would deposit a substantial proportion of their liquid sterling funds with the Central Bank in the form of *interest-bearing* balances repayable in Irish currency. The interest paid should be such that the commercial banks would not suffer loss by reason of keeping their liquid reserves mainly with the Central Bank rather than in London. As much as possible of the clearing of cheques between banks should be effected by drawing on the deposits with the Central Bank, which should itself act like a London discount house by investing these deposits on a short-term basis. It is understood that a proposal for the settlement of bank clearing balances through the Central Bank is being actively pursued by the Central Bank with the Irish Banks' Standing Committee.*

(iii) The change outlined in (ii) would increase the resources available to the Central Bank for the exercise of the rediscount functions, under section 7 of the Central Bank Act, 1942, by which it can fortify, on a temporary basis, the reserve ratios of the commercial banks. An increase in the resources of the General Fund of the Central Bank is particularly desirable in view (a) of the imminent depletion of the existing resources of that Fund through the reduction of the Grant Counterpart deposit, (b) of the growing need of the commercial banks for rediscount facilities to ensure the liquidity of Exchequer Bills, Government securities generally and trade bills and (c) of the reduction in the banks' independent sterling reserves which the change would necessarily entail. The question whether the new arrangement can facilitate maximum economic progress without balance of payments difficulties should be fully tested before

* Arrangements came into operation on 1st November, 1958 for the settlement of domestic clearances through the Central Bank.

any consideration is given to encroaching upon the existing reserves of the Legal Tender Note Fund. If, however, the proposal regarding commercial bank deposits with the Central Bank is not made effective, it would be desirable that some portion of the existing sterling reserves of the Legal Tender Note Fund be made available to augment the resources of the General Fund.

(iv) Generally, in the matter of central banking, evolution rather than revolution should be the guiding principle.

17. The extent to which the foregoing suggestions might free resources for domestic capital formation is considered in Chapter 4.

18. Improvements in banking, however desirable in principle, can be safely introduced only if all concerned act always in a reasonable manner and with the country's long-term interest in mind. It must be realised that the availability of credit will not of itself activate development and that the exercise of financial responsibility may require unpopular measures of restriction as often as it admits of liberality and expansion.

CHAPTER 4

DEVELOPMENT RESOURCES AND NEEDS

General

1. Productive enterprises will not be started merely because capital is available. But they cannot be carried through without capital. Even though money may be a lubricant rather than a prime-mover, no programme of development can be regarded as realistic which is not founded on a reasonable assessment of the resources likely to be available to finance it. An assessment of this kind is by no means an easy matter. It involves predictions about the course of savings and the availability of external capital to which no certainty can be attached. But, whatever the difficulties and uncertainties, the assessment must be made.

2. The approach adopted has been to make optimistic but still, it is hoped, reasonable assumptions as regards the probable availability of capital, whether from home or external sources. The need for economic expansion is too great to excuse the rejection of any productive development prospects merely because it is not absolutely certain that the necessary capital will be available from home sources. The emphasis, of course, is on "*productive development*". There is no doubt that a list of extremely doubtful or wasteful projects could be made, calling for much more capital than the community is ever likely to have at its disposal, or could afford to service if spent in that way. This study, however, is concerned only with objects of capital expenditure offering a fair prospect of being productive and beneficial to the national economy. For projects of this kind every effort must be made to raise the necessary capital: it would be justifiable to borrow from abroad if internal resources were inadequate. It would seem, indeed, that the real risk is not that excessive capital indebtedness may be incurred but rather that the scale on which worthwhile projects are set in motion may not, for some years at least, be large enough to satisfy the general desire for increased employment and living standards. At the outset productive ideas may well be scarcer than capital. As a momentum of productive development got under way, however, a more favourable psychological atmosphere would develop, more faith would be shown in the country's future, there would be a greater readiness to take risks and initiate new enterprises, while, at the same time, a greater supply of capital might be expected to accrue from current savings.

31

3. To measure the probable supply of capital to meet development needs over the next five years, it is necessary to examine the prospects under the following heads:

(i) current savings;

(ii) external reserves and investments; and

(iii) external borrowing.

This is done seriatim in the remainder of this chapter. Attention is then given to the no less important questions of:

(a) the possible development needs of the private, as distinct from the public, sector; and

(b) the extent to which the capital which may be available for the public sector can be reserved for *productive* projects, allowing both for automatic and for deliberate reduction of non-productive public investment.

The general principle observed throughout is that, consistent with reasonable social outlay, there should be the *maximum* of productive development, private and public, so as to secure the highest possible level of useful employment and economic activity. At the same time, the need for economy in the use of capital is stressed, some general suggestions being offered in this context. At this point attention is being confined to capital, although, as indicated earlier, other things, including enterprise and education, hard work, technical skill and good management, may be no less essential to national development.

4. Lest there should be any feeling that to the three sources of capital mentioned in paragraph 3 a fourth should be added, namely, credit creation, it is well to dispel this notion right away, because this cannot be an independent source of capital. Resources could be raised in this way only at the expense of one or more of the three ways specified in paragraph 3. Credit creation cannot be a real source of capital except by setting idle resources to work or by attracting resources from consumption. The second of these is covered by "current savings". Setting idle resources to work would, in our circumstances, lead immediately to increased imports. If balance of payments deficits were caused, they could be financed only by drawing on external capital or by incurring external debt.

Savings

5. No estimate of the future course of savings can safely be made without regard to the actual trend in recent years. First, however, it is necessary to be clear as to what is meant by savings. In general, savings represent the excess of income over what

is spent on current consumption. This is clear enough for the individual, whatever about the difficulty of measuring the excess. The savings of corporate enterprises are their undistributed profits after provision for depreciation (as allowed for tax purposes) and after payment of tax. Increases in the life funds of insurance companies are regarded as part of personal savings. So also is the value of any increase in livestock numbers on farms and of the physical increase in stocks held by unincorporated businesses. Whenever one is concerned about *monetary* savings, however, it is necessary to exclude savings which take the *physical* form of increases in stocks, whether of animals or of goods.

SAVINGS, 1938 AND 1947/57

	Savings and Provision for Stock Appreciation				Less Stock Appreciation	Current Savings
	Personal	Public and Private Companies	Public Authorities	Total		
	£ million					
1938	7·4	4·7	3·0	15·1	n.a.	15·1
1947	2·8	10·0	4·5	17·3	—7·1	10·2
1948	9·5	10·2	5·1	24·8	—0·3	24·5
1949	16·4	12·7	5·0	34·1	—0·8	33·3
1950	11·7	14·7	3·6	30·0	—13·0	17·0
1951	7·7	14·6	—5·0	17·3	—18·8	—1·5
1952	30·6	12·0	1·6	44·2	—1·3	42·9
1953	43·2	14·2	—3·8	53·6	+2·9	56·5
1954	31·4	15·6	—3·5	43·5	+0·9	44·4
1955	20·4	14·3	—2·1	32·6	—3·3	29·3
1956	27·2	13·4	—1·5	39·1	—7·0	32·1
1957	48	15	—2	61	—6	55
Total 1947/57	248·9	146·7	1·9	397·5	—53·8	343·7

The deduction for "stock appreciation" is in line with the similar deduction made in computing national income and is made for the following reason. As income in the accounting (as distinct from the national income) sense is taken to include any increase at the end, as compared with the beginning, of a year in the value of an unchanged volume of stocks, savings would also include this "stock appreciation" element if it were not positively excluded. The deduction for "stock appreciation" is, therefore, made to ensure that only the value of any increase in the *physical* volume of stocks is reckoned as "savings". It may also be desirable to explain that saving (or, as is more usual, dissaving) by public authorities is measured by setting their current revenue against their expenditure on *current* goods and services, subsidies and transfer payments. A saving in this sense could occur if, for instance, the deficit on current account were less than the allocations out of current revenue for redemption of debt.

33

6. The table brings out clearly a point already touched upon in Chapter 2, namely, the irregularity in total savings. They range from a dissaving of £1.5 million in 1951, which was an exceptional year in many respects, to savings of £56.5 million in 1953. The table shows, moreover, that fluctuations in personal savings are almost entirely responsible for this irregularity. Even if savings in monetary form only are considered, the irregularity still persists, as the following figures for recent years show:—

Current Savings (exclusive of changes in stocks)

			£ million
1953	...	...	50.0
1954	...	....	49.6
1955	...	...	19.3
1956	...	...	40.1
1957 (provisional)	...		56

The average of monetary savings for these five years was £43 million but, if the two preceding years (1951 and 1952) are included, the average is reduced to £36 million. Figures for certain categories of monetary savings are given in Appendix 4 and these give the following totals for 1953 to 1957:

			£ million
1953	...	...	42.4
1954	...	...	30.9
1955	...	...	23.9
1956	...	...	26.4
1957	...	...	36.0

The average by this different *and incomplete* compilation is roughly £32 million. When such great fluctuations occur, it is dangerous to rely much on averages as an indication of future possibilities. Still, as a prediction must be made, one would hope for at least £45 million of monetary savings as a yearly average for the next five years even if no improvement were secured in the average rate of increase in real national income. This would allow for the disappearance of the present exceptional surplus in the balance of payments. Indeed, if the present level of capital formation were to be maintained, it would entail the re-emergence of a small external deficit.

7. A word is necessary on the means by which savings are made available for investment. Some current savings are directly invested by the savers themselves but, for the most part, investment is done by others so that investment funds must be raised by them from the public and from the financial institutions with which the public lodges its savings. If current savings are to be effectively mobilised for capital

development, private and public, the methods adopted to raise money for capital purposes will need the full support of the public and of financial institutions. Savings are at present garnered for investment in various ways—through National Loans and other public issues of stocks and shares, through Savings Banks, Savings Certificates, Prize Bonds, Insurance Companies, Building Societies and the Commercial Banks. These are legitimate and orthodox ways of collecting savings, in contrast with the forced saving which (through budget surpluses or through deliberate inflation) is effected in some countries. All these voluntary forms of saving need to be encouraged, and uninformed criticism, e.g., of the amount and frequency of public issues, discouraged. Moreover, so far as savings accumulate in the commercial banks, it is appropriate that they should be channelled, either directly or through underwriting commitments, into Government and other public authority securities as well as into domestic advances and other investments for productive purposes.

8. Procedural matters aside, the question is whether the present low and inadequate level of savings can be raised. That it is low by West European standards requires little demonstration. The following table shows how much—or rather, how little—of our national income we, as a community, save by comparison with certain other countries:

SAVINGS AS A PROPORTION OF NATIONAL INCOME IN CERTAIN COUNTRIES

Country	1950	1951	1952	1953	1954	1955	Average 1950/55
	Percentage						
Belgium	4·4	11·3	10·9	8·1	n.a.	n.a.	8·7
Denmark	14·1	13·0	15·5	16·3	13·2	14·5	14·4
Ireland (U.N. Definition)	2·0	−3·2	8·4	10·6	7·8	4·0	4·9
Ireland (Official) ...	4·9	−0·4	10·5	12·7	9·9	6·3	7·3
Italy	12·8	13·1	9·4	10·7	12·5	14·9	12·2
Netherlands	17·1	18·6	20·6	22·9	23·5	24·2	21·2
Norway	14·8	24·2	21·4	16·5	17·7	19·8	19·1
United Kingdom ...	7·3	7·1	6·2	7·4	9·0	9·9	7·8
United States	15·0	14·5	11·2	10·2	9·0	11·4	11·9

NOTE: In the U.N. system of national accounts emigrants' remittances are considered to be a capital transfer and are not part of national income. An annual payment to the British Government, treated as a current transfer in the official figures, is considered to be a capital transfer in the U.N. system. The figures for savings derived on the basis of the U.N. definitions are, therefore, lower than the official figures by the amount of net emigrants' remittances less the annual payment to the British Government.

9. The insufficiency of our current savings as a basis for national capital formation on the scale which would be necessary to enable us even to follow, at some distance, the rising standards of living in the rest of Europe was pointed out in paragraph 25 of Chapter 2 and is

further developed in paragraph 13 of this Chapter. This overall insufficiency of savings makes it highly desirable that as great a proportion as possible should be applied to productive capital investment. While non-productive public capital investment now shows a downward trend, the level of investment in productive activities is still extremely low. Since 1953 gross fixed asset formation in industries producing transportable goods has been about £10-12 million annually. When allowance (perhaps not even adequate allowance) is made for depreciation it would appear that net fixed asset formation is about £6-7 million per annum in these industries. This low figure of net fixed asset formation in an important sector of the economy is paralleled by relatively low profits and by the virtual absorption of personal savings to finance the public capital programme. In recent years about one-half of total fixed asset formation has been financed through the Exchequer. In such circumstances, there is clearly need for a large directly-productive element in the State capital programme, whether it take the form of State enterprise or assistance to private producers.

10. The prospects of obtaining a higher level of savings in the future are not encouraging. Personal savings appear to be conditioned by the varying propensity of the community to spend rather than by any steady disposition to save. Having regard to the relatively low level of income per head compared with other West European countries, to the absence of any large body of wealthy citizens and to the growing anxiety about inflation, it will be difficult to persuade the community voluntarily to save a sufficient part of current income. Exhortations and inducements may do no more than arrest a decline.

11. Any large and sustained increase in savings is likely to result only from an increase in real national income providing the community at once with more money to spend on current consumption and with more money to save. In turn, an increase in real national income requires the productive investment of present savings to ensure the utmost expansion of productivity in industry and agriculture. Increases in industrial productivity would make additional resources available for investment both directly (through increased profits) and indirectly (by raising real incomes and savings). Increases in agricultural productivity would lead to greater savings by farmers, taking the form not only of direct investment in livestock, farm buildings, equipment, etc., but also of increased monetary savings which could be used for capital formation by other sectors of the economy. In paragraph 6 it was estimated that monetary savings would run at an average rate of £45 million during the next five years, assuming that real national income rose no faster than in recent years. Allowing for the expansionist effect on real national income of carrying out the proposals in

36

this study, it may not be too optimistic to expect that out of the addition which they will make to real income in each year £2 million will be saved. This would mean a progressive rise over the next five years in monetary savings from £45 million per annum to £55 million per annum, giving an average annual rate of £50 million.

12. The next step is to enquire how far £50 million per annum will go, assuming this level of savings is realised. It may be said, roughly speaking, that it would maintain the present level of public and private investment, without any draw on external capital or any external borrowing. In 1957, when monetary savings were £59 million, i.e., £9 million greater than the assumed annual average for the next five years, we had a surplus in the balance of payments of £9 million. In 1958 some adverse forces will be at work, including the full effects of the latest round of wage and salary increases and a probable falling-off in cattle exports. But it would be pessimistic to assume that any considerable deficit will emerge, and a savings figure of between £45 and £50 million would not be improbable. In future years, if reasonable financial and wage policies are observed, if the terms of trade do not turn markedly against us, if production does not fall off and if spending does not greatly increase, current savings, taking one year with another, may be sufficient to maintain the present amount of capital expenditure while maintaining equilibrium *over the period* in the balance of payments. It may be that the balance of payments will go wrong temporarily but, taking the five year period as a whole, fluctuations—both in external payments and in savings—may not push us much off balance. This, at any rate, is a chance we should take and we should not be frightened by any manageable deficit in the balance of payments into restricting *productive* capital investment.

13. The possibility that savings may suffice to support the *present* level of investment gives no great comfort, though it may allay some anxiety. The present level of gross investment is low by comparison with other West European countries—it represents about 12% of gross national product against an average of 20% for O.E.E.C. countries generally. Taking 1949 as starting-point, our gross national product had risen only 7½% by 1956 compared with 21% for Britain and 42% for O.E.E.C. countries generally. The rate of increase in real output here has, therefore, been only about 1% per annum compared with 5% in Western Europe generally and 2¾% in Britain. If we are not to fall further and further behind in the race for better living standards, a great increase in the yearly volume of productive investment is essential. The recent rate of increase in output is rather less than the rate at which the population would rise if fertility remained constant and emigration ceased altogether. In other words, there could never be any improvement in the present standard of living if emigra-

tion ceased and output increased only at the recent rate. A higher rate of increase in output is essential if we are even to hold the population we have, not to mention increasing it by reducing the rate of emigration. If the possibilities of increased productive investment are present and we cannot reasonably hope to finance the increase from current savings, must we abandon the effort to make Ireland a viable economic and political entity? Obviously not, so long as we can look to other possible sources of capital. It is now time to examine the possibility of recourse to (a) the external reserves and investments in Irish hands and (b) external borrowing.

External reserves and investments

14. External assets represent a particular form of past savings which (unlike savings embodied in domestic assets) can be utilised to supplement the *current* flow of goods and services produced by the economy. They can be drawn upon, subject to important qualifications, to augment current savings in the financing of domestic investment.

15. The effective repatriation of external assets involves an import of foreign goods and services and the deliberate incurring of a deficit in the balance of payments. If investment and not consumption is to benefit, this deficit must enlarge the flow of goods and services available for *capital formation*. General economic policy must try to ensure that the deficit is used to supplement rather than replace current savings, though the practical difficulty of doing so is formidable.

16. External assets fall readily into two main categories—external *investments* held by the private sector and external *reserves* held by monetary authorities. External *investments,* as long as they are not sold voluntarily by their owners, or used directly to purchase imports, are not available to finance balance of payments deficits. It is true that in so far as their owners can be induced to sell these investments sterling becomes available, either directly or through the banking system, to finance imports but it would be imprudent to base policy on the likelihood of this taking place on a significant scale.

17. External *reserves* are held by the Central Bank (£92.2 million at end 1957, including £6.3 million in the form of gold and £8.8 million in U.S. dollar securities), the commercial banks (£90.5 million) and departmental funds under the control of the Minister for Finance (£13.2 million). The total at the end of 1957 was about £196 million. Our external reserves do not compare in quality with those of many other countries. The total comprises items (e.g. long-term external securities) which in other countries are excluded from the category of reserves; and it includes some items (notably the external advances of the com-

mercial banks) which are illiquid, and others (e.g., the assets of the Legal Tender Note Fund) which are not immediately available as external reserves. Having regard in particular to the illiquid nature of some of the components, the effective (i.e. readily realisable) amount of the external reserves at the end of 1957 was of the order of £150 million.

18. Further analysis of our external reserves shows that:—

(i) the " front-line " of external reserves (i.e. those held by the commercial banks) represent approximately 30% of the banks' deposits within the State and, subject to what is said in Chapter 3, are no more than a " minimum safe level " for the commercial banking system as a whole;

(ii) the external reserves held by departmental funds have been reduced to minimal proportions and, in any event, should properly be regarded as secondary reserves since they are held primarily as a small (10%) liquidity reserve against demand liabilities—deposits in the Post Office Savings Bank and in Trustee Savings Banks, Saving Certificates and Prize Bonds;

(iii) over seven-eighths of the external reserves of the Central Bank are held in the Legal Tender Note Fund and are, therefore, not immediately available to finance external deficits as long as that Fund (in the absence of an application by the Central Bank under the Currency (Amendment) Act, 1930) is closed to domestic securities;

(iv) any relaxation of the investment provisions governing the Legal Tender Note Fund must perforce be cautious and gradual, and must take place when the balance of payments is satisfactory, if the paramount need of preserving confidence in the currency is to be served.

19. Caution is also enjoined by the fact that we have no objective criterion by which to determine whether, and, if so, to what extent, our external reserves are in excess of requirements. We know from experience that both our imports and our exports can fluctuate in an embarrassing way from year to year and that balance of payments difficulties of an acute kind can emerge suddenly.

20. It was, in effect, suggested in Chapter 3 that if *productive* development requires more capital than can be obtained from home sources, i.e., from current savings, suitable domestic assets might be accepted as backing for *future* issues of Legal Tender Notes. This proposal would obviate the immobilisation within the Legal Tender Note Fund of external reserves at present held by the commercial banks

which would otherwise have to be surrendered to the Central Bank to pay for new Legal Tender Notes. These reserves would then be available to finance external deficits incurred to step up domestic capital formation. If the note issue continues to increase at the *average* annual rate which obtained in the period from 1951 to 1957, this provision would set free external reserves amounting to some £3½ million annually—though the annual figure might, on 1951/57 experience, vary from a nominal amount to about £6 million.

External Borrowing

21. The greater part of Ireland's external indebtedness consists of assets of various kinds held in Ireland by externs. These assets include branches of foreign companies operating in Ireland, shares in companies registered in Ireland and land, houses, ground rents, land bonds, etc., owned by outside interests, mainly British. Since 1947, the State has borrowed $128 million under the European Recovery Programme (Marshall Aid) and the balance of payments figures for the years to 1954 indicate a sharp rise in external (sterling) indebtedness on private account. The indications are that the flow of external capital into this country has been reduced in the last two to three years.

22. Apart from the dollar borrowings under the European Recovery Programme, the external indebtedness of the Government comprises investment by externs in national loans and a small terminable annuity payable to the British Government under the Damage to Property (Compensation) (Amendment) Act, 1926. The Irish currency equivalent of the Marshall Aid loan at the rates of exchange in operation at the time of borrowing was £40.7 million. The devaluation of sterling in 1949 increased the Irish currency equivalent of the indebtedness to £45.8 million. The first capital repayment was made in 1956. The final payment is due in 1983. The total value of Irish Government securities held by non-residents is approximately £20 million while the outstanding liability to the British Government under the Damage to Property (Compensation) (Amendment) Act, 1926, was £3.7 million at 31st December, 1957.

23. State-sponsored bodies have for the most part sought little of their capital requirements from external sources but the shortage of domestic capital in recent years forced some of them to seek accommodation abroad. Tea Importers, Ltd., and Grain Importers succeeded in financing part of their import requirements by the discounting of bills abroad while Irish Shipping, Limited, and Bord na Móna raised small external loans. External capital has also been obtained by the Air Companies.

24. As regards future possibilities of supplementing capital

40

resources by external borrowing, the world-wide shortage of capital, which is accompanied by high lending rates, would make it extremely difficult for this country to raise funds independently on any of the world capital markets. To attract investors in the principal markets to an Irish issue a higher rate of interest would have to be offered than in the case of issues by more prosperous countries and by international financial institutions such as the World Bank. The market in an Irish security would be relatively narrow and this would tend to discourage extern subscribers. Issues in New York or Zurich would have to be underwritten and serviced in dollars and Swiss francs, respectively, and foreign commissions and the exchange risk would have to be taken into account in calculating the total service charges.

25. There are a number of specialist international lending institutions which are possible sources of capital. In particular, there is a possibility of obtaining assistance, if needed, from the World Bank which Ireland joined in August, 1957. The Bank has lent over $4,000 million to 49 countries since it began operations in 1947. The scale of its operations has been expanding in recent years. In the year ended 30th June, 1958, it lent $711 million, of which $99 million went to European countries. The interest rate charged by the Bank on its loans depends on the terms on which it can itself borrow. On the basis of its current lending rates the Bank cannot be regarded by any means as a source of cheap money. Furthermore, the Bank normally lends only the foreign exchange requirements of investment projects. Nevertheless, assistance might, with advantage to the economy, be secured from the World Bank for the financing of productive capital development. The Bank makes loans only to Governments or to other borrowers under Government guarantee. Very few loans have been made to private manufacturing firms, although the Bank in recent years has made a number of loans to private financing institutions. In principle, however, the Industrial Credit Company, which lends to private firms, would be eligible to receive loans guaranteed by the Irish Government.

26. Other possible sources of capital are the Development Loan Fund and the Export-Import Bank which are agencies of the United States Government. The Development Loan Fund was established in 1957 to assist the financing of projects, either public or private, which contribute to the economic growth of less developed countries; this assistance is granted only when capital is not otherwise available on reasonable terms. Assistance may take the form of loans or guarantees, but not of grants or direct purchase of equity securities. The Fund prefers to finance only the foreign exchange cost of a project. The aim of the Export-Import Bank is to promote American exports of capital goods and at the same time to further the political aims of the United States and the Western World in general.

41

27. Investment by *private* foreign interests will be required on a considerable scale if the policy of concentrating on the production of goods for export is to be successful. Positive steps are being taken to encourage such investment. Three years ago, the Industrial Development Authority began a drive to attract direct investment to Ireland by residents of Switzerland, Germany, Belgium, Netherlands, Britain and the U.S.A. A number of factories are in production or are being built as a result of this drive, which is continuing. The Control of Manufactures Acts have been amended to reduce the restrictions on foreign investment. The taxation and other incentives towards industrial expansion which have been introduced in recent years are available to foreigners who establish industries in Ireland. It is the policy to make arrangements to secure that foreign investors will not be liable to double taxation.

28. Exchange control presents no obstacles to external investment. Dividends, interest and profits on all investments may be freely transferred to the foreign investor's country in the appropriate currency. Capital received in foreign currency may be repatriated at any time and this right also extends to appreciation of capital.

29. In order to facilitate external private investment in Ireland the Government signed an Agreement with the United States Government in 1955 under which the United States Investment Guarantee Programme was extended to Ireland. As a result, residents in the United States investing in Ireland may obtain guarantees from the United States Government covering them against (a) the risk of inability to convert into dollars the capital invested and earnings thereon and (b) the risk of their investment being expropriated.

30. A further stimulus to private investment would be provided if Ireland joined the International Finance Corporation.* This institution is an offshoot of the World Bank and was established in 1956 to assist in the financing of private enterprise in member countries. Assistance to private enterprise by the World Bank is in effect restricted by the stipulation that its loans must be made to Governments or be backed by a Government guarantee, and the Corporation, which will conduct its business solely with private enterprise, is intended to fill this gap.

31. In the Corporation's own view its primary function is to demonstrate in concrete form that soundly conducted investment in the less-developed areas can be highly profitable, and so to stimulate the flow of private management and capital into such investment. It intends to concentrate its operations for the time being in the fields of manufac-

* Ireland became a member of the Corporation in September, 1958.

turing, processing and mining, which exert the greatest impact on employment and stimulation of associated activities.

32. Membership of the Corporation would assist the efforts at present being made to attract foreign investment to Ireland. In the first place, the possibility of obtaining financial assistance from the Corporation would encourage foreign firms to explore opportunities of profitable investment here and, secondly, the Corporation itself would help to bring these opportunities to the attention of American and other foreign industrialists seeking an outlet for their funds.

33. It is understood that Ireland would be eligible for assistance. The capital of the Corporation is, however, limited and it has responsibilities in connection with member countries in all parts of the world. By reference to the subscriptions fixed for other countries it would appear that Ireland's subscription would be of the order of $350,000.

34. The construction of the oil refinery at present proceeding in Cork represents the largest single investment in Ireland by outside interests. Three oil companies are concerned and the total investment is of the order of £12 million, including £9 million for the construction of the refinery.

35. The general arguments for external borrowing are:

(a) it enables development to go ahead more rapidly than would otherwise be possible; countries with low incomes, which leave little margin for saving, would be condemned perpetually to low standards of living in the absence of external borrowing;

(b) a factor linked to the consideration in (a), and of particular relevance to our conditions, is that technical competence and marketing technique usually accompany foreign investment;

(c) projects financed by external investment are more likely to be economically justifiable. The external lender will not normally be influenced by sentiment or by pressure to relieve social disabilities. The realistic basis on which foreign loans tend to be made is exemplified by the fact that there has been no default on any of the 214 loans so far made by the World Bank;

(d) foreign investors have a stake in the borrowing country's prosperity.

36. Against these advantages, the following disadvantages which are inherent in external borrowing should not be overlooked:

(a) it entails an exchange risk where the lender insists—as is nearly always the case—that the loan be expressed and serviced in his own currency. This risk is a real one as it is only the countries with the strongest currencies that are likely to have capital to lend abroad;

(b) unlike internal borrowing, the cost of external borrowing by the Government is not reduced by the amount of tax charged on the interest;

(c) dependence on foreign capital would involve, to a certain extent, the transfer of control of industry to foreign hands, especially when the investment takes the form of the establishment of branches by firms abroad. In the event of a trade recession involving loss of export markets the reduction in output might be concentrated on the branch establishment, especially if it should be less efficient than the parent firm;

(d) while payment of interest on internal borrowing merely re-distributes domestic real income, payment of interest on external borrowing gives command over domestic output to externs; external borrowing, therefore, unless productively invested, creates financial difficulties for the borrowing country. Experience with Marshall Aid borrowing provides a warning of this danger.

37. There can be no doubt where the balance lies in assessing these pros and cons against the background of Irish conditions. The expansion of the Irish economy in the last 30 years has depended on and has been financed in the main by national savings—current and past. These savings have not been sufficient to cope with the requirements of an under-developed economy and, at the same time, to meet the arrears of social development needs, mainly housing, which faced the State on its establishment. Investment in Ireland has for years been insufficient to ensure economic progress at even the average rate for the rest of Europe. Increased investment in productive enterprise is essential and, if sufficient capital is not available from home sources, every effort should be made to obtain it from abroad on reasonable terms. The rate of progress could be considerably accelerated by an inflow of external capital directed to types of development which would increase the country's productive capacity and which would bring with it new techniques and methods.

38. It is important to stress that any external borrowing should be spent on projects which will develop our productive capacity and sustain and strengthen our economic position and external purchasing power.

Our external account is already burdened with growing charges in respect of interest and repayments of principal on past external borrowing which must, in the last analysis, be provided out of our export earnings. Any addition to our external payments resulting from new borrowing abroad—unless offset by a corresponding increase in external earnings—would intensify our external payments difficulties and this in present circumstances would tend to curtail internal credit. Borrowing from abroad except for adequately productive projects, apart from being objectionable in itself, might result in less money being available for capital purposes from home sources.

39. In the event of external borrowing becoming necessary, it would be preferable to borrow from international institutions like the World Bank, the International Finance Corporation or any financial agency established in connection with the proposed Free Trade Area. The expert personnel of such institutions would carefully appraise all projects from the viewpoint of economic development.

Conclusions

40. Summing up, therefore, as to the prospective supply of money for capital purposes, public *and private*, it is tentatively estimated that:

(1) on average, £50 million per annum might be supplied by current savings;

(2) if (1) were insufficient to meet the demand for capital for *productive* purposes, £3½ million per annum on average might be supplied at the expense of external reserves; and

(3) supplementary capital for productive projects, to an extent not possible to define, might be supplied by external borrowing, primarily from international institutions but partly also by way of direct participation of externs in new industrial enterprises.

As the present rate of investment could be continued on the basis of (1) above, the additional capital under (2) and (3) would enable new investment to be undertaken above the present level.

41. It has been emphasised already not only that new investment should be productive but also that national progress depends on a higher proportion of existing investment being of that character. An opportunity for raising the proportion of productive investment will be afforded by the decline in existing forms of public investment over the next five years. The extent of this decline is estimated in Appendix 5. It will be seen that it is expected to average nearly £2½ million a year, dropping from £40.74 million in 1958-59 to £30.98 million in 1962-63. The fall in capital expenditure of the various transport under-

takings, which is due to completion of existing programmes, is particularly noticeable—from £6.07 million (£7.83 million in 1957-58) to £1.02 million. The decline under the heading of building and other construction is also significant, housing and allied services being the principal item accounting for the fall. Private housing needs have been largely met, while local authority housing programmes have already been completed in a number of areas and are expected to be completed in all areas outside Dublin within three or four years. Indeed, references in the course of the Dáil debate on the Local Government Estimate for 1957-58 (Dáil Debates of 8th May, 1957, Col. 1006) indicate that there has been over-building by some local authorities. In Dublin, the Corporation's housing programme should be completed within five or six years. The period could be much shorter if heavy emigration from the Dublin area and the significant increase thereby caused in the surrender of tenancies on municipal housing estates should continue. Apart from this automatic decline in public investment, some deliberate re-allocation as between non-productive and productive investment is possible and desirable and proposals in this connexion will be made in later chapters.

42. Productive enterprises, private and public, should have first claim both on such new capital (above the current level) as may be available in future and on the capital which will be set free in future years by the decline in social investment. Up to this, however, private development, notwithstanding various forms of State encouragement, has been very inadequate. This may have been due in part to the absorption of most of the available savings by public authorities and to heavy taxation of profits, though this can scarcely be the whole explanation. It has been advocated in Chapter 3 that financial policy should be directed towards reducing the weight of direct taxation in the hope of stimulating enterprise and initiative. In addition, policy should aim at leaving more savings available for the private sector to work on and providing liberally for the capitalisation of the Industrial Credit Company so that it will be able to finance extensions of existing industries and new industries. No industrial project with worthwhile prospects, particularly export prospects, should be frustrated by lack of capital. A minimum of £2 million a year of State finance for the Industrial Credit Company is provided for in this study. It is expected that the banks and insurance companies will also provide finance for the company, and if—as is hoped —still further capital is needed for productive projects, that the company will obtain the necessary funds from international institutions. Apart from its participation in the provision of capital for the Industrial Credit Company, the State can also help private industrial enterprise directly by continuing to provide capital grants for the development of new industries with export prospects.

46

43. However liberal the financial facilities made available for industrial (or agricultural) development, there must be doubt whether an adequate demand for additional capital will emerge at once in the private sector. The figures already quoted of net annual capital investment in industry (apart from depreciation reserves) and the fact that the Industrial Credit Company has contrived to do with only £½ million or so of fresh capital per annum show how disappointingly low the current demand for industrial capital is. The demand will need to be stimulated through the promotional activities of the Industrial Development Authority and the vigorous co-operation of the Federation of Irish Industries. For some time to come, however, it is probable that a demand for productive capital will have to be generated in the public sector if the objective of maximum development, private and public, is to be attained. In this study the principle is followed of allowing both for additional capital for the private sector and for the undertaking of new public investment of an economic kind. It is not unreasonable to assume that sufficient capital may be obtainable to realise the possibilities of development discussed in this study. Rough estimates of what these possibilities might cost over the next five years are presented in the final chapter.

Economy in Capital

44. Before this chapter is concluded, reference must be made to the desirability of economy in the use of capital. So that the best possible use may be made of available resources and costs kept at a minimum, all reasonable steps should be taken to conserve existing capital assets and avoid extravagance in capital expenditure. Economy and efficiency in the use of capital are necessary to achieve maximum reconciliation of the concurrent demands for capital for economic and social purposes. Policy should be framed to encourage the maintenance in good condition of houses, factories, machines and equipment, and to avoid duplication of investment in schools, offices and other forms of capital. Preservation of the national stock of houses would be greatly helped by the progressive abolition of rent control over private lettings. Other directions in which economies may lie are indicated in the remaining paragraphs of this chapter.

45. In regard to schools, an inter-departmental committee is being set up to examine the possibilities of making economies by prescribing standards and integrating the national and technical schools building programmes. As these programmes are still far from complete, it is important that every effort be made to secure the maximum integration, arrangements being made as far as possible for the use of the same accommodation. Even the siting of separate national and technical schools at the same place would yield savings in respect of various services that could be shared (sanitary services, footpaths, etc.). There

should be similar possibilities of integration of accommodation requirements between the local offices of the various countrywide services, e.g., the Post Office, E.S.B., C.I.E., Social Welfare, Garda Síochána.

46. Peak demand for various services which is confined to very short daily or seasonal periods entails substantial capital investment in plant, equipment, etc., which is lying idle for the greater part of the year. This applies particularly to transport, electricity, roads and bridges, hotels and restaurants. The heavy capital investment required by these peak demands is, of course, reflected in the cost of the services to the consumer, and a more even spread of demand would not alone give large savings in capital, which would be available for other forms of development, but would also reduce the prices of the services to the user. It would obviously be quite impracticable to spread demand evenly over the whole day or whole year but price incentives should be used to smoothen the incidence of demand and other expedients employed to secure savings, without significant sacrifice to the individual.

47. For instance, opening hours in the morning and closing hours in the evening could be staggered systematically. This could be achieved to a substantial degree in the Dublin area, in which by far the greatest problem exists, by co-operation between Government Departments, the Corporation, E.S.B., other public bodies and private firms employing large staffs. The interests of most shops and of their customers would be better served if they opened an hour later in the morning and closed an hour later in the evening. Even if this were done by certain classes of shops in rotation on, say, two days a week, there should be quite a relief to C.I.E. and the E.S.B. The periods for later opening and closing could well be extended to, say, $1\frac{1}{2}$ hours during the summer time, in the interests of tourists and others who are far better served in this respect in Continental countries. Luncheon hours could also be staggered over the hours 12 to 3 p.m. A system of staggered hours for civil servants has been in operation in London for some time and a special committee set up by the Minister of Transport has been studying the extension of the system to private employees. Half-days could be staggered over the whole working week; they already differ in some degree. Some of the factories and offices operating on a five day week and closing down on Saturdays could close instead on Mondays. In all such adjustments the co-operation of the staffs and of the trade unions would, of course, be essential. A fair measure of such co-operation could be secured by suitable explanations and publicity which would stress the ultimate benefits to the whole community.

48. As the mid-July—mid-August period is the peak season for foreign visitors to Ireland and as the capital cost of providing bedroom accommodation is particularly high, we should encourage our own

people to take their holidays outside that period. Moving school holidays to an earlier or a later period would help; so also would a better spacing of public holidays. Long-distance travel should be relatively dear during the peak summer period and relatively cheap outside the peak periods. With such inducements it should be possible to reach positive understandings with trades that traditionally close down for holidays during the peak period to close down outside that period. This would relieve home pressure on our hotels and guest-houses and enable them to cater for greater foreign demand without extra investment.

CHAPTER 5

AGRICULTURE—GENERAL SURVEY

Position of Agriculture in the Economy

1. The importance of agriculture in the Irish economy can be gauged from the fact that over the five years 1952-56 it accounted for an average of 31% of the total national income and engaged just under 40% of the total number at work.

Area of Agricultural Land

2.* Of the 17 million acres of land in the State some 11¾ million are classed as agricultural. The remaining 5¼ million apart from 360,000 acres of woodland, vary from marginal to waste, but over wide stretches are capable of improvement. The actual figures of agricultural land returned in the annual enumeration show some variation over the past hundred years:—

Year				Area of crops and pasture Million Acres
1851	...	...	...	12.00
1901	...	...	...	12.52
1906	...	...	...	12.22
1931	...	...	...	11.73
1939	...	...	...	11.61
1951	...	...	...	11.59
1957	...	...	...	11.77

The peak acreage recorded was 12.97 million in 1872; the lowest 11.55 million in 1945. The decline in the recorded acreage during the past century is attributable partly to changes in the headings under which returns are made and partly to a gradual change in standards: much of what was formerly returned as " pasture " has now become "grazed mountain ".

3. It is to be expected that the extensive land rehabilitation programme of recent years would produce a significant increase in the total area of agricultural land. Up to 31 March, 1957, the total acreage rehabilitated under this programme was 617,000. It is not possible to say how much of this is reclamation of waste land and how much improvement of land already cultivated.

* In this and following paragraphs figures relating to the 19th century have been inserted to give some idea of the long-term trend. These figures should, however, be read with caution and the comparisons between one century and another should not be pressed too far since the validity of the figures may be largely dependent on a subjective assessment by the enumerator.

4. In 1957, some 15% of the total area of crops and pasture was used to grow grain, root and green crops, a further 16% produced hay and the balance of 69% was used for pasture. In other words, 85% of the area under crops and pasture was devoted to grass. The immediate pre-war (1939) position was substantially the same.

5. One hundred years ago tillage accounted for at least 29% of the total crops and pasture, hay for 9% and pasture for the remaining 62%. There followed a steady decline in the tillage area, which reached its lowest point in 1932, at 1.42 million acres. The present tillage area is about 1.7 million acres and the fall of 1.8 million acres since 1851 has been mainly in corn crops (especially oats), potatoes and turnips.

6. For the past fifty years, however, there has been little substantial change in the relative proportions of the main land uses. The principal change has been a transfer of about half a million acres from " pasture " to "mountain land"; this might be described as a lowering of the farming " watermark " in mountain areas.

7. International comparisons of land use (averages for the years 1952 to 1955) show up the particular importance of grass in the Irish agricultural economy:—

Country	Tillage i.e. Ploughed (a)	Temporary Grassland (b)	Permanent Grassland (c)	Arable Land (a)+(b)	Agricultural Area (a)+(b)+(c)
	%	%	%	%	%
Ireland	15	15 (35)	70 (50)	30 (50)	100
Benelux	53	5	42	58	100
Denmark	67	24	10	90	100
France	48	15	37	63	100
Germany (Fed.) ...	59	2	39	61	100
Italy	75	17	7	92	100
Netherlands	44	2	54	46	100

8. The dual figures for Ireland are given to facilitate more accurate comparison with other countries because our " permanent pasture " cannot be classed as non-arable. In the international tables published, " arable land " denotes ploughed land plus *temporary* grassland, a term used in Ireland to mean the sum of rotation pasture under five years old and first year's hay. This is in reasonable accord with definitions proposed by the Food and Agriculture Organisation. However, a substantial proportion of " permanent pasture " in Ireland is very definitely arable in the sense of capable of being tilled, and may in fact be tilled over a longer rotation period. The lack of international agreement on

the definition of "temporary grassland" makes exact comparison difficult. The dual figures for Ireland, therefore, represent the range resulting from broad and narrow definitions of temporary grassland. It is quite definite, however, that the proportion of grass to tillage is far higher in Ireland than in the other countries quoted.

9. A caveat must be entered against drawing close comparisons with other countries. Our demographic, economic, climatic and soil conditions do not permit of exact parallels being drawn with other European countries. New Zealand, because of its low population and type of production, more nearly approximates to our own position, but the area of pasture in New Zealand is approximately 31.5 million acres (against our 8.1 million), of which some 17.5 million acres are under artificially sown grasses, leaving some 13 million acres under naturally established grass, or what is more usually regarded in this country as permanent pasture. The total New Zealand area under tillage and tree crops is only 1.2 million acres.

10. Clearly, the primary product of Irish agriculture at present is grass. As a natural consequence, the main activity of the farming community is the production of grazing animals and ancillary live-stock. Some 85% of the land under crops and pasture is, and has been for many years, devoted to grass; of this grass area, only some 1.7 million acres, or 18%, consists of "temporary grassland". In other words, only 18% of our grass is cultivated as a crop—most of it a poor one at that, consisting of grasses with a low carrying capacity and producing hay with a low nutritive value. The remaining 83% of our grasses are "permanent" in the sense that longer—usually much longer—intervals than five years elapse before they are ploughed, and, while permanent grass is not necessarily poor, its general quality is low. On the quality of grassland depends the number of livestock which can be fed and exported and this is a most important factor in the Irish economy.

Livestock Population

11. *Cattle:* During the past hundred years cattle numbers in the State have increased by 1½ million to 4½ million in 1956, a record figure. (The figure for June, 1957, shows a slight reduction.) About 1 million of this increase occurred by 1901 and the remainder since then. During this period of one hundred years the number of milch cows has remained almost stationary at 1.1 to 1.2 million so that the increase (mainly due to improved fertility and reduced calf mortality) has been confined to cattle produced for export or home slaughter. This emphasis on meat production is a reflection of economic forces, in particular the demand of the British market for live animals to be fattened in Britain.

12. *Sheep:* The sheep population has fluctuated considerably over the past hundred years. The highest figure ever recorded was in 1868, when it reached 4.6 million. In 1900 the figure stood at 4 million: by 1923 it had declined to 2.7 million, it jumped to 3.6 million in 1931, fell gradually to 2.1 million in 1948 (the lowest figure since 1851) and has risen steadily every year since then, the 1957 figure being 3.7 million—the highest since 1909.

13. *Pigs:* Pig numbers are subject to greater and more rapid fluctuations than sheep. Up to 1939 the number oscillated $\frac{1}{4}$ million either side of the million mark. It fell to 380,000 in 1944, the lowest figure on record, but recovered steadily to 960,000 in 1954. In 1955 and 1956 the number declined to 750,000 but the latest figure (June, 1957) stands at 907,000.

14. *Poultry:* In 1847 poultry numbers stood at 6 million. By 1915 they had reached 20 million. Though they fell subsequently they had returned to that figure by 1939; the war years, however, brought a drop to 17 million in 1947. A peak of 22 million was reached in 1949 but for 1957 the number stood at less than 15 million, the lowest since the beginning of the century.

15. *Horses:* As might be expected, horses, which numbered between 400,000 and 500,000 up to 1945 have given way since the war to the tractor, the number in 1957 being 261,000.

Crop Yields

16. The tillage area, representing only some 15% of our agricultural land, is devoted as to two-thirds to grain crops and one-third to roots and greens. In assessing crop yield figures, or indeed, any figures purporting to give " average " data for Irish agricultural phenomena, it should constantly be borne in mind that, in this context, " averages " have little meaning. The results of the Farm Surveys have confirmed other indications that the variability of returns of all types from Irish farms is very great. There is no representative farm in any main class in Irish agriculture. Furthermore, the statistics of crop yields available are not such that reliance can be placed on their absolute magnitude; they should, rather, be regarded as indicating *trends*. This applies particularly to oats and root crops used mainly for animal feed. The estimated yields given for hay are also open to question. In the case of wheat, independent particulars of deliveries to mills enable a satisfactory check to be made, while the sugar beet figures are accurate. There is no reason to believe, however, that the qualifications attaching to Irish agricultural statistics do not apply also to those of other countries; international comparisons should, therefore, only be taken as an indication of the order of magnitude involved.

17. With these caveats entered, the trends in crop yields over the past hundred years may be summarised thus (two five-year periods have been taken, in order to eliminate as far as possible the variations between bad and good years): —

Percentage increase in crop yields between 1847-51 *and* 1952-56

					%
Wheat	...	...	...	...	77
Oats	...	...	...	...	43
Barley	...	...	...	...	37
					—
	Total Corn Crops			...	57
Potatoes	...	...	...	...	60
Turnips	...	...	...	...	7
Mangels	...	...	...	...	6
Cabbage	...	...	...	...	26
					—
	Total Roots and Greens			...	39
Hay	...	...	...	...	3

Even having regard to the qualifications attaching to the early statistics, it is reasonably certain that there has been little, if any, improvement in the hay yield over the century. This is particularly regrettable because the total area under hay, amounting to almost 2 million acres, is greater than the total area ploughed. At most, only a quarter of the 2 million acres can be considered as having been sown within the preceding five years. It has, indeed, been stated that the general attitude towards grass and hay is to regard them as gifts of nature requiring no encouragement or cultivation.

18. The poor showing of the yields of turnips and mangels, too, is to be noted. These crops play an important part in stock feeding.

19. The variation in yield per acre for various crops is as follows:—

Wheat :	from	14	to	30	cwt.	averaging	22–25	cwt.
Oats :	,,	12	,,	30	,,	,,	20	,,
Barley :	,,	12	,,	35	,,	,,	22–26	,,
Sugar Beet :	,,	6	,,	18	tons	,,	10	tons
Mangels and Turnips :	,,	10	,,	30	,,	,,	18	,,
Potatoes :	,,	6	,,	13	,,	,,	7–9	,,

The farmers who get low yields are, of course, in the majority, and consequently the average yield for most crops tends to be nearer the lowest than the highest figure. This is another indication of the capacity for improvement in production which is common to most branches of Irish agriculture.

Pasture Yields

20. Information about pasture yields is extremely limited: it was not until 1956 that studies were begun on the carrying capacity of Irish grasslands. Following are figures for 1951-52 of average output of pasture here and in other countries:—

Netherlands :	26·2 cwt. starch equivalent per acre
Denmark :	22·3 ,, ,, ,, ,, ,,
England :	16·7 ,, ,, ,, ,, ,,
Ireland :	14·0 ,, ,, ,, ,, ,,

The Social Structure

21. Of the 379,000 holdings in the State in 1955, over 65,000 did not exceed one acre and cannot be regarded as farms. The remaining 314,000 were divided as follows:—

SIZE OF HOLDING	NO. OF HOLDINGS '000s	% OF TOTAL
1— 5 acres	26	8 ⎫
5— 10 ,, ...	30	10 ⎬ 27
10— 15 ,, ...	29	9 ⎭
15— 30 ,, ...	84	27 ⎫ 47
30— 50 ,, ...	63	20 ⎭
50—100 ,, ...	53	17 ⎫
100—200 ,, ...	22	7 ⎬ 26
Over 200 ,, ...	7	2 ⎭
All holdings above 1 acre	314	100

Of the total, 27% did not exceed 15 acres, 47% were between 15-50 acres, while 26% exceeded 50 acres. Generally speaking the larger the holding, the smaller the proportion of agricultural land: on holdings under 30 acres, crops and pasture cover more than 90% of the total area, but on those of 200-500 acres the figure is two-thirds, while on those over 500 acres, it is reduced to one-third.

22. There has, over the past forty years, been a steady trend towards consolidation: the number of holdings of 1-15 acres has been almost halved, while those in the 30-50 and 50-100 ranges have increased in number and area. There has been little change in the 100-200 acre group, while both the numbers and acreage of those over 200 acres have fallen, the area for which they account being almost halved. The steady movement, therefore, is towards the creation of farms in the 30-100 acre range, which now comprise 45% of the area of crops and pasture. These figures give little support for the popular belief that Ireland is predominantly a country of small farms—small, e.g., in comparison with the farms in Holland or Denmark—and that this is a factor retarding progress. It is also worth remarking that, unlike some continental countries, Ireland does not suffer from "fragmented" holdings, apart from some areas in the west. On the other hand, the

55

extreme variety of soil types in the country at large and the combination of poor soil and dense population in congested districts are not duplicated among our European competitors.

23. In the 1951 Census, 235,000 persons were returned as "farmers". The difference of 81,000 between this figure and the number of holdings of one acre and over in the same year represents, in the main, the number of holdings owned by people whose principal occupation is not that of "farmer", e.g., agricultural labourers, shopkeepers, etc.

24. The average age of farmers in 1951 was 55 for men, 62 for women. More than three-quarters of the men and all but one-ninth of the women were 45 or over; more than one-quarter of the male farmers and almost one-half of the female farmers were over 65. Male farmers were, on the average, about 9 years older than employers, managers and self-employed persons in non-agricultural occupations. The significance of this factor as an obstacle to progress in Irish agriculture needs no emphasis but, nevertheless, should not be exaggerated. Irish farmers have shown themselves responsive to economic and other stimuli.

Labour Resources

25. The relative importance of agriculture as a source of employment in the Irish economy is illustrated by the following figures:—

PERCENTAGE DISTRIBUTION OF PERSONS AT WORK

	1926	1936	1946	1951	1953	1955	1957
Agriculture* ...	53·4	49·6	46·2	40·7	38·9	38·5	38·2
Other production	13·4	16·8	18·5	23·7	24·5	25·3	24·9

The following census figures give an indication of the total labour force engaged in farming and its composition:—

PERSONS AT WORK IN FARMING AND STOCK-BREEDING

	Total at work		Farmers		Relatives Assisting		Employees	
	Males	Females	Males	Females	Males	Females	Males	Females
	Thousands							
1926	522·8	121·5	220·8	48·5	190·9	71·3	111·1	1·7
1936	499·1	106·2	212·2	46·5	185·0	59·0	102·0	0·7
1946	478·1	80·8	207·5	42·0	165·0	38·0	105·7	0·8
1951	418·5	67·3	198·8	35·9	140·0	30·9	79·9	0·5

* Including forestry and fishing (figures insignificant).

56

26. These figures illustrate clearly the drift from the land: in 1926-36 the decline in numbers of males was spread fairly evenly over all three categories—farmers, relatives and employees; from 1936-46 the " relatives assisting " group accounted for the bulk of the decline, while in 1946-51 relatives and employees showed the heaviest losses. Among females, the largest movements have always been in the " relatives assisting " group.

27. The Emigration Commission, in examining these figures, found that from 1926-46 the decline in males was mainly on farms under 15 acres, but from 1946-51 all sizes of farms lost about the same proportion of their male labour force. They also found that the loss of members of families was mainly on the smaller farms, while that of employees was mainly on the larger farms.

28. The actual magnitude of the drift from the land in more recent years can be gauged from the following: —

NUMBER OF MALES ENGAGED IN FARM WORK ON 1ST JUNE ('000s)

1946	1951	1952	1953	1954	1955	1956	1957	1958
519·6	452·7	441·3	420·8	421·3	418·4	409·3	401·9	400*

*Provisional.

The discrepancy between the above figures for 1946 and 1951 and those given in paragraph 25 is explained by the fact that the census figures relate to April, when agricultural employment is lower than in June.

29. These figures suggest that, after a period of relative stability from 1953 to 1955, the movement of male workers from agriculture has recommenced. However, if figures for temporary employees (which fluctuate from year to year) are omitted, the annual decline from 1946-53 averaged 12,200, while from 1953-56 it averaged 4,700. It is worth noting that the corresponding figure for the period 1926-46 was 4,300. Nevertheless, the total decline in permanent male workers in agriculture in the decade 1946-56 has been just short of 100,000 and in the six years 1952-57 has been 51,800.

30. The volume index of gross agricultural output (including turf, but excluding changes in livestock numbers) has, to base 1938-39 as 100, increased from 100.2 in 1950 to 110.2 in 1955; the 1956 figure was 110, the figure for 1957, 120.1. The figures, to the same base, for 1936-7 were 105.4 and for 1946, 99.2. The modest increase in output registered has been achieved by a considerably diminished labour force, though not without the help of extensive mechanisation: the number of tractors on Irish farms increased from 2,000 in 1939 to over 32,000 in 1956.

31. It is fairly well established that the volume of under-employment in Irish agriculture has always been considerable. The Emigration Commission considered that by European standards the volume of output could be produced by two-thirds of the number of workers. Since 1850 the volume of agricultural output has increased by some 25%, while over the same period the total rural population, which is an indicator of the trend in agricultural working population, decreased by about 60%, so that the output per worker rose by some 200%, though it is still low by European standards.

The Farm Surveys

32. In assessing the results of the first two Farm Surveys, the tentative nature of these results should be borne in mind: firm conclusions cannot reasonably be drawn until several years' results are available. With this qualification, the investigations have confirmed a number of impressions previously held about Irish farming, and have measured factors which were merely the subject of assertion formerly. What they have shown, above all, is the great variability of output and income per acre in every category of farm size. In the 1955 Survey, farms were classified into three groups by efficiency—the middle one representing approximately the average national position, the lower one being definitely below the national average, and the higher one to show what can be achieved even under present conditions and to show how this might be done.

33. As is well known, the number of specialist farms in the country is not large. On the basis of the 1955 Survey, it is estimated that of all farms over 5 acres, some 14½% are subsistence (i.e., where more than 40%-50% of output is consumed on the farm); of the remainder, 12½% are mainly crops, 16½% mainly cattle, 9% mainly dairying and 8% mainly pigs and poultry. The remaining 54% of non-subsistence farms are " mixed " farms, including general mixed farms as well as those with either crops, cattle, dairying or pigs and poultry as the main enterprise.

34. Generally speaking, the larger the farm size, the smaller the output and income per acre, the smaller the income per £100 total output, but the larger the income per unit of labour. In all the size groups, mainly dairy and mixed dairy farms gave the highest returns to labour. Crop farms were second, all other types were intermediate, *with cattle farms generally last of all,* even where the farms were large.

35. The inferior earnings from cattle farming are shown up in other findings; of the mainly cattle farms in the 1955 Survey, 52% were in the lower income group, 35% in the middle income group and only 13% in the higher income group. In contrast, mainly crop farms had a repre-

sentation of 24%, 19% and 57% in the lower, middle and higher income groups, while mainly dairying farms had 11%, 29% and 60% respectively. Each unit of labour on the mainly cattle farms earned on an average about £60 p.a. less than similar workers on the mainly crop farms, and over £80 p.a. less than on dairy farms.

36. At first sight this is rather disturbing. Cattle are our largest single export, receiving no subsidy or artificial aid, and it is little exaggeration to say that our survival as an economic entity depends on our ability to supply an increasing number of cattle for the export market. On the results of the Farm Surveys, there appears to be a definite economic incentive to farmers to get out of cattle and into crops and dairying, the export prospects for which are poor. This deduction, however, would not be sound; the Farm Survey figures reflect the present *extensive* system of cattle farming and are no guide to what could be achieved by a greater intensity of cattle production based on improved grasslands. As is shown elsewhere in this study, the greatest scope for increased agricultural output lies in the increased production of meat from improved grasslands.

37. The following is a summary of output based on the 1955 Farm Survey from the different enterprises on 30-50 acre farms:

TYPE OF FARMING

	Mainly Crop	Crops Mixed	Mainly Cattle	Cattle Mixed	Mainly Dairying	Dairying Mixed
	Output per Farm (£)					
Crops	556	346	44	78	43	125
Cattle	143	226	261	220	168	206
Dairy Produce ...	84	104	48	102	503	412
Pigs	51	87	20	39	62	139
Poultry	62	75	46	64	73	65
Sheep and Wool	21	62	34	38	5	16
Other	40	45	22	30	20	21
Total Output ...	956	943	476	570	874	985

These results indicate that there are many Irish farms which could increase their output of crops, pigs and poultry, without any reduction in their cattle, while most farms could increase their output under all heads, particularly if the grasslands were improved. This, of course, immediately poses the problem of marketing the surplus produce (apart from cattle) which would ensue from such an increase in output. The selling of such surpluses, particularly of dairy produce, would undoubtedly present a problem—milk and butter surpluses are common in most European countries to-day. Marketing aside, one of the factors that makes our agricultural produce uncompetitive is its high cost, which in turn is mainly due to a low level of production. The possibilities of improvement under the headings of grass, hay and crops have already been adverted to. Milk yields also afford scope for an increase which would reduce the cost of dairy produce and make its export less uneconomic. Our agricultural resources, animate and inanimate, could be used with greater efficiency and economy. A far higher output could be achieved in most lines at a disproportionately small rise in cost, the net result being an overall reduction in costs of production with a consequential increase in selling power.

38. The overriding necessity of Irish agriculture is to break out of the vicious circle of low production at high cost, which, together with inferior marketing arrangements, renders many products unsaleable save with a subsidy. This position in turn discourages capital investment, enterprise, and improvement in techniques which would render low-cost production possible. The possibilities in the principal sectors of the agricultural economy are now examined.

CHAPTER 6

GRASSLANDS

Importance

1. Our grasslands are our greatest potential for increased output and export. They comprise 85% of the area under crops and pasture, and on the efficiency of the production and use of grass depends the volume and quality of livestock and livestock products, which are, and have been for many years, the sheet-anchor of our export trade.

Low level of fertility of Irish pasture soils

2. A sufficient supply of nutrient elements and lime in soils is now universally recognised as one of the major factors in crop production but there is little doubt that our pastures have been depleted of nutrients over the past 100 years or more. Apart altogether from the lack of fertilisers, there were many adverse social factors which discouraged farmers from raising the fertility of their land : the system of tenure, for example, was such that any attempt at soil improvement was liable to be penalised by an increase in rent. Another contributory factor may well have been the contraction in the area under tillage over the past 100 years. In any such movement it is usually the most easily worked, and often the best, fields of a farm that are retained for tillage; this may have been one of the causes of the secular increase in crop yields and the relegation of pasture to the more intractable land. During the last 50 years, although these adverse factors have in part disappeared or been mitigated, the pattern of depletion and deterioration has continued, though on a less pronounced scale. Writing in 1948, G. A. Holmes, a New Zealand expert who was employed by the Department of Agriculture to survey and report on our grasslands, reported that

> "In fencing, water supply, drainage, cultivation, liming, fertilising and re-grassing . . . . Ireland is still largely virgin country . . . . I saw hundreds of fields growing just as little as it is physically possible for the land to grow under an Irish sky . . . . . It is a miracle that some of the land is able to grow grass at all."

The progress achieved since then (substantial though it be) has not eliminated the force of his remarks.

Pasture Output

3. Although information about the carrying capacity of our pastures is limited, it is clear that the present level of production is low and the

possibilities for increased output great. An O.E.E.C. Mission which visited Ireland in 1953 reported that

> " . . . . . eighty-one per cent. of the feed requirements of all farm stock in Ireland is derived from grassland . . . . . If it is allowed that the yield from rough grazings is one-sixth that of the grasslands, then the yield from grassland would be 2,500 fodder units per hectare (i.e. 2,200 lb. per acre). Under the climatic conditions of Ireland and with a reasonable standard of grassland management, the yield could easily be raised to 4,000 fodder units per hectare."

4. This conclusion is supported by the figures of pasture output for 1951/52 (expressed in cwts. of starch equivalent per acre) quoted in Chapter 5, paragraph 20, viz., Netherlands 26.2, Denmark 22.3, England 16.7 and Ireland 14.0. Specific studies of pasture output were not undertaken in Ireland until 1956. These showed an average figure of 16.4 cwt. for that year, while the figures for 1957 show an average of 17.9 cwt. Particular instances show variations of from 4 to 40 cwts. starch equivalent—the latter an exceptional figure, but an indication of the possibilities. It is of considerable interest that a number of figures ranging from 25 cwt. to 35 cwt. starch equivalent output per acre have been obtained on old pastures properly fertilised. These figures indicate that, from the technical aspect, an easily attainable target is a 50% increase in the national average yield from pastures.

Principal means of improvement of pastures

5. The improvement of pastures depends on the application of scientific farming techniques to their cultivation. The principal means of improvement open to Irish farmers are increased use of lime and fertilisers, particularly phosphates, and better management of grasslands. The returns to be obtained from such techniques in Ireland are proportionately greater than in any other Western European country, not only because of the relatively poor condition of our grassland but also because our soils are very responsive to fertilisers and our moist climate is particularly well suited to the growth of grass.

6. Although the use of fertilisers has increased in Ireland in recent years, the quantities being used are still far below the optimum. The fertilising of grasslands is in particular neglected; by comparison, the fertilising of tillage land, while still below the desirable level, is in general reasonably satisfactory. The following paragraphs examine the present lime and fertiliser status of Irish soils, and the prospects of their improvement.

Lime*

7. Ground limestone is not a fertiliser; it is a slow-acting agent, the function of which when applied to grassland is to bring into being a basic

---

* Most of the data in this section on lime and fertiliser use and requirements is taken from Walsh, Ryan and Kilroy: *A Half-Century of Fertiliser and Lime Use in Ireland*, a paper read before the Statistical and Social Inquiry Society of Ireland, March, 1957.

condition in the soil (neutralisation of excess acidity) which is essential for the full development and proper functioning of the clover plant. Clovers supply (or " fix ") the nitrogen which is essential for the sustained vigorous growth of the grass plants; this fixation takes about two years in old pastures. Clovers are, besides, valuable sources of certain mineral elements for animals, elements which they have a high capacity to absorb from fertile soils. They are, moreover, rich in protein. Under Irish conditions an adequate liming programme is of special importance. Because of the moist climate there is, for much of the year, loss of lime through drainage and the light texture of a great portion of our soils increases this loss.

8. Lime was intensively used and probably over-used in this country up to the 1870's. Its use then declined due to the introduction of fertilisers which gave quicker and more spectacular results; social and economic reasons also contributed to this decline. A picture of lime use in more recent times is given by the subsidy scheme operated by the Department of Agriculture from 1934 to 1951. Under this scheme an average of 46,500 tons of lime was distributed each year. This probably accounted for most of the lime applied and annual consumption during this period can scarcely have exceeded the equivalent of 100,000 tons of ground limestone per annum. With the introduction of the ground limestone scheme in 1951 the position changed radically. The quantities distributed under this scheme are as follows:—

				tons
1952/3	...	...	...	545,500
1953/4	...	...	...	694,000
1954/5	...	...	...	839,000
1955/6	...	...	...	1,128,300
1956/7	...	...	...	985,700
1957/8 (estd.)	...	...	...	1,250,000

(These figures include sugar factory lime distributed under the scheme, equated at 2 tons factory lime=1 ton ground limestone.)

9. Recent surveys carried out by the Department of Agriculture have revealed that in counties where the soil is derived from limestone the proportion of soils with a *moderately* satisfactory lime content is only about 60%. These include Counties Limerick (69%), Kildare (66%), Offaly (64%), Dublin (62%), Westmeath (54%) and Roscommon (52%). Where the soils are mainly derived from non-limestone materials the figures are far lower: Counties Cavan (15%), Monaghan (16%), Leitrim (19%) and Wexford (12%). It is obvious from these figures that lime status is at an extremely critical level in the non-limestone soils and that even on soils derived from limestone the position is far from satisfactory. This is contrary to common belief but can be attributed to the continual

downward leaching of lime in the soil by rain. The overall picture is that some 60% of our soils are deficient in lime.

Lime requirements

10. Holmes calculated in 1948, on the basis of a preliminary survey made by the Department of Agriculture, that altogether between 12 and 20 million tons of ground limestone would be required to raise our deficient soils to their proper calcium level. A recent survey by the Department puts the figure at 17 million tons. In addition, it is believed that some $1\frac{1}{2}$ million tons of ground limestone are necessary to replace the annual loss caused by leaching and otherwise. The amount being distributed under the ground limestone subsidy scheme is, as yet, not sufficient to do this. Holmes calculated that an annual distribution, over a 15-year period, of 3 million tons of ground limestone was urgently required to make up the arrears and at the same time to make good the annual loss.

Fertilisers

11. The primary nutrients necessary in soil for healthy crop growth are nitrogen, phosphorus and potassium. These are generally applied in the form of such fertilisers as sulphate of ammonia, ammonium nitrate, superphosphate, basic slag and muriate of potash, and through the medium of farmyard manure.

12. Information on the quantity of fertilisers used before 1900 in Ireland is scanty; it is known, however, that superphosphate was not used in any quantity until the late 1850's. The main fertiliser applied during this early period was guano which was used until the 1870's when supplies were exhausted. Since the quantities used were small and were applied almost entirely to tillage crops the effect in building up soil nutrient can be taken as negligible. There is no evidence that potash was used in Ireland before the end of the nineteenth century; in fact, even in 1904 the total amount of potassium contained in imported fertilisers was only 469 tons. It is equally certain that little or no nitrogenous fertilisers were used by Irish farmers before 1900. The data available since 1900 shows on the whole a consistent loss of nutrients, both nitrogenous, phosphatic and potassic, in the soil.

13. In 1948 Holmes judged that

" In any attempt to estimate the fertiliser requirements of Irish grasslands one is dumbfounded by the magnitude of the problem . . . In some counties the soils are so deficient in phosphate that cattle show clinical symptoms of aphosphorosis . . . . As all land in Ireland may be presumed to be phosphate deficient to a greater or lesser extent no money spent on phosphate can be considered wasted."

It is only fair to say that the Department of Agriculture has found difficulty in recent years in locating for the Spring Show an animal showing clinical aphosphorosis, but surveys since 1950 have shown that only 10% of our soils can be regarded as satisfactory in phosphate content. The best potassium levels have been found in counties where the soil is heavy and poorly drained (in other words, where it is of little productive use), while the overall average indicates that approximately 50% of our soils are deficient in this element.

14. The backlog of fertiliser deficiency is large and is increasing steadily each year. The extent to which we have fallen behind accepted practice in other countries is shown clearly by the following table (the figures are in terms of kilograms per hectare of agricultural land applied in 1956-57 and are taken from an O.E.E.C. study on fertilisers in Europe):—

	Nitrogen	Phosphate	Potash	Total	Total Agricultural Area
					(hectares)
Belgium	50	61	88	199	1,751
Netherlands	82	49	66	197	2,308
Germany	37	40	62	139	14,197
Denmark	32	35	56	123	3,066
United Kingdom ...	25	30	25	80	12,570
France	14	27	20	61	28,663
Ireland	3	12	9	24	4,688
Average for 17 O.E.E.C. countries	17	22	20	59	

This shows clearly how far we are behind other European countries in fertiliser use. Even in the United Kingdom, where climate and conditions generally approach ours, some eight times more nitrogen, two and a half times more phosphate and three times more potash per statute acre are used than in this country.

15. Details of fertiliser use for different crops in this country are not available but it can be taken as reasonably certain that, apart from a few limited areas, practically all the farmyard manure and fertilisers available are applied to tillage crops. A survey made in the spring of 1957 by officers of the Department of Agriculture confirmed this. The most striking finding was the invariable use of manures—whether farmyard or fertiliser—on root crops; cereals, too, it was found, are usually manured, especially in tillage counties. It was further noteworthy that the least manuring of cereals occurred in the dairying districts. Little more than half the 1956 hay crop and only 36% of permanent pasture received any fertiliser whatsoever. As is unavoidable in such surveys, the fields surveyed were on the more progressive farms. It can be taken, therefore, that the general position for grassland is, in fact, much worse than is shown by these figures. This neglect of grassland is an extremely serious matter.

Fertiliser Requirements

16. The nutrients required annually by our soils if they are to produce optimum economic yields have recently been estimated as follows:—

	Nitrogen (tons)	Phosphorus (tons)	Potassium (tons)
Total needed	71,000	114,000	170,000
Now used	15,000	25,000	40,000

In these estimates allowance has been made for the supply of nutrients to the soil by farmyard manure. Generally speaking, it may be taken that fertiliser use is only about 20% of the economic optimum, compared with 65% in Denmark, 75% in Belgium and almost 100% in the Netherlands.

17. A great increase in low-cost output is possible even if the application of fertilisers should fall short of the optimum. The response in terms of output (and quality of output) per unit of lime and fertiliser applied is higher here than in any other country in Europe. This is so not only because of the low levels of use at present but also because of the more favourable Irish climate and the generally more responsive nature of Irish soils.

Fertiliser policy

18. Nitrogen is one of the key nutrients in obtaining the desired increase in production from grassland, and by far the cheapest source of nitrogen is the clovers present in pastures which are properly and adequately fertilised with phosphates and potash. Because of the present lack of phosphates, and to a lesser extent of potash, pasture output is not only *directly* retarded to a very serious extent, but is also *indirectly* retarded by the low level of nitrogen fixation by clovers. To remedy this and to bring about increased low cost production, the first requirement in a balanced fertiliser policy is a very substantial increase in the use of phosphates, followed by potash, while increasing, where necessary, the present use of lime. Such a programme would bring about a very substantial increase in summer production of grass and would make possible a greatly increased conservation of grass for winter use in the form of silage and hay. With the introduction of improved grassland management techniques, the next development should be the use of nitrogenous fertiliser for spring and autumn production.

19. It is not enough, however, to rehabilitate old pastures if proper use is not made of them by modern techniques of grazing and if care is not taken to maintain their output by proper attention to weeding, drainage and reseeding. In this regard, there seems to be a conflict of expert opinion on the merits of reseeding old pastures. It

has been maintained by some that the building-up of soil fertility over a number of years by adequate applications of lime and fertiliser will itself result in the complete dominance of high-quality grasses and clovers. Others maintain that, without reseeding, a programme of lime and fertiliser application will merely mean an increase in the natural excess of grass in mid-summer, without either raising its quality or extending the grazing season. This is a question that obviously requires determination one way or the other. A controversy on this matter could only distract attention from the programme of pasture rehabilitation which is so obviously of the highest priority.

20. A complete soil survey of the whole agricultural area would be desirable. Some general surveys have been made which have revealed that the predominant characteristic of Irish soils is their variety. A greater number of soil types has been found within the confines of a single field in Co. Tipperary than exist in the whole of Holland. Each of these types may require different treatment. It is obvious that a comprehensive programme of pasture rehabilitation requires far more detailed information on our soils than is at present available. A programme of pasture improvement is now a matter of such national urgency, however, that it cannot wait for the compilation of a general soil survey, which could take many years. Both must be pressed ahead with all possible speed.

Grass conservation
21. The provision of adequate quantities of good quality hay and silage must be a rational part of a grassland improvement programme. A major defect of present farming practice is the low level of animal nutrition in the winter and early spring months. A great deal of the ill-health of our cattle during the winter months is attributable to malnutrition. It is unnecessary to labour the point, but it is clear that inattention to winter feeding affects every aspect of cattle-rearing from milk yields to beef quality. At present silage-making is practised very little in many areas, although it has long been shown that a high degree of self-sufficiency in winter feeding can be achieved on any farm at a low cost through the adoption of modern silage-feeding techniques.

22. The conversion of our grasslands to high-quality pastures with a long grazing season presents no insurmountable technical difficulty. If the farming community can be educated to the proper use of improved pasture—through better management, hay-making and silage conservation—then an easily attainable target is a 50% increase in the national average output per acre of grassland and it is little exaggeration to say that the stock-carrying capacity of our grasslands could be doubled with a far from proportionate increase in costs.

Conclusions

23. The following considerations should have the greatest influence on agricultural policy in the immediate future:

(a) The predominance of grass—and the production of grazing animals—in our agricultural economy; 85% of the area of crops and pasture is under grass, and livestock and livestock products make up 75% of total agricultural output;

(b) the great extent to which our external purchasing power, and therefore our industrial production, employment and general living standards, depend on exports of meat (live and processed);

(c) the fact that our grasslands are seriously neglected and starved of fertilisers;

(d) the great potentiality of increased and profitable production of meat for export, dependent on an improvement in grasslands;

(e) the possibility of a substantial improvement in grasslands over the next decade, provided farmers are induced to apply the appropriate quantities of lime and fertilisers and to improve grassland management.

24. The form which State aid to agriculture should take in future, in view of the considerations just mentioned, is discussed in Chapter 12, where special emphasis is laid on the importance of subsidisation of phosphatic fertilisers. A vigorous drive to rehabilitate our grasslands could achieve notable results over the next few years. Departmental and local advisory services have been directed in recent years towards convincing the farmer of the need for, and the benefits to be derived from, such a programme. This campaign should be intensified, since much more remains to be done. Pasture improvement would lead a general advance on the agricultural front, in particular by increasing the carrying capacity of grasslands, raising the demand for cattle to graze on those grasslands and thus offering an inducement to both dairying and other areas to keep more cows for breeding purposes. A general and marked advance on the agricultural front would generate greatly increased activity and employment in the Irish economy as a whole.

CHAPTER 7

CATTLE

General

1. We have seen that our grasslands, the foundation of the agricultural economy, are producing far less than they could. It is not surprising, therefore, to find that the cattle industry is not giving the output of milk and beef of which it is capable. Pasture improvement can expand this output by increasing the number of cattle grazing in the fields. But there are other means of boosting production which are no less effective and no less urgently desirable.

2. Better—by which is meant more intelligent—feeding would subdue the wasteful rhythm of summer abundance and winter privation which marks the life of cattle from birth to beef. A more intensive assault on the main cattle diseases would also raise the output figures. A more rational organisation of the existing rearing and marketing arrangements would eliminate losses which at present may be unobtrusive but which are nonetheless real, large and damaging to the national economy. Finally, and this, indeed, governs the whole structure of the industry, there is the question of the breed, or breeds, of cattle best suited to the nation's requirements.

3. Some attempt is made in what follows to examine the principal sectors which appear to the lay observer to be most in need of, and most responsive to, overhaul; *marketing* problems are discussed in the next chapter. None of the ideas or suggestions put forward is novel or revolutionary. They are repeated here because the present is an appropriate time for review. The European Common Market is in being, a Free Trade Area is likely to follow. If we go into the latter, it will be on the back of our main exporting industry, which is meat, both live and processed.

4. The market for Irish agricultural output is more or less evenly divided three ways, into consumption on the farm, home consumption off the farm, and exports. In the case of cattle, however, over 80% of the output is exported. Of total agricultural exports, three-quarters consist of cattle, live or processed. Of these agricultural exports 60% go to Great Britain and a further 20% to the Six Counties. Of the country's *total* exports, over one-third consists of live cattle (valued at £36 million in 1956 and £46 million in 1957) and nearly one-half of

cattle and cattle products. The picture that emerges, therefore, is that the viability of the Irish economy is heavily dependent on cattle and cattle products, that in cattle production the export interest is paramount and that, for cattle exports, the United Kingdom is almost the sole customer. Since the home demand is fairly stable, any percentage increase in the output of cattle becomes immediately available as a greater percentage increase in exports; an increase in cattle output of 50% (an attainable target) would mean an increase in the export availability of over 60%, worth at present prices some £25 million.

Pasture Capacity

5. Specific information on the carrying capacity of Irish pastures is extremely limited. Some indication of pasture yields in terms of starch equivalent per acre has already been given (Chapter 5, para. 20) and in assessing these figures it may be taken that 6 lbs. starch equivalent equals 1 lb. beef or 1 gallon of milk. The present average output per acre of pasture in terms of starch equivalent (18 cwts.) supports an output of 3 cwts. of beef or 340 gallons of milk per acre. It is quite possible with a moderate programme of pasture improvement to raise this average to 24 cwts. starch equivalent per acre (some of our best pastures already produce 38 cwts. starch equivalent) which would mean an output of 4 cwts. of beef or 450 gallons of milk per acre. In experiments conducted by the Department of Agriculture at Johnstown Castle an output of beef of over 5 cwts. per acre has already been attained on poor to average soil, so that the raising of the national average to the figure quoted is by no means impracticable. Yet this would mean an increase of almost 50% in the output of cattle and cattle products. If this increase had to be bought at a heavy price in land reclamation, or fertiliser input, it would be of little use. It is beyond doubt, however, that the increase could be achieved more easily and at lower cost in this country than by any of our European agricultural competitors. The greater part of our 8 million acres of permanent pasture receives little or no manurial treatment. Large areas of good soil are carrying very inferior pasture. Not only could pasture output be increased but unit costs of production could be reduced significantly.

Milk Yields

6. Two sources are available for milk yield estimates—the Agricultural Output returns and the Farm Surveys. They compare thus:—

1955 Milk Yield per Milch Cow (Gallons)

Region	Farm Survey	Agricultural Output
East and Midlands	420	439
South	496	485
North and West	352	355
State Average	448	448

70

An indication of what is possible, even under present conditions, is given by the performance of cows as reported by the cow-testing associations. The average yield of these cows has risen from 537 gallons in 1938 to 627 in 1956. The number of cows under test in these associations is, of course, less than 5% of the total and *ex hypothesi* they are of better quality than the average; the national average itself has, however, been increasing, although slowly, over the years:—

Year	Yield (gallons per cow per year)
1934/5—1938/9 (av.)	376
1945—1948 (av.)	387
1949—1952 (av.)	416
1953	440
1954	444
1955	448
1956	476
1957	500

The increase in the 1956 and 1957 figures can largely be attributed to unusually favourable weather, though it is evident that some improvement in feeding and management is also taking place.

7. By comparison, the *national* averages for other countries in 1955 were: New Zealand 544, England 614, Denmark 736, and Netherlands 825. The difference between the Irish and New Zealand figures may seem small, but it should be remembered that the average butterfat content of New Zealand milk is over 5% against our 3.5%, so that the output of *butterfat per acre* is 180 lbs. in New Zealand against about 60 lbs. here. These figures, however, do not permit of unqualified comparison. The New Zealand figure is achieved mainly with the Jersey breed, which gives a high butterfat output, but whose progeny would be of little use for the production of beef. The Dutch and Danish figures are compiled on the basis of lactation periods somewhat longer than ours. The English figure reflects the high proportion of concentrates fed to cattle in that country, a system of feeding which would be quite uneconomic here.

Cattle Breeds

8. One of the most commonly advocated methods of increasing milk yields is improvement of cattle breeds. Livestock policy in this country has for many years been based on the dual-purpose Dairy Shorthorn. The Department of Agriculture has, by exhortation and through its bull premium and artificial insemination schemes, actively promoted this breed. The wisdom of this policy has been questioned on many occasions, particularly in recent years by some farming organisations. It was the subject of consideration by the Committee of Inquiry on Post-Emergency Agricultural Policy which reported in 1946 and which argued, as others have done before and since, that in order to achieve exports of dairy produce, low cost milk production must be attained. The average milk yields of our cows need to be

71

increased. On the other hand, regard must be had to the importance of the beef sector of the agricultural economy and the extent to which it depends on the dairying side for its prosperity.

9. The 1946 Committee pointed out that agricultural produce formed some 60% of our total exports but dairy produce only 10% of our agricultural exports (the dairy produce percentage is now much less, despite heavy subsidisation). Equilibrium in the balance of payments and the earning of foreign currency to buy industrial raw materials and finished goods have traditionally depended to a great extent on ability to sell fat and store cattle in the British market. The whole agricultural economy of the dry stock farming areas is dependent on the regular receipt of surplus young cattle born and reared in creamery counties. The surplus male progeny of the Dairy Shorthorn cattle bred in the creamery counties make quite good " stores "—though it has been argued* that the beef producers are enabled to receive cheap calves from the small dairy farmers because the latter bear a disproportionately high share of the total cost of producing beef animals and receive a disproportionately low return. The Committee argued that if the creamery districts went over to dairy breeds, it would mean a cathartic change in the agricultural practice of the dry stock areas. This could hardly be achieved without serious dislocation and economic loss to the country as a whole. Accordingly, the Committee came down on the side of the Dairy Shorthorn, holding that any advantage to be gained through higher milk yields from the introduction of dairy breeds would be outweighed by the low value for store or fattening purposes of so much of the progeny as would be unsuitable for breeding stock. They added that there was no evidence pointing to incompatibility in the Dairy Shorthorn breed between reasonably high milk yields and good beef-producing characteristics. The Committee apparently only gave consideration to the purely dairying breeds as an alternative to the Dairy Shorthorn—they do not seem to have examined the possibilities of *other* dual-purpose breeds.

10. Dr. John Hammond of the Cambridge School of Agriculture was engaged by the Minister for Agriculture in 1955 to survey cattle breeding policy. He reported: —

> " I have no doubt that the bulk of the cattle should be of dual-purpose type . . . The dairy exports, however, strike me as being rather low for a country with dual-purpose type cattle. I would, therefore, favour an increase in the Friesian breed, provided that the dual-purpose type is used, but would be averse to the use of purely dairy type cattle such as the Jersey or Ayrshire, which would lower the quality of the store cattle."

Dr. Hammond also suggested that, where the type of Shorthorn is not good or is milking badly, herds should be up-graded with Friesians.

* J. J. Byrne in *Studies,* Spring, 1955.

It has, however, been argued that, where such conditions obtain, they are due to low standards of feeding and management and that, in such conditions, it is unlikely that up-grading would bring about an improvement.

11. It is not yet possible definitively to compare the Friesian and Shorthorn from the point of view of milk production or general efficiency under Irish farming conditions. Until recently, no scientific examination of their relative merits had been carried out here, though comparisons of yields based on records of the cow-testing associations show the Friesians to give over 30% higher butterfat output than the Shorthorns. The results so far available from the scientific tests indicate that at the end of the first year the Friesian weighs considerably more than the Shorthorn but takes, on average, six weeks longer to mature which means, of course, that the Friesian costs more to feed—though whether this would be true on a " per lb. of beef " basis is not so clear. As regards the marketability of the carcase, the advantage is in favour of the Shorthorn, but only to the extent of 1%, which must be regarded as indeterminate. Furthermore, it is claimed that the Shorthorn is more suitable from the point of view of conformation and maturity for the production of the small joint now in favour. From these tests, however, the dual purpose Friesian does seem to give higher milk yields than its Shorthorn counterpart. It is worth mentioning that, as far as the production of beef is concerned, these results do not tally with the findings of the statistician who, in an article in the *Irish Farmers' Journal**, claimed that experiments carried out on a farm in Co. Wexford clearly established the superiority of the Friesian, both on a weight-for-age basis and for providing lean joints on slaughter. General experience of both breeds so far suggests that the average Friesian is just as good for beef production as the Shorthorn, and gives considerably more milk. To reach a final determination of their comparative merits, it is urgently necessary, in view of the economic importance of the question, that further detailed and scientific investigations be undertaken.

12. The making of such experiments, and official policy generally, might be taken to postulate that the dual-purpose cow, of whatever breed, should remain the cornerstone of our cattle economy and that any improvement can take place only within the existing, or another, dual-purpose breed. This implies that our system of cattle production should remain divided between dairying areas which produce surplus young cattle, and dry stock areas which purchase them for fattening. These are, in effect, arguments for maintaining the existing situation and, as such, must be searchingly reviewed.

13. The argument which has often been put forward that yields of up to 800 gallons of milk can be obtained from a Dairy Shorthorn cow

* 26 January, 1957.

which can yet produce a good beef calf is true, but only within limits. Such performance has been obtained from some Shorthorns under test by the cow-testing associations. These associations, as noted above test less than 5% of all milch cows and it can be taken that such cows are better bred, fed and managed than the average. It is quite another matter to suggest that this performance can be repeated among Irish cattle at large. The Irish dual-purpose Shorthorn is not dual-purpose in the real sense of the term: hitherto, it has been primarily a beef producer with a low milk yield. In latter years, however, the practice of locating dairy Shorthorn bulls at A.I. stations—very few beef Shorthorn bulls have been used since 1948—is reported to be producing progeny of a reasonably good dairy type without, apparently, impairing their beef characteristics. It has, however, been suggested that the genetical antecedents of the present Irish Shorthorn are so confused that the breed is no longer homogeneous, and that grading-up to achieve higher milk yields will be a lengthy and tedious process.

14. From time to time the argument has been heard that if the Irish Dairy Shorthorn were replaced in the dairy districts by specialised dairying breeds, the number of cattle necessary to produce our dairying needs would be greatly reduced and more land would be freed for beef production. That milk production from specialised breeds could be far more profitable for the dairying community is evident: it has been calculated by Dr. Henry Kennedy that the milk output of the Shorthorn would have to be raised to 1,000 gallons before her profitability could be compared with that of a 600-gallon Jersey. Equally, no matter how much one favours the grading-up for milk of the Shorthorn, it cannot be advocated as a solution to the problem of producing low-cost milk: specialised dairy breeds are clearly more economic for the dairy farmer. It has been claimed that if the dairying areas went over to these breeds, the losses accruing to them from the unsuitability of dairy-breed calves for fattening might be outweighed by the gains in greatly increased milk production from a far smaller number of cattle costing much less to feed and maintain, with the prospect at last of a viable dairying industry.

15. On the other hand, the case for retaining the Shorthorn breed in dairying areas rests on the necessity of furnishing a supply of suitable calves for fattening in the dry stock areas. This argument has been advanced often and with much force. The 1946 Committee reported that

> " The activities and welfare of all classes of livestock farmers in this country are mutually interdependent. Interdependence is the result of long, natural and spontaneous development in search of the most profitable methods of production and disposal of livestock."

Dr. Hammond, too, was impressed by this division of functions between the dairying areas, which produce and rear the calves (generally to about six months), and the dry stock areas which fatten them for marketing. Even if this counter-argument is accepted, it must be recognised that the present division of functions, however traditional and convenient, does not result in the optimum development of *both* the dairying and the cattle industries. At the dairying end the evidence is rather of unduly high production costs which make profitable marketing extremely difficult and operate, therefore, to discourage the expansion of output.

16. Even to say that the present is the most economical method —from the national viewpoint—of producing *beef* requires rather more evidence than is available. The economic efficiency of the geographical division of the industry, under which cattle trek their way from Munster through Connacht to Leinster before being finally exported, must be questioned. Dr. Hammond, it is true, was impressed by what apparently struck him as a domestic application of the doctrine of comparative costs. He said : —

> " In a country like Ireland with a large number of small herds and farms, working capital for the farmer is often a very difficult proposition. A good supply of milk from his cow, which is paid for monthly, is essential to give him the working capital he requires. With beef, the turnover of capital is much slower but the system of apportioning this between rearer (for six months), grazier (for one year) and ' stores ' keeper (for one and a half years) seems a good one, for it offers a quicker turnover for each with more capital outlay and slower turnover as the cattle get older; thus proceeding from the small farmer with least capital to the larger farmer with more capital at his disposal."

Others, however, have been less impressed. During the animal's perambulations around the country, it loses weight and condition from the repeated walkings to fairs; at these fairs it is exposed to inclement weather, hardship and the risk of infection; add to this the regular winter losses from malnutrition and the price paid for the system which has evolved over the past hundred years is a formidable one.

17. It may help to set out the position statistically. There are some 1,200,000 cows in the country, most of them in the dairying areas. They have an average life of 6 years, so that some 200,000 heifers are required annually for replacements. This involves the breeding of some 400,000 calves of the dairy type of which half will have to be disposed of as store bullocks. The remaining 800,000 cows are at present crossed with beef bulls to produce calves for the export market. This means that there are three related questions to be considered. The first is the ability of the breeding cows to produce beef cattle at a first cross with a beef bull. The second is the suitability for

the beef trade of the 200,000 or so dairy-breed bullocks. The third is the yield of dairy produce from the breeding stock to produce a profit for the dairy herds. These matters are so closely interlinked—particularly in the dairying areas—that one cannot be stressed save at the expense of the others.

18. Viewed in relation to the possibility of rapid improvement in national real income, the zoning of the country into beef and dairying areas is a long-term proposition of doubtful practicability. During the year 1957 we exported a total of 824,172 store and fat cattle. Allowing for deaths, this would represent the progeny of approximately 1 million cows per annum, whereas the total number of cows in the beef areas is about 500,000. To produce the present output of store and fat cattle outside the dairying districts it would be necessary to double the number of cows in the beef-producing areas of the country. This does not take into account the number of heifers required for replacement purposes in the beef areas. It is evident that the zoning of districts into beef and dairying areas would present an almost insuperable problem if we were, at the same time, to try to maintain, let alone increase, cattle and beef exports. In any event it would be impossible, except by compulsion, to bring about a change in the south to purely dairying breeds. The present system of farming in that area is based on dairying, and farming income derives not alone from milk sold to the creamery and the pigs produced on the skim milk, but also from the dropped beef calf which at present commands a high price.

19. When we turn to the non-dairying districts, the possibilities of early improvement in the situation are evident. The only way to increase significantly the number of cattle or beef for export is to increase the number of breeding stock. An obvious way of doing this is to persuade the graziers in the beef areas to breed their own calves, preferably from specialised beef breeds. High prices for calves and young stores may ultimately force them to do this; it is noteworthy that many of the grazing lands were under-grazed in 1957, because of difficulty of obtaining stores at an attractive price. This is one form of breed specialisation that would be of great benefit to the nation. If the breeding stocks were increased in beef areas and if breeds were orientated towards specialised beef breeds in conjunction with a programme of pasture improvement and winter feeding, it should be possible to produce, in greater numbers, a better beef animal reared straight through from calf to maturity. This need not involve converting all the present good beef lands in Leinster to breeding; it could be achieved mainly by extending, through a programme of pasture improvement, the present breeding areas to the currently poor lands in the west, from which suckled calves would move to the first-class grazing in the east and be brought to maturity quickly. This would be in conformity with the objective—discussed in Chapter 8 —of utilising surplus milk in the rearing of calves.

20. This brings up another question of importance: to increase the profitability of beef production, it is highly desirable that stores should be brought to maturity at an earlier age. The elimination of the present periodic setbacks in the life of the store beast would help to achieve this. Without any radical alteration of the present system, it should be possible to reduce the travelling time of the beasts and the loss of time and condition consequent on attendance at fairs. The substitution of auction marts, where animals are sold by quality and weight, for fairs would speed the transfer of beasts from seller to buyer and would impress upon the producer the importance of bringing them to the peak of condition whatever their age. Some progress has already taken place on these lines, particularly in the south, and there is reason to believe that this development will spread throughout the whole country. This cannot come too quickly. It is worth remarking that a small but increasing proportion of the store cattle at present exported is little over two years old, but this seems to be more in response to a British demand for beef of that age than to their maturing earlier.

21. The export prospects for our meat are good; those for milk products (particularly butter) are extremely poor. In this context, the case for continuing the present structure of the industry is not convincing. Clearly, what is required is not the production of yet more milk from a larger herd composed of specialised dairying breeds, but the more economical production of a marketable supply from fewer dairy cattle which the improvement of milk yields would make possible. Equally, although we require an increase in beef output, we do not want the concurrent expansion in the dairy herd which would be inevitable under the present system. It is clear that a rapid expansion of beef output requires an increase in the number of breeding stock. *One of the chief means of achieving this is by the expansion of breeding in the beef-producing areas.* If this took the form of specialisation in beef breeds, it would result in high-quality beef matured at an early age. The rearing of these calves on whole-milk would prevent the emergence of any surplus milk problem, and both cow and calf could finally be disposed of as high-class beef. As regards the dairying areas, the system of farming practised in those areas postulates a continued reliance on a dual-purpose breed, but this should not rule out an increase in the number of breeding stock kept in these areas primarily for beef production. The scientific investigations which must precede a proper appraisal of the problem of which is the best dual-purpose breed are still in the initial stages. It is important that this question be decided. If a modification of official breeding policy is found necessary, it cannot be undertaken too soon. The bovine tuberculosis eradication scheme (discussed separately below) offers an opportunity for the gradual re-orientation of breeding policy, through the introduction of replacements for reactors, which it would be a national tragedy to miss.

22. Breeds and their complexities aside, however, it is clear that, even within the present structure of the industry, the scope for improvement in milk yields—and consequent lowering of the cost of production per gallon—is considerable. The first and easiest way of improving milk yields is by better feeding. The 1946 Committee estimated that the average yield of the dairy cows of the country could be raised by at least 120 gallons a year by improved feeding methods alone and added that:—

> " The first limiting factor in milk production is the low level of feeding rather than the low milking capacity of the cow. Until a radical change in the feeding of dairy cows is brought about, the adoption of higher breeding standards and the provision of improved services for combating disease will be largely neutralised."

It is readily conceded that high-cost feeding is no answer to our problems. Feeding need not, however, be more expensive, if it is more intelligent. The proper cultivation and conservation of grass could give a cheaper foodstuff than any now used. Even to-day, proper silage-making is a novelty in too many parts of the country: this is clearly a matter where agricultural instruction can palpably raise the standard of cattle husbandry.

23. The under-feeding of dairy cattle curtails milk yields: the winter shortage of food and the poor body condition at spring calving-time means that the first five or six weeks of pasture are spent in improving (or rather, restoring) the cows' condition instead of in producing milk. This, together with the decline in pasture productivity in autumn, curtails the lactation to a period which allows only a moderate yield of milk. This concentrated production period has, of course, profound effects on costs of production of dairy produce. Dr. Hammond has calculated that a cow yielding 320 gallons a year (not much less than the yield of many Irish cattle) uses 56% of her food merely to keep alive and only 44% of it for milk production; and Dr. Henry Kennedy has suggested that the body-maintenance figure for a 400-gallon cow can be as high as 70% (this would apply particularly to the Shorthorn, which is a large-framed animal). On the other hand with a cow giving 850 gallons a year only 35% of the food she consumes is used to keep her alive and 65% goes for milk production. Clearly, the present high cost of producing a gallon of milk is due at least in part to the methods of dairy husbandry which confine to the few summer months the milking period of a cow which, properly fed, could remain in good production for up to 45 weeks of the year. It is equally clear that the cost of production of butter is affected by the system which squeezes 60% of our butter production into four months of the year, leaving plant and personnel inefficiently utilised for the remaining eight.

78

Diseases

24. Another potential source of increased yields is, of course, an improvement in cattle health. An indication of the possibilities can be gleaned from estimates made* by Mr. P. Harnett, M.R.C.V.S., of the Department of Agriculture. He estimated the losses in milk alone due to internal parasites, mastitis, infertility, abortion and tuberculosis at nearly £3½ million a year, and computed the *total* loss each year through cattle diseases at over £18 million. Though the figures for mortality of calves under one year have shown a gratifying reduction from the pre-war level—from about 7% to 2% at present—there is such considerable scope for further improvement in the health of our cattle herds that it may prove profitable to devote a larger proportion of State aid to this purpose. This question is referred to in Chapter 12—State Aid to Agriculture.

Bovine Tuberculosis

25. A special word must be said about the eradication of bovine tuberculosis from cattle herds. This is perhaps the most immediate and outstanding problem facing the cattle industry at the present time. A programme of eradication has been in operation in Britain since 1934, and that country is now within sight of complete clearance: at present 90% of Scotland and Wales is clear of the disease and 70% of England. The whole of Britain is scheduled to be clear of the disease by 1961 and the programme is at present running ahead of schedule.

26. This means that we stand to lose our chief market unless we can satisfy the British that our stores are free of tuberculosis. At present, store cattle which have passed a single tuberculosis test within 14 days of shipment are allowed into " clean " areas in Britain but they must be isolated there for 60 days and pass another test before being allowed into an attested herd. This is an interim arrangement and it cannot be regarded as a substitute for the complete eradication of the disease from our herds which is a matter of the greatest urgency.

27. Our programme of clearance began on 1st September, 1954, and has progressed as fast as technical resources will allow. Eradication is proceeding by areas—clearance, intensive, and general—and the movement of cattle between clearance and other areas is controlled. From the end of March, 1958, Co. Donegal and all areas west of the Shannon have been declared clearance areas. All cattle in these areas must be tested annually, all reactors must be cleared, and cow byres must be disinfected. The Department of Agriculture provides free testing and professional advice and is prepared to purchase all reactors at current market prices. In intensive areas, which comprise Counties Cavan,

---

* In a paper read before the Statistical and Social Inquiry Society of Ireland—March, 1956.

Monaghan, Kerry, Cork and Limerick, and "Greater Bansha" in Co. Tipperary*, the Department provides free annual testing and professional advice, and purchases cow reactors at current market prices. In the rest of the country, an Accredited Herds Scheme is operated under which participants receive an initial and final herd test free of charge; herds reaching a prescribed standard are registered as accredited herds and allowed direct entry to attested areas in Britain.

28. The expansion of the Scheme in recent months and the exhaustion of the American Grant Counterpart provision will add substantially in future years to the net cost, already close to £1 million a year. So far, about one-quarter of the total cattle population and about one-third of the herds in the country have been tested. The average incidence of tuberculosis is 17% for all cattle and over 25% for cows. It is obvious that the physical task of replacing reactors will be no less than the problem of meeting the capital cost involved; the programme of eradication will also have repercussions on our export potential.

29. Along with the eradication scheme a programme of installation of pasteurisation plant in all creameries is being put into force. This is being done with the help of American Grant Counterpart moneys and from the 1st January next the installation of such machinery will be compulsory.

30. A serious limitation on the progress of the scheme and, indeed, on the elimination of cattle diseases generally, has been the shortage of veterinary personnel. This is being overcome as far as possible by the use of suitably trained lay personnel, under veterinary control, on certain defined duties in meat factories, etc., so that veterinarians may have more time to devote to the many important tasks that only they are qualified to perform. It is vital that sufficient areas should be cleared of the disease by 1961 to safeguard our export trade in live animals. Even apart from the export interest, clearance will be of enormous value in raising the general standard of health of our cattle; tuberculosis-free animals may be expected to have a higher standard of resistance to other cattle diseases. In this way, although the primary result of the campaign will be to raise the quality of our beef, it should have a secondary effect in improving milk yields. Farmers generally have complained that it is often their highest-yielding milch cows which have proved to be reactors.

* By November, 1958 the intensive measures had been extended to Counties Kildare, Kilkenny, Louth, Meath and Westmeath.

CHAPTER 8

CATTLE PRODUCTS

1. Milk and beef are joint products, though not necessarily produced in an inflexible ratio. In Chapter 7 it was argued that, even assuming the continuance of the dual-purpose Shorthorn in the dairying areas, a significant increase in cattle exports could be obtained by increasing the number of specialised beef breeding stocks in the non-dairying areas. It must be accepted, however, that increased production of meat will entail some increase in milk production. Already more milk is being produced than can be absorbed at home, whether in the form of milk or of butter and other milk products. Most of the milk available for export is being exported in the form of butter, which requires heavy State subsidisation. If essential State aid is to be provided for other sectors of agriculture, to say nothing of industry or tourism, more milk must be used in the rearing of calves, the cost of producing butter for export must be reduced and, at the same time, as much as possible of the exportable milk must be diverted from butter towards more economic export lines. To ease the transition, a limited and gradually declining butter export subsidy could be tolerated, provided advances were being made, in the fields of production and marketing, towards increasing the volume of exports of milk products which could be sold at a profit.

Milk and Milk Products

2. Total milk production has been increasing steadily for some years:—

				Total production (million gallons)	Yield per cow (gallons)
1938/9	...	...	...	484	381
1951	...	...	...	485·7	408
1952	...	...	...	478·6	413
1953	...	...	...	516·5	440
1954	...	...	...	534·0	444
1955	...	...	...	536·7	448
1956	...	...	...	565·2	476
1957	...	...	...	616*	500*

* Provisional.

This increase is chiefly attributable to the improvement in the average milk yield per cow. While advances in feeding techniques have helped, the increase in yields is mainly due to measures financed by the Exchequer, which have resulted (chiefly through artificial insemination) in an improvement in both the genetic constitution and the health of the milch cow herd. It is clear that if the measures advocated in Chapters 6 and 7 are carried into effect, we may expect an even greater increase in the years to come. The economic disposal—from a national viewpoint—of the growing output is, therefore, an increasingly urgent problem.

3. The present methods of disposal of the country's milk production are shown by the following figures:—

UTILISATION OF TOTAL MILK PRODUCTION

		1955	1956	1957
			As % of total	
Used in the production of				
Creamery butter	...	35·9	38.8	40·4
Farmers' butter	...	21·6	21·0	22·4
Consumed by persons	...	20·0	18·9	17·6
Fed to livestock	...	14·1	12·9	12·6
Used in other industries	...	8·4	8·4	7·0
		100·0	100·0	100·0

The milk intake of creameries has been as follows:—

				Total	Used in the production of butter
				Million	Gallons
1937–1939 (average) ...	...	...	207·5	193·8
1953	...	...	231·8	180·1
1954	...	...	240·3	201·2
1955	...	...	237·1	192·7
1956	...	...	262·5	219·1
1957	...	...	289·6	248·8

4. Of the 1957 milk intake at creameries, 86% was used in the production of butter. The problem of disposal of butter stocks surplus to home requirements has recently been examined in detail. It is sufficient to restate the essential factors:—

(i) Most of the additional milk output in recent years has been manufactured into creamery butter. The number of cows on farms supplying milk to creameries, and the number of creamery milk suppliers, have increased in recent years. As home consumption of butter has fallen recently (though still well above pre-war levels), the increasing output must be disposed of in export markets. At present, and for some time at least, this can be done only at a loss by comparison with the home market return. The loss is so great—on exports of the 1957-58 season's production it is estimated at £2.5

million—that the rest of the economy would suffer if it had indefinitely to bear, either in higher taxes or prices, a subsidy of this magnitude.

(ii) The principle to be aimed at in the disposal of milk is that production above home requirements should be disposed of, in whatever form, at the best price obtainable on the export market without State subsidy. Since our competitors in the British market now subsidise their dairying exports to a greater or lesser degree, this ideal may not be attainable in the immediate future but the subsidy must be kept to a minimum and should be used to the best advantage, which is not necessarily to subsidise *butter* exports.

(iii) State assistance should be arranged so as to leave creameries an incentive to find the most economic outlets for surplus milk and to leave suppliers an economic choice between delivering their milk to creameries or using it themselves to rear calves.

(iv) With this in view, it has been decided that, while the Exchequer will bear in full the losses on the export of creamery butter produced in the 1957-58 season, the State subsidy in respect of exports of butter produced in the 1958-59 season will be limited to two-thirds of such losses. The remainder will be contributed by the dairying industry—by means of a levy on butter production.

Producers now face the reality that butter exports do not realise the prices which home consumers are compelled to pay and it is to be hoped that they will take an active interest in ensuring that the gap is narrowed, as far as possible, by efficient marketing of milk abroad in the most economic forms.

Liquid Milk Consumption

5. Our present liquid consumption compares as follows with other countries: —

	Gallons per head per year (1956)
New Zealand	45·1
Switzerland	43·9
Sweden	39·7
Netherlands	37·5
Ireland	36·9
U.K.	32·1
U.S.A.	29·9
Denmark	26·7

The prospects of raising the Irish figure—which is already high by international standards—are not bright. Consumption generally is falling, save in countries where it is already low. The Irish figure has increased by only 1.6 gallons over the last four years, during which period the British figure, despite an expensive 'drink more milk' campaign, has shown a steady if slight decline. Though there seems little hope of increased consumption of liquid milk, the farmers' organisations should be encouraged to run a publicity campaign as a contribution to the solution of the problem of the disposal of growing milk supplies.

Livestock Feeding

6. It is in this direction that the greatest possibilities lie. If dairy farmers—and indeed farmers generally—could be persuaded to feed whole milk to calves, many problems would be solved. The milk surplus could be absorbed, and—more important from the national viewpoint—*better* beef calves could be reared more quickly to maturity. It is, indeed, on this basis that any programme to extend breeding to the west and midlands must be carried out.

7. The great stumbling block to converting dairy farmers to feeding milk to their calves is, of course, their dependence on the monthly creamery milk cheque as their main source of cash. This has also coloured the objections to curtailing the butter subsidy. It is significant that despite the increase in total milk output in recent years —and despite the increase in livestock—the quantity of whole milk fed to livestock has been static for some time past at 70/75 million gallons. What is often overlooked, however, is that the average milk cheque has increased by at least 3% every year since 1953 and is increasing according as the milk yields of cows increase. It is greatly to be desired that dairy farmers should realise that it would be better for both themselves and the country if this annual increment in their cash income were invested in the rearing of better beef calves; a change in this direction is, in fact, essential, since the dairy farmer's monthly cheque is at present dependent on a subvention, to which there is a definite limit, from the general taxpayer. It is understandable that the farmer should prefer a sure and immediate return from the creamery to a more long-term and less assured return from milk-fed cattle. The " sure return " from the creamery has, however, only been made possible in recent years by heavy State assistance and, even under the modified arrangements introduced this year, could not withstand a continued increase in milk intake. It is important to convince the farmer that what is involved in the present proposal is not a choice between the creamery cheque on the one hand and the feeding of whole milk to cattle on the other, but rather an adjustment at the margin which will prevent additional milk output from reaching the creameries and prejudicing even his present milk cheque.

8. Some time ago the Irish Creamery Milk Suppliers' Association favoured the feeding of more whole milk to livestock (though in recent

months they have criticised·the proposal) and they and other farmers' organisations should be given every encouragement to induce farmers to adopt this course. The County Committees of Agriculture and the local advisory services could also assist in the achievement of this desirable objective.

Chocolate Crumb

9. Apart from butter, the largest industry based on milk processing is the manufacture of chocolate crumb, exports of which in 1957 amounted to £4.5 million (£4.0 million of which went to Britain). Expansion of this industry would be of great value to the balance of payments, as virtually all the increased production would be for export, either as crumb or as finished chocolate.

10. Production of chocolate crumb for export is spread over eight producers and, despite some price fluctuations, has remained fairly stable in recent years at the equivalent of 23-24 million gallons of milk a year, though it fell by about 10% in 1957. This country provides 92% (1956) of Britain's imports of crumb, so that any material increase in production here would have to be exported largely to new markets. To achieve this would require a more dynamic approach from the producers.

11. In what way could the State help towards increasing exports? As a diversion of milk from butter production to crumb production would result in some saving in subsidy, a subvention to the crumb industry which would absorb part of this saving could be justified from the viewpoint of the Exchequer. Apart from certain objections to this proposal, price may not, in any case, be so much of a limitation on exports as the fact that British needs are already well supplied and the largest Irish producers have, therefore, no readily available market for increased production. Unfortunately, the crumb process for the manufacture of chocolate is not in general use outside Britain, but there are crumb factories in Canada and some Irish crumb exporters have endeavoured during the past two years—with some promise of success—to interest other Canadian chocolate manufacturers in using the process with the relatively cheap Irish crumb. Efforts have also been made to interest Western German chocolate manufacturers in Irish crumb, but the present German import classification of the product would cause it to be subject to heavy duty. Recent attempts to have this classification modified to the benefit of the Irish crumb industry have failed. Nevertheless, it would seem worthwhile to have the general export possibilities investigated by Córas Tráchtála; if this investigation shows the prospects to be favourable, it would be desirable to make

capital available, if required, so that the Irish producers could expand output for new markets.

Cheese

12. In view of this country's tradition of dairy farming, it seems strange that our total exports of cheese in 1957 amounted to only £20,370 and even this was more than offset by cheese imports of £30,855. In the same year, Britain imported cheese to the value of £25.1 million, of which New Zealand provided £15.9 million. Research and development work on this product should be well worth while; so would a sales and publicity drive aimed at capturing a much larger share of the British market. Attention should also be directed (e.g. by encouraging the farmers' organisations to run a publicity campaign) to increasing home consumption of cheese, which is deplorably low. Some of the blame for this must be placed on the manufacturers, whose products, unless improved in quality and range, will never sell in the quantities necessary to make a substantial contribution to the solution of the milk problem. Some slight improvement has been noticeable in recent years, but much more is needed. Exchequer and technical assistance should, if necessary, be provided to manufacturers anxious to improve the quality of their product. The matter must be considered, however, in its proper perspective. The present output of the Irish cheese industry absorbs only about 6 million gallons of milk, so that even a 100% increase in output—assuming it could be disposed of profitably—would contribute little to the solution of the problem. This does not, however, detract from the importance of making an urgent effort to increase output and sales.

Other Uses

13. The prospects in other fields are not promising. The main outlets (accounting for some 10 million gallons of milk each year) are:—

(1) *Ice Cream :*

The question of increasing the milk content of ice cream sold in this country has been examined, but it has not proved practicable to do so. Any increase would, in any event, have only negligible results on the butter surplus problem.

(2) *Cream :*

Our cream comprises the bulk of fresh cream imported into Britain and only the comparative insignificance of the amount involved in the context of the British market has prevented opposition to its importation by the Milk Marketing Boards. There have, indeed, been rumblings of discontent over the situation among British farmers, as the most profitable outlet for the present huge surplus of British milk is in the form of cream. There may be some scope for exports elsewhere, and

86

home market consumption might be increased by preventing the sale or incorporation in food of artificial cream.

(3) *Full-cream Milk Powder :*
We already have a substantial share of the British market in this commodity.

(4) *Skim Milk Powder :*
There is excessive plant capacity in this country for the production of skim milk powder, much of it of recent installation. There is a surplus of this commodity on the British market at present and New Zealand has been asked to reduce her exports to Britain in the future.

(5) *Condensed Milk (including Tinned Cream) :*
The British demand for this product is not sufficient to justify production on a larger scale for that market. There is an unsatisfied demand for condensed milk and milk powder in Far Eastern countries but export prospects are limited by the low *per capita* incomes in the countries in question and the relatively high price of our products. If our costs can be reduced and if economic conditions improve in these regions, export possibilities should improve, but there are other hurdles to surmount: the overseas trade is largely in the hands of international cartels which have considerable influence on local trade policies.

14. The general objectives must be (1) to reduce, by every possible means, the cost of production of milk and (2) actively to encourage the diversion of milk away from butter making towards more remunerative outlets. In so far as financial assistance is needed to achieve these objectives and State aid is insufficient, there is ground for expecting the cattle industry to make some contribution to the maintenance of the dairying industry, on which it is so dependent. If the demand for meat is rising, and the demand for milk and milk products is static or rising less steeply, it would be reasonable to expect that the more prosperous beef sector would contribute towards the survival of the less viable dairying sector. Any such contribution would merely be a recognition of the fact that, in the last resort, the subsidisation of agricultural products must come in the main from the agricultural industry as a whole.

Beef and Mutton
15. The key to agricultural expansion lies in a dynamic grasslands policy and a greatly increased output of cattle and sheep on the basis of better and cheaper grass. What, it may be asked, is the future of

the live and dead meat trade? The answer must obviously be sought in export markets. A continuance of the secular movement of economic progress in the world at large (despite possible periodic or local recessions) would, as in the past, result in increased consumption of meat. Most of the world's population is still seriously underfed, and their diet to a large extent consists of low-grade, starchy foods. The economic progress of underdeveloped countries, on the basis of past experience, implies advances on the industrial rather than the agricultural front; it is unlikely, therefore, that any advance in material progress in those countries could be accompanied for a considerable time to come by domestic self-sufficiency in meat. In the shorter run, our main meat markets will continue to be found nearest home, and forecasts of likely demand rest on a more solid foundation. Allowing for the present British policy of increasing domestic beef production, one can say that, as far as store cattle are concerned, the British market will absorb all we can produce—and the maintenance of the link with domestic cattle prices there will ensure a profitable return, provided, of course, that we eliminate bovine tuberculosis. As regards the dead meat trade, Britain and the Six Counties imported nearly 574,000 tons of beef and veal in 1957, and as their per caput consumption of beef is not only still below the 1938 level but is only half the U.S.A. and New Zealand figures, our basic market is, as yet, nowhere near saturation point. Furthermore, the O.E.E.C. have estimated that consumer expenditure on meat in its 17 member countries should by 1960 be 20% over the 1955 level. A study of the available information leads to the conclusion that the demand for beef (live or dead), mutton and lamb should not only be maintained but should gradually expand. The importance of the British market to Irish producers of both live and dead meat, and the importance of the Irish supply to Britain argue for a joint approach to the problem by both countries. A bilateral beef policy would be of mutual benefit and would accord with modern internationalism in economic affairs.

Exports

16. The relation of livestock and meat exports to our total exports is shown by the following figures:—

	1955 (£m.)	1956 (£m.)	1957 (£m.)
Total domestic exports of all commodities	106·6	103·6	127·0
Fat Cattle	9·3	11·0	4·8
Store Cattle	26·5	25·1	40·6
Milch Cows and Springers	·4	·3	·3
Total Cattle	36·2	36·4	45·7*
Sheep and Lambs	1·0	1·0	1·0
Beef	7·6	6·7	8·6
Mutton and Lamb	·9	1·5	1·4
Total cattle and sheep exports, live and processed ...	45·4	45·6	56·7

* It should be noted that imports of cattle, which are usually negligible, amounted to £5·1 m. in 1957.

It will be seen that in the past three years total live cattle exports were about 35% in value of total domestic exports of all commodities.

17. Exports of beef, mutton and lamb to Britain and the Six Counties amounted to £5.86 million in 1956 and £4.39 million in 1957. These figures are negligible in relation to exports by such countries as New Zealand and Argentina, whose total exports of meat to Britain and the Six Counties in 1956 were £60.13 million and £41.61 million, respectively. It should be remembered, however, that our very large live trade in cattle has no counterpart in the economies of those countries.

18. The immediate limiting factor on the expansion of the dead meat trade to Britain is the pull of cattle into the store market because of the link with the British guaranteed price. While this link also affects fat cattle exports to Britain, these also have a marketing advantage over dressed beef because

(i) freight charges on live beasts are lower because dead meat involves specialised handling and transport;

(ii) there is an inadequate market for offals here and they must be exported in frozen form to Britain where they sell at a discount as compared with fresh offals;

(iii) fat cattle slaughtered in Britain are retailed as fresh home-killed beef, which normally earns a premium over chilled beef imported from this country;

(iv) the established channels of trade are mainly for cattle on the hoof, and there are important interests, in both Britain and Ireland, concerned to maintain the present position.

An indication of the effect of these disabilities is given by costings, made in 1953 on behalf of the meat exporters, of trial consignments of fat cattle and carcase beef sent to Britain, which showed that the extra cost of exporting dead beef (even allowing for receipts from offals, hides, etc.) was about $1\frac{1}{2}$d. a lb. or, say, 70/- a beast. In present conditions, therefore, the beef export trade tends to be increasingly dependent on markets other than Britain, though this would not necessarily be the case if cattle production and exports increased substantially. As regards mutton, the live sheep or lamb does not travel well, so that the dead meat trade is relatively more developed, exports to Britain and the Six Counties in 1957 being valued at £1.25 million, as against £1.0 million for the live trade.

19. Exports of canned beef go almost entirely to Britain. While they are not insignificant, they are of declining importance; the 1957 figure of £2.1 million compares with £4.6 million in 1952. This trade

is based mainly on the cows retired annually from the country's dairy herds, and is largely in the hands of a few specialist manufacturers. Our share of the British market has become attenuated because of the increase in supplies of meat of all kinds and also because alternative outlets for this type of animal have grown considerably in recent years.

20. Store cattle exported to Britain fit into the British pattern of farming and, when fattened there for not less than three months, qualify for the guaranteed payment under the British fat stock guarantee scheme, abated by 3s. 6d. per live cwt. This arrangement will continue for at least three years from the 28th March, 1956, unless there is a material alteration in conditions, such as a fundamental change in the British system of guarantees. It has had a beneficial result in maintaining Irish cattle prices and in encouraging output, but has operated to limit to some extent the development of the dead meat trade. If some arrangement of a similar nature could be extended to the meat trade there would be obvious advantages; in particular, an expansion in meat production for export would create productive work both in the trade itself and in the many ancillary industries.

21. The development of the meat industry is not hampered by inadequacy of plant and equipment. Registered slaughtering premises are in a position to handle any foreseeable numbers of livestock. While the export figures testify to the relative competitiveness of existing production, there can be little doubt that unit costs could be reduced even further by the wider spread of overhead charges which would result from a bigger throughput at these plants.

22. One indirect way of aiding the expansion of the dead meat industry would be to speed up the bovine tuberculosis eradication scheme, as sound cow beef from slaughterings under that scheme can be used for canning and manufacturing, and the current market abroad for cow beef is buoyant. It is, in fact, a highly developed one, both in Europe and the U.S.A., though hampered by governmental restrictions on imports, especially in some European markets. State aid might be provided to help finance technical research into such questions as——

(a) freight charges and methods and the use of containers;

(b) the greater use of by-products, e.g., glands for the pharmaceutical trade;

(c) improved marketing methods, e.g., the pre-packaging of meat. It might also be desirable to encourage slaughtering companies to purchase their own farms; apart from improving the supply position, this would help to bring the benefits of company organisation to stock farming.

23. In view of the fluctuations in the supply and prices of live-stock, there would be some advantage in an organised purchasing system based on contractual arrangements with graziers to ensure regular supplies for slaughter. While such an arrangement would benefit the slaughterers, its value to the farmers is less obvious, except insofar as the elimination of the middleman might permit the payment of higher prices. It would be difficult to determine in advance a suitable price which would be adequate to offset offers by other buyers and ensure a timely supply at the factory. It might, how-ever, be possible to come to some long-term arrangement with the larger graziers and cooperative organisations. This is a complicated matter which would require detailed examination by the interests concerned

CHAPTER 9

PIGS AND BACON

General

1. Although there are some large-scale pig farms in Ireland, most pigs are produced from units of one or two sows on small farms. Pigs are prolific breeders: the period of gestation of a sow is four months, and the average litter produced is about ten. The pig population is, accordingly, capable of rapid increase or decrease—though Dr. Robert O'Connor has shown* that farmers increase pig production more slowly than they reduce it—and the high rate of turnover of the pig population (about ten months would cover the total period between the mating of the sow and the slaughter of the progeny for bacon) means that improvements in breeding, feeding and management can bring rapid results.

2. The predominant characteristic of the pig trade is one of severe fluctuation. Studies have shown that many factors influence the numbers of pigs produced—current market prices for pigs, prices of pigs relative to other agricultural products, quantities of pig feed available, price of pig feed, the pig/food price ratio, incidence of disease, etc. Of these, the most important influences on pig numbers are the quantity of food available and the price of pigs. The scarcity of supplies of maize during the war was followed by a reduction in the number of pigs to 380,000 in 1944, the lowest on record, while it has long been recognised that a heavy potato crop in any year is followed by a subsequent increase in pig numbers about eighteen months afterwards. The increase since 1956 in pig numbers is probably attributable to the high guaranteed export price for grade A bacon.

3. Actual production of pigs and their disposal has been estimated as follows for recent years:—

ESTIMATED PIG PRODUCTION (NUMBERS)

Year	Home Consumption	Exports	Total
1953	815,000	382,000	1,197,000
1954	903,000	518,000	1,421,000
1955	936,000	296,000	1,232,000
1956	899,000	147,000	1,046,000
1957	933,000	323,000	1,256,000

The home market demand, it will be seen, does not vary greatly, any

* In a paper read before the Statistical and Social Inquiry Society, December, 1953. This paper also contains a review of the literature on the subject.

fluctuations in the numbers produced bringing greater proportionate variations in the quantities exported.

4. The final destination of the pigs produced in 1957 is estimated to be as follows: —

Used in
Curing (bacon and ham) ...		1,027,000
Pork		105,000
Sausages, etc.		43,000
Slaughtered on farms		81,000
Total output		1,250,000

Breeds

5. Official faith has hitherto been pinned on the Irish Large White and the importation of boars of other breeds has not been permitted. In particular, the Department prohibited until recently, on veterinary grounds, the importation of the Landrace pig, thought by many to provide a superior and more economic product than the Large White. This prohibition did not prevent the smuggling of Landrace pigs over the Border and recently the Department has recognised a *fait accompli* by permitting importations under licence; a Landrace Herd Book has been established to ensure that only high-quality animals of the breed are admitted. A controversy has raged for some years over the comparative merits of the two breeds, but this question can be finally decided only by scientific testing. The first pig progeny testing station in Denmark (which specialises in Landraces, but will not permit their export) was founded in 1907. Our first progeny testing station began operations in January, 1958, with a capacity of less than 200 pigs (although a smaller pilot station has been in operation for about four years at Ballyhaise Agricultural School). A projected second station has not yet advanced beyond the planning stage.

6. The aim of progeny testing is first to find the strains which produce the best pigs and then to disseminate these strains among the producers at large. It is one thing to have high-grade bacon from pigs tested at the testing stations; it is another to raise the *general* quality of Irish bacon. It is not that the general quality is low. The export price guarantee scheme for grade A bacon, introduced in April, 1956, has already made a significant contribution to raising standards; the proportion of pigs received at the bacon factories *in the main bacon weight range* is now 70% on average, compared with 54% for August-December, 1955 and 62% for the year 1956. Even yet, however, little over 55% *of all pigs produced* are grade A so that there remains plenty of room for improvement. It is important for this reason that progeny testing be pushed ahead with all possible speed, and that the second progeny testing station be erected without delay.

7. It is to the export market, of course, that we must look for the disposal of increased pig production, and success depends on our offering high class bacon at competitive prices. Exports of pig products (including bacon, pork, hams, canned hams and sausages), which in 1957 were valued at a total of £4.9 million have been increasing over the last few years, but they are still below the 1953 peak of £7 million. Despite the increase, our share of the British market is still very small. Total imports of bacon and pork into Britain in 1957 amounted to 7,153,000 cwts. valued at £86.8 million, the principal supplying countries and the amounts being as follows:—

	cwts.	£ m.
Denmark...	4,480,000	56·1
Poland ... .·. ...	979,000	11·2
Netherlands	739,000	8·9

Imports from these countries have to bear a 10% tariff which does not apply to Irish bacon.

Guaranteed Prices for Pigs and Bacon

8. Under the guaranteed price scheme bacon curers are at present guaranteed a minimum price of 327/- per cwt. delivered in Britain (i.e., about 307/- per cwt. ex-factory) for grade A bacon on the basis of their paying a minimum price of 235/- per cwt. deadweight for grade A pigs and 230/- per cwt. for grade B.1 pigs deadweight. The Exchequer contribution for 1957-58 towards supporting these prices (assisted by a levy of 10/- per bacon pig paid by curers) was originally estimated at £190,000 on an assumed average price of 270/- per cwt. for Irish bacon in Britain. The bacon market in Britain was, however, very depressed during the latter part of 1957 and the early months of 1958, mainly as a result of abundant supplies of British and Danish bacon, and the price for Irish bacon, which averaged about 276/- per cwt. from January to August, 1957, fell later to as low as 210/- to 230/- per cwt. Although there has been a recovery of prices in Britain, it seems unlikely, on present indications, that the average price realised for our bacon in Britain will exceed about 240/- or 245/- per cwt. in 1958-59. As in the case of milk, the present uneconomic returns on the export market have not brought about a fall in production; on the contrary, because of the operation of the guaranteed scheme, deliveries of pigs to factories in the opening weeks of this year were over 50% higher than at the beginning of 1957, though the cessation of cross-border smuggling has also contributed significantly to the heavy home supply.

9. This situation required an increase in the Exchequer subsidy for 1957-58 from the amount of £190,000 previously calculated to £787,000. Reductions in the guaranteed prices for pigs by 5/- a cwt. and an

94

increase in the levy on all pigs converted into bacon, both to take effect from 1 July, 1958, will leave the level of Exchequer subsidy in 1958-59, at the current level of production, at £650,000. If production should increase, or the average price realised for our bacon exports be lower than expected, the demand on the Exchequer could be far greater. This is not a healthy base for the expansion of the industry, particularly in the light of the keen competition that must be expected in export markets.

10. The export market may be divided into three sections: pork, bacon and manufacturing. Although an over-simplification, it is an indication of the problem to say that the pork market requires pigs at about five months old, the bacon market at $6\frac{1}{2}$ months old and the manufacturing market at eight months old. In conditions of over-production, the seasonal pork market, having first choice, takes its requirements and leaves the surplus to flood the bacon and manufacturing markets, with consequent depression of prices. The problem is exacerbated by the fact that the British market for bacon (in practice our sole export market) is very inelastic, absorbing about 10,500 tons a week, and quite small variations of supply around that figure can cause disproportionate fluctuations in price. A further complication from the point of view of the Irish producers is that both in the U.K. and Denmark the pig population has been increasing rapidly in recent years. This increase in supply has brought about a glut in the British bacon market, so that the prices realisable are at present uneconomic for even the most efficient producer. It should not be overlooked that British pig production is subsidised to the extent of £40 million a year.

Costs

11. As regards Irish producers, it appears reasonable enough that they should be assured a measure of stability of prices for pigs so that they may not be at the mercy of the violent fluctuations which are so characteristic of the bacon trade. At the same time, regard must be had to economic realities. We cannot fix prices to suit ourselves or world markets; neither can we sustain exports by placing undue burdens on the home consumer and taxpayer which would hamper development of the economy in other directions, and which would merely grow heavier as production and exports increased. Our present costs of production are much too high. The main item in these costs is, of course, the price of feeding stuffs. There is a wide variety of feeding stuffs for pigs: maize, barley, wheat, oats, potatoes, offals, skim milk, brewers' grains protein cakes/meats, fodder beet, domestic swill, etc. This variety, the absence of any market price for such items as skim milk and swill, variations in the types of balanced rations fed to pigs, all make for great differences in production costs. In general, however, our costs are too high for successful competition with a large and highly efficient supplier such as Denmark.

12. The important movement in recent years has been the rapid growth in barley production and its substitution for maize in pig feeding. The following tables illustrate the trend:—

IMPORTS OF BARLEY AND MAIZE

	Barley Imports		Maize Imports	
	000 tons	£000	000 tons	£000
1951	1	29	200	5,907
1952	2	87	143	4,493
1953	0	3	193	5,437
1954	46	981	170	4,269
1955	22	608	224	5,472
1956	26	631	111	2,745
1957	34	841	16	408

HOME PRODUCTION OF FEEDING BARLEY

	Sold	Retained by Growers	Total
	000 tons	000 tons	000 tons
1952/3	30	114	144
1953/4	45	75	120
1954/5	21	68	89
1955/6	50	84	134
1956/7	100	74	174
1957/8	150	117	267

13. The difficulty about home production of feeding barley is that such a high proportion of it is grown as a cash crop. Less than half of it is grown (1957-58) in the pig-rearing areas where it is most needed. Successful barley growing, moreover, requires limed soil and fertiliser, and, therefore, a degree of capital outlay often beyond the capacity of the small farmers who comprise the country's main pig producers. The fact that few small farmers are in a position to wait for their return until pigs reared on barley are eventually slaughtered accounts for much of the barley being grown for cash; a good deal of the cash crop, however, comes from large farms in the south. Since it has been found necessary to restrict maize imports to absorb the home barley crop, the combination of a high guaranteed price for barley and the high costs of drying, storage, handling and transporting the barley to pig fattening areas, keeps production costs unduly high. The question of the price of barley and the problems of a wheat surplus are discussed in Chapter 10. Here it may be remarked that since barley is merely a raw material in pig production, its price should be governed by that of the end product.

14. It is clear that concentration of fattening in areas where barley is grown would reduce significantly the cost of rearing pigs, and it is on

this basis that the support or guarantee price structure for pigs should be established. Improved varieties of barley have been developed in recent years and, with proper liming and manuring, feeding barley can now be grown in any part of the country on land suitable for growing oats. Thus, farmers in most if not all counties could engage in pig production on an economic basis by growing their own requirements of barley. Equally, if the large growers in the south, who are mainly responsible for the considerable local surplus of barley which is grown for cash and has to be marketed at high cost in the north and west, went in for pig fattening on a large scale, a much sounder basis for the pig industry could be laid, and our chances of holding and expanding our share of the British and other markets would be much enhanced. The ideal of the entire barley crop being consumed locally as pigfeed is unlikely to be attainable in practice, but it should remain the general aim of policy.

15. A greater degree of specialisation by farmers in pig production, including particular attention to feeding and management, would raise the general level of efficiency and thereby improve the quality of bacon. The more extensive operation of pig farms by bacon factories and the participation of the larger creameries in pig fattening would be welcome developments.

16. It is in this general context that the long-term basis of State assistance to the pig industry should be fixed. In the case of wheat, the Exchequer subsidy will disappear after 1958-59, while a definite limit has been set to Exchequer subsidy of butter. No such limit obtains in the case of bacon. There is provision for adjustment of the guaranteed price and the curers' levy at six months' notice, but to bring the bacon subsidy into line with the general principles governing produce subsidies outlined in Chapter 12 and already adopted in the case of butter, some more definite curb is required to the contingent liability to the Exchequer. It has been suggested that this could be achieved by linking the guaranteed price for pigs to a guaranteed barley price, provided that the latter was kept in line with world coarse grain prices. Such an arrangement, however, would be unwieldy in practice. Besides, it does not take account of the British market price for bacon, which in practice determines the size of the loss to the Exchequer. The object of achieving a self-supporting guaranteed price structure may be unattainable with present depressed (and subsidised) export prices, but in more stable market conditions it would be easier of achievement if Exchequer assistance were directed towards cheapening feed rather than guaranteeing high prices. This merely emphasises the point that barley prices should be governed by pig prices and not *vice versa*. Perhaps the best solution in the long run—if it could be achieved—would be a link with the British price structure in consideration of the general

desirability of the coordination of agricultural policies in the two countries.

Modernisation of Bacon Factories, etc.

17. There are about 40 bacon factories in the country and they give employment to some 3,600 persons. They have capacity well in excess of present output, though the capacity could be better distributed in relation to supplies of pigs. Expansion of output could, therefore, be achieved without any significant increase in capital investment. Modernisation may, however, be desirable in many cases and there is scope for the installation of up-to-date machinery and equipment for the expansion of such lines as pre-packaged bacon, cooked hams, pork luncheon meats, sausages, etc. There is a demand for canned hams in the dollar area and elsewhere but expansion of this line is dependent on the availability of appropriate refrigeration services. Development of these and similar lines should be particularly encouraged in view of the greater degree of processing involved.

Research and Marketing

18. To maintain and increase efficiency, to keep abreast of technical progress abroad and to develop new lines, constant research is necessary. A full-scale unit for general research work, including the experimental production of bacon, other pig products and by-products, is desirable. The unit might be financed jointly by the State and the industry, and might with advantage be operated in conjunction with the research for the beef and mutton trades recommended in Chapter 8. Research in both industries into production, marketing, advertising, etc., should be co-ordinated as far as possible.

19. The committee which has been established to advise on the marketing of agricultural produce will no doubt fully investigate the marketing problems involved. It may, however, be permissible to suggest here that a more centralised marketing of pigs, based on a system of contracts with farmers, may have distinct advantages for all concerned. One final point: as far as bacon is concerned, we are largely only marginal suppliers to the British market; even in present conditions of heavy production, we are supplying only about 600 to 700 tons a week. As a result, when supplies become plentiful, the price of Irish bacon tends to fall more heavily than prices for the larger and more regular supplies. The following prices per cwt. for Irish and Danish bacon in the British market illustrate this clearly:—

1957				Irish	Danish
June	...	...	...	312/-	318/-
July	...	...	...	264/-	280/-
October	...	...	...	210/-	250/-

Maintenance and expansion of our exports to Britain require continuity of supply and ability to secure standing orders. The home consumer should, if necessary, go short so that export continuity might be preserved. We cannot hope to progress on the basis of sporadic incursions into export markets, conducted mainly at times when losses are more likely than profits. It is the producer—and the country—that can supply in times of scarcity as well as times of glut that finds pig production profitable.

CHAPTER 10

OTHER ASPECTS OF AGRICULTURE

1. It is not the intention of this study to review all the problems of agricultural development. A comprehensive examination would, for example, have to consider such matters as the possibilities of expanding horticulture and fruit farming (the industrial aspects of which are discussed in Chapter 17), the prospects of developing an export trade in early vegetables, table poultry and pedigree cattle and expanding the trade in thoroughbred horses, and the effects of land division policy. Before passing on, however, to the questions of agricultural education and State aid generally, a few remarks may be made on wheat, barley (already touched upon in Chapter 9, paras. 12 to 14) agricultural credit and the improvement of agricultural trade relations with other countries.

2. The place of wheat and barley in agricultural production may be seen from the following figures:

AREA UNDER TILLAGE (EXCLUDING FLAX AND FRUIT)

	1947	1949	1951	1953	1954	1955	1956	1957
Corn Crops					*Million Acres*			
Wheat	0·58	0·36	0·28	0·35	0·49	0·36	0·34	0·40
Barley	0·15	0·16	0·17	0·19	0·16	0·21	0·24	0·32
Oats	0·83	0·69	0·62	0·57	0·53	0·55	0·53	0·46
Total ...	1·56	1·21	1·07	1·12	1·19	1·12	1·11	1·18
Root and Green Crops ...	0·72	0·66	0·62	0·62	0·61	0·59	0·59	0·57
Total Tillage ...	2·28	1·87	1·69	1·74	1·80	1·71	1·70	1·75

3. Since the ending of compulsory tillage the area tilled has been more or less constant with, if anything, a tendency to decline. The comparison with other countries given in Chapter 5, paragraph 7, shows that the area under tillage in Ireland is relatively low. This is, of course, associated with the concentration on livestock and milk production off grasslands and the particular suitability of our climate for the growing of grass. Most of the tillage crops are fed to animals; the only major crops for human consumption are wheat, potatoes and sugar beet. The place of tillage in the agricultural economy is, therefore, secondary to grass but it is nevertheless of considerable importance as a steady source of cash income. Moreover, greater cultivation of tillage crops, especially roots and barley, would be a necessary complement to an increase in

the carrying capacity of grasslands and the better conservation of grass for winter feeding.

Wheat

4. Until 1958, farmers had a guaranteed market, at a guaranteed price, for all the millable wheat which they produced. Apart from short and exceptional periods, foreign wheat is substantially cheaper than Irish wheat, and national wheat policy has, therefore, involved higher flour and bread prices for the consumer. The price of imported wheat, however, does not in all cases reflect the full costs of production and, while this may be immaterial in so far as the consumer is concerned, the farmer is legitimately entitled to protection against subsidised imports. The encouragement of some wheat growing can be defended on security grounds but the main justification of wheat policy rests on the general proposition that the home market should be reserved to the home producer. Wheat growing has become so accepted and so important a part of the agricultural economy that any *major* reversal of policy at this stage would be very difficult. Wheat is the farmers' most important cash crop and with the declining importance of oats is becoming the most important tillage crop. The expansion of the acreage under wheat has been partly responsible for the very considerable post-war investment in farm mechanisation, and a substantial reduction in that acreage would have unfortunate repercussions. Home production of wheat helps to reduce imports but its effect on the *balance of payments* is not so obvious since, if wheat were not grown, the land would be put to alternative use.

5. Until recently the guaranteed price could be fixed without fear that it would evoke a supply of Irish millable wheat in excess of demand—in other words, the guaranteed price and the guaranteed market were not necessarily inconsistent. In the cereal year 1957-58, however, a combination of increasing yields (the mill intake per acre is now 60% greater than the pre-war average), a high acreage, an unusually high carry-over of stocks and a falling demand for flour, produced a situation in which supplies of Irish millable wheat greatly exceeded the amount which could be used in the production of flour. The surplus has to be sold for animal feed or otherwise disposed of, at an estimated loss to the Exchequer of £1.45 million.

6. The new " married price " arrangements announced for wheat of the 1958 harvest are designed to avoid a recurrence of this burden on the Exchequer. The guaranteed price will extend only to 300,000 tons of dried Irish wheat. If mill intake exceeds this figure the balance will be sold for animal feed or exported and the effective price received

by growers will be determined by the *total* receipts for the sale of wheat, whether for the production of flour or otherwise. The loss on surplus wheat will therefore be spread over all wheat growers.

7. It remains to be seen how the new system will work out in practice. It involves forecasting not alone the total wheat intake but also the anticipated loss on the intake in excess of 300,000 tons of dried wheat. These forecasts will have to err on the safe side if an "uncovered" loss is not to emerge, and it would not be surprising if they became the subject of contention and acrimony. Furthermore, if a substantial surplus occurs in any year, it will be difficult to avoid *some* reduction in the guaranteed price in the following year with a view to bringing the demand for, and the supply of, Irish millable wheat closer together. The alternative would be to attempt to achieve the same result through the farmers' fear that, if the *nominal* guaranteed price were left unchanged, the effective price would have to be reduced substantially to cover losses on surplus wheat.

8. The new proposals have the advantage of taking fully into account—though on an estimated basis—the *entire* wheat crop and, therefore, the losses likely to arise on surplus production, but in the long run they are not likely to be more effective or acceptable, and are certainly bound to be more difficult to administer, than "straight" variations in the guaranteed price. Admittedly, there is no assurance that guaranteed prices, in the absence of a system of contractual wheat growing, will evoke the amount of wheat required. Provided, however, that price policy is flexible and adaptable it should be possible to achieve a tolerable concordance between supply and demand and thus avoid the present indefensible position in which good land is diverted to the production of wheat for animal feeding. Part of the trouble in 1957-58 was caused by the high level of stocks at the beginning of the year; if in future years stocks are maintained at normal levels our new expanded grain stores should be able to accommodate any *temporary* excess of supply over demand, provided that in years when the excess is large the guaranteed price is adjusted downward for the following year. Correspondingly, in years when supply falls short of the target the guaranteed price for the following year should be adjusted upwards.

9. The adoption of the "married price" arrangement may, of course, work out satisfactorily but if experience this year proves other-wise, it is suggested that a *flexible* guaranteed price policy should be adopted in future years. One of the factors which would render the "married price" plan more acceptable to farmers—and possibly easier to administer—would be an increase in the basic amount (at present 300,000 tons) of dried wheat in respect of which the *full* guaranteed

price would be paid. It is true that the reduction in the extraction rate to 72% will increase the demand for Irish wheat but it appears to be the intention to revert to an extraction rate of 80% at the end of the present cereal year. In recent years the percentage of Irish wheat used in the grist has increased significantly and the present percentage of 79% actually exceeds the percentage (about 75%) contemplated in the Government's decision that 300,000 tons of dried Irish wheat should be used for milling purposes. If the percentage is to be raised further, it will be necessary to press ahead vigorously with the investigations into the technical milling and baking problems arising from the extended use of Irish wheat. These problems were referred in 1955 to the Institute for Industrial Research and Standards which has already reported some progress. As Irish wheat is much dearer than imported wheat, an increase in the percentage of Irish wheat used in milling grists would entail, for consumers, the unwelcome prospect of higher flour and bread prices, but, provided the increase were technically feasible, it would be consistent with the basic principle of reserving the *home* market for domestic suppliers.

10. The difficulty of ensuring that, for any given guaranteed price, the supply of Irish wheat would not prove excessive, could be solved by a contractual system of wheat growing. There are, of course, objections of a general nature to any contractual system, but these do not seem to have prevented the successful operation of contractual systems for sugar beet and malting barley. Admittedly these analogies should not be pushed too far since conditions are different in the case of wheat, where there are about 70,000 individual growers, some thirty final purchasing agents and (what is more significant) a danger of over-production. These, however, are differences of degree which do not *entirely* rule out of consideration a contractual system of wheat growing and, in fact, it might be argued that the greater number of purchasing points would enable a contractual wheat system to cover a much larger area than in the case of sugar beet and malting barley. It would be prudent to obtain the views of the milling industry (which favours a contractual system) and of the farmers' associations most immediately concerned on the feasibility of introducing such a system, if the "married price" arrangement proves difficult to administer or is otherwise unsatisfactory in its operation. The minimum requirement is that contractual wheat growing should be encouraged as much as possible. Wheat is an industrial raw material and wheat growing should be operated *as far as possible* on business lines.

11. The same considerations also point to the desirability of raising the general level of the quality of Irish wheat and of securing a more orderly marketing of Irish wheat. Developments in recent years have placed a premium on top-quality wheat and imposed penalties on poor-quality wheat. Thus the bushelling requirements for top-grade wheat

have been increased, bonuses have been paid for wheat with a moisture content of less than 25%, and penalty deductions have been authorised where the moisture content exceeded 26%. These developments might, with advantage, be continued with a view to encouraging the growing of top-quality wheat—an objective which is all the more desirable in view of the present tendency to excess production and the high price which the consumer is paying for flour made from a grist containing a high percentage of Irish wheat. Finally, only those varieties of wheat which are suitable to Irish soil and climate should be sown. The investigations carried out by the Institute for Industrial Research and Standards have shown that some of the varieties used are quite unsuitable; fortunately, these varieties are not grown to any significant extent.

12. As regards marketing, the concentrated intake of wheat at the mills in the first two months of the cereal year has imposed a severe strain on drying and storage equipment. The post-war increase in this equipment has relieved the strain considerably but only at the expense of a comparatively uneconomic use of the equipment throughout the year as a whole; the increase in the acreage under feeding barley may ensure its more economic use. More orderly methods of marketing wheat are nevertheless desirable. In recent years inducements, by way of bonuses for late deliveries, have been held out to farmers to withhold their wheat from the market in the opening weeks of the cereal year. These inducements—though substantial—have not proved very effective and, indeed, are hardly likely to be successful as long as wheat production exceeds requirements. It has been stated that the inducements might be more effective if farmers had facilities for holding wheat for an extended period and were allowed to dry it and sell it on a dried basis; credit facilities on the security of the crop might have to be provided to make this feasible. The millers have, hitherto, objected to this proposal on the grounds that the wheat should be dried by them or under their control, to prevent its being damaged in the process. Here again the large increase in the wheat crop calls for a reassessment of points of view in the light of changed circumstances. Any such reassessment must take into account the extent to which farmers elsewhere dry wheat, the fact that the increased output of feeding barley may require the installation on farms of drying equipment which could also be utilised for drying wheat, the possibility of cooperative grain drying and the undesirability of building up drying facilities in excess of national requirements.

Barley

13. Barley for malting purposes is grown under contractual arrangements made between the growers and brewers and this portion of the crop does not enter into the general grain market save insofar as barley unsuitable for industrial purposes is diverted to feeding.

14. The question of feeding barley is, as was indicated in Chapter 9, inextricably bound up with pig production. To avoid high drying, storage and transport costs, the ideal arrangement would be to have all feeding barley used in the area in which it is grown, but its importance as a cash crop for so many farmers (less than one-half the crop is retained by growers) makes this difficult to achieve, at least for the present and certainly as long as a minimum price is guaranteed. As was indicated in Chapter 9, the ideal would be that the large-scale growers in the south who are mainly responsible for the considerable amount of barley that comes on the market would themselves raise pigs, thus reducing the commercial surplus and that the farmers in the north and west would grow more barley for consumption on their own holdings.

15. The attraction of a guaranteed floor price helps to ensure that home requirements will be met, with consequent advantage to the balance of payments; the increase in production in recent years has displaced the annual importation of some 150,000 tons of feeding stuffs. As against this, it must be remembered that as a feeding stuff *barley is merely a raw material* in the production of livestock. It is on the sale of our livestock and livestock products that our economic future depends and anything that tends to raise, or even to render more rigid, farmers' costs of production is to be deprecated. There is, therefore, a strong case for allowing the price of the end product—in this case pigs—to govern the price of barley.

16. The difficulties of the present position are mainly attributable to the extent to which barley is grown as a cash crop. Drying, storage and transport costs inflate the ex-farm price of barley with the result that *purchased* native barley is at present £4 to £5 a ton dearer than the imported variety (the price of which is subsidised by the countries of origin) though, for the farmer who uses his own barley, the foreign barley is dearer than the native barley. To overcome these difficulties, the aims of policy should be:—

1. to free the price of barley (thereby removing some of its attractions as a cash crop and giving the larger barley growers some incentive to convert the grain into pigs instead of cash) leaving the market price to be determined by the price of pigs; and

2. to persuade pig producers to grow their own barley requirements.

The aim should be to ensure, as far as possible, that barley is used locally for animal feeding. There are undoubtedly difficulties in the way of attaining this objective. Some growers may prefer to sell the grain because they need the cash at harvest time; in such cases appropriate credit arrangements seem necessary. In other cases, lack of storage on the growers' farms may present difficulties; here it may be necessary to encourage the erection of farm buildings or to facilitate the farmer in obtaining access to local or cooperative storage.

17. In giving effect to this policy, two points are of great importance. First, care should be taken that the growing of feeding barley, which has been developed with much effort over a number of years, does not decline. Second, the removal of price support for barley will not be practicable until a method has been devised which will ensure that, as a cash crop, barley is not replaced by wheat, thus adding to our wheat problems. A contractual system for wheat, as suggested above, should remove this danger.

Agricultural Credit

18. At present there might be said to be a conflict of opinion on whether or not there is a significant unsatisfied demand for agricultural credit, at least by farmers who, on any reasonable definition of the term, are credit-worthy. Certainly, little use has been made of some of the special credit schemes introduced in recent years. At the same time, it cannot be assumed that, despite the present substantial recourse to merchant, hire-purchase and bank credit, existing facilities and resources would be adequate to finance a substantial increase in production. If pastures are to be improved and full advantage taken of their increased stock-carrying capacity, if the present beef areas are to be encouraged to produce their own calves and rear them to maturity, if farmers are to be induced to withhold their barley from the market and to use it instead for pig feeding, if adequate farm buildings and grain storage are to be provided, if some form of farm apprenticeship scheme is to be introduced and if young farmers are to be encouraged to rent farms, it is clear that arrangements must be made to ensure that any consequential increase in the demand for agricultural credit can be met in full and without delay. In the case of some farmers, a traditional reluctance to incur debt may be the greatest obstacle to increased production, and it may be necessary to convince them of the net financial advantage of borrowing to finance a greater volume of output.

19. An examination is currently being made of agricultural credit facilities with a view to making recommendations for unified or coordinated arrangements having, as their primary object, the encouragement of increased agricultural production. The problem need not, therefore, receive extensive treatment in this study but the following points are noted for consideration:—

  (i) The partial rationalisation of the agricultural credit structure achieved in 1955, when schemes operated by the Department of Agriculture were transferred to the Agricultural Credit Cor-

106

poration, should be extended by simplifying and, if possible, unifying the present multiplicity of credit schemes operated by the Corporation, the emphasis being laid on "production" schemes operated in close association with the local agricultural advisory service.

(ii) The security conditions stipulated by the Corporation should be relaxed in view of the favourable bad debt experience to date (admittedly due in the main to rising prices since 1939), the State guaranteeing the Corporation against financial loss. As between a small volume of credit, involving few bad debts but associated with a low level of production, and a larger volume of credit possibly involving some losses from bad debts but facilitating an expansion in agricultural production, the choice should be quite clear. Security conditions cannot be relaxed to cater for the marginal farmer but there is little point in introducing credit schemes which are subject to conditions which many of the farming community cannot satisfy.

(iii) The funds required to finance an expansion of agricultural credit should be readily available to the Corporation from the banking system and, if necessary, from the Exchequer. It would be heartening—and wholly appropriate—if the minimum annual demand henceforth for industrial and agricultural credit were at least equivalent to the £3½ million on average of external reserves which would be set free by the proposal in Chapter 4 (paragraph 20).

(iv) There should be close working relationships between the Corporation and the commercial banks and the possibility might be examined of devising a system in which local bank branches would act as agents for the Corporation. This system—which would require the utmost goodwill between both parties—would help to give the Corporation a clearer picture of local conditions. Close liaison with the advisory services would also help towards this end, though care would be needed to maintain the independent status of the instructor.

(v) A further point to be considered is the extent to which hire-purchase institutions are at present meeting the credit needs of farmers and whether the Agricultural Credit Corporation should not enter this field. It is understood that this matter, which presents considerable difficulties, is being examined by the Corporation.

(vi) History affords no support for the belief that cooperative credit societies could be successfully established, but it might be possible to encourage existing creamery and other cooperative societies to extend additional credit to their members to finance increased production.

Agricultural Trade Relations

20. The importance of finding markets for our agricultural produce underlines the need for satisfactory external trade arrangements. Government intervention in agriculture and in agricultural trade in all countries is nowadays so widespread and deeply rooted that inter-governmental relationships are vital to, and indeed inseparable from, the question of maintaining and increasing external markets for our agricultural produce. An increase in agricultural productivity leading to increased export potential could be largely negatived in the absence of satisfactory trading relationships with the countries to which we export our produce. As there seems to be little doubt that Britain will continue to be the main importer of agricultural products in Europe, our agricultural trade relationships with that country will continue to be very important. We must, however, endeavour to maintain and increase markets for our products outside Britain. So far as Western European markets are concerned, it will be necessary to ensure that, with the advent of the Common Market and the Free Trade Area, our export position *vis-à-vis* those markets does not deteriorate but is in fact improved. In the Free Trade Area negotiations, therefore, our aim must be to broaden the scope for increased agricultural exports to the continental countries and to ensure that there will be no disimprovement in our existing arrangements with Britain.

CHAPTER 11

AGRICULTURAL EDUCATION AND INSTRUCTION

1. It is a matter of the highest national priority to raise the standard of Irish farming skills. This calls for an improvement and extension of the existing facilities for agricultural education and instruction. An analysis of these facilities reveals certain defects and inadequacies and underlines the need for a new approach, not prejudiced by the controversies of the past.

2. For reasons discussed below, an improvement in farming skills over the next five years or so must be achieved largely through the advisory services. The advisory services, however, will not become fully effective until the farmer has the understanding of the basic sciences which only an adequate education can supply. The broadening and deepening of the educational system will take many years to accomplish, but if only because of the time-lag involved before aspiration can become achievement, it is important that no time be lost in giving our educational system an agricultural bias. Agriculture has for too long been the Cinderella of the educational household, from primary school to university. Unless we are prepared to accept indefinitely the consequences of this—a rather low standard of production, and therefore of living, compared to most of Europe, and a common tendency to regard farming as an occupation inferior to that of clerk—it is of paramount importance that this most fundamental problem be tackled now.

3. Appendix 6 contains a brief survey of the facilities for agricultural education and instruction available at present. In the following pages an assessment is made of the means by which they can be improved and extended.

Primary Schools

4. The Commission on Vocational Organisation noted in 1943 that there was a considerable divergence of opinion on the wisdom or, indeed, the usefulness of teaching agriculture in primary schools. It commented that a formal scientific course obviously could not be taught in primary or even in secondary schools, but that the fundamental notions of the basic sciences underlying agriculture, and the necessary foundation for subsequent scientific training in agriculture, are both interesting and extremely useful for children in primary schools who will become farmers.

The Commission underlined this by pointing out that the vast majority of children receive no post-primary education—out of a total population of 397,000 between the ages of 12 and 19 in 1951, only 50,000 were in secondary schools and some 20,000 in day vocational schools. While admitting the validity of this point, it is well to recognise that it may be very difficult to integrate agricultural education with general education at the primary level, save in the most elementary fashion. In 1954, only 2.7% of the pupils in primary schools were over 14. Obviously the majority of the children could not take any useful part in the practical work of a school garden, but children of average intelligence should be able to benefit from a course in nature study from the age of 12 upwards; in fact nature study was a compulsory subject in rural primary schools until 1934, though it was actually taught in only a fraction of these schools. The teaching of nature study is, undoubtedly, the most effective means of giving a rural bias to primary education, and there seems no convincing reason why the subject should not be taught in rural primary schools (as is the case in almost every country in Europe) with the basic object of giving children an understanding of the importance, the wonder and the dignity of country life. Since this must be achieved without overloading the already heavy curriculum, it may involve a reassessment of the time given to other subjects, including Irish. The problem of teachers is, admittedly, a considerable one, for if the subject is to have a worth-while educational value it must be taught by people who are themselves interested in it. This in turn means that the subject must be well imparted in the preparatory and training colleges. The fact that this will take time merely underlines the necessity for tackling the task without delay. In the meanwhile, much ould be done in the primary schools with the aid of a good reader. It is painful to recall that almost a century ago an elementary text book of agriculture sold 30,000 copies within two years of publication, while at the time of the Recess Committee (1893) a similar textbook was widely used in national schools. What is now the Albert Agricultural College was established in 1838 by the Board of National Education as a model farm to train national teachers in agriculture so that a course of practical agricultural education might be grafted onto the ordinary curriculum of the elementary schools.

Vocational Schools

5. When vocational education was in its infancy, it was considered by many that the main functions of the rural vocational school should be the teaching of agriculture and domestic science. The Commission on Vocational Organisation endorsed this view which was not, however, accepted by the earlier Commission on Technical Education. While the aim might be a laudable one—though many would disagree—events have proved that it is not practicable. Education, of whatever type, is regarded by all parents as a means of advancing their children, both socially and

110

economically. A school which merely prepared girls for household work and boys for farming (one of the lowest income groups, as th. Farm Surveys have shown) would never succeed, and in fact, in the early years of the system, some vocational schools had to close down for lack of pupils until the curricula were broadened. The fact that such a high proportion of rural children must migrate reinforces the case. The aim of the subjects taught in these schools must be educational and cultural as well as utilitarian; their purpose is to continue the education of girls and boys of whom a fair proportion, because of origin and environment, are likely to remain on the land, either managing a home or working a farm.

6. A more valid complaint by the Commission on Vocational Organisation was that the Department of Agriculture, which has always claimed the sole right to organise adult education or instruction in agriculture, had no function in regard to the teaching of rural science in vocational schools, and it attributed this situation to the competing claims of different Departments. Unfortunately this criticism is still largely true and the Department of Agriculture remains almost completely divorced from these schools. Wherever the blame may lie, it cannot but be a cause of national concern that the Department responsible for agricultural policy is not more closely associated with the furtherance of agricultural knowledge in these schools, or that, in the past, some of the most successful projects in these schools have had to be introduced almost by subterfuge. The rural vocational schools will never realise their full potential—and it is immense—for rural education, nor will the advisory services be fully effective, until the activities of Departments in this respect are fully coordinated.

7. Generally speaking, the rural vocational schools have, or should have, three functions: first, to provide day courses of a specially directed nature for young people, second, to provide evening courses for the adults of the district, third, and perhaps most important, to become centres which can train people to live a full and contented life in rural surroundings. To do this, the school must be closely linked to the lives of the people, must be their training centre, their social meeting place and their source of culture. An interesting example of what has been done in this regard was shown at a conference of rural science teachers held in April, 1956, when a review was given of the progress achieved by the school at Grange, Co. Sligo. In 1943 the total effective attendance at day courses in this school was only 17. Apathy, misrepresentation and failure of the local people to understand its real purpose were partly the cause. By 1954, as a result of a drive to provide suitable courses, to integrate its work with that of the surrounding area and to develop the social side of the school life, the average attendance had been raised to 50 and it had become the focal point

111

of the activities of the area. During the twelve sessions 1943-55, a total of 172 boys completed two full years' attendance at day classes in the school. Of these, 30% returned to work on the land and were still there in 1956, 44% went to non-farming jobs in Ireland and 26% emigrated. ˙ While the figure of 30% for those who remained on the land may not seem very substantial, it is not discreditable if one considers that the majority of pupils attending these schools do so for the express purpose of getting away from the land, and that even those who do not are tempted to leave farming when they realise that education offers them the opportunity.

8. This, indeed, is one of the main weaknesses in the system of rural vocational education: typically, only about 30% of the boys return to farming and, in fact, most of the pupils go to the schools with the express intention of being educated for non-agricultural occupations. This is the product of a parental attitude of mind which regards education after 14 as unnecessary for those seeking a living on the land and which will change only when it becomes widely accepted that schooling can and does increase agricultural incomes. This attitude obviously will take many years to correct—though there have been welcome signs of enlightenment in the last few years—and meanwhile the problem is not eased by the total exclusion of rural subjects from primary education. In spite of all this, however, the rural vocational schools have had an influence on rural life out of all proportion to the numbers attending classes.

9. Perhaps the greatest weakness of the system is its small coverage. Only some 5,000 boys attend rural science classes, and a still smaller number return to the land. Apart from the effects of apathy or prejudice, the numbers are affected by the substantial group of parents who send their children to secondary schools in search of a higher social status. Yet it is in vocational education that there are best prospects for an advance in agricultural education. The vocational organisation is more flexible than the primary and secondary systems and those concerned with it are imbued with an enthusiasm which, in the large areas of rural Ireland where the system is still a novelty, gives something of a missionary character to the work involved. These schools, furthermore, can fulfil a most important function in becoming the social centres of rural areas. The effects of an advance on this front would be felt far beyond the field of education. A glimpse of what is possible can, indeed, already be seen: the initiative in establishing local branches of Macra na Feirme has in many cases come from the rural science teachers. This organisation has achieved more in young-farmer education in the past five or six years than decades of conventional instruction.

10. Most educationalists would agree that there should be a system of continuous education from boyhood to manhood, and would regard

the education given by the vocational schools as inadequate since the pupils generally finish the continuation course at less than 16 years of age. Few farmers, however, can afford to keep their sons at day schools after the age of 16. The rural science teachers attempt at present to fill the gap by evening discussion groups but this does not fully meet the need. Something more is required—perhaps a programme of further education designed to integrate with local farm life and conditions. Meanwhile it might be possible, by cooperation between the rural science teacher and the agricultural instructor, to provide a further two or three years' basic part-time education during the slack winter months; this would bring the instructor into close contact with the pupils and would lay the basis for a closer instructor-farmer relationship.

11. More rural vocational schools are needed to bring this form of education within reach of the pupils—an important point in rural areas where the pupils cannot be expected to have mechanical transport at their disposal. This need not involve an enormous building programme. Of the 4,900 national schools in the country, nearly 2,500 are in remote areas, far from the smallest town. It would be merely to make the maximum economic use of available resources and personnel if these were used by the vocational teachers to teach rural science to post-primary pupils after normal school hours. It can readily be realised that this would not be possible on a large scale: many of these buildings are unsuitable for this purpose; rural science is not, in any event, a subject likely to thrive in isolation. Separate buildings for vocational education may ultimately prove to be essential in most cases but this will necessarily take time; meanwhile, the benefits of rural post-primary education could, with the goodwill and co-operation of the national school managers, be spread more widely than at present.

12. A marked expansion in the number of rural science teachers would also, of course, be required. The shortage of graduates, and the steady loss of rural science teachers to other occupations, has in the past led the Department of Education to provide a two-year training course of its own for teachers in the subject and more than half the present number of rural science teachers are products of these courses. The Department does not expect to have to hold these courses in future as the number of agricultural undergraduates has shown a sharp rise in recent years. There has been a steady loss of graduate teachers, however, both to Departmental inspectorates and the advisory services, which pay higher salaries, and the extent of this movement may be judged from the fact that of the 34 rural science teachers who resigned since 1952, all but one went to one or other of these occupations. While a graduate is not *ipso facto* a good teacher, experience has shown that graduates have many advantages over their non-graduate colleagues. In view of the importance of rural science in relation to national progress, it is desirable that the salaries and conditions of service of

rural science teachers should be sufficient to attract (and retain) graduates of the proper calibre.

13. The question presents itself: why should rural science be taught only to boys? It is highly desirable that the scientific basis of the family's occupation should be as familiar to the farmer's wife as to the farmer himself, and indeed, when the farmer has not the requisite knowledge, it becomes essential. The difficulties of introducing agricultural education into girls' schools at primary and secondary levels are at least as great as in the case of boys, but in the vocational schools considerable progress could be made in a relatively short time. Girls in vocational schools are taught domestic science—a great deal of it, in fact. The reports of the Department of Education indicate that up to fourteen hours a week are spent on the subject. While domestic science is essential for girls, it is not apparent why at least some of this time could not with advantage be devoted to rural science. Such a change could be implemented in a comparatively short period: there is a rural science teacher in almost every rural vocational school. It would also, for that reason, ensure the maximum use of the present limited number of rural science teachers. If this should throw unreasonable burdens on these teachers, the problem could be met to a large extent by dispensing them from their present obligation to teach other subjects—a dispensation which, incidentally, would enable the teacher to plan his extra-curricular activities with maximum benefit to the surrounding area and its inhabitants. If a concerted drive were made over the next five years to spread agricultural education among the rural population by improving the teaching of rural science in vocational schools, the effect on agricultural productivity could be very significant. Its secondary effects would reach even further afield in preparing the way for the shaping of primary and secondary education on an agricultural basis and in creating the much-desired love of the land which would discourage migration.

Agricultural Schools

14. At the time these schools were established it was doubted whether farmers could afford to be without their sons for the 11 months over which the courses extended and it was feared that such training would tend to encourage the pupils to pursue a career elsewhere than on a farm. In fact, while courses at these schools, particularly in latter years, have been well attended, it cannot be said that there is a widespread demand for this type of education. The schools of the Department of Agriculture, as a result, have tended to become less institutions of teaching than of research and investigation. The private schools continue to be widely regarded by the farming community as preparatory colleges for the Universities or as training grounds for posts with the Department or elsewhere. Whether this attitude will change with time is doubtful; the best hope seems tc

lie in the provision of shorter courses which can be availed of more easily by young working farmers. Clearly, there is little use in looking to these schools as a source of improvement in general agricultural education: they barely scratch the surface of the problem.

Secondary Schools

15. Of over 60,000 pupils in secondary schools less than half come from urban surroundings: in 1953-54 some 24,000 came from the four Counties (including County Boroughs) of Dublin, Cork, Limerick and Waterford. This means that some 21,000 boys and 15,000 girls in secondary schools come from rural families, yet very few of the boys and none of the girls are taught the fundamental sciences underlying farming. Agricultural Science, as a subject, can never become part of the general secondary curriculum, if only because a farm is required for the proper teaching of the subject. What can be done, however, is to increase the amount of teaching in basic science subjects, something which is of even greater importance when viewed out of its merely agricultural context. Economic progress to-day depends to a considerable extent on a broad scientific education among the population at large. The secondary schools have academic functions not directly related to rural life but these functions can be performed just as well through the basic sciences as through other subjects, and no good reason is apparent why the fundamentals underlying an industry which provides 30% of the national income and employs nearly 40% of the total working population should not be taught to *all* children, of whatever background. This is a matter that requires early attention, for it is at the secondary level that the proper groundwork of detailed physical, chemical and biological knowledge necessary for a thorough agricultural education can be laid.

Agricultural Instructors

16. While agricultural instructors can perform admirable work, their numbers are insufficient by comparison with other countries. There are some 235,000 farmers in the State, or about 1,300 per agricultural instructor. If the graduate advisors under the Parish Plan are included, the figure becomes 1,200. While considerable progress has been made in post-war years in strengthening the advisory services, the present figure of 200 general advisors will have to be increased to 300 if we are to have one instructor for every 800 farmers—a reasonable target and one adopted in Britain. Since all the instructors are graduates, the rate of increase depends on the numbers graduating each year. The output of agricultural graduates has been hampered by the inadequate accommodation, staffing and equipment at the Universities but has increased considerably in recent years (in 1958 about 80 students will graduate). Over the period 1950-57 just over half the graduates took up local advisory work as a career; most of the remainder entered the service of the Department of Agriculture.

17. A proper advisory service is not, however, merely a matter of numbers. The quality, training and practical experience of the advisors in agriculture is all-important and it is to be feared that standards in these respects are not high enough. Moreover, it is necessary to remember that even a good graduate is not *ipso facto* a good agricultural instructor. Training in advisory work, whether at undergraduate, postgraduate or in-service level, should be as accepted a requirement for an instructor as training in education is for a secondary teacher. Unfortunately, this is not insisted upon.

18. The mechanics of the advisory service also require reconsideration. It is anything but clear that the best use is being made of the material at the disposal of the County Committees of Agriculture. There is but one Chief Agricultural Officer for each county, a post which, incidentally, is the only promotion open to instructors. Since the Chief Agricultural Officer is generally an advisor to a district within the county and, in addition, performs the functions of secretary to the County Committee of Agriculture, his supervisory work is necessarily restricted; in fact the instructors are virtually independent in their own districts. Some supervision is exercised by Departmental inspectors, but, apart from the fact that their numbers have not kept pace with the growth in the local advisory services, they have no direct control over the instructors and their influence rests on persuasion rather than authority. This situation is not conducive to the effective operation of the advisory services. The alternative solutions are either to organise effective supervision of the district instructors within the present framework or to bring all the advisory services under unified central control after the manner of the Parish Plan. For a number of reasons, however, the latter is not likely to prove feasible and it would seem better to strengthen the supervision exercised by the Chief Agricultural Officers over their subordinates.

19. The Department's Parish Plan, which was intended, by the appointment of a graduate advisor to every three parishes, eventually to cover the whole country, is more or less moribund. The object of the plan was an admirable one—it was described by O.E.E.C. as a most forward step in the improvement of agricultural advisory work in Europe—but since these advisors are employed directly by the Department, the possibilities of duplication and friction between the County Committees and the Department inherent in the plan are great. It is not clear that the object of the scheme could not be achieved as readily by strengthening the local services on the same lines. In the meantime, the existence of two parallel schemes of instruction contributes little to the solution of the problem. A final decision on the future of the Parish Plan should form part of a rationalisation of all advisory services.

20. There can be little doubt that a reorganisation is overdue. In the Department of Agriculture itself, there are at least three

groups of officials who perform some advisory services: the Land Project supervisors, the Farm Buildings supervisors and the Parish Agricultural Advisory Agents (who operate in the former Congested Districts). In addition to the county instructors in general agriculture, there exist county instructors in horticulture and poultry-keeping. While some attempt is made to coordinate the activities of these officers, it is not unknown for a farmer to be visited over a short space of time by four or five officials, some seeking basically the same information. It is obvious that greater coordination (and some degree of integration) of these services would increase their efficiency.

21. The initiative shown by one or two cooperative societies in employing agricultural advisors for their own members is welcome, but it is open to several objections from the national viewpoint, chief of which are the possibility of the instructor's isolation from the main advisory body and the danger that the local viewpoint may not coincide with that of the central authority on matters affecting policy. These, however, are difficulties to be met and overcome; it would be a pity if such a development were to be stifled for lack of adequate liaison with the central authority.

22. The present decentralisation of the advisory services may have some administrative drawbacks, but it has the advantage of close association, through the County Committees of Agriculture, with representatives of the local farming community. This advantage will not be fully realised if—as has happened in the past—the Committees include persons whose knowledge of, or interest in, farming is secondary. It is important that only the most suitable persons should be appointed to these Committees.

23. The training of an agricultural instructor must, essentially, be broadly based. Not only must he have a satisfactory knowledge of the various technical aspects of agriculture and of their economic implications for farm management but, in addition, he must have a thorough understanding of people and be a good public relations officer. In the conditions of Irish agriculture the advisor has to deal, not only with a wide variety of problems, but with a wide variety of farmers with varying capacity for management. These requirements underline the need for special training in advisory work and for making available to the local instructor a specialist advisory service. In the past, the lack of such a specialist service has seriously affected the efficiency of the agricultural instructors and other advisory officers. It is only through such a service that the results of research, investigation and development work can be brought to bear on farming in the shortest possible time and the problems of the individual farmer brought to the notice of the specialist. A specialist service already exists in nucleus form in the Department of Agriculture but requires to be greatly expanded. The

relationship between a centralised specialist service and the local advisory service will obviously require to be carefully defined. The establishment of An Foras Talúntais, specifically charged with disseminating the results of research work to the advisory services, affords an excellent opportunity for overhauling and expanding these services.

24. To sum up, it can be said that the present system of control of the advisory services is not conducive to their efficient operation. A greater degree of supervision is necessary since at present the individual instructor has too much independence of action. The instructors themselves need special training in advisory techniques, particularly in public relations and farm management. The number of advisory officers needs to be increased by 50% if their advice is not to be spread too thinly over too many farmers. Finally, the whole system must be backed by a specialist advisory service. These are not sophisticated refinements of a dispensable nature; they are reforms essential to the proper functioning of an efficient and effective advisory service.

Universities

25. The importance of the agricultural graduate should be apparent from what has been said already. The graduates form the base on which an extension of agricultural education must be built. As already noted, there has been in recent years a considerable increase in the numbers taking the agricultural degree courses. The following tables summarise the trend:—

NUMBER OF AGRICULTURAL GRADUATES (PRIMARY DEGREES)

				1953/54	1954/55	1955/56	1956/57
U.C.D. ...	...	...	...	16	23	29	47
U.C.C. ...	...	...	...	5	3	3	11
T.C.D. ...	...	...	...	2	2	2	4

TOTAL NUMBER OF AGRICULTURAL UNDERGRADUATES

		1953/54	1954/55	1955/56	1956/57	1957/58
U.C.D. ...	...	208	241	264	313	300 (prov.)
* U.C.C. ...	...	31(49)	34(78)	58(92)	43(112)	32(117)
T.C.D. ...	...	10	22	20	20	31

* Figures in brackets represent students pursuing Dairy Science Course (including Diploma Course)

	1945/46 to 1948/49	1949/50 to 1952/53	1953/54 to 1956/57
Average annual number of agricultural undergraduates in U.C.D.	132	112	259

The numbers of undergraduates in U.C.D. at present indicate that, for the next few years at least, between 70 and 80 will graduate in agriculture each year.

118

26. Until recently, the main impediment to an expansion of the advisory services was the shortage of agricultural graduates; the recent increase in the number of these graduates has, however, led to the paradoxical situation in which an inadequate advisory service exists side by side with some unemployment amongst agricultural graduates. The situation is likely to get worse, for even if the advisory services are expanded to the optimum, it is doubtful if employment can be provided —as instructors, rural science teachers or departmental officials—for 70 to 80 graduates annually. Obviously the long-term implications of this trend require to be carefully assessed. Meanwhile, it is vital that if the present unemployment amongst agricultural graduates is due to any unwillingness on the part of County Committees of Agriculture to appoint additional instructors, ways and means be found of overcoming that unwillingness. Recent legislation empowering these Committees to strike higher rates for advisory services has removed one barrier.

27. Numbers, however, are not enough. The quality of the graduates is all-important and the available statistics suggest that the recent increase in the number of graduates has not been paralleled by an improvement in quality. In 1953-54 twelve of the sixteen primary degrees in Agriculture conferred in U.C.D. were honours degrees; in 1955-56 ten out of twenty-nine reached honours standard, while in 1956-57 only fourteen out of forty-seven graduated with honours—and there is no indication that this is due to the raising of examination standards. Over the same period the number of post-graduate degrees conferred in the faculty has declined from four in 1953-54 to one in 1956-57.

28. It would be impossible to exaggerate the importance of the Universities in any system of agricultural education: they stand at the apex of any such system, and there would be little use in reforming and co-ordinating the remaining media if the main centres of education did not make their full contribution. It is now a matter of the utmost importance that the agricultural faculties in the Universities should be strengthened.

29. The first step should be an immediate raising of the standard of entry into the agricultural faculties, which have not, in the past, been getting enough student material of the right type. This may in part be due to the fact that some of the entrants have not adequate practical experience on a well-worked farm. Practical experience is essential, particularly in the case of graduates who intend entering the central or local advisory services.

30. The second step must be to raise the status of the agricultural faculties in the Universities. It should be a recognised aim, both of

119

Universities and State, that agriculture should have a high place among university faculties. This can scarcely be said to be the case at present. In so far as U.C.D. is concerned, the physical isolation of its Agricultural Faculty from the rest of the College has, no doubt, contributed to this position, one of the results of which has been that in the thirty years of the faculty's existence no travelling studentship in agriculture has been offered by the University. Students at T.C.D., U.C.C. and U.C.G. take two of the four years' B.Agr.Sc. degree course at U.C.D., while the Dairy Science faculty at U.C.C., although in a relatively healthy condition, is rather too specialised to be of great importance in the field of general agricultural education.

31. It is generally admitted that the State grants towards the agricultural faculties, particularly that of U.C.D., have been less than generous, but the Universities themselves are not entirely blameless in the matter. For many years no effort was made to seek additional State assistance for the Faculty of Agriculture at U.C.D. Although the number of agricultural undergraduates increased fifteen times between 1925-26 and 1956-57, the number of technical academic staff remained unchanged. We have now reached a point where we cannot afford *not* to have a healthy and expanding agricultural faculty and, with the establishment of An Foras Talúntais, the time has come to reassess the rôle of the Faculty. If An Foras Talúntais is to achieve really useful results as a research establishment, it must have both a trained staff—who seem likely to come in increasing numbers from pure science faculties—and a trained corps to disseminate the results of its researches, a corps which it should be the function of the agricultural faculties to provide.

32. The State can do much to attract students of the right calibre into the agricultural faculties. The main outlets for these graduates are as research workers, county instructors, departmental inspectors or rural science teachers and it must be borne in mind that the conditions of service and the opportunities available to graduates influence the number and quality of undergraduates coming forward.

General

33. Apart from State and State-aided media, the various agricultural representative bodies form a ready channel for imparting knowledge to the ordinary farmer. The most important from this point of view is Macra na Feirme, with its junior branch Macra na Tuaithe, whose main aims are to create a demand for education and to organise it among their members. Nothing but good can come of this. There are many other associations, however, through which much could be achieved by organised courses of lectures and demonstrations and of which full use is not at present being made.

120

34. Under the Public Libraries Act, 1947, the Library Council has power to assist local authorities to improve their library services. The Council is supported by State grants, but no tangible efforts have yet been made to carry out this particular function. This is one form in which a palpable improvement in general rural education could be achieved for a comparatively small outlay. The extension of a travelling library service throughout the country could give the ordinary farmer the means of self-education almost literally on his own doorstep.

35. A necessary part of the education of any young farmer is practical farming experience. Here, the virtual impossibility in Ireland of renting land for a period of years is a definite barrier. In December, 1957, proposals devised by the National Farmers' Association and Macra na Feirme were put forward as a basis for discussion of the problem. In brief, these were that a two-year course in rural science followed by a year at an agricultural college should prepare a youth for a four-year apprenticeship with approved farmers at the standard agricultural wage, after which the Land Commission, on being duly satisfied with the applicant's abilities, would allot a 50-acre farm on a rental basis for a probationary five-year term, when the land would be vested and purchased by annuity. The proposed scheme, which would be aided by State moneys, presents many difficulties, but there appears to be a need for some arrangement whereby, on the one hand, the aspiring farmer could serve an apprenticeship on progressive farms and, on the other, the young farmer could rent land until he was in a position to buy a farm, if he so desired. These are two separate questions, and the latter raises problems of agricultural credit which are referred to in Chapter 10.

36. Perhaps a more effective method of achieving the same object would be to increase the supply of farms for sale. There is evidence that many young farmers have, through considerable effort on the part of themselves and their families, raised the necessary capital only to find their ambitions thwarted by the scarcity of farms coming on the market. It is a matter of concern that young men of industry and ambition should thus be denied the opportunity of practising their farming skills, while at the same time so much good land is persistently abused under conacre and agistment lettings. It has been suggested that such land should be compulsorily acquired by the Land Commission for resale. This might not be the best solution to the problem, but some method of forcing such land onto the market should be devised. It is paradoxical that the State should expend so much money on reclamation of poor land when, at the same time, so much first-class land is not contributing effectively to production.

37. Clearly, the State can do a great deal, even in the short run, to

raise the present standard of agricultural education and instruction. The real barrier, however, is the attitude of the rural community. Education is too widely regarded in rural Ireland as irrelevant to farming. The problem is in the first instance essentially one of public relations for the agricultural and educational authorities, and must be treated as such. Education has to be " sold " to rural Ireland. Close contact with, and encouragement of, the various agricultural associations as media of education must be developed. The help of rural parish priests would be invaluable. There is a truly monumental task ahead, but the way is reasonably clear and there is no reason why a widely-based plan of agricultural education and instruction carried out with enthusiasm and drive, and clearly seen to be accorded a high degree of national priority, should not create in a relatively short time what could be our greatest national asset—a corps of well-educated farmers.

Chapter 12

STATE AID TO AGRICULTURE

1. An analysis of existing forms of State aid to agriculture is a necessary preliminary to deciding how resources can best be found to stimulate the improvements advocated in this study, especially the pivotal improvement in grasslands. The object is not to find grounds for a reduction in State aid to agriculture. This, at the present stage of development, would not be economically justifiable. The aim is rather to see whether the existing total of aid could be more effectively allocated, bearing in mind the urgent need to expand production at lower unit cost. Indeed, so great is this need that an immediate increase in State aid appears to be justified to secure it. This is allowed for in assessing the capital required to give effect to the recommendations in this study.

2. Some forms of State aid to agriculture cannot readily be measured in money terms but are nonetheless important—the home market price supports for wheat, sugar beet, bacon, milk and butter, in particular. Supports of this kind are provided in many countries to cushion farmers against the price fluctuations which are a feature of food markets and in some they have the further purpose of re-distributing incomes in favour of the agricultural sector of the economy. The scope for both these purposes is much more limited in Ireland than in industrialised countries like the U.S.A. and Britain, where incomes generally are much higher and the farming community forms a smaller proportion of the total population. It can, at the same time, be accepted as desirable that farmers' incomes here should be under-pinned, as far as home sales are concerned, until a policy of producing, at lower unit cost, for the export market has become firmly established. The home market is small and if the income of farmers, and of the community generally, is to be raised, it can only be by producing more for export. Unless the cost of what farmers produce for export is brought below the price realised on the export market, the income they receive from exports will not bring a corresponding increase in national income but will represent, in part, merely a transfer of income, through subsidies financed from taxation, from other sections of the community. There will always, in these circumstances, be a tendency to regard increased production and increased exports, not as deserving unqualified encouragement, but as liable to create serious fiscal problems.

3. It has already been explained in Chapter 3 that a climate favourable to national development will be created only when direct taxation can be lightened and that this depends, amongst other things, on subsidies being kept to a minimum and being used only where their temporary support is clearly necessary to secure a significant and permanent increase in *economic* production. As was said, there is no sector of the economy strong enough not merely to advance itself but to carry another sector permanently on its back. Clearly, unlimited subsidisation of exports could not be superimposed on the costly supports already given to production for the home market. This has been recognised by the policy decisions already announced in relation to wheat and butter. Bacon producers, too, have accepted a cut of 5/- per cwt. in the guaranteed price of bacon, though this will not become effective until July next and may leave a gap of as much as 90/- a cwt. between the guaranteed and the export prices. The point to realise is that, broadly speaking, subsidies of final products treat the symptoms—inability to sell without loss in world markets—but leave the disease—high production costs—uncured.

4. The table given below summarises the headings under which *actual State outlay* (as distinct from price supports borne by the consumer) benefits agriculture; further details are given in Appendix 7. For the reasons just given, it should be examined with particular reference to the desirability of directing expenditure away from subsidising final products and towards reducing production costs. It is also necessary to consider broadly whether other existing forms of State aid represent the most useful or the most productive means of spending such capital as will be available in future for agricultural development.

STATE AID TO AGRICULTURE, 1958/59
(Figures are net of relevant Appropriations-in-Aid)

	£	£
Subsidies of final products :		
Butter	1,400,000	
Wheat	800,000	
Bacon	650,000	2,850,000
Subsidies to reduce production costs :		
Ground Limestone	448,000	
Superphosphate	200,000	
Petrol	40,000	688,000
Drainage, land reclamation and general improvement schemes :		
Arterial Drainage	695,000	
Land Project	2,482,000	
Other drainage schemes	57,000	
Improvement of Land Commission estates ...	594,000	
Other improvement schemes	511,000	
Gaeltacht and Congested Districts schemes ...	229,000	4,568,000

124

	£	£
Elimination of disease, livestock improvement, etc. :		
Bovine t.b. eradication	1,061,000	
Pasteurisation plant	300,000	
A.I., milk production and livestock improvement	77,000	
Administration of improvement and regulatory Acts	192,000	1,630,000
Grants towards farm buildings, etc. :		
Farm buildings and water supplies	720,000	
Poultry houses and equipment	47,000	
Orchard planting	4,400	771,400
Education, research, advisory and technical services :		
Education	373,000	.
Research work	246,000	
Advisory services	324,500	
Rural organisations	25,600	
Technical services	147,000	
Departmental capital expenditure on land and buildings	114,500	1,230,600
Land Annuities :		
Halving of land annuities	720,500	
Bonus to vendors and other costs	117,200	837,700
Relief of Rates :		
Agricultural Grant		5,620,000
		£18,195,700

5. Without going into detail, an obvious case exists in principle for : —

(i) contracting the amount devoted to subsidisation of final products; and

(ii) enlarging the provision for reduction of production costs, since the problem of Irish agriculture is to *produce in quantity at prices competitive in export markets.*

The subsidy on disposal of surplus wheat should not recur after 1958-59 as an arrangement has been made whereby the loss incurred on the disposal of supplies surplus to home requirements of flour will be met by abating the guaranteed price paid to growers. But no similar term has yet been set to the Exchequer liability for export subsidies on butter and bacon. Reference has already been made to the minor reduction in the bacon export subsidy. If the gap between the guaranteed and export prices remains so large, a further reduction may well be necessary. In the case of butter, the Exchequer has limited to two-thirds its commitment to subsidise exports of butter produced in 1958-59. This contrasts with 100% subsidisation of exports in 1957-58. A limited and gradually diminishing subsidisation of butter exports could be accepted as a contribution towards ensuring the success of a grasslands improvement policy. If more cattle are to be produced for profitable export, without subsidy, more cows must be kept for breeding and more milk may come forward for disposal, even if, as is hoped, more is used directly in the rearing of calves. It would be short-sighted to reject outright any idea of an export subsidy for milk products, if the effect were to discourage farmers from keeping more cows. The desideratum is that the breeding stock should be expanded, the number of young grazing animals in the fields increased and, at the same time, milk production costs per gallon lowered so as to permit, if possible, of profitable export of butter and other milk products but, at any rate, of export at minimum loss. The potentialities of increased export of meat are too great to be surrendered because of any rigid objection to the subsidisation—on a limited and reasonable scale—of the milk by-products. Moreover, in view of the subsidised and, therefore, depressed foreign markets for butter and some other products, a limited policy of subsidisation of exports could be justified if progress were being made in reducing our production costs. There may, therefore, be ground for retaining *temporarily* a measure of subsidisation of butter and bacon.

6. A strong case exists for: —

(a) diverting a substantial part of Land Project expenditure to increase the provision for more urgent and more immediately productive purposes, especially the subsidisation of phosphatic fertilisers for grasslands;

(b) diverting much of the expenditure on "other improvement schemes" (mainly road works) to increase the provision for farm buildings;

(c) strengthening the educational and advisory services as recommended in Chapter 11;

(d) increasing the amount expended on research and, in particular, on progeny testing, as recommended in Chapter 7;

(e) not halving the annuities in any future cases of land division since the full annuity represents a lenient assessment of what the land will bear, in bad as well as good years;

(f) gradually transforming the Agricultural Grant into forms of aid more directly serving to lower production costs, e.g., subsidisation of fertilisers and increased provision for research (especially in relation to pasture and soil improvement), education, advisory services, development of progeny testing and marketing. A beginning should be made by fixing the Grant at £5 million, thus freeing over £600,000 for subsidisation of phosphates.

The reallocation recommended at (a) and (f) above should make a sum of about £1 million available annually to reduce the cost of fertilisers. To this the Government might consider adding £1 million a year for ten years as a further investment in stimulating a rapid increase in production at lower costs.

7. A clear understanding is necessary of the basis on which a policy of temporary, but intensive, subsidisation of fertilisers is advocated. The room for improvement of grasslands, and the capacity of improved grasslands to carry more cattle and sheep and, therefore, to provide more meat for export, have been explained in Chapters 6 and 7. A policy of subsidisation of fertilisers as a means of increasing what we produce from grass can be justified only if it reduces unit costs of production sufficiently to enable farmers to sell increasing quantities in competitive export markets without further aids. The increase in farming profits must come from an increase in sales. The trouble at present is that, for many products, home market prices and production costs are so high that sales abroad at the prices foreigners are prepared to pay are completely unattractive. It would be quite unjustifiable to encourage, with State aid, the use of fertilisers, the improvement of grasslands, the carrying of more stock and the production of more milk, if the result of State assistance in these directions were to generate greatly increased output which itself had to be disposed of with State aid. State aid at the production end can be justified as being for the economic benefit of the community only if this *temporary* boost to production results, through a permanent lowering of costs per unit of output, in competitive selling prices which, taking account of the higher turnover, bring farmers a bigger net income than before. As future agricultural and national development depends on it, every effort must be made to win the understanding and cooperation of farmers in this policy of increased output, reduced costs of production, lower prices but higher total profits.

8. The eradication of major livestock diseases would normally rank high in the list of demands for additional State capital but the limiting factor, at present, is professional personnel; all available veterinarians are likely to be fully engaged for some time to come in the bovine tuberculosis campaign, but an increasing number of lay personnel are being used for non-professional duties. The early elimination of bovine tuberculosis is so fundamental to the survival of our cattle trade that

some way must be found of getting around the manpower difficulty. The first requirement is to prepare a programme showing what *must* be done if we are to keep more or less in step with the British, and in the light of this programme to estimate manpower needs and the Exchequer subvention necessary in the immediate future. These requirements should then be discussed with the veterinary profession which should be invited to submit suggestions as to how the limitations of personnel might be overcome.

9. A word of explanation may be necessary for the views implicit in paragraph 6 (a). In general, State aid should be concentrated on achieving as quickly as possible the most advantageous use of *existing* agricultural land. This is where the greatest potential lies. Encouraging the increased use of fertilisers and the better management of grasslands is the most effective way of securing over the next decade a great increase in agricultural output and national economic activity and this should be the prime object of State aid to agriculture. Until a much higher proportion of existing agricultural land is being used to full advantage, the question of adding to the area of agricultural land by arterial and field drainage is of secondary importance. In paragraphs 10-12 the particular grounds for switching some of the finance now devoted to the Land Project to the subsidisation of fertilisers are stated. As regards arterial drainage, the position is that the policy of having three major and one or two minor schemes always in progress entails an annual outlay of close on £1 million to cover administrative and engineering charges, wages and materials and the maintenance, repair and replacement of machinery and plant. The cost must be regarded as high when it is borne in mind that it represents, in recent schemes, from £40 to £60 per acre of land improved and that the improvement in the annual value of the drained land is reduced to a very small net amount when allowance is made for the cost of maintenance. There does not seem to be any good ground for increasing this form of State aid to agriculture until more immediate needs are fully met.

10. Next to the Agricultural Grant, the Land Project is the largest single item of State aid to agriculture. Between its inception in 1949 and the end of 1957, expenditure on the Project amounted to £17 million of which some £10 million represents grants to farmers and payments to contractors, and £1.1 million expenditure on lime and fertilisers. That a great deal of this expenditure has been productive to some degree there can be no doubt. An examination of the operation of the scheme, however, gives rise to grave doubts whether this proportion is very high. Under Section A of the Project, the farmers carry out the reclamation work themselves, aided by a grant of two-thirds the cost of the work, subject to a maximum of £30 an acre. In fact, only some 10% of grants under Section A reach the maximum, and the average

grant paid since the initiation of the Project is only £10 an acre. This means that the average investment by the farming community under Section A is only £5 an acre. Making allowance for other factors, such as lack of initiative, the main reason for this low figure must be that ordinary economic criteria would not justify a greatly higher investment.

11. The results of Section B of the Project are, incidentally, an illuminating illustration of the different standards adopted when the State foots the bill. Under this Section the Department undertakes the work, obtaining a contribution from the farmer (paid by additions to his land purchase annuities) of two-fifths of the estimated cost, subject to a maximum of £12 an acre. In addition, the farmer pays 50% of the estimated total cost over and above £42 an acre, provided that works estimated to cost over £60 an acre are not undertaken save in exceptional circumstances. In practice, even this limit is overrun where, in the event, the work turns out to be more costly, and in fact cases have come to light where the reclamation cost as much as £300 an acre. Section B of the Project accounts for about £900,000 a year. An expenditure of more than £40 an acre on reclaiming marginal land would be difficult to justify on present returns from farming. Yet over 80% of the work undertaken under Section B costs more than that. It is clear that farmers are using Section B merely to have stretches of land which are sub-marginal reclaimed at minute cost to themselves.

12. No detailed analysis of the economic returns from expenditure under the Land Project has ever been made. In its absence, conclusions about its merits must be somewhat indeterminate. Clearly, where drainage is the limiting factor to production, the expenditure may be highly productive. It is not enough, however, to point to the thousands of acres now carrying heavy crops, where only rushes grew before. One must ask " at what cost?" If, as seems clear in the case of Section B, the cost is uneconomic, the Land Project is merely a case of misdirected State aid; indeed, to the extent that, even under Section A, farmers carry out small reclamation works merely to qualify for the State grant, it is fast becoming a social service. In the circumstances, it would be reasonable to terminate the acceptance of applications under Section B from some date in the near future; allowing for the backlog of applications, which would take about 12 months to clear, and for diversion of applicants to Section A, this should release an average of about £500,000 a year for more directly productive purposes. Moreover, a review of the results of the Project as a whole ought to be made as soon as possible. The Farm Survey organisation could be used to determine the effects in a representative sample of cases.

13. It has been suggested in paragraph 6 (b) that increased provision be made for farm buildings by diverting to this purpose part at least of

the money (£511,000 in 1958-59) now being spent on various minor schemes in rural areas. Under the schemes for farm buildings and water supplies, grants are given to farmers towards the cost of erecting new byres, piggeries, barns, etc., and of providing piped water supplies on farms. The average grant given is £30-£35, which represents about one-quarter of the cost of materials and, perhaps, one-eighth of the total cost of a new building. Grants are also given towards the labour costs of repairing existing buildings, within a limit of three-fifths of the grants for new buildings. So far, these have accounted for a negligible fraction of the total expenditure on the scheme, but the recent increase in the grants from 50% to 100% of the labour cost of repairing cow byres may alter the picture. State expenditure on these schemes in recent years has amounted to about £650,000 a year, which would indicate a total investment (taking account of construction costs) of nearly £5 million a year on these items. The value of, and necessity for, this investment and the desirability of providing for an increase are self-evident. The heavy annual losses from animal diseases are attributable in part to bad housing of stock, particularly cattle; and effective progress in the elimination of bovine tuberculosis depends on the segregation of reactors and young stock. More byre accommodation, and improvement of existing accommodation will be needed if the number of cows is to be increased and also if, as is greatly to be desired, the areas which at present import young stock from other areas start producing calves themselves. The increasing mechanisation of Irish farms demands adequate accommodation for the shelter and repair of machinery. It was estimated in 1947 that on over 80% of all agricultural holdings new and improved farm buildings were urgently required, and on only about a quarter of these holdings have any improvements yet been carried out under these schemes. Even where the existing buildings are otherwise satisfactory, in many cases poor layout, by increasing labour costs, reduces efficiency and negatives the contribution of good buildings to productivity.

14. The suggestion in paragraph 6 regarding the Agricultural Grant is not novel. Much attention has been focussed recently on this sub-vention and on the question of its efficacy as an aid to agricultural production. The employment allowance (some £1.3 million out of a total of £5.62 million) is a wage subsidy, introduced in the early thirties as an inducement to farmers to increase the amount of their hired labour. It was never an effective inducement and in the conditions of to-day is a complete anachronism. The number of workers in respect of whom the allowance is given has declined by over 30% since its inception though it might, perhaps, be claimed that it slowed the exodus; it is more than likely that the allowance is claimed fraudulently in many cases with consequent demoralising effects; and there is no evidence that it has ever had any beneficial effect on production.

15. The Capital Investment Advisory Committee recommended that the Grant should be made available to farmers by way of a scheme for the provision of vouchers for fertilisers and lime instead of by direct rate relief. There is, undoubtedly, a strong case for transforming it gradually into more specific aids to increased production and a beginning might be made by diverting at least £600,000 to fertiliser subsidisation in 1959-60. The progressive transformation of the Agricultural Grant is one of those changes (referred to in Chapter 1, paragraph 10) which may be more easily accepted in the context of a comprehensive and rational programme of development, involving a substantial net increase in State aid for agriculture.

CHAPTER 13

FISHERIES AND MARINE PRODUCTS

I. *Sea Fisheries*

Introduction

1. There are many speculative features about the sea fishery industry. Owing to the natural hazards of the sea and the seasonal and cyclical movements of fish the industry is constantly faced with the problem of large surpluses in the summer months and small and uncertain catches in the remainder of the year. Careful planning and organisation of production, processing and distribution are, therefore, necessary. Irregularity in the supply of prime quality fish and fluctuations in price impede the development of a steady consumer demand. On the other hand, there is little inducement to fishermen to make the necessary effort to increase catches so long as there is a risk of large quantities being left unsold. To overcome this difficulty, there must be some assurance that landings will be absorbed at remunerative prices. The British White Fish Authority has introduced a surplus fish marketing scheme for Northern Ireland and Scotland. This scheme provides for payment of a minimum first-hand price for unsold fish. These payments are made from a fund whose income is derived from a levy on landed fish payable by licensed producers and from the proceeds of disposal of surpluses. The scheme has the further purpose of ensuring greater utilisation of surplus fish and encouraging the development of processing. The problem of surpluses has been dealt with by the distant-water trawler companies in England and Wales by the fixing of minimum prices and the laying up of a proportion (5% in 1956-57) of trawlers during the summer period. In this country the problem might be tackled by : —

(a) the establishment of fishmeal plants to deal with gluts, particularly of herring and mackerel;

(b) the setting up of additional plants for quick freezing, cold storage, smoking and other processing with a view to regulating supplies to the consumer. These plants might also be used to develop a processing trade in fresh-frozen canned and bottled fruit and vegetables; and

(c) the development of an export trade, especially in packaged frozen fish.

Production

2. The development of sea fisheries in the post-war period will be evident from the following figures for landings of wet fish (excluding salmon):—

Year				Quantity cwt.	Value £
1938	....	....	....	171,186	133,734
1950	....	....	....	214,236	442,309
1956	....	....	....	377,367	787,160
1957	....	....	....	532,475	907,119

Notwithstanding the improvement the figures for 1956 and 1957 are very low by comparison with, say, Scotland where landings in 1956 totalled nearly 4,000,000 cwts. valued at £10.3 million. There has also been a substantial increase in landings of shellfish, valued at £34,000 in 1938, £87,000 in 1950 and £240,000 in 1957, over 90% of which are exported. The comparable 1956 figure for England and Wales is £1,025,000 and for Scotland £509,000.

3. The increase in production has resulted in a better trade balance. The quantity of all kinds of fish and fish preparations imported declined from 176,000 cwts. valued at £337,000 in 1938 to 47,000 cwts. valued at £419,000 in 1957 while exports of sea fish (excluding salmon) increased in the same period from 74,000 cwts. valued at £54,000 to 258,000 cwts. valued at £622,000 (including £330,000 for shellfish), a figure which contrasts with the landed value given in paragraph 2 above.

4. The comparatively low level of landings, exports and home consumption indicate that there is considerable scope for development. Consumption per head of the population here is one of the lowest in Europe: it is less than half that of Britain and only about one-fifth that of Denmark. There should be a good prospect of higher sales on the home market; this, indeed, is a necessary basis for a prosperous export trade. Export markets in Britain, Germany, the United States and other countries are promising. For instance, 3.5 million cwts. of fish and fish preparations valued at £33 million were imported into Britain in 1957 of which our share, consisting largely of fresh salmon, was 170,000 cwts. (more than 50% increase on 1956) valued at £855,000. There are substantial direct landings from foreign fishing vessels in Britain. These foreign landings are subject to a 10% customs duty which also applies at present to direct landings from Irish ships but not to ordinary trade imports from this country. Legislation to amend the Customs Code has been enacted in Britain and a technical provision of this legislation will have the effect of removing the 10% duty on Irish landings after 1st January, 1959. This will give us an

advantage over the other European countries concerned—Germany, Iceland, Denmark, Belgium and the Netherlands—and should provide a useful stimulus for Irish fishermen. At the same time it must be borne in mind that British landings from inshore and near and middle water fleets are subsidised. The acquisition of new boats and engines is also subsidised to the extent of 25% to 30%. While the distant-water trawlers operate without any subsidy, there is reason to believe that such trawlers operate at a loss, the losses being met from profits on other activities of the trawling companies, e.g. wholesale and retail distribution and transport. The more profitable course for this country might, therefore, be to concentrate on the export of processed fish rather than avail of the withdrawal of the 10% duty on direct landings to Britain.

5. As regards shellfish, about twice as many lobster and other species were landed in the early thirties as are being landed now. Takings from present inshore fishing grounds could be increased by 75% to 100% without endangering the conservation of the fish. The limiting factor is the uncertainty of securing remunerative markets abroad. The exploitation of new beds would scarcely be feasible until certain minor marine works are carried out for the improvement of landing facilities.

6. The slow development of the sea fisheries industry in this country has been attributed to the following factors : —

(a) policy emphasis on inshore fishing and protection rather than on fishing in more distant waters. This has contributed to the irregularity and inadequacy of supplies and to the high prices which have restricted home consumption; it has also resulted in failure to acquire sufficient modern fishing boats and the experience of operating them;

(b) inadequate investment in processing plant for quick freezing, curing and canning;

(c) lack of wholesale and retail outlets, with little or no interest in exports; and

(d) lack of training and training facilities.

The Food and Agriculture Organisation has been approached with a view to the engagement of a consultant with the following terms of reference :—

(1) to review the present state of the Irish sea-fishing industry with the object chiefly of developing it as an export industry and especially

(2) to advise on the measures to be taken

    (a) to increase and train the manpower;

    (b) to develop catching power and processing;

    (c) to facilitate marketing, and

    (d) to attract the necessary capital.

7. Policy in regard to the size and type of boats to be acquired is the key to the problem. The total number of boats engaged in fishing in 1957 was 2,211, comprised as follows:—

Motor-boats, 15 tons gross (about 40 feet in length) and over	186
Motor-boats less than 15 tons gross	419
Other boats (sail and row-boats)	1,606

With a fishing fleet of this size and composition there is no hope of competing with other countries, which have developed large fleets of modern trawlers. The British fleet, for example, consists of over 800 seine net fishing boats (mostly over 40 feet in length), 560 near and middle water boats (70 feet to 140 feet) and 255 distant-water trawlers (140 feet and over). This does not take account of sail and row-boats operating inshore.

Bord Iascaigh Mhara

8. Responsibility for the improvement and regulation of the sea fishing industry has been placed on An Bord Iascaigh Mhara. The Board is engaged in various activities including boat-building, auctioning of fish for direct consumption and processing. It has four boatyards, eight ice plants, six processing stations and various depots throughout the country. The Board also operates three offshore fishing vessels on which there has been capital outlay of some £95,000. The vessels were purchased in 1952 but their engines proved unsatisfactory. One was re-engined in 1956 and its landings of fish in 1957 amounted to 4,800 cwts. valued at £21,000. The other two have recently been re-engined and all three should soon become fully effective. The Board's estimate of capital requirements in the next three years is on a modest scale: 1958-59, £190,000; 1959-60, £250,000, and 1960-61, £250,000. Increased investment under the following heads should be productive:—

    (1) Extension of the hire purchase scheme for motor fishing vessels and gear (the number of such vessels the subject of hire purchase transactions at 31st March, 1958, was 111 valued at approximately £485,000 while 12 further boats valued at £107,000 were under construction);

(2) Installations for handling, marketing and distribution (e.g. freezing, smoking, curing and filleting plants, storage and distribution centres and transport).

Of the boats issued on hire purchase up to 31st March, 1958, only twelve were 55 feet in length and over. British trawlers operating in near and middle waters (Faroes, North Sea, West Scotland, Irish Coast, English and Bristol Channels) range from 70 to 140 feet. Boats of less than 70 feet in length are not suitable for fishing at any distance off the Irish south and west coasts and it seems clear that there will be no further substantial increase in catches until these waters can be fully exploited. Apart from the question of capital, there are two main obstacles to the development of a fleet of large-sized boats—the shortage of harbours with proper accommodation and handling installations and the lack of trained skippers.

Dock Accommodation

9. Advice is being obtained by the Fisheries Division from a harbour engineer of international repute on the harbours most suitable for development. In Britain millions of pounds have been spent on the provision of dock facilities designed for the rapid handling and storage of catches and their speedy transport to the consumer. In Grimsby, for example, there are three fish docks with a water area of more than 60 acres and a covered fish market occupying an area of over 300,000 square feet.

Training

10. The need for trained skippers is being met by a nautical training scheme which has been arranged with the cooperation of Galway Vocational Education Committee. The course will last 40 weeks, 20 weeks on one of the Board's offshore vessels and 20 weeks ashore. At the outset it is proposed to take on eight fishermen for training, four on each of two of the Board's offshore vessels which will engage in fishing in the ordinary way with four trainees substituted for two of the usual deckhands. This may appear to be a small number but the output of trained skippers must be kept in line with the number of boats likely to become available. Arrangements are being made to obtain the services of a highly skilled Icelandic skipper to tutor our fishermen in modern methods. The need for training schemes in this country is underlined by the fact that in Britain fishermen's training schemes are operated—by trawler owners' associations.

Distant-Water Trawlers

11. It is necessary to consider whether it would be possible to provide a trawler fleet on the lines of the British distant-water fleet

operating from Hull, Grimsby and Fleetwood. This fleet consists of 250 trawlers of 140 feet and over which travel great distances (up to 3,000 miles round trip) at speed, and catch large quantities of prime quality fish. Catches in 1956 totalled 8.56 million cwts. with a quayside value of £21.7 million (i.e. 50% by weight of total British landings). The industry is run by private enterprise and no grants or loans are given towards the construction of the trawlers. Catches are also excluded from the white fish subsidy payable to inshore and near and middle water fishermen. The capital cost of the distant water trawlers ranges from £200,000 to £250,000 each and they are fitted with every possible device including electronic aids for navigation and the finding and catching of fish. Owing to the enormous capital that would be required for even a small fleet of these trawlers, the present unsuitability of our fishing harbours for the accommodation, maintenance and handling of the trawlers and the shortage of trained personnel, it is clear that, at least in the earlier stages, large scale development of the sea fishery industry in this country must be based on boats in the 70-foot class. Trawlers of this size would be suitable for fishing in any waters off the Irish coast and it would seem preferable and more economic in our circumstances to exploit these waters rather than the more distant fishing grounds. Landings by all countries from waters around the Irish coast in 1955 totalled 2,860,000 cwts. against total native landings of less than 500,000 cwts. There is, therefore, considerable scope for increased fishing in our own offshore waters at lower capital and running costs and with much less risk than in distant waters.

Canning

12. It has been reported that large quantities of fish caught in Irish waters are being canned at continental ports and it is difficult to understand why no fish canning industry in this country has so far prospered. A number of proposals for the establishment of fish-processing plants are, however, at present under consideration. In the south-west of England there are several factories engaged in the canning of pilchards and sprats. The value of output is comparatively low but there are substantial imports into Britain from South Africa and there may be possibilities for developing this industry here. If private interests cannot, by encouragement and assistance, be persuaded to build up a large-scale fish canning industry, it appears desirable that An Bord Iascaigh Mhara should consider doing so. Consideration might also be given to the possibility of inducing foreign fishing companies to land their catches in this country for processing and subsequent export.

Other Processing

13. The Board already engages in smoking—for the production of kippers—and quick freezing. There are, however, substantial imports of kippers. Home requirements could be met from home sources if imports were effectively restricted. Apart from a small duty there is

no restriction on the import of kippered and smoked fish. There appear to be good prospects of developing an export trade in quick-frozen packaged fish to continental countries, and perhaps the United States.

Fishmeal

14. In the industrial sphere the main prospect is the manufacture from herring and mackerel of (a) fishmeal, for use as a feeding stuff, and (b) oil, mainly used in the manufacture of paints, varnishes and other materials. In 1957 we imported more than 2,000 tons of fishmeal valued at about £130,000 and it should be possible to increase consumption substantially. Furthermore, there is a big demand for fishmeal abroad. In 1957 Britain imported 109,000 tons valued at £6.7 million.

15. The Board had planned to establish three fishmeal plants on the coast to yield in a normal season of 100 days per year about 3,000 tons of meal in all. The estimated capital cost of the three plants was £120,000. It was proposed to establish one in Donegal in 1956-57, one in the west Cork area in 1957-58 and one on the south-west coast in 1959-60. When the Board was about to initiate its plans for the Donegal factory foreign interests submitted a proposal for the establishment of the industry at Killybegs. Work has begun on the site of the factory; it will probably be completed and ready for production this year.

Marketing and Distribution

16. One of the main difficulties of expanding the home market is the problem of distribution in midland areas. With this in mind, the Board proposes to provide depots with cold storage facilities at Longford and Kilkenny. There is a depot of this kind at Limerick already and it has helped considerably to increase consumption in areas in Counties Limerick, Clare and Tipperary where fish was seldom eaten previously. The Board expects that when its processing stations at Killybegs, Galway, Schull and Dingle are in full operation plentiful supplies of frozen and processed fish will be available to supply the proposed depots. No detailed study of export markets has been carried out. Provision has, however, been made, as part of the Fisheries Technical Assistance Programme, for visits abroad by trade representatives to make precise appraisal of consumer taste in continental markets. These studies will be undertaken in conjunction with Córas Tráchtála, Teoranta. Provision is also included in the programme for visits at official level to the continent for study of marketing, distribution and export organisations.

Research and Experiment

17. An exploratory boat is being designed to promote the scientific exploration of fish stocks generally around our coast. In Britain there

is considerable research and experiment into such matters as freezing at sea, the manufacture of gutting machines for use on trawlers at sea, methods of smoking and curing, etc. No opportunity is lost of taking advantage here of research and experiment carried out by British biologists and technologists. But we should not fail on that account to move towards having our own research establishments and programmes. Up to now it has not been possible for the scientific staff attached to Fisheries Division to undertake research in many spheres in which research must be undertaken if investment in fisheries is to be assured of optimum productivity. This would require the strengthening of the professional staff and the provision of buildings and equipment.

Ancillary Trades

18. A thriving sea fishery industry would also bring prosperity to other trades such as the building and repairing of boats. It would stimulate other industrial activity such as the manufacture of packing boxes and fishing equipment. The indirect employment given would be considerable.

II. *Inland Fisheries*

19. Salmon (including sea trout) and eels are the chief freshwater fish exported. Exports of salmon, which fluctuate considerably according to runs of fish and suitability of conditions for netting, amounted in 1957 to 15,710 cwts. valued at £534,000—much the same as the average for the preceding ten years. Exports of eels in 1957 came to 2,400 cwts. valued at £31,000, about the average for recent years. Salmon and sea trout as well as other freshwater fish such as brown trout and coarse fish are also important as a tourist attraction. There are also some exports of trout, pike and perch with prospects of further development.

20. A five-year plan for fishery development was announced in 1957 by Bord Fáilte Éireann. This plan was prepared by the Inland Fisheries Trust in conjunction with the Board. It contains proposals for the improvement and development of coarse fishing, game fishing and sea angling. The primary aim is to open up fishing waters and to facilitate access by anglers to the waters, to clear coarse fish from selected salmon and trout rivers and lakes, to restock where necessary, and to provide living accommodation in the areas concerned.

21. For coarse fishing the principal operations will be in the Shannon and Erne areas, the Rivers Barrow, Nore and the Cork Blackwater system, waters in the Sligo, Drogheda and Dundalk areas and various canals, representing in all about 70% of the total exploitable

waters. Coarse fishing is a branch of angling which is assuming increasing importance as a tourist attraction; there are, it is estimated, 3 million coarse-fishing enthusiasts in Great Britain alone and it is hoped to attract an increasing number of these to this country in the coming years. To this end a publicity campaign on lines similar to that proposed for sea angling (par. 28 below) is planned but it will, if anything, be on a more extensive scale. In the case of game fishing it is proposed to open up, rehabilitate and restock lakes in Clare, Cork, Galway, Kerry, Mayo, and Donegal, and this programme, coupled with the plans of the Inland Fisheries Trust and the Electricity Supply Board, will represent almost 100% of total exploitable waters.

22. The inland fisheries development plan is estimated to cost £155,000, spread over the next five years. This will be borne by Bord Fáilte Éireann from its grant-in-aid. In addition, the Board will bear the cost of ancillary works (such as improvement of access roads, erection of piers, shelters, etc.) which are necessary if angling amenities are to be fully exploited. It is not possible at this stage to give an estimate of the cost of such works. The Inland Fisheries Trust, whose grant-in-aid has been increased from £12,500 in 1957-58 to £20,000 in 1958-59, will continue with its work in its own waters. The Trust's operations are primarily concerned with the improvement of brown trout fishing in waters owned or leased by it. The work of the Electricity Supply Board on the improvement of salmon stocks, mainly in the River Shannon area, will be coordinated with the plan and that Board will continue its operations on an intensified scale.

23. The Fisheries Division has in hand plans for improvement works on a number of rivers. The works, mainly of an engineering nature, are designed to give salmon access to new spawning grounds and it is hoped that this will bring about an improvement in the runs of salmon in the rivers concerned. In some cases the aim will be to induce runs of fish in rivers at present relatively barren. It is intended that portion of the cost involved will be met out of the Salmon Conservancy Fund, private interests contributing where appropriate. As well as benefiting anglers the increase in stocks of salmon in rivers and lakes will result in an increase in supplies in the estuaries where the salmon are netted for the export trade.

24. A fish farm has been established at Roscrea by the Inland Fisheries Trust with the help of a capital grant from the National Development Fund. The farm will make available brown and rainbow trout, bream, rudd, tench and carp for the stocking of suitable waters and will also supply fish to angling clubs and produce supplies of rainbow trout for sale for table use. It is hoped that the proceeds of the

sale of these fish will contribute substantially towards the cost of operating the farm, which will carry out research on problems of fish biology. Production of trout for export alive or processed is an industry of considerable importance in Denmark and the exports of farmed trout from that country in 1956 amounted to £2½ million. An Irish firm has indicated its intention of establishing a commercial trout farm near Woodenbridge, Co. Wicklow. Investigations have shown that rivers in this country are especially suitable for trout farming.

25. It is intended to persuade farmers in suitable areas to adopt pond fish culture as an adjunct to farming and material is being gathered on the economics of small-scale operations. It may be necessary to offer some inducement by way of grant for the construction of ponds.

26. There is a good demand in Britain and elsewhere for smoked and jellied eels. Eels are already exported alive from this country and processed abroad. Irish rivers are, it appears, among the best sources of eels in Europe and there should be considerable scope for increasing exports. Development of this trade has been hindered by existing statutory restrictions on methods of capture but amending legislation is contemplated which should facilitate trade and lead to a significant increase in exports. The possibility of establishing eel farms is being examined by Fisheries Division and provision has been made under the Technical Assistance Programme for study tours in continental countries which specialise in eel culture.

III. *Sea Angling*

27. It is proposed under the five-year plan to carry out a general survey of resources around the entire coast and in particular to investigate, with the help of foreign experts, the possibilities of big game fishing off the south and west coasts.

28. It is also proposed over the next few seasons to bring teams of sea anglers here to sample the possibilities of various Irish coastal centres. Films will be made and the sport publicised.

29. An idea of the tourist potential of the sport can be inferred from the estimate that there are some 500,000 sea anglers in France and a corresponding number in Belgium and the Netherlands. In Britain the sport has become highly developed and scores of sea angling clubs have been established. In the United States the number of sea anglers is reckoned at 5,000,000. These figures suggest that the sport offers excellent prospects of extending the very short holiday season in many seaside resorts.

IV. *Marine Products*

30. Marine products include alginates, carrageen and seaweed meal. Arramara Teoranta, a State-sponsored body, is at present engaged in (a) the processing of sea rods and (b) the production of high-class carrageen. A number of other firms is engaged in the production of seaweed meal.

31. Sea rods are gathered off the western coast, mainly Galway and Mayo, by the local people and when dried out by them in the open are brought by Arramara for further drying and milling to their factory at Kilkieran, Co. Galway. The resultant meal, which is the raw material for alginates, is sold to a British company, Alginate Industries Ltd. (which is a substantial shareholder in Arramara) to be processed in their factories in Scotland. The market abroad for sea-rod meal is bouyant and production could, with advantage, be increased. The question whether the final processing could be done by Arramara Teoranta has been examined from time to time, but economic operation on a commercial scale presents considerable difficulties; as the home market is very limited, there is the further problem of securing adequate export outlets against competition from established foreign manufacturers. It should be noted, however, that a private firm has recently undertaken the production of alginates.

32. There appear also to be possibilities of developing markets for animal feeding stuffs produced from other types of seaweed; this is a matter which should be investigated further. Every effort should be made to develop such markets, if necessary through the medium of Arramara Teoranta.

33. As regards carrageen, it appears that there is a good demand in Great Britain, on the continent and in America provided the purchasers can be assured of consistently high quality and regularity of supply. The carrageen is required abroad not so much for food or medicinal use as for industrial processes. Arramara has recently installed a plant for the mechanical cleaning of carrageen and efforts are being made to find new markets on the continent. These developments might be intensified.

CHAPTER 14

FORESTRY AND FOREST PRODUCTS

State Forestry

1. Forestry in this country is predominantly a State activity: plantations total 327,000 acres and all but 90,000 are State-owned. The State planting rate has risen from 12,500 acres in 1952-53 to 20,000 in 1957-58. It is proposed to plant 22,500 acres in 1958-59 and 25,000 in 1959-60 and subsequent years. The programme envisages the growing of sawlog crops on a 50-year rotation. Small dimension timber (i.e., timber required for pulp, etc.), so far as not obtainable from the thinning of the acreage necessary for sawlog production, would be produced from plantations grown on a rotation of, say, 30 years. Work in the forests and on the supply of road materials at present provides employment for approximately 5,000 and it is expected that this figure will increase to about 13,000 at the turn of the century.

2. An annual planting rate of 7,000 acres would suffice for present domestic requirements of sawnwood and pulpwood but if consumption were to increase to the much higher Danish levels the produce of an annual planting programme of 17,500 acres would be absorbed on the home market. It follows that, in either case, export markets will be needed for the disposal of much of the output expected from the planting programme which is being carried out. The rapid increase in world population and literacy gives promise of increased outlets for timber and timber products, including newsprint—always assuming that technological advances do not lead to timber being superseded by other materials to any appreciable extent. In 1955 Europe as a whole had a net import balance of 6 million cubic metres of industrial wood and wood products; sawnwood imports, which stood at under 2 million cubic metres in 1954, had risen to over 3 million in 1955. Although Europe had a net export balance of woodpulp in 1955 of 0.93 million metric tons, this represented a fall on the export figure for the previous year, which was 1.24 million. Average European consumption of industrial wood is considered low compared with North American consumption. Because of its proximity, Great Britain is, of course, our most important export market for timber and timber products. Great Britain's forest programme aims at supplying only 35 per cent. of her total estimated consumption, and progress towards this objective has been at less than the desired rate. Accordingly, if we can provide timber at competitive prices, it seems a reasonable expectation that our surplus

143

could be absorbed on the British market. Pulp products appear to have better export prospects than sawlog timber because of their increasing importance in industrial production.

3. The important part that could be played in our economy by a prosperous forest industry may be gauged from the following figures showing the net import excess for timber and timber products in the years 1956 and 1957:—

	1956	1957
Imports	£	£
Timber (including tropical)	4,897,092	2,882,333
Timber manufactures	1,123,934	1,247,224
Pulp and Waste Paper :		
Woodpulp	1,401,905	1,244,481
Other	112,250	180,735
Paper and paper manufactures ...	5,110,859	4,610,461
Total Imports	12,646,040	10,165,234
Total Exports and Re-exports ...	2,403,573	2,461,207
Net Import Excess ...	10,242,467	7,704,027

4. Forestry could be considered economic if the sale of crops yielded enough to repay the capital cost, with compound interest. The long production cycle and current high interest rates make this a difficult test. With some reservations regarding western peat areas, climatic and soil conditions in Ireland favour rapid and sustained growth of trees; rural wages are comparatively moderate and there is a reasonable expectation that satisfactory markets will be available to absorb the output in due course. Besides, forestry offers the attraction of providing, in rural parts, especially in the west, a substantial amount of employment, yielding tangible future wealth. This useful employment is provided where there is little economic activity at present and emigration is rife. Forestry fits harmoniously into the agricultural pattern of our economy and, like agriculture, it is virtually independent of imported raw materials for its development. Provided, therefore, the financial implications were not prohibitive, the continuance of a forestry programme on the basis of an annual planting of 25,000 acres would have much to commend it.

5. Total State expenditure on forestry prior to 1950-51 amounted to £4 million, which was provided from revenue except to the extent that budget deficits had to be financed from borrowing and afforestation expenditure contributed to those deficits. From 1950-51 to 1957-58, inclusive, the sectors of forestry expenditure classified as capital and met by borrowing amounted to £6.3 million. In 1956, costings of productive forestry expenditure and estimates of revenue were made. These were based, *inter alia*, on the existing prices for crops grown on a 50-year rotation. From these calculations emerged the discouraging

conclusion that a loss of around £500 per acre per rotation (allowing for interest charges) might be expected. It appeared that the moneys invested in the forestry programme would produce a return of no more than $2\frac{1}{2}\%$ per annum. An active campaign to reduce costs was instituted in 1956 and has been intensified since 1957. Substantial economies have thereby been effected: savings under all heads are estimated at £$\frac{1}{4}$ million per annum. On the recommendation of a firm of industrial consultants, an incentive bonus scheme is being introduced and is calculated to achieve savings in the cost of labour of about 20% on 1956 levels. Measures to secure savings in other directions are also in hands.

6. The review carried out in 1956 was based on estimates of timber yields that were known to be unreliable. A more accurate appraisal of yields is in progress but, since it will not be completed for some time, the yield figures assumed in 1956 must, with some modification, be used for the purpose of the present study. Prices paid by Irish users for pulpwood and spruce poles are, in general, well below import levels. This is, to some extent, the result of the excess of supply over demand. Certain developments are, however, taking place which may lead to an expansion of the present activities of Irish firms engaged in production of paper, cardboard and other wood products, a modification of the imbalance between supply and demand and, consequently, better prices for the produce of State forests. It is assumed that prices for pulpwood will rise to general import levels and prices for sawnwood to those paid for imported timber. The latter are currently about 50% above Irish levels. It is expected that 50-year-old crops will begin to be felled in 1959-60 and that as much timber as possible will be sold standing. Taking account of these assumptions about revenue, in conjunction with those in paragraph 5 about expenditure, the Department of Lands estimate that total receipts will exceed total expenditure (other than interest) by approximately £670 per acre over a 50-year rotation. It is a notable feature of the calculations that receipts to the extent of 80% of the total are expected to arise in the final year.

7. The net financial yield derived from the calculations mentioned in the preceding paragraph is $5\frac{1}{4}\%$ per annum on the total outlay. Compound interest calculations at $5\frac{1}{4}\%$ would result in a loss of around £30 per acre, but it is estimated that this would be offset by the residual value of land and roads available for the next rotation. This means that, if the cost assumptions are realised and there is, in fact, a market at the expected prices for the timber available, a 50-year sawlog rotation could be secured without loss if the compound interest rate did not exceed $5\frac{1}{4}\%$ on *all* outgoings.

8. The excess of expenditure over revenue in 1958-59, inclusive of Allied Services but excluding expenditure on private forestry, is estima-

ted at £1,914,000, of which £1,110,000 is reckoned as capital. A gradual decline of the excess to £1,225,000 in 1971-72, with an accelerated decline thereafter producing a revenue excess (£286,000) for the first time in 1974-75 is anticipated. Over the period 1958-59—1974-75 the total excess of expenditure over income will have exceeded £23 million. It has been calculated that, on a 50-year rotation, net revenue will increase progressively after 1974-75 until virtual peak at approximately £17 million is reached in 2009-10 with the final crop of the first annual 25,000 acres. The Department of Lands have stressed the pitfalls in attempting a financial projection over such a period, particularly having regard to the speculative nature of many of their assumptions and calculations, especially those relating to the timber yields anticipated. If the assumptions and costings prove to be over-optimistic, net revenue would not accrue until much later and would increase more slowly.

9. The Department of Lands have made an examination of the probable demands upon the State for capital for forestry purposes and of Exchequer expenditure and revenue over the period 1957-58 to 2009-10. Taking into account the capital (i.e., *borrowed* State moneys) of £6.3 million already invested in forestry prior to and including 1957-58, the financing of the present programme envisages investment of (borrowed) State capital rising to an aggregate of £21,618,000 by 1973-74 at the rate of approximately £1 million per annum. After 1973-74 new capital will be provided from forestry revenue. It is assumed that net forest revenue will be used to repay the capital debt until the total debt is cleared. The peak charge on Exchequer revenue, including interest on the capital investment, would be £1.38 million, reached in 1968-69. By 1982-83 net forestry revenue would suffice to meet all the interest on capital and in the following year would enable a start to be made on capital repayments. By 1994-95 the entire net forestry revenue (£3,465,000) would accrue as current revenue to the Exchequer, i.e., borrowed capital will have been repaid by 1993-94.

10. Because of the substantial employment it provides in areas which are largely bereft of other economic activity, a continuance of the present planting programme would be warranted, notwithstanding the heavy financial burden on the Exchequer for some years to come, if there were a reasonable expectation that the financial outcome envisaged by the Department of Lands would be realised in practice. The Department's expectation that timber production on a sawlog rotation could be successfully financed in face of an interest rate not exceeding $5\frac{1}{4}\%$ on *all* outgoings must be taken with reserve in view of the doubts about many of the calculations and assumptions which they are at pains themselves to emphasise, but it would scarcely be over-optimistic to expect a return of that order on that portion of the expenditure classified as capital for budgetary purposes. This would involve, in effect, treating

the " non-capital " expenditure in the Forestry Vote as a social service until such time as the level of forestry revenue would make demands on the Exchequer for this purpose no longer necessary; according to the Department's calculations, this situation would be reached in 1972-73 and the total net draw on Exchequer revenue (excluding interest on capital) from 1957-58 up to that year would amount to £8,750,000. This course is justifiable not only because of the social advantages of afforestation but also because, unlike other forms of social outlay, it would automatically come to an end in about fifteen years and would meanwhile help to produce real national wealth.

Private Forestry

11. Afforestation has been almost wholly a State responsibility, the contribution made by private enterprise, even with State aid, being very small. In the years preceding 1929, the scale of private planting did not, it is believed, exceed 200 acres a year. State aid was introduced in 1929, the planting grant being fixed at £4 an acre; this was increased in 1943 to £10 an acre and to £20 in 1958. In the period 1930 to 1942 the average annual area of private planting was about 130 acres. In the period 1943 to 1955 the average was about 250 acres. Over the past few years the trend has been upwards, reaching 424 acres in 1957-58. The higher rate of planting since 1943, which has been concentrated in the post-war years, appears to have been due, in the main, to the replanting conditions attaching to licences for felling, which was carried out on a large scale during the war.

12. The planting grant of £10 an acre which applied until recently was based on 1943 costs. The increase in the grant to £20 was justifiable as an inducement to increased planting. The grant does not apply to poplar cultivation, but a special Poplar Grant Scheme is proposed. Steps are being taken to bring home to the agricultural community the advantages of private planting and the facilities which the Department of Lands can put at their disposal in this connection. On many farms there are some pockets of suitable land which could be devoted to the production of high-quality timber. Under proper management these pockets, which as a rule are too small for State development, would, in fact, be capable of giving higher timber yields per acre than can be secured from the type of land acquired for State forestry.

13. It is not possible to subject private planting to an economic analysis on the lines of that undertaken in relation to State forestry. The quality of land, the size of plantations, marketing circumstances and the extent to which extra paid labour would be employed in tree cultivation are too variable to permit of general calculations. In practice, timber felling on small, privately-owned woodland areas is timed by economic requirements on the farm rather than by

normal considerations of forestry rotation. Private woodlands do, however, constitute a capital reserve which can be called upon by the owner, when required, to finance improvements in his holding.

Forest Industries

14. The import figures given in paragraph 3 above show that, *prima facie*, there is much scope for the sale of Irish timber and timber products on the home market. In this connection allowance must be made for the fact that some categories of our imports (e.g., tropical timber) could not be replaced by Irish products but there is no apparent reason why inroads could not be made upon imports by greater development of the industries concerned with timber and related products. So far as disposal of timber surplus to domestic requirements is concerned, it would obviously be more valuable, both in terms of employment and aid to the balance of payments, to have as much processing as possible carried out prior to export.

15. With the exception of a few sawmills operated by the Department of Lands, which are of minor importance, the timber and paper industries are in the hands of private enterprise. The output of State forests consists largely of thinnings and is likely to take this form until, in years to come, an appreciable amount of mature timber may be expected. Irish industrial firms are using about 60,000 tons of thinnings per year (out of a total annual production of 100,000 tons) in the manufacture of paper and wallboard. Most existing firms have immediate plans for increasing production and, in addition, there are proposals for new industries involving the use of native forest products. The capital required for the establishment of these enterprises is substantial in each case.

16. It is understood that, latterly, the Irish timber trade has been devoting more attention to the processing of native timbers for constructional and other purposes. Kiln-drying facilities have been installed by a number of firms and there has been a growing confidence in the use of native timber for many purposes for which only imported timber was previously regarded as suitable. Certain types of home-grown timber are being much more readily accepted by architects and building contractors as a suitable substitute for imported timber and the Department of Local Government are encouraging greater use of native timber in housing schemes. Some of the more prominent firms in the Irish timber industry are understood to be actively concerned with measures aimed at popularising the use of Irish timber for purposes hitherto served by imported products.

17. If it is decided to continue planting a high acreage each year, it is important to ensure that no measure likely to assist in

providing profitable markets for the produce of these plantings is ignored or overlooked. The development of native industries, having the twofold object of meeting, as far as possible, home requirements at present served by imports and of exporting the greatest possible proportion of our surplus in the manufactured rather than the raw state, is eminently desirable. The establishment of a State-financed Forest Products Development Board had been suggested in this connection but this proposal was deferred and a working committee, representative of the pulp and paper manufacturers, set up under the auspices of the Industrial Development Authority. It is possible that the committee —which will furnish its report soon—will recommend that increased quantities of thinnings expected to become available over the next ten years would best be disposed of by existing users stepping up their requirements over that period. In the light of these developments, State intervention at the present juncture appears unnecessary but the position will obviously need to be kept under review having regard to the importance of finding satisfactory outlets for the increasing quantities of timber expected to become available.

CHAPTER 15

INDUSTRY—INTRODUCTORY SURVEY

1. Before considering the problems that lie ahead of Irish industry it may help to glance at the manner and extent of its development in recent times. On its establishment, the new Irish State was comparatively under-industrialised. It found itself without industries to supply such essential items as boots and shoes, clothing, furniture and other household goods. The number of persons engaged in non-agricultural production in 1926 was only 164,000 (or 13.4%) of all persons "at work", as compared with 647,000 (or 53%) engaged in agriculture. In other words, the number employed in industry and similar production was only a quarter of the number of agricultural workers.

2. As a first step towards fostering the growth of native industry a policy of protection was introduced. This policy, which was intensified in 1932 with a view to accelerating the rate of industrial expansion, was accompanied by the Control of Manufactures Acts, 1932-34. These Acts were intended to secure that, as far as possible, Irish nationals would control and finance new manufacturing enterprises and would be protected against foreign industrialists who, in the absence of controls, would have been free to set up competing units here to capture the home market.

3. The extent of the success of these measures is indicated in the tables in Appendix 8 which summarise the development of Irish industry since 1926. Expressed in real terms, the volume of production (base 1953=100) showed more than a three-fold increase from 33.6 in 1926 to 104.0 in 1957 (the 1955 figure was 107.8). The average number engaged in all industries covered by the Census of Industrial Production was 220,000 in 1957 or 117,000 more than in 1926, while employment in transportable goods industries stood at 149,000 as compared with 61,000 in 1926.

Financing of Industry

4. The annual amount of private investment in Irish industry is small. As mentioned in Chapter 4, gross fixed asset formation in industries producing transportable goods has recently been only £10-£12 million a year. The *net* figure, after allowing for depreciation, can be only £6-£7 million a year. There is the further evidence that of the new capital of £146.4 million known to have been raised by the issue of

marketable securities in the six years 1952-57, inclusive, only £6.6 million related to issues other than those of public authorities. Not only is total capital formation relatively low, but the proportion devoted to manufacturing and construction compares unfavourably with that in other O.E.E.C. countries.

State Enterprises

5. Any review of Irish industry, however brief, would be incomplete without mention of the contribution by State-sponsored bodies to the development of the economy. In 1956-57 industrial employment (excluding seasonal employment) was afforded to as many as 15,300 by such concerns as the E.S.B. (8,500), Bord na Móna (4,900) and Comhlucht Siúicre Éireann (1,900). The State has been directly responsible for about one-eighth of the additional industrial employment of about 125,000 created between 1926 and 1956. In addition to the foregoing, an *industrial* personnel of about 8,350 is employed by the companies which have been taken under the auspices of the State, viz., C.I.E. (6,200), G.N.R. (1,700) and Irish Steel Holdings (450). Furthermore, some 4,200 workers, classified as "industrial", are serving in Government Departments. It has also to be remembered that much of the output and employment in the building, furniture and ancillary industries is generated and supported by State policy in regard to housing, hospitals, schools and social investment generally.

Industry and the Economy : Present Position

6. The relative importance of manufacturing and closely related activities as a source of employment is borne out by the following figures for the year 1957:—

NUMBER OF PERSONS AT WORK *

Branch of Economic Activity	Thousand	Percentage
Agriculture, etc.	436	38·2
Manufacturing industry	184	16·1
Other production	100	8·8
Services, etc.	422	36·9
	1,142	100·0

* The figures for industrial employment quoted in this paragraph relate to all persons engaged in industrial production, whether covered by the Census of Industrial Production or not.

Although the number at work in *all* industrial production (not merely manufacturing) in 1957 (284,000) was considerably lower than the number at work on the land, industry as a whole almost rivalled agriculture in the contribution it made to the national income. Over the five-year period from 1952 to 1956, it accounted for about 24% of the total national income, whereas the contribution of the larger agricultural

151

population in the same period was not very much higher at 31%. This reflects a higher output per person engaged in industry.

7. Industrial employment has grown considerably since 1926, but its expansion has not been nearly sufficient to absorb all those leaving the rural areas. Even though industry as a whole is now the source of about one-quarter of the national income it will be noted that the country is still much less industrialised than O.E.E.C. countries generally for which the corresponding figure is close on 40%.

8. Despite a policy of decentralisation, quite a noticeable feature of Irish industry is its concentration in the Dublin and Cork areas in which 2,441, or 52% of the total of 4,761, industrial establishments were situated in 1954. Over one-half (123,500) of all industrial personnel covered by the Census of Industrial Production (233,400) were engaged in production in the same two areas.

9. The most recent analysis of establishments according to the number engaged in each is that for the year 1952. It may be assumed, however, that the pattern, as set out in the following table, has not changed appreciably in the meantime.

TRANSPORTABLE GOODS INDUSTRIES

Establishments classified according to number of persons engaged

Number of persons engaged in each Establishment	Establishments		Net Output	Persons Engaged	
	Number	Percentage	Percentage	Average Number	Percentage
Under 20	2,106	61·0	10·0	17,232	12·3
20–49	741	21·5	14·5	23,366	16·7
50–99	314	9·1	13·6	21,596	15·5
100–249	187	5·4	20·1	28,978	20·7
250–499	78	2·3	18·9	25,925	18·5
500 and over ...	24	0·7	22·9	22,732	16·3
Total ...	3,450	100·0	100·0	139,829	100·0

From these figures it will be seen that the number of establishments employing 50 and over was 603, representing 17.5% of a total of 3,450. These larger establishments accounted for 75.5% of net output and 71.0% of total employment in transportable goods industries. Twenty-four establishments providing employment for 500 or more were responsible for 22.9% of net output and 16.3% of the total number of persons engaged. We have only a small number of big industries and the loss of even a few would have serious repercussions on total production and employment. At the other end of the scale we find very many small enterprises: 82.5% of all establishments employed less than 50 persons each, giving rise to 24.5% of the net output of transportable goods and 29.0% of total employment. One consequence of the overwhelming predominance of small-sized units of production is that most firms cannot afford to advertise extensively in export markets, undertake large-scale research or incur heavy outlay on the introduction of improved production methods. The experience of other countries proves, however, that smallness and inefficiency are not necessarily synonymous.

10. As to the nature of industrial production in recent years, details of output and employment in the transportable goods industries (which consist almost entirely of manufacturing concerns) are contained in respect of the year 1955 in Appendix 8, while the following figures set out its pattern and progress: —

PRODUCTION OF TRANSPORTABLE GOODS

Industrial Group	Percentage share of total net output in 1955	Volume in 1957 (Base 1953 = 100)
Food, beverages and tobacco ...	37·4	93
Clothing	8·1	93
Textiles	9·9	111
Paper and Printing	9·3	119
Metal and Engineering	13·4	113
Other	21·9	107
Total ...	100·0	102

The output of transportable goods may also be analysed under the following main heads: —

	1955 Percentage of total net output
1. Producers' equipment and materials for capital goods	15·3
2. Consumers' capital goods	8·3
3. Consumer goods or materials therefor	76·4
Total ...	100·0

11. These figures underline the great extent to which manufacturing industry is concerned with the provision of consumer goods, mainly for the home market. Imports of materials for further production (other than agriculture) expressed as a percentage of total imports rose from 36% in 1929 to 53% in 1957, while the proportion of consumer goods imported declined from 45% to 23% over the same period. As outlets for expansion in this sphere become less numerous, manufacturing concerns will, if they wish to expand output, have to turn more and more to export markets where they will have to bear the full brunt of international competition.

12. Exports of manufactured goods at present represent only a small percentage of total exports. Agricultural produce, including fresh, chilled and frozen meat, accounted for £71.9 million or 57% of the total domestic exports of £127.0 million in 1957, while many of the " other exports " valued at £55.1 million had some domestic agricultural content, e.g.

	£m
Beer	5·7
Chocolate crumb	4·5
Butter	4·5
Bacon and hams (not tinned)	4·2
Tinned beef	2·2
Leather	1·4

Other exports of manufactured goods in 1957 were:—

	£m
Apparel	2·7
Vehicles	2·4
Paper and cardboard	2·0
Machinery and electrical goods	1·1
Woollen and worsted woven fabrics ...	1·1
Yarn and thread of wool or hair ...	1·1

Conclusion

12. The process of transition, which commenced with the establishment of the Irish State, from a predominantly agricultural to a more balanced economy is still far from complete. The acceleration of that process is one of the major problems facing the Irish economy. Further industrial development, accompanied by the raising of agricultural output and purchasing power, is the best means of coping with the problems of unemployment and emigration. It is not so much a question of obtaining capital as of securing the necessary enterprise and technical competence, the " know what " as well as the " know how ". There is no evidence that any really good project has hitherto been stifled through lack of capital. For future development capital will be necessary but the real shortage is of ideas. These may have to come in part from external sources and are likely to fructify only if domestic conditions and policy are favourable to profit-making, and direct taxation is relatively light.

CHAPTER 16

ASPECTS OF INDUSTRIAL DEVELOPMENT

Promotion of Industry

1. The arrangements for the promotion of industrial development should be as comprehensive and effective as we can make them. At present the following seven public authorities and agencies are providing assistance for, or are concerned with, the promotion of manufacturing industry: —

    (i)   *Department of Industry and Commerce*
concerned with—

> the promotion of industry generally (excluding initial proposals in a specified list of cases dealt with by the Industrial Development Authority); tariffs, quotas, company law, Control of Manufactures Acts, trade agreements, general policy in relation to turf, electricity, etc.

    (ii)   *The Industrial Credit Company, Ltd.*
concerned with—

> the financing of industry by subscribing for or underwriting issues of shares by public and private companies, giving loans or guarantees of loans, advising on the most suitable means of raising capital, etc.

    (iii)   *The Industrial Development Authority*
concerned with—

> initiating proposals, for submission to the Minister for Industry and Commerce, for the creation of industries in certain specified fields; attracting foreign industrialists for the purpose of setting up new industries or associating in the development of existing industries; the making of grants towards the cost of buildings and other works for new industries in areas other than those covered by An Foras Tionscal (see below). The grants are subject to a limit of two-thirds of the cost of the buildings and other works or £50,000, whichever is the smaller. There is an aggregate limit for grants of £2.0 million. The Authority also has powers to investigate the effects of protection for industry and to review tariffs and quotas at the request of the Minister for Industry and Commerce but these powers have not so far been widely exercised.

    (iv)   *An Foras Tionscal*
concerned with—

the making of grants for industrial development in the following counties only: Donegal, Sligo, Leitrim, Roscommon, Mayo, Galway, Kerry and parts of Clare and Cork; has power (not used so far) to acquire land, to construct factories and provide ancillary facilities; may give grants for such acquisition and construction and also in respect of roads, bridges, harbour works, machinery and equipment, houses, the training of workers, etc. Grants for machinery and equipment are subject to a limit of 50 per cent. of the cost but there is no cash ceiling limit and there is no cash or percentage limit for grants for other purposes, except that the aggregate for grants under all heads must not exceed £4 million.

(v)   *Gaeltarra Éireann*

concerned with—

the fostering of industry in Gaeltacht areas; operates tweed and toy factories, organises cottage knitwear industries and markets the various goods; has now been established as an independent board, a grant of £220,000 being fixed for 1958-59.

(vi)   *Córas Tráchtála Teoranta*

concerned with—

the promotion of exports and for that purpose has the duty of encouraging and assisting the better production of exportable commodities.

(vii)   *The Institute for Industrial Research and Standards*

concerned with—

scientific research to promote the utilisation of natural resources and the discovery and improvement of technical processes; the testing of and the formulation of standards for commodities and processes.

2. It would be unwise for a small country such as ours, limited in capital resources, in industrial tradition and in executive and technical skills, to disperse, over too many agencies, the responsibility for the promotion of industry. In some other countries one general development or promoting body covers all the important aspects of industrial development, including the provision of capital funds in various ways, the establishment and the operation of industries, the provision of executive and technical personnel and the training of staffs. There are certain advantages in having one centralised body with comprehensive powers rather than separate bodies with limited powers operating in different or overlapping parts of the same field. Even with the maximum coordination of the activities of separate bodies, the fact of their separate existence denies to each the broad overall picture that would

be available to a more central body and must militate against common policy both in general and particular instances. In principle, bodies with comprehensive powers should be able to operate more expeditiously and effectively over the whole field.

3. It would, however, be going too far in the direction of rationalisation and centralisation to suggest that we should have one unified industrial development and finance corporation dealing with all aspects of industrial promotion. There are compelling reasons for a separate industrial credit body performing the specialised functions of the Industrial Credit Company in providing equity and loan capital for industry and acting as an underwriting and issuing house. Up to the present there has been some overlapping of functions in this respect between the company and the Department of Industry and Commerce, which has operated the system of guaranteed loans under the Trade Loans (Guarantee) Acts Under arrangements now being made, the provision of assistance, whether by loan or guarantee, will normally be a matter for the Credit Company in future, thus giving a desirable centralisation of functions. If the present system of grants were eventually replaced by interest-free loans with, say, a ten years' stay on the commencement of repayment, the Industrial Credit Company could appropriately assume the administration of such loans. The Company's effectiveness would probably be enhanced if it were able to provide a technical advisory service for the industries assisted by it; this may already be under consideration.

4. Allowing that the Gaeltacht is a special case and needs individual treatment, it should be possible for Gaeltarra Éireann, under the general directions of Roinn na Gaeltachta, reasonably to meet the needs of that case. Other remote areas may also have special natural advantages in the spheres of tourism, fisheries and afforestation and their potentialities in these respects can be exploited by Bord Fáilte Éireann, An Bord Iascaigh Mhara and the Department of Lands. For industrialisation generally, remote areas do not, on a realistic appraisal of our conditions, appear to have any good case for special treatment through the medium of a separate body.

5. Some degree of rationalisation could be effected in relation to the administration of grants. There are strong grounds for separating the grant-giving from the promotional function. If An Foras Tionscal continues in being, the administration of grants should be transferred to it from the Industrial Development Authority. An Foras Tionscal should have responsibility for grants in respect of the country as a whole, leaving the Industrial Development Authority as the specialist promotional agency.

6. Close liaison between the bodies concerned with the development of industry and the expansion of industrial exports is desirable.

Inter-board representation could be further extended to this end; there is already a liaison of this kind between the Industrial Development Authority, the Industrial Credit Company and the Institute for Industrial Research and Standards.

7. The promotional activities of the Industrial Development Authority would—as indicated in Chapter 4, paragraph 43—need the vigorous support of the Federation of Irish Industries. The Authority might consider to what extent it would be practicable to construct factories for sale or letting. In the Six Counties, by arrangement with industrialists or even in advance of such arrangements, the Ministry of Commerce builds factories for lease or sale. The Northern Ireland Development Council has reported that the availability of factories is a definite advantage.

Financing of Industrial Credit Company, Limited

8. As the principal State-sponsored agency for the provision of capital for industry, the Industrial Credit Company is in a particularly important position and clearly should have adequate funds available to enable it to discharge its functions. New arrangements now in train will make it possible to finance the company in future by direct advances from the Central Fund as desired or by State guarantees to banks, insurance companies, etc. providing loan capital. Following recent negotiations the commercial banks have agreed in principle to contribute between them capital to the extent of £1.8 million by way of guaranteed loan stock. This initial supply of bank capital will be used up largely in redeeming existing overdrafts of the company and directly financing liabilities under existing bank guarantees. It is usual for banks in other countries to contribute heavily to central agencies financing industry and it is to be hoped that our banks and insurance companies will in future be a substantial source of funds for the Credit Company. As was indicated in Chapter 4, paragraph 42, provision is made in this study for a minimum of £2 million a year of State finance for the company; the possibility of the company being a medium for the investment of extern institutional finance in Irish industry was also mentioned.

9. The company has also the power to raise funds by the operation of investment trusts and unit trusts, though the restricted market in Irish industrial investments has hitherto made it impracticable to use them. Such trusts are being operated successfully in other countries and have the advantage, assuming the securities held have possibilities of capital growth, that they offer at least some protection against long-term depreciation in the value of money. At least one English unit trust fund operates a thrift plan offering participation to small savers on the basis of savings as low as 5/-. Arrangements might be made with the larger industrial and other employers, or through trade unions, for weekly or monthly

subscriptions which could be channelled into a unit trust fund. Workers would thus be helping directly to finance industry and at the same time would share, to some extent, in its ownership and participate in its profits; the Industrial Credit Company would also be assisted to stimulate the market in Irish securities which has never been a large one and is currently depressed. Recent publicity suggests that there is a favourable climate amongst workers for this type of development. It is a form of saving and profit-sharing which is deserving of every encouragement. The spread of ownership of industry throughout the community is, of course, very desirable. It would help in its turn to spread a sense of responsibility and enlightened self-interest on the part of workers.

Decentralisation

10. It has been general policy for many years to favour the decentralisation of industry with the aim of bringing to areas away from the larger centres of population some share in the employment and other advantages resulting from industrial development. It is time to consider whether this is a correct policy to maintain in the conditions which we are now facing.

11. First, it must be noted that unless there are particular advantages in doing so, such as availability of raw materials locally (as in the case of fish meal plants), entrepreneurs will not normally site their factories in areas remote from good ports. Special inducements are necessary which are costly to the economy; thus, the size and scope of the grants provided by An Foras Tionscal are much wider than those provided by the Industrial Development Authority. Additional initial costs may arise from the lack of local facilities (factory sites, access roads, sanitary services, etc.). There may also be increased continuing costs. Raw materials may have to be transported to remote areas and the finished product must be transported to the main centres of home population or, if for export, probably to the main harbours near to these centres. This may involve two additional sets of transport costs and, in many cases, transport charges represent a very significant element in total costs. To offset these additional costs, increased tariff protection is often necessary with consequent reaction on the cost of living of the home consumer, who is likely in turn to seek compensation in higher wages or profits.

12. Further, the lack of a local pool of skilled labour is another initial difficulty in getting industry under way. There will also be continuing difficulties in retaining the best of the skilled labour which will tend to move to the more prosperous centres where the opportunities and scales of reward are greater and more of the amenities now generally sought after in modern life are available. Much

as we may regret this tendency of workers to migrate or emigrate to the larger urbanised districts, we cannot in practice escape from it.

13. Since the home market has been largely catered for, further industrial development must depend largely on exports. Tariffs and quota protection are at best only of limited use in this context. A realistic appraisal indicates that if we are to have any hope of success and, indeed, are not deliberately to add to our already severe handicaps, we must site our industries at, or convenient to, the larger centres of population where internal and external transport facilities are best and supplies of skilled and unskilled labour, fuel, water, etc., are readily available. This is not to ignore the possibility that there *may* be special economic advantages in doing otherwise in certain cases. Even with such siting, transport costs to and from external markets will be a heavy handicap on our exporters as compared with their competitors who are, in most cases, better placed in such matters as capital resources, experience and techniques.

14. In our present circumstances, with virtually the whole country undeveloped, it seems wasteful to subsidise remote areas specially by providing more extensive grants. Special subsidisation of this kind entails additional burdens on the community as a whole and retards progress in the most suitable areas where concentrated effort could give better results.

Protection and Foreign Participation in Irish Industry
15. Accepting that our further industrial development must be largely on the basis of production for export markets and that in any case the coming of freer trade in Europe in one form or another must be faced in due course, we can no longer rely on extensive tariff or quota protection. Neither can we afford to retain the controls we have been exercising against foreign participation in the ownership of Irish industries. The new legislation amending the Control of Manufactures Acts will remove some of the obstructions to foreign participation. Even, however, if the Acts were completely repealed, certain other handicaps would remain, e.g., the smallness of the home market, scarcity of natural resources and of skilled personnel, heavy transport charges and distance from export markets. It may reasonably be expected that foreign industrialists coming to Ireland would bring with them skills, techniques and " know-how " that we need. A readiness to welcome foreign capital is a necessary complement to efforts to secure foreign participation in industrial development. If foreign industrial investment in Ireland does not rapidly increase, a more radical removal of statutory restrictions should take place.

16. Continuous and widespread publicity is essential if any measure

of success is to be achieved in attracting manufacturers from abroad. This implies advertising in suitable publications in Britain, America and elsewhere and, perhaps, through the medium of radio and television.

Development of Foreign and Home Markets

17. Córas Tráchtála Teoranta has not up to recently engaged in the promotion of exports to Britain to any great extent but arrangements are now in hand to broaden its activities. This is desirable since the British market offers special opportunities and should receive particular attention. Irish exporters generally lack the finance and initiative to mount large-scale advertising campaigns on their own and it is essential for success that Irish goods be advertised widely through such powerful media as the press, radio and television. Córas Tráchtála could promote such advertising energetically and continuously for selected Irish products or groups of products, the exporters contributing to the cost to a reasonable extent.

18. Apart from the development of markets abroad, there is also the important question of the development of the home market. In this respect, a determined effort should be made to break down the prejudices that still exist against Irish goods even where they compare reasonably in quality and price with the imported article. A widespread, continuous publicity campaign which would bring home to all workers and employers that it is in their own interest to give preference to Irish goods, should yield results. In such a campaign it would be important to enlist the active support of the trade unions, educationalists and others in a position to influence large numbers of people. A determined effort should also be made to secure the cooperation of wholesalers and retailers and to eliminate difficulties in the way of stocking Irish goods by these traders.

Research

19. The full development of industry here will require considerable fundamental research based on our natural resources, a type of research which is unlikely to be adequately covered in the research programmes of private industry. It is to be expected, therefore, that the State should foster the provision of facilities for research work, for disseminating the results obtained, and for training research workers.

20. The Institute for Industrial Research and Standards is already performing much useful research work, particularly since the limit of its annual State grant was increased to £35,000 under the Industrial Research and Standards Act, 1954. This work has included the following investigations: —

    (a) the production of bread containing a high percentage of Irish wheat;

(b) new production processes for Comhlucht Siúicre Éireann Teoranta;

(c) examination of the properties of carrageen on behalf of Gaeltacht Services;

(d) examination of samples of clay and shales from different areas to determine their suitability for the production of bricks, tiles, etc.

This type of investigation, which lies between pure research and day-to-day testing and standardisation work, is most desirable but it should form part of a systematic programme.

21. In a recent book*, a study is made of a cross-section of significant inventions over the past fifty years with a view to assessing the relative importance of the various inventive agencies, ranging from the independent individual inventor to the elaborate research institutions which are a feature of most industrial countries nowadays. The study indicates that opinion is divided as to the best means of securing important technical advances, and that the prudent course is to maintain a multiplicity of types of research organisations. In this country the universities, the Institute for Industrial Research and Standards and the manufacturing firms are the main agencies concerned with research. Of these, the first-named is more likely to be concerned with pure scientific research than with problems of industrial research, but scientific research, whether basic or applied, leads in the direction of invention and improved industrial processes. In our present circumstances, it behoves us to make the best of all agencies at our disposal. Comment has been made from time to time about the disproportionate number of arts and medical graduates being produced by the universities and the desirability of greater concentration on training and research in scientific subjects. It has also been contended that more research should be undertaken by industrial firms or groups of such firms and that they could well afford to do this. It would be advisable to review the organisation and available resources of the Institute in order to ascertain whether these are adequate to provide all the services which the nation requires in this sphere. The Institute has only a small technical staff and could, probably, increase this staff and expand its activities if given the necessary funds.

22. Some beneficial results for our economy might be achieved by examining, in the light of the foregoing comments, the respective con-

---

* J. Jewkes, D. Sawers and R. Stillerman, *The Sources of Invention.*

tributions being made in this field by the Universities, the Institute and manufacturing firms. In regard to the latter, the Federation of Irish Industries would, no doubt, be able to offer valuable assistance.

23. In connection with the Scholarship Exchange Scheme financed from Grant Counterpart funds, it seems advisable, in our particular circumstances, to ensure that emphasis is placed on research and training having a bearing on production.

24. Another State body which may be mentioned in this connection is the Geological Survey Office. Reference is made in another part of this study to certain mineral exploration projects, including a coal prospecting scheme which the Geological Survey Office is undertaking with the aid of a sum of £80,000 from the Grant Counterpart Fund and which aims at increasing anthracite production from the present level of 160,000 tons to 250,000 tons a year. The Geological Survey normally works on a relatively modest budget of less than £10,000 a year which seems sufficient for little more than its normal mapping and survey work. Additional finance would make possible more intensive prospecting by modern methods, particularly for materials which are now much sought after, such as radioactive minerals, silica for silicone production, etc.

Industrial Efficiency, Productivity and Technical Education

25. Organisational ability and working efficiency are among the most critical factors in economic development. Some countries with meagre natural resources, e.g., Switzerland, have made very considerable economic progress and have obtained high standards of living because of determination and skill in creating and managing commercial and industrial enterprises. If the best use is to be made of investment in industry here, and we are to exploit foreign markets successfully, the general level of efficiency and productivity must be raised; to achieve this, there must be an adequate supply of trained managers, supervisors and skilled workers generally. In so far as we lack these and cannot provide them quickly, we should endeavour to get them from abroad.

26. An incentive to improve efficiency and productivity is available to manufacturers in the form of State grants towards the cost of technical assistance projects, for which purpose there is a provision of £130,000 for 1958-59. Under the scheme, up to one-third of the cost of approved projects may be recouped to the manufacturers. The reduction in tariffs which membership of a European Free Trade Area would entail would also help to promote increased efficiency and productivity.

27. So far, this country, unlike the majority of O.E.E.C. countries, has not a national productivity centre, activity in this sphere being carried on under the aegis of the Department of Industry and Commerce. The work of that Department will, it is hoped, be augmented shortly by a committee under the auspices of the Irish Management Institute. Ireland is the only O.E.E.C. country which is not an active member of the governing body of the European Productivity Agency or of the Agency's Productivity Committee. If we played a greater part in the Agency's activities, we could reasonably hope to receive, at comparatively little cost, an increased share of its technical assistance allocations.

28. The Irish Management Institute has recently published a report on education and training for management and has set up a management development unit with the aid of Grant Counterpart Funds. The work of the Institute in attempting to improve the quality of management in Irish industry deserves the fullest support. It is desirable, however, that increasing attention be given to the specialised techniques which are sometimes referred to as the tools of management, e.g., supervision, work study, operator training, costing, personnel management, office organisation and methods, etc. A scheme known as Training Within Industry for Supervisors, which originated in the United States in the early 1940s and has since spread throughout the world, has proved a most effective means of developing supervisory skills. In this country, Training Within Industry has been used by a few companies since about 1950 and is now available to smaller concerns through the High School of Commerce, Rathmines. Work study, in so far as it is used by Irish industry, seems to be largely restricted to the development of incentive schemes of remuneration; elsewhere it has proved even more fruitful in other fields such as rationalisation of procedures, economy in the handling of materials, improvement of management controls, etc. An Irish Work Study Society has been formed within the past two years to foster the knowledge and practice of work study and the Rathmines High School of Commerce is in course of establishing a School of Work Study. There is scope for the extension to other centres of the specialised courses conducted by the Rathmines School of Commerce.

29. The place of vocational education itself in the life of the nation requires careful examination. The question of improving and extending the system in rural areas is discussed in Chaper 11. In urban areas, a different approach is obviously required if the courses are to take cognisance of the essentially industrial environment and outlook of its pupils. Care must be taken, however, that the fundamental education given in these schools is not swamped by purely technical training and instruction, important though these are; the problem is one of maintaining a correct balance. The present curricula of urban schools seem

unduly weighted by art and hobby courses. While it is appreciated that there is a definite demand for courses in such subjects, it is desirable that the amount of time devoted to them be not excessive and there seems no reason why the fees charged should not reflect more fully the economic cost of providing them.

30. There is a case for developing and broadening the work of the Employment Exchanges by the provision of a full-scale placement and advisory service for workers, particularly young workers. At present, the Exchanges concentrate on such activities as the routine registration of unemployed workers, notification of vacancies to such workers and the distribution of unemployment benefit and other social assistance payments.

31. In the spheres of scientific, technological and technical training generally, we have probably much to learn from the experience of other countries. In Britain there is a three-tier system of technical education consisting of local and regional schools and finally colleges of advanced technology, the latter providing courses for diplomas in technology. The lines of British development should prove helpful to us in deciding the form and manner of extensions suitable to our conditions.

32. The direct annual cost of vocational services to the Exchequer is now of the order of £1¼ million per annum. While any significant extension of the services would probably entail additional cost, some economies should be possible, at least on the side of capital investment in school buildings, through a degree of integration with the national school system (see Chapter 4, paragraph 45). Some savings may also be possible through modification of the present high standards of technical school building.

Restrictive Labour Practices
33. Information about the extent of restrictive labour practices is incomplete but various instances of such practices have come under notice from time to time. In general they refer to the refusal of workers and their trade unions to allow the use of improved materials or equipment or the free entry of apprentices into industry. Examples are the insistence of the trade unions on the continued use of obsolete and expensive loading and unloading methods at Dublin and Limerick ports. In Dublin the dockers refuse to handle container traffic (with certain exceptions) and also will not allow the operation of modern ramp loading services for vehicles. Another example in Dublin is the case of the "ghost" cattlemen who are paid for *not* travelling on the cattle boats to the Continent. Yet another example is limitation of apprenticeship recruitment in the printing trade.
34. Restrictive practices of these kinds—and the adoption in some

cases of rather low output standards—have a significant bearing on the cost of production and distribution and on the general development of the economy. With the rapid improvements in skills and techniques and the progress of automation throughout the world, the matter will be of even greater importance for the future, and it would be worthwhile investigating the whole field with a view to devising means to eliminate or reduce restrictive practices as far as possible. It may be argued that, by and large, we are no worse off in this respect than many other countries but if we are to develop exports, we must do better, at least in *some* respects, in order to offset the disadvantage from which we suffer as compared with our foreign competitors.

35. In any approach to the subject the general attitude of workers and trade unions is, of course, crucial. In the final analysis, the only effective preventive to ill-informed opposition to measures which are ultimately for the good of the national economy and of the workers themselves is better education. Probably much could be done to reduce this harmful antagonism by a more adroit introduction of new methods and in particular " getting it over " to the workers that the initial dislocation will be followed in the long run by increased national prosperity in which they will share. The trade unions in the U.S.A. and Britain appear now to be adopting an enlightened attitude towards the changes necessary to secure higher productivity. It should be possible to obtain a similar reaction from the unions here in the context of general measures for the development of the economy. The participation of union officials in programmes of the European Productivity Agency is a welcome step in the right direction.

36. Joint machinery for the conduct of relations between employers and workers is not well developed in this country. There are only about a dozen standing joint committees or industrial councils and most of these appear to deal only with wage questions. The Industrial Relations Act, 1946, includes provisions designed to encourage the establishment of joint industrial councils but these provisions have had little or no success. There is a definite need throughout industry for organisations of this kind which would deal fully and continuously with such questions as restrictive practices.

CHAPTER 17

CERTAIN INDUSTRIES BASED ON AGRICULTURAL
PRODUCTS*

Biscuits and Cakes

1. The biscuit industry was once one of our strongest export industries, sending its products all over the globe. In 1929 exports of biscuits exceeded £500,000 and imports were only £11,000. Exports had declined by 1940 to £298,000 while imports increased to £19,000. In 1957, exports were valued at only £86,000 (of which £84,000 went to the Six Counties) while imports were valued at £120,000. The substitution of an import trade for a once flourishing export trade is most regrettable. The development of an export business would be most helpful from the employment and balance of payments aspects. If capital should prove to be a limiting factor, the Industrial Credit Company should be able to provide the necessary facilities under the arrangements proposed in this study.

Processed Vegetables, Fruit, etc.

2. This country is so close to the British market that most of our exports of fruit, vegetables, etc., can reach that market in a fresh or virtually unprocessed condition and thus attract good prices. The main development possibility here seems to lie in improved production, marketing and distribution techniques in the agricultural sphere. There should be some scope—in association, perhaps, with the freezing and processing of fish—for the development of a substantial processing and export trade in fresh-frozen, canned and bottle fruit and vegetables, fruit juices, soups, sauces, jams, etc. Such exports are at present relatively small, as the following figures for 1957 indicate:—

Commodity	Value of Exports
	£
Fruit, canned or bottled	37,000
Fruit pulp	95,000
Vegetables in air-tight containers	3,000
Salad cream	59,000
Jams and marmalades	8,000

* Milk products, beef and mutton have been dealt with in Chapter 8 and bacon in Chapter 9

167

Britain imports relatively little tinned or bottled fruit and vegetable preparations of the type we could provide. This is not to say that a market for processed vegetables could not be developed in Britain. The main prospects for export development seem, however, to be in new markets, particularly in the less developed countries whose consumption of food may be expected to increase in future years. A promising beginning has been made in exports of pre-packed vegetables to self-service stores in the West Indies.

3. The Irish food processing industry is at present based almost entirely on the home market. Production figures for 1955 were:—

Commodity				Factory Value
				£
Fruit, tinned or bottled	...	...	...	76,587
Canned vegetables	...	....	...	612,653
Soups or purées ...	...	...	...	119,185
Jams and marmalades	...	...	...	1,377,634

Judging by the lack of variety of vegetables and fruit supplies, particularly in provincial towns, there should be room for further expansion of the industry on the home market as well as in the export field.

4. Some of the reasons for the lack of development in this industry may be gleaned from a " Report on the Handling, Processing and Storage of Fruit and Vegetables and on the Canning, Bottling, Chilling and Freezing of Fruit and Vegetables, etc." which was furnished in 1952 by an American technical assistance expert. The following were some of his conclusions:—

    (a) Farmers need to be encouraged to plant suitable fruit trees, vegetables, etc.

    (b) There should be a greater use of home-produced glass jars instead of tins.

    (c) There is need for improvement in the quality of tinned and bottled goods and there is need for standards of identity, quality and fill of containers.

    (d) Standards of factory lay-out are poor.

    (e) The firms concerned should cooperate in the establishment of a canners' school and information service.

    (f) Present labelling is inadequate.

5. As the ingredients (fruit, vegetables, sugar) should be readily and

cheaply available, this country should be in a favourable position to develop the food processing industry. The machinery required would not appear to be very expensive so that the capital cost of developing the industry should not be heavy. The main requirements are improved production and marketing methods and the development of new markets. For the purpose of stimulating increased and more efficient production of fruit and vegetables, contact with the producer could best be effected through the County Committees of Agriculture who at present employ 58 horticultural instructors.

6. It is understood that a few proposals have recently been received by the Department of Industry and Commerce from private interests in this country who propose to engage in the canning of fruit and vegetables, or the freezing of vegetables, both for the home market and for export.

7. The experience of Comhlucht Siúicre Éireann, Teoranta, places that company in a favourable position to engage in the development of the processed fruit and vegetable industry. It is understood that the Company have tentatively considered, from time to time, the possibility of doing so but have not reached any final conclusions.

Sweets, etc.

8. As regards manufactured products based on milk and sugar—other than chocolate crumb which has been considered in Chapter 8—a fairly large export trade has already been developed in chocolates, sweets and toffee (£613,000 in 1957). This is a trade in which high quality, attractive wrapping and presentation are of as great importance in the export field as price. The sweet factory operated by the Dairy Disposal Company in Limerick might, if it were organised to concentrate on an attractive higher-grade product, play a pilot role in the exports drive. The fact that it is operated by a State-sponsored body would facilitate any direct capital investment that a reorganisation might require.

Brewing and Distilling

9. Brewing and distilling are among the few traditional industries that survived in Ireland in the free trade era following the Act of Union; they have continued to operate successfully without protection. Due to the enterprise and efficiency of A. Guinness, Son and Co., Ltd., brewing has for many years given a good account of itself in the export trade, total exports of stout and porter in 1957 amounting to 1.12 million standard barrels valued at £5.68 million. On the other hand, exports of spirits have been disappointing when one considers not only the very considerable investment of capital and skill in this old-

169

established industry but also the industry's independence of imported raw materials.

10. In the years 1937, 1938 and 1939 exports of spirits (mainly whiskey) averaged 230,000 gallons a year with an average annual value of £179,000. The main export markets and the average annual exports to them were as follows:—

	Average Annual Exports, 1937–1939	
	galls.	£
Britain...	136,000	110,000
Six Counties	48,000	37,000
U.S.A....	44,000	30,000

In the post-war period exports of whiskey grew steadily from 1948 to 1951, reaching a peak in the latter year of 438,000 gallons valued at £558,000. They declined steeply in the next three years but have since begun to recover, the main increase being in exports to the Six Counties. The following figures illustrate the changes:—

	Six Counties		Britain		U.S.A.		Total (All Destinations)	
	galls.	£	galls.	£	galls.	£	galls.	£
1950	118,000	155,000	254,000	286,000	29,000	60,000	405,000	508,000
1951	123,000	160,000	280,000	324,000	27,000	58,000	438,000	558,000
1954	53,000	86,000	40,000	58,000	23,000	51,000	127,000	224,000
1956	62,000	116,000	24,000	39,000	40,000	91,000	150,000	300,000
1957	90,000	178,000	32,000	53,000	39,000	90,000	194,000	383,000

11. While total exports of whiskey are now above the pre-war level in value (because of higher prices), they are still below that level in volume and they are 50% less in volume than in 1950-51. Current exports are, indeed, trifling in relation to British exports and, in particular, to the size of the American market. In 1957 British exports of whisky were valued at a total of £52.1 million of which £28.6 million went to the U.S.A. Córas Tráchtála, Teoranta, believe that whiskey has virtually unlimited sale prospects in the U.S.A. and that it could also sell well in Canada. The distillers have recently come together to finance, with the aid of Córas Tráchtála, Teoranta, an advertising campaign intended to widen their foothold in the American market and are meeting with sufficient success to encourage hope of building exports up to the £1 million mark in that market in a few years' time. In 1957-58, Córas Tráchtála contributed £21,000 from their grant-in-aid to a joint publicity campaign directed towards the U.S. market and a larger provision has been made in the 1958-59 budget for the same purpose.

170

12. So far the main effort to increase exports has been directed to the U.S.A. but on the basis of pre-war and early post-war trade, the British market should have potentialities despite the increased competition from Scotch whisky which was in short supply immediately after the war. With determination we should be able to win back a worthwhile foothold. The existence of a large Irish population in Britain suggests a potential market which nearness and good communications should make it easier to exploit. The question of expanding our exports to Britain and the Six Counties deserves special investigation by Córas Tráchtála.

13. If the distillers find difficulty in building up their own export organisation, it might be possible for them to come to an arrangement with Guinness whereby they would have access to the appropriate services of that concern's export organisation for sales promotion and marketing purposes. The Industrial Credit Company might be approached if expansion in export trade gives rise to a greater need for capital, e.g., in connection with the holding of stocks of whiskey for maturing, than the distillers can themselves meet.

14. There appear to be possibilities for developing exports of gin. Difficulty in regard to flavour does not arise and as gin does not have to be matured for long periods it has the advantage over whiskey that production can be increased rapidly. The Cork Distilleries Company has been producing gin, as well as whiskey, for many years. Another distilling firm—John Power & Son, Ltd.—has recently announced its intention to produce, mainly for the export market, a high-quality distilled dry gin.

Leather and Leather Products

15. Leather should be a product of prime importance in an economy such as ours which is so largely dependent on the cattle and meat trades. The industries based on leather (mainly situated outside Dublin) are already fairly large, as the following figures, relating to production in 1956, show: —

(a) Boots and Shoes:

Gross Output	...	£6.5 million
Persons employed		5,913

(b) Other Manufactures (handbags, cases, wallets, straps, saddlery, etc.):

Gross Output	...	£0.5 million
Persons employed		638

171

16. A fairly big export and import trade is done in hides, leather and leather products. The following figures relate to 1957: —

Exports

	(£000)
Cattle hides and skins, undressed ...	365
Sheep and lamb skins, undressed ...	131
Other hides and skins, etc.	34
Leather	1,423
Other leather manufactures	7
Boots, shoes, etc.	911
Total Exports	2,870

Imports

	(£000)
Cattle hides, undressed	519
Other hides, etc., undressed	47
Leather	658
Leather manufactures	24
Boots, shoes, etc.	135
Total Imports	1,383

17. The IBEC report on the industrial potentials of Ireland calculated that the slaughter here of cattle worth £20 million would make available an additional £3.5 million of hides for local processing, which, since the fellmongery and leather trade adds some 41% in net product to the cost of materials, might contribute another £1.4 million of processing activity. If the finished leather were made into boots and shoes (in which the net product adds about 70% to materials cost) the final addition to the national output might be of the order of £8.3 million. While such calculations must be treated with reserve, they give an indication of the large expansion in the leather industry which could follow from increased home killings of cattle. Existing capacity for leather tanning and shoe manufacturing is in excess of requirements. If, however, the available quantity of hides should increase significantly as the result of increased home slaughtering of cattle, there might be some opening for productive investment in the leather industry directed towards new export markets. There should also be some scope for the production of finer leathers for home consumption.

18. The fact that leather is imported for manufacturing purposes indicates some shortage of the better quality leather, or of some varieties of leather. It should be possible to offset this shortage to some extent by research into improved tanning, etc., methods. Such research should help the industry to recover some of the markets lost to rubber and other substitutes. There appears also to be scope on the agricultural

side for improving the quality of hides and skins by reducing the damage done by insects, diseases and injuries; for example, it has been estimated that 70% of hides from cattle slaughtered here are warbled with a loss of about 15/- each, which works out at a total annual loss of about £250,000.

19. Further improvements in design and finish would help to promote exports of leather products such as shoes, gloves and handbags. A leather development centre on cooperative lines, which would be concerned with research, development and design should be a help here. Alternatively, the Institute for Industrial Research and Standards might specially investigate the position.

CHAPTER 18

TURF

Production

1. Exchequer advances to Bord na Móna for turf development and ancillary activities total some £12 million. Advances for the first development programme, now amounting to £6.4 million, were interest-free up to 1952 and advances for the second development programme, which now total £5.0 million, were interest-free prior to 1955-56; the Board is currently paying interest on all advances. The Board has also raised a loan of £0.5 million from A. Guinness, Son & Co., Ltd., to meet part of its requirements in 1957-58 and 1958-59. It is estimated that to complete the present development programmes further borrowings from the Exchequer or other sources of the order of £1.2 million will be necessary in each of the years 1958-59 and 1959-60 and that £0.5 million will be required from such sources in 1960-61, these amounts being additional to sums available from the Board's own resources.

2. The Board's production of turf has expanded to 1½ million tons a year, production in the last two years being:—

	Machine Turf Tons	Milled Peat Tons	Total Tons
1956/57	829,000	290,000	1,119,000
1957/58	820,000	652,000	1,472,000

Under the existing programmes production is planned to rise in the next few years to an annual rate of approximately 3 million tons, made up of 1 million tons of machine turf and 2 million tons of milled peat. Of this output some 0.5 million tons of machine turf and 1.2 million tons of milled peat are for supply to the E.S.B. for use as fuel in the generation of electricity. The balance of the machine turf (0.5 million tons) is intended for sale for industrial, commercial, domestic and institutional consumption, and of the milled peat (0.8 million tons) for manufacture into briquettes for sale in that form.

3. In the case of milled peat the estimated requirements of the E.S.B. (at 1.2 million tons) are over 1 million tons a year less than the original estimate owing to the failure of demand for electric current

to expand as expected. In view of the reduction in the E.S.B.'s requirements two new turf briquetting factories are being constructed at an estimated cost of £1.8 million and these will absorb about 600,000 tons of milled peat annually. In addition, the existing briquetting factory at Lullymore has been modernised and its future annual requirements will be 150,000 tons of milled peat. The three factories are, therefore, expected to absorb 750,000/800,000 tons of milled peat yearly, representing 250,000 tons of briquettes.

4. Experience with milled peat to date has indicated that it is a cheaper fuel than oil for electricity generation and the setback arising from the failure of the demand for electric energy to come up to expectations is, therefore, particularly unfortunate. The current development programmes extend to upwards of 100,000 acres of bog. A further 300,000 acres could be exploited with the methods at present in use, though production costs would tend to be higher as the remaining bogs are smaller. Nevertheless a significant addition to the country's wealth and employment would appear possible. The Board now gives employment to about 7,000 persons at the peak period of its production season. The question of stimulating the demand for electricity which is discussed elsewhere is therefore of great importance in the context of the further exploitation of the nation's turf resources. Outlets for turf must, however, also be looked for in other directions.

Turf for Domestic and Industrial Use
5. Production of briquettes has up to the present fallen far short of demand but, as indicated above, arrangements have been made to step up production very substantially. It would appear prudent not to contemplate any further expansion in this sector before 1960-61, when the two new briquetting factories will be in operation and it will be possible to make an assessment of future demand.

6. Recent experience as regards the general demand for machine-won turf has not been so encouraging. In 1956-57 sales of machine turf to domestic, institutional, industrial and commercial consumers (other than the E.S.B.) amounted to 300,000 tons but much more could have been sold given the necessary demand. Stocks were in fact accumulating, though this is partly accounted for by the postponement of the commissioning of the E.S.B.'s new sod-peat-fired generating station at Lanesboro arising from the slow growth in demand for electricity. In 1957-58 sales, other than to the E.S.B., rose to about 330,000 tons, following the initiation of a special publicity campaign by Bord na Móna, but stocks are still heavy. Further expansion of this market should be possible and is, indeed, urgently necessary. Keen competition must be expected to continue from coal, oil and gases such as " Calor " and " Kosangas ". To step up—and even to maintain—sales, the Board will have to maintain persistent and widespread publicity. Special

attention will also need to be paid to easing the delivery, storage and handling problems of consumers. Continuing research into the production and introduction of better turf-burning apparatus will be necessary. Factories and institutions in particular need modern storage and stoking facilities, as well as up-to-date burning apparatus, to get the full benefit of machine turf, which Bord na Móna claims to be cheaper than coal, and it should pay the Board to arrange a general hire-purchase system to encourage the installation of such facilities. Public institutions which find difficulty in installing turf-burning apparatus because of the high initial cost should be facilitated in the matter of loans for the purpose; it appears that an investment of the order of £200,000 would meet the cost of changing over to turf for the main public institutions now using imported fuel.

7. There may also be opportunities for the export of turf to the Six Counties from the more conveniently situated bogs.

Other Development
8. Proposals for the establishment of a fertiliser industry using milled peat as a raw material are discussed in another chapter. It may be noted here that such an industry requiring annually, as it would, up to 150,000 tons of milled peat and 80 million units of electricity, would be of considerable help to the further development of both Bord na Móna and the E.S.B. A sum of over £300,000 has already been expended in development work and further expenditure estimated at £550,000 would be necessary to complete development for the purpose of a fertiliser industry.

9. Bord na Móna operates a peat moss factory at Kilberry, Co. Kildare. Production has expanded steadily in recent years and is now running at an annual rate of 200,000 bales, sales being valued at £120,000. The bulk of the output is exported. Expenditure, amounting to £230,000, on the expansion of peat moss production, is planned for the period 1958-59 to 1961-62. There may be further prospects in this line depending on experience over the next three or four years. The high cost of packaging materials and lack of adequate shipping facilities tend to make it difficult to compete in export markets but these are problems which time, persistent attention and the gradual development of the trade may solve. The Board has also been developing a fermented soil conditioner called " Humona ". This is still largely in the experimental stages; it is to be hoped that it will offer possibilities for exploitation.

10. Turf may be used as a raw material for the manufacture of a wide variety of products. Examples are peat wax, peat coke, activated carbon, domestic gas and oil. Activated carbon is used in the chemical

176

and rubber industries and is, in fact, being manufactured in the Six Counties from turf supplied by Bord na Móna.

11. The Industrial Development Authority, in cooperation with Bord na Móna and interested private concerns, has been investigating the possibilities, technical and commercial, of establishing industries producing such items as wax, coke and carbon. So far, however, no definite proposal has materialised, one of the principal difficulties being that of securing a sufficiently large market for the product. The Board is also investigating the possibility of producing town gas from milled peat. These activities are deserving of every reasonable encouragement. In order that private enterprise may be assisted it is desirable that Bord na Móna should undertake or arrange for more intensive research into the possibilities of developing new lines as well as new and improved techniques. A welcome step in this direction is the arrangement which has recently been made between the Board and A. Guinness, Son and Co., Ltd., to finance jointly the establishment of a Chair of Microbiology at University College, Dublin. While research may be costly, the Board is well-established and it should have no great difficulty in allocating a sizable annual sum for the purpose. There is an existing research station which could be expanded as necessary. Information does, of course, become available as to new discoveries and advances in techniques in other countries, but a virile body that has already pioneered the way in some respects may rightly be expected to continue to do so.

12. It would appear desirable that the Board, or, if necessary, a separate public agency, should establish pilot plants for likely new lines and be prepared to carry out initial development and exploitation of markets. This might be done in participation with private interests, or in advance of such participation, if time would otherwise be lost. The Board or a separate agency could proceed with large-scale development of promising lines even if there were no prospect of private participation.

Liaison between Bord na Móna and the E.S.B.

13. As the fortunes of Bord na Móna are largely bound up with those of the E.S.B., the closest coordination of programmes and co operation generally between the two Boards is obviously necessary. With these objects in view the existing Joint Technical Committee which deals with joint problems on the technical level might be upgraded to include the Chairman of the E.S.B., the Managing Director of Bord na Móna and the chief engineers and senior finance representatives of both bodies. Such a committee would be in a better position to secure coordination and cooperation on all fronts.

CHAPTER 19

FERTILISER INDUSTRY

Introduction

1. There are three main groups of artificial fertilisers: phosphatic, potassic and nitrogenous. Examples are, respectively, superphosphate, muriate of potash and sulphate of ammonia. Ordinary (single) super-phosphate is made here in substantial quantities by grinding imported rock phosphate to a fine powder and mixing with sulphuric acid, but concentrated (triple) superphosphate, used mainly in compounds and requiring treatment of rock phosphate with phosphoric acid, is not manufactured here. There is no manufacture of potassic fertiliser and little scope for it, as potassium salts are not found in this country. Small quantities of nitrogenous fertiliser are derived as a by-product of the gas industry. The establishment of an oil refinery at Cork opens up possibilities of expansion in the Irish fertiliser industry.

2. The following table shows the increase in imports of fertilisers in 1957 as compared with 1938: —

Imports	1938		1957	
	Tons	£	Tons	£
Superphosphates	5,922	19,416	66,998	1,220,217
Rock Phosphate (unground)	80,263	118,126	73,387	546,439
Basic slag	21,798	54,415	44,337	402,140
Muriate of Potash	4,289	32,169	100,574	1,486,484
Sulphate of Ammonia	31,410	211,548	62,082	1,142,695
Ammonium Nitrate	—	—	14,909	278,831
Natural fertilisers n.e.s.	2,042	14,268	3,989	78,771
Compound manures	2,522	16,610	1,581	74,362
Other fertiisers (including phosphates n.e.s.)	22,268	71,118	13,517	364,566
	170,514	537,670	381,374	5,594,505

3. The need for greatly increased use of fertilisers, as the quickest and most effective means to increased agricultural production at lower unit cost, has been explained in Chapter 6; and, in Chapter 12, it has been proposed that provision be made for a temporary but intensive programme of subsidisation to promote, in particular, the increased application of phosphatic fertiliser to grasslands. This is based on the expert opinion that in undertaking an improvement in soil fertility the most urgent need is for considerably more lime and phosphate. It is hoped that subsidisation of phosphatic fertilisers on the scale suggested in Chapter 12 (i.e., £2 million a year) would result in an immediate and

progressive expansion in the purchase of such fertilisers. The next development in a balanced fertiliser policy would be the encouragement of the use of potash, followed by nitrogenous fertiliser for spring and autumn production of grass.

Superphosphates

4. Home production of single superphosphate in the fertiliser year ended 30 June, 1957, was 152,000 tons and imports in the same period for compounding totalled 25,000 tons, making a total of 177,000 tons. The principal manufacturing firm has erected a new factory in Cork; when this factory comes into production, present demand for single superphosphate will then be capable of being met entirely by home manufacturers, with a small margin to meet expansion in demand. Triple superphosphate is not manufactured here and imports in 1956-57 came to 32,000 tons. The manufacturing capacity of the industry will allow for some increase in present demand; if the hopes placed on the proposed subsidisation programme are realised, there will be ample scope for further expansion.

Nitrogenous Fertilisers

5. The present use of these fertilisers is about 80,000 tons per annum (mainly sulphate of ammonia) as against the 400,000 tons or so which would be necessary to approach the level of average consumption in O.E.E.C. countries. Nitrogenous fertiliser was (and still is) applied in this country mainly in the form of sulphate of ammonia, although the use of ammonium nitrate fertilisers has increased steadily since they were introduced on the Irish market in 1952. Since 1946 investigations have been proceeding under the aegis of Ceimicí, Teoranta, into the possibility of establishing a plant for the manufacture of nitrogenous fertiliser requirements from native raw materials. These investigations, which were pursued in consultation with foreign firms, were initially directed towards the production of sulphate of ammonia and later to ammonium nitrate production.

6. In 1953 Ceimicí Teoranta submitted a report recommending that ammonium nitrate should be produced, using milled peat or anthracite duff in conjunction with limestone as raw materials, the factory to have an output of 100,000 tons per annum. This recommendation was confirmed in a detailed report, prepared after consultation with Dutch consultants and furnished in 1954 at the request of the Government. An investigation of the position in the Netherlands and other countries had shown that there was a marked preference there for ammonium nitrate, mainly because of the lower cost of production and the absence of the soil acidification which may result from continued use of high doses of sulphate of ammonia. The company stated that anthracite duff or oil were alternative raw materials to milled

peat for the proposed industry and suggested that, if these fuels were used, the factory should be located near a seaport.

7. Consideration of the matter has recently crystallised in a proposal to establish a nitrogenous fertiliser factory at Shannonbridge to produce ammonium nitrate fertiliser using milled peat from the nearby Blackwater bog, which has already been partly developed by Bord na Móna for the production of electricity. Until this proposal is further developed, however, detailed estimates of capital and production costs will not be available and it would be premature to attempt any conclusive assessment of the economics of the project. Some of the considerations involved are indicated in the following paragraphs.

8. A home industry manufacturing nitrogenous fertiliser would be a desirable project if it could (without subsidisation) supply the Irish farmers' requirements as cheaply as they could be supplied by imports and could export any surplus production without loss. The advantages of such an industry include the saving obtainable by importing raw materials rather than finished products, the security afforded in times of emergency and the employment and training which would be made available in a new and important field. As indicated in paragraph 4, when the present expansion programme is completed all the single superphosphate *now* required will be available from home sources. If nitrogenous fertiliser based on native fuels were also manufactured here our requirements of these two fertilisers would be reasonably secure and a basis would be laid for further developments in the production of chemicals.

9. On the other hand, while it has been estimated that ammonium nitrate fertilisers based on milled peat could be produced more cheaply than imported nitrate or sulphate of ammonia, it is unlikely that the economic output of the factory (100,000 tons) would be absorbed on the Irish market for some years. The current demand for all types of nitrogenous fertilisers is of the order of 80,000 tons per annum. A factory producing 100,000 tons of ammonium nitrate per annum would, therefore, be faced with the initial disadvantage of having to sell its surplus production on export markets in competition with large-scale British and Continental producers. However, Irish ammonium nitrate would, under the existing Trade Agreements, be entitled to customs-free entry into British markets and the factory would not be tied to the conversion of all its ammonia into ammonium nitrate. It is claimed that an annual output of less than 100,000 tons of ammonium nitrate would be economic, provided the remaining ammonia or nitric acid production could be disposed of to phosphate manufacturers for conversion into the newer complex fertilisers, viz., nitrophosphate and ammonium phosphate.

CHAPTER 20

ELECTRICITY

Development

1. Investment in the development of electricity and ancillary services through the medium of the Electricity Supply Board is now in the region of £100 million, including £23 million for rural electrification. About half of this investment has been made in the last five years; two-thirds of it have been financed by Exchequer advances. With the exception of sums totalling almost £2 million made available as subsidy towards rural electrification, the E.S.B. is paying interest on the Exchequer advances and is also repaying the advances themselves over a period of fifty years. The balance of the investment has been financed by the Board itself, principally by borrowings from internal sources (viz., renewal and replacement provisions and superannuation funds) and by means of public stock issues.

2. Further development over the next five years is estimated to require £26 million; this figure provides for the completion of rural electrification within that period, bringing total investment under that head to some £30 million. Of the amount of £26 million, some £15 million is expected to be found from internal sources and from the balance of the proceeds of the recent £5 million public stock issue, leaving a further £11 million to be raised.

3. It will be seen that, despite the magnitude of the investment which has already been made, the capital requirements of the E.S.B. continue to be large. The development programme, as outlined in a White Paper published in 1954, was based on an estimated annual average growth in demand for electric current of 13.4 per cent., i.e. on an expectation that demand would double itself every five and a half years. This was related to experience in the pre-war and early post-war years. The expectation of such a rapid growth was not realised and early in 1956 the generating programme was revised downwards on the basis of an annual growth of 9 per cent., but this has again been too optimistic. In 1955-56 growth was only 7.6 per cent. and in 1956-57 only 4.7 per cent. It has risen to 7.7 per cent. in 1957-58 (equivalent to a doubling of demand about every nine and a half years) but this rise may have been exceptionally stimulated by the severe weather conditions in the March quarter of 1958. As heavy demand cannot be expected from the bulk of the new consumers remaining to be connected (i.e., persons

in the poorer rural areas) and as there is severe competition both in town and country from oil and gases, there is no good reason to suppose that there will be a greatly increased rate of growth in the near future unless a rapid expansion of the economy occurs.

4. In recent years the provision of generating capacity has run ahead of the country's requirements, and the E.S.B. has surplus capacity, over and above a reasonable reserve for contingencies, which would enable it to supply current of 400-500 million units a year in excess of the present demand of about 1,775 million units. This alone would suffice for almost four years of growth of demand at last year's rate. The period of excess capacity will be prolonged by the completion of new generating stations now under construction. The heavy excess investment in plant adds to fixed charges and represents a deadweight burden on the E.S.B.

5. Heavy investment by the E.S.B. without a commensurate rise in revenue has meant a steep rise in the proportion of capital charges (interest, sinking fund and depreciation) to revenue. In 1951-52 capital charges represented 30 per cent. of revenue and likewise 30 per cent. of working expenses; they now represent about 50 per cent. in each case, or over £6 million a year, and will continue to rise.

Rural Electrification

6. Apart from the over-capitalisation resulting from the provision of excess generating plant, a serious burden is also being imposed by the loss incurred on rural electrification. This amounted to £552,000 for 1957-58 which profit on other operations reduced to a loss of £180,000. The capital cost to date averages over £100 per rural consumer without including any element for generating cost. Now that only the more remote and less populous areas remain to be connected, rural electrification will become more and more uneconomic according as it progresses; it is estimated that the annual loss on rural electrification will be up to £1¼ million by 1963, assuming completion of the scheme by that time. To ease the burden on the E.S.B. it has been decided to recoup by Exchequer subsidy 50 per cent. of the capital charges arising from the completion of the scheme.

7. Subsidisation will not, of course, solve the problem. It will merely transfer part of the loss from the electricity consumer to the taxpayer, i.e. from Peter to Paul. The case might be made that the general consumer of electricity is as good a mark as the taxpayer; indeed, viewed as a vehicle of taxation, the electricity bill is as effective, convenient and equitable as any other. The primary consideration is that if more of our national resources are to be applied to productive development, uneconomic investment must be curbed.

The investment of £23 million in rural electrification since 1946-47, resulting in the supply of electric power to 75 per cent. of rural areas, represents a generous contribution from the nation's resources towards providing a desirable amenity as well as a means of increasing agricultural production. In fact, on most farms, the use of electricity is virtually confined to domestic purposes; it contributes more to comfort than to output. No material increase in agricultural production can be expected from the extension of supply to the remoter areas. These factors suggest that the rate at which further areas are connected should be adjusted so as to keep pace with an improvement in the Board's general finances, thus moderating the losses falling on the general electricity consumer and the taxpayer.

Stimulation of Demand for Electricity

8. The measures suggested in different parts of this study with a view to expanding the economy and providing higher living standards should have the effect of accelerating the growth of demand for electric current. This would make it possible to complete rural electrification fairly rapidly without additional strain on the Board's resources. Consideration should be given to the possibility of arrangements with the Six Counties which would provide an export outlet for current generated here. The export of current to Britain would not be possible because of the high cost of underwater cable but a feeder cross-border line could be constructed without difficulty and at relatively small cost. The new oil refinery at Cork which is expected to commence operations in 1959 will require a substantial amount of electricity annually. The power requirements of a nitrogenous fertiliser factory based on milled peat would be substantial; the actual consumption would depend on the process adopted and might be as high as 60/80 million units a year. It is clear that industries using large quantities of electrical energy would be of great assistance to both the E.S.B. and Bord na Móna, apart from their other benefits to the economy.

9. The Board is no longer in the position in which it was during the war and early post-war period of having an unlimited demand for its product. Like Bord na Móna, it must be prepared to meet the keenest competition from other sources of energy. It follows that the maintenance and intensification of sales pressure for electric current, particularly directed towards industrial and agricultural users, is essential. In this connection joint publicity with Bord na Móna should be an advantage to both Boards in some sections of their activities.

10. The use of electricity for agricultural purposes is still extremely small and additional efforts appear necessary to increase it. Publicity brought home directly to farmers and their wives is needed to break down their natural conservatism. Amongst other ways of stimulating

demand in rural areas, the Board has cooperated in the equipping of a few pilot farms with electrical apparatus; this activity could well be extended.

11. Similar scope exists for the promotion of electrical soil heating for horticultural production; this is already widely publicised by the Board. This country is backward in the production and use of out-of-season vegetables, fruit and flowers and this suggests that the Board, in cooperation with the Department of Agriculture, the County Committees of Agriculture and other interested parties, should sponsor in various centres full-scale pilot greenhouses using electricity to the maximum and fitted with modern grading and packing equipment.

12. Continuous sponsoring of pilot schemes for new uses of electricity in the industrial and commercial sectors is also desirable. It is not enough merely to advertise new uses: their success in practice must be shown. The standardisation of electrical components and accessories is a field in which the E.S.B., in cooperation with the Industrial Development Authority and the Institute for Industrial Research and Standards, could take further action with profit to itself and to the Irish electrical industry.

Research and Efficiency

13. The size of the national electricity undertaking, and its repercussions, direct and indirect, on the whole economy make it most important that its efficiency should be of the highest. Research and efficiency go hand in hand, the one promoting the other. While the E.S.B. may hope to maintain efficiency and progress by keeping in close touch with developments abroad and arranging to take the earliest advantage of new discoveries and improvements in techniques and methods, there will always be fields in which independent initiative and effort would be beneficial. In Britain the Central Electricity Authority sponsors research in numerous universities and technical colleges for which purpose it has allocated £60,000 a year; it also contributes on a substantial scale to various research and efficiency bodies. It further arranges for the commercial development and exploitation of inventions and operates on its own account a wide engineering and utilisation research programme.

Fisheries

14. The E.S.B. operates or has rights over fisheries in the various rivers developed or being developed for hydro-electric power. The main fisheries are those in the Shannon; they include salmon, eel, trout and coarse fisheries. In general, none of the fisheries operated by the Board has operated profitably to date, the loss on the Shannon fisheries

being £11,000 in 1955-56 and £9,000 in 1956-57. The accumulated loss on these fisheries as at 31 March, 1957 was £47,000. Since hydro-electric development does considerable damage to fisheries in the first instance, the preservation and development of fisheries in such rivers is not an easy matter. The Board is carrying out a long-term programme to rehabilitate stocks of salmon in the Shannon and, as has been mentioned in Chapter 13, is also concerned, in conjunction with the Inland Fisheries Trust and Bord Fáilte Éireann, in a five-year plan for fishery development relating to trout and coarse fish.

CHAPTER 21

STEEL, SHIPBUILDING, TELEPHONES AND ENGINEERING

Steel and Steel Products

1. The only steel-producing plant in this country is that operated at Haulbowline, Co. Cork, by Irish Steel Holdings, Ltd., a State-sponsored body with a nominal share capital of £100 which purchased the assets of a privately-owned concern in 1947. The Company is engaged in (a) the production of steel ingots from open-hearth furnaces fed largely by native scrap, (b) the conversion of ingots into billets and a limited range of finished sections and (c) galvanising and corrugating imported steel sheet. The Company's capital requirements have been provided by bank overdraft (£300,000 State-guaranteed) and by profits ploughed back into the industry. Guaranteed bank accommodation to the extent of £150,000 was replaced in 1957 by a long-term State-guaranteed loan from an insurance company. The industry employs about 500 people.

2. The galvanising and corrugating plant was installed by the present company to extend its activities in accordance with a decision taken by the Government in December, 1953. The company had also under consideration the construction of a sheet rolling mill (of which some parts had been acquired with the original assets) which would enable the company to manufacture from imported sheet bars the steel sheet now imported for galvanising, etc., and to provide steel sheets for firms engaged in the manufacture of metal containers, domestic hollow-wear, metal furniture, rainwater goods and general sheet metalwork.

3. The industry has had to face some serious handicaps. Its location on a small island has added to the cost of raw materials (though the new oil refinery may ease one problem) and transport of labour is another heavy item. While the company has been following a policy of modernising the existing plant, its resources are limited and any considerable expenditure in this connection could best be undertaken as part of a project for increased production. The industry is one of the smallest steel-producing concerns in the world, yet it has to produce for a limited home market a fairly wide variety of sections and sizes, some of which are frequently ordered in small quantities with consequent production problems It thus lacks the advantages of those

steel plants in Britain and elsewhere which specialise in a limited number of lines to meet the large-scale requirements of the heavy engineering
industries, e.g. shipbuilding, armaments, motorcars.

4. Notwithstanding its disabilities, the Irish company has been
successfully conducted, the annual net profit in recent years being of
the order of £55,000 to £70,000 before payment of income tax and
around £35,000 after payment of tax. Apart from the skill and resource
displayed in dealing with technical problems, factors in the firm's success
have been the low initial price of the plant, the tariff protection enjoyed,
the export restrictions on scrap metal and the opportunities afforded
until recently by a sellers' market. As well as supplying the home
market for the limited range of products manufactured, the company
has also exported to different parts of the world, but the continuance
of exports depends not only on the volume of home demand but on
market conditions abroad outside the company's control.

5. The Government have approved in principle proposals submitted to the Minister for Industry and Commerce by the company for
major extensions of the steel works at Haulbowline. The company is
proceeding to prepare detailed plans, based on its proposals, for
further consideration by the Government. The proposals include provision for :—

(1) The extension of the steel works, including the enlargement of
the existing furnaces from a maximum annual output of 23,000
tons of ingots to 61,200 tons, with an increase from 3 cwts. to
15 cwts. or even higher in the weight of the ingots cast from
the molten steel.

(2) The erection of a blooming or cogging mill to convert the large
ingots into blooms, billets and sheet bars. The blooms would
be re-rolled in this mill into 8/9,000 tons of large sections,
including joists, channels, tees, rails, etc. The annual quantity
of finished and semi-finished sections produced by the mill
would be about 55,000 tons.

(3) The completion of the partially erected sheet mill. Sheet bars
produced in the blooming mill would provide the raw material
for the sheet mill.

(4) The mechanisation of the existing merchant bar mill so as to
achieve greater versatility and reduction of costs.

6. The capital cost of the proposed developments is provisionally
estimated at £2 million and it has been suggested that, in so far as the

capital cannot be raised by borrowing either at home or abroad, the State should provide all the fixed capital requirements by the purchase of shares in a reconstructed company rather than by loan capital carrying a fixed rate of interest, which would add £2 10s. per ton to the costings assumed under the scheme. The production of finished products from the works at full capacity would be almost double the present optimum, and employment would be increased from about 500 to 740 persons. It is estimated that the development plan would take three to four years to implement.

7. While the principal purpose of the proposed development is to make the industry more economic, an increase in demand for steel is also envisaged. Such an increase might be expected to result from progress in national development as the consumption of steel in this country is at present relatively low. The company considers that there are good prospects of selling the bulk of the finished products on the home market and that the remainder could be exported, save in periods of exceptional recession of demand abroad.

8. Even having regard to official prices, i.e. those normally quoted abroad, protection is essential to preserve the home market (the period of the Korean War, when Irish steel was priced lower than foreign steel free of duty, was quite exceptional). As a result of economies in production expected to arise in time from the proposed development, the company hopes, in the long run, to be able to sell in competition with foreign steel at normal official price levels, but during the period of transition before the expanded industry is running efficiently to full capacity, could not dispense with protection.

9. The development plan is envisaged as the first phase in a process of expansion leading eventually to the establishment of a major steel industry which would produce pig iron from imported ore and which would have a greatly extended range of finished products, as well as some important by-products. The final phase would involve very heavy capital expenditure and would be feasible, in the view of the company, only on the basis of foreign investment which could more readily be attracted if the development now proposed had been successfully accomplished. Closer estimation, in association with expert consultants, of the capital cost and further consideration of the technical problems involved may lead to modifications in the present scheme. Steel-making is a basic industry in a modern economy and the type of employment which it provides for skilled operatives and for graduates in engineering and science should be fostered if at all practicable. The question is not whether a new industry should be established but whether the nucleus that already exists can be improved and expanded on an economic basis.

Tinplate

10. Imports of tinplate and tinned plate in 1957 totalled some 6,000 tons valued at about £500,000. In addition, tinplate manufactures were imported to the value of over £800,000. In 1957 Britain exported over 14,000 tons of cans and tin boxes of which about one-third were consigned to this country; we were by far Britain's best customer for these articles in that year. It is of interest to note that the International Bank for Reconstruction and Development has decided to make a loan of $960,000 to Italy to cover the cost of imported machinery and equipment for the establishment of an electrolytic tinplate factory, the total cost of the project being $2.9 million including working capital. The proposed plant has an estimated production capacity of 24,000 tons per year. In the beginning, however, it is contemplated that production would be at only 50% of capacity, 100% capacity being reached after 2 years' operation. It is estimated that about 30% of output will be exported to countries in the Mediterranean market.

11. It has been calculated that the Italian project should be able to break even while operating at 40% of capacity, i.e., producing 9,600 tons annually. These figures would appear to show that the market here is sufficient to justify the setting up of a small plant, though the Italian project may have advantages (e.g. the use of natural gas) which the Irish venture would lack. There is the major difficulty that the principal raw materials (steel and tin) would have to be imported (Italy will have to import the tin only). Tinplate is produced from de-seamed sheet bars, cold rolled from "clean" ingots and it is understood that the ingots at present produced at Haulbowline are not sufficiently "clean" to ensure good tinplate. Irish Steel Holdings had under consideration the possibility of manufacturing tinplate but the advice of their consultants in 1954 was unfavourable. It is understood that the Company is giving further consideration to the question in the working out of its detailed plans for future development.

Shipbuilding and repairing

12. There is at present a glut of world shipping, particularly in the charter trade, with the result that a growing tonnage is being withdrawn from service and laid up. Ships are still being launched in exceptionally large numbers from the world's shipyards but it is not surprising to find that cancellations of orders are spreading. Typical of this situation is the case of Great Britain whose shipbuilding yards accounted for 17% of the world total of new shipping launched in 1957 but where, on the other hand, shipping laid up for lack of employment totalled 864,000 gross tons at end April, 1958, as compared with 32,000 gross tons at the beginning of 1957. There has also been a substantial increase in the total number of ships under repair, including a sizable tonnage which

would not have been put in for repair if employment were available for it. This suggests that in present circumstances the prospects lie in ship-repairing rather than ship-building.

13. It is necessary, however, to look at the possibilities of developing, even in a limited way, the shipbuilding industry at Dublin. In view of the likelihood of a scarcity of orders from abroad, the question must be examined on the basis that the Irish industry would have to depend on Irish shipping companies and Irish Shipping, Limited, in particular, for orders.

14. It is very doubtful whether orders from Irish companies would be sufficient to ensure full-scale operation of a shipbuilding industry. The total tonnage of the fleet operated by Irish Shipping, Limited, is 140,000 tons consisting of 19 vessels; there still remains one vessel, a tanker of 18,000 tons, to be delivered about the end of 1960. All these vessels have been built in the past ten years. Assuming the company can compete with sufficient success in the charter industry to warrant keeping their full fleet in service, it would hardly be necessary, with a fleet of only 20 vessels, to place more than one order every year to meet replacements. An Irish dockyard could not be assured of even this one order. No Irish shipyard has the capacity at present to build ships of the size required by Irish Shipping, Ltd.

15. It has been claimed that Haulbowline Dock, including its outer basin, was—until recently at least—the longest in the world. It is, moreover, well situated in being the nearest point within reach of any ship in difficulties over a large area of the North Atlantic, as well as being close to the new oil refinery with which many large tankers will no doubt be trading. With the trend towards bigger ships and the scarcity of large dry dock facilities in these islands, the scope for development of the Haulbowline Dock is promising and the proposal by Dutch interests to establish a major ship-repairing industry there deserves encouragement. If such an industry were successfully established it would provide a useful basis for the promotion of a shipbuilding industry. The new graving dock at Dublin should also play its part in establishing this country as a ship-repairing centre.

Telephones

16. Telephone capital works, viz., development and extension of the telephone system as distinct from the day-to-day working, are financed by moneys issued under the Telephone Capital Acts out of the Central Fund. The advances are raised from the Post Office Savings Bank Fund and are repaid to that Fund by terminable annuities charged on the Vote for the Department of Posts and Telegraphs.

17. Shortage of capital to meet public requirements has, in the past, necessitated curtailment of telephone capital expenditure. Reference to the Post Office Commercial Accounts over the past years shows that such expenditure has much to commend it as a commercial proposition. There is normally a surplus after meeting interest charges, depreciation and superannuation provisions. Apart, however, from the case that can be made for increased telephone expenditure from a purely commercial standpoint, the extension of the telephone system is desirable in that it contributes to greater efficiency in production and distribution and it provides, without any net charge on the Exchequer, a desirable social amenity, particularly in rural areas. This country is, in regard to telephone development, far behind other countries with a comparable standard of living, and there is every reason to expect a continued and steady demand for telephones for as long as can be foreseen.

18. The present approved telephone capital programme involves a capital investment of approximately £1.5 million per annum for the four years ending 1959-60. Due to capital shortage the Department of Posts and Telegraphs have deferred in certain cases the introduction of automatic equipment at rural exchanges. Capital requirements could be of the order of £2 million a year, or more, if policy decisions were taken to expand rather than curb development.

19. The most recent figures available show that the operating and engineering staff employed full-time on telephone work is 3,750. The provision of additional capital would not necessarily lead to a proportionate increase in permanent employment as, owing to the limitation imposed on telephone capital expenditure, there has been a concentration to a large degree on the work of connecting subscribers. Such work has had the triple merit of having a high labour content, being more immediately remunerative and satisfying the more clamant demands for telephones. Greater availability of capital might result in more emphasis being laid on the extension of automatic methods and laying of underground cable, the advantages of which would be more long-term in character.

20. It should be noted, however, that a diminution in the volume of employment is unlikely, even when development is concluded. Maintenance work will tend to increase following the growth of plant and, although the introduction of automatic working at individual exchanges results in staff savings, this is usually more than offset by an increase in the labour force throughout the country to cater for normal growth of traffic. On the other hand, recent developments may make it possible to extend automatic methods

191

to long distance traffic, at present handled manually, with resulting economies in staff.

21. An increase in the yearly allocation of capital for telephone development to, say, £2 million would be justified in view of its self-sustaining nature and other merits. On the basis of an increase in the annual allocation to £2 million there would be a total capital expenditure of £10 million over the next five years as against £7.5 million, approximately, on the present basis. Such an increase in capital expenditure would raise the question of the scope for home manufacture and assembly of telephone equipment.

22. Considerable progress has already been made in replacing imported by home-produced telephone equipment. The position now seems to be that there is little likelihood that the bulk of the remaining imported items could be economically produced here. Equipment is being made in the Post Office factory and by private firms, but the work done consists largely of assembly operations. The Industrial Development Authority, in consultation with the Department of Posts and Telegraphs, have been discussing the matter with manufacturers. It is understood that proposals for the manufacture of telephone hand sets may emerge as a result of these discussions but it is not yet known to what extent full manufacture, as distinct from assembly, will be undertaken.

Public Engineering Workshops

23. The engineering workshops of C.I.E. at Inchicore and those operated until recently by the G.N.R. at Dundalk and now being operated by a separate State-sponsored company (Dundalk Engineering Works, Limited) have been employing between them a staff of some 3,500 persons. In view of the cessation of a number of cross-Border rail services by the G.N.R. and of the projected general re-organisation of rail and other public transport services throughout the State, it must be expected that a large part of this labour force will become redundant so far as the needs of the public transport system are concerned. These engineering works could provide a nucleus for engineering activities in which the country is very much lacking. Neither of the workshops is modern and their organisation and efficiency would need to be improved.

24. The new company operating the Dundalk works is about to formulate long-term plans for development. Various proposals have been under consideration, one of them relating to the partial manufacture and assembly of a small motor car with a view to developing an

export trade. The amount of capital which the company will require has been estimated tentatively at anything up to £1¾ million. In the export of cars the most severe competition would, of course, have to be faced from the bigger and long-established car manufacturers who have enormous resources, automatic plants and world-wide sales and servicing organisations. This suggests that the best hope of success for the new company in this line would lie in the active participation of established external manufacturers whose technical knowledge and various other resources could be availed of to build up a market abroad.

25. Experience with the Dundalk Engineering Works should be helpful in considering possibilities for the C.I.E. workshops. It would appear worth while examining whether the heavy repair work of State and State-sponsored concerns could with advantage be centralised at Inchicore; a certain volume of work of this nature is already being done separately by such bodies as the Office of Public Works, the E.S.B. and Bord na Móna. Centralisation might provide at least one fairly large unit having reasonable prospects of economic operation, capable of handling the main engineering work of public bodies and also of contracting for outside work.

26. It would, of course, be essential to bring the workshops to the maximum degree of efficiency. If this were done, the prospects of further development would be enhanced and it might be possible to attract external engineering interests to participate in new ventures. A Technical Assistance grant towards the cost of employing a firm of industrial consultants to survey the workshops has been approved. Generally, in the consideration of proposals for the establishment of industries requiring engineering skills, it would be well to bear in mind the desirability of utilising the resources of C.I.E. workshops and skilled personnel.

Precision Instruments and Electronic Equipment

27. There is reason to believe that light engineering industries could be established here on an economic basis, as the quantity of raw materials required is relatively small, and the freight costs to export markets of the finished products would be low compared to the value of the goods themselves. In Britain there are many small firms which, having developed special applications of electronics, are flourishing concerns with excellent export records. It has been contended that such small firms are at a disadvantage in so far as they cannot supply the whole gamut of automation equipment, but in fact they often provide some equipment essential for automation which is not available anywhere else in the world. These small firms concentrate on new products and, for this purpose, engage relatively large research

staffs which operate at a level of efficiency and intensity of effort seldom found in the research departments of large organisations. The only possibility for this country in this field of industry is to concentrate on speciality products which have an assured market and play a vital part in the development of electronics and precision instruments.

28. The watch industry does not appear to provide any immediate prospect. Imports of complete clocks and watches in 1957 were valued at little more than £200,000 while imports of parts (presumably required for assembly or repair work) were valued at only £30,000. It appears that an extension of assembly work is the most that could be hoped for in the foreseeable future. Apart from the lack of skilled technicians, watch manufacturers in other countries are understood to be most reluctant to permit the export of parts for assembly outside their own factories. On the whole, therefore, the prospect of establishing a worthwhile manufacturing industry is remote.

29. A firmly-established radio industry produces most of the popular makes of domestic receivers, including V.H.F. models. Irish-manufactured components are used to an extensive degree and one concern does a substantial export business. Three of the radio manufacturing firms are also engaged in the part-manufacture and assembly of television receivers; one of them produces extensively for export. Short-wave telecommunication equipment is also produced in considerable quantity by one firm, largely for export.

30. Subject to further study of the economics of the operation, there is a prospect that Aer Lingus may undertake in their own workshops the extensive work of overhauling turbo-prop engines at present done for them by a British company; this would involve a capital investment of about £150,000. This change-over, if decided on, would not take place for another twelve to eighteen months. It is very unlikely that Aer Lingus would get any significant work on the overhaul of engines belonging to other airlines. In the present state of underemployment in the aircraft industry in Britain it is unlikely that Aer Lingus would have any worthwhile opportunity to engage in the manufacture of aircraft component parts for outside firms; the extent of the manufacturing which they could undertake or have undertaken in this country on their own behalf is strictly limited.

CHAPTER 22

MINERAL DEVELOPMENT

1. This country does not possess commercial mineral deposits of substantial extent but a number of small deposits is being worked at marginal profit. The mining of metal ores is a particularly uncertain venture because of the variability of world prices. Profits and production tend to fluctuate with world conditions.

Production

2. The Census of Industrial Production, 1955, gives the following figures for mining production (excluding quarrying of stone, slate, sand and gravel):—

NET SELLING VALUE OF GROSS OUTPUT

Product	1954	1955
	£	£
Coal :—		
Anthracite	666,815	667,254
Semi-bituminous	160,981	208,781
Briquettes	26,172	8,778
Lead ores and concentrates	108,545	246,669
Zinc ores and concentrates	53,306	106,540
Gypsum	94,032	94,840
Other Products	28,419	41,847
Total value of minerals raised :	1,138,270	1,374,709

The average number of wage earners engaged in mineral production in 1955 was 1,727, of whom 1,315 were engaged in coal mining.

3. Exports of mineral products were as follows in 1957:—

Product	Value
	£
Coal	139,460
Gypsum	103,246
Barytes	47,542
Lead ore and concentrates	164,426
Zinc ore and concentrates	43,079
TOTAL :	497,753

A feature of these exports was that only a small amount went to Britain, the bulk going to Continental countries.

Exploration

4. During the fifty years prior to the last war, minerals exploration and development in Ireland were on a negligible scale. The Minerals Development Act, 1940, aimed at stimulating prospecting and mining and gave the State power, where necessary, to acquire privately owned minerals which were not being worked. Since 1941 the State, through Mianraí, Teoranta, has spent over £1 million on minerals exploration schemes, e.g., for copper and pyrites at Avoca (£543,000, repayable from the profits of St. Patrick's Copper Mines), for coal at Slievardagh and phosphates in Co. Clare (£576,000, written off in 1947) and for gypsum at Kingscourt (£35,000).

5. The State has in recent years granted special tax concessions for mining, the most important of which are contained in the Finance (Profits of Certain Mines) (Temporary Relief from Taxation) Act, 1956, and the Finance (Miscellaneous Provisions) Act, 1956. As regards mining of copper, lead, zinc, pyrites, barytes, gold and silver, profits from the operation of new enterprises which commence production within five years from April, 1956, are completely exempted from income tax and corporation profits tax for a period of four years from the date on which production commences; for a future four years one half of the profits will be exempted. As regards coal mines, one half of the profits of new mines will be exempted from income tax and corporation profits tax for a period of ten years from 1956; this concession also applies, in the case of existing coal mines, to profits from increased production over the volume achieved in the year ended 30 September, 1956. Special tax allowances are also provided in respect of capital expenditure on mine development and in respect of depreciation of equipment in a mine, quarry or smelter.

6. These taxation incentives have encouraged large-scale exploration —costing over £2 million—by Canadian and other external interests in the past two years. The recent sharp recession in world metal prices has, however, caused the cessation of active prospecting and development in most areas except at Avoca, Co. Wicklow, and at Allihies, Co. Cork.

7. The geological mapping of most of the country was done almost a century ago and there have since been revision surveys from time to time. While it is unlikely that any major occurrence of minerals has escaped attention, it is possible that more modern techniques of exploration would yield some results. In many areas, rocks are hidden under coverings of glacial drifts, soil, turf, etc., and there is the possibility that other mineral deposits may exist which do not outcrop to the surface. A detailed geophysical examination, concentrating on the location of mineral deposits, might be worth while. The geophysical examination so far carried out here has, in the main, employed only the

magnetic and gravity surveying methods. There remain various other techniques such as electrical and seismic methods and aero-magnetic surveys. Reference is made in Chapter 16, paragraph 24, to the possibility of the Geological Survey undertaking more work of this nature if additional funds were available to it.

Coal

8. The coal deposits of Ireland seem to offer most scope for development in present circumstances. Our total annual consumption of coal is of the order of 1.5 million tons, of which about 200,000 tons are anthracite. Imports, which until recently have come almost entirely from Britain, amount to about 1.26 million tons a year, costing approximately £10 million. Total annual home production at present is about 240,000 tons, of which 160,000 tons are anthracite and 80,000 tons semi-bituminous. The value of home production is now over £1 million a year and employment is provided for about 1,450 men.

9. There are three coal fields which contain seams of coal which can be worked economically:—

(a) The Leinster coal field covering about 70 sq. miles is estimated to contain about 70 million tons of extractable anthracite. Present production is about 100,000 tons a year.

(b) The Tipperary coal field covering about 12 sq. miles is estimated to contain about 5.5 million tons of extractable anthracite. Present production is about 60,000 tons a year.

(c) The Connacht coal field covering about 12 sq. miles is estimated to contain 8.5 million tons of semi-bituminous coal. Present production is about 80,000 tons a year, most of which will be absorbed by the new E.S.B. station at Arigna which is scheduled to begin generating this year.

While it is clear that our collieries cannot produce our requirements of bituminous coal, our anthracite needs could be wholly met from home sources and a net export surplus developed.

10. Under the American Grant Counterpart Agreement regarding technical assistance projects, a sum of £80,000 has been provided for a three-year scheme of exploration, the aim being to provide information about coal deposits which would form the basis for an expansion of anthracite output from the present 160,000 tons to 250,000 tons a year. The Geological Survey originally proposed a larger scheme, costing £160,000 in all, with the aim of expanding production to 300,000 tons a year but this was modified because of the limited Counterpart funds available. In view of the balance of payments and employment considerations, it seems desirable that, if the preliminary results of the approved scheme are not discouraging and if full cooperation is forth-

coming from the owners of the deposits, the Exchequer should supplement the Counterpart funds to the extent necessary to prove deposits which would form the basis of an annual production of at least 300,000 tons. Such an expansion should provide additional employment for up to one thousand men. Experience suggests that when minerals are proved by exploration it is easier to interest private enterprise in commercial working.

11. Apart from lack of knowledge of the precise location of the deposits, the main limitation on production here is that the coal requires modern mechanical cleaning. To provide for increased production it would be necessary for the owners to incur capital outlay on the installation of coal cleaning plant. Test work would have to be undertaken to produce low-ash domestic fuel, a high calorific value pulverised fuel for industrial use, or low-ash carbon, which has various industrial uses. Further tests might also be required to indicate suitable methods of adapting industrial and institutional heating appliances to the use of anthracite. Some, at least, of this test work might be performed through the Institute for Industrial Research and Standards.

Molybdenum

12. Molybdenite ore is the source of the metal molybdenum which is used as a hardener in high-speed tool steel. There is only one molybdenite mine operating in Europe—in Norway where annual production is about 200 tons. The main source of the ore is in the U.S.A. The only known deposits of molybdenite in Ireland, situated at Murvey, Co. Galway, were explored some years ago under a technical assistance scheme. The results of the exploration have not been published but it is understood that it has been proved that there occurs at Murvey at least 250,000 tons of rock containing an average of 0.13% molybdenite at a maximum depth of 100 feet from the surface. The deposits in Norway contain 0.2% of molybdenite which is considered to be the minimum warranting commercial working but possibly the taxation concessions available here, and the high price of the final product, might make our deposits—small though they appear to be—attractive to commercial operators.

Oil and Natural Gas

13. The technical information at present available does not point to the likelihood of finding commercially exploitable oil and gas reserves here. Enquiries made by foreign companies suggest, however, that it may be possible to have an exploration of some areas made if liberal royalty and taxation arrangements were granted in the event of commercial development. It would be necessary to enact legislation to bring all oil and gas rights in the country into State ownership.

CHAPTER 23

TOURISM

1. The following figures of income from tourism proper give a picture of the value of the industry in recent years: —

Year	Gt. Britain and Six Counties £m.	Overseas Visitors* £m.	Total £m.
1953	13·0	2·2	15·2
1954	13·1	3·7	16·8
1955	12·8	4·0	16·8
1956	13·4	4·3	17·7
1957	12·6	4·3	16·9

* These are mainly tourists from the dollar area who returned from Ireland direct to countries other than Britain or the Six Counties. Some expenditure of tourists from the dollar area is also included in the preceding column.

Earnings from visitors other than tourists, and other income, totalled £15.5 million in 1957 as follows: —

		£m.
Visitors to relatives	... ...	7·5
Business visitors ...	... ...	2·9
Others	... ...	3·0
Adjustment in respect of receipts of certain Irish transport companies	... ...	2·1
		15·5

Thus income from tourism and travel totalled some £32.4 million in 1957 compared with a total of £31 million in 1955. The expansion has been very modest bearing in mind the potentialities of tourism and the decline in the value of money.

Loan and Grant Facilities for Hotel Improvement

2. The Tourist Traffic Act, 1952, provided for a scheme of State-guaranteed loans within an aggregate limit of £3 million for the purpose of improving or increasing tourist accommodation and improving amenities and services at holiday resorts. The scheme included grants to cover interest on the loans for a period of three years. It was not, however, very successful, the total actually guaranteed being only £¼ million. The comparative failure of the scheme in respect of tourist accommodation has been ascribed by Bord Fáilte Éireann to the onerous conditions

imposed in the agreement required to be entered into by the borrower and the Minister for Industry and Commerce as guarantor and to the delay involved in effecting such agreements. Amendments of the scheme (including an extension to five years in the period covered by the grants for interest charges) have been agreed with the Board; and the Tourist Traffic Act, 1957, provides for the continuance of the scheme for a further five years and for the extension of the grants in relief of interest charges to loans raised by hotels otherwise than under a State guarantee. It is hoped that these changes will result in greater capital expenditure of benefit to the tourist trade. These benefits have been extended by the same Act to motels.

3. Because of the heavy capital cost of new accommodation in relation to the number of weeks' occupancy in seaside resorts, it has been agreed in principle to provide State grants towards the provision of additional hotel bedrooms. Similar financial encouragement could with benefit be extended towards the provision of accommodation in angling districts.

4. A general point to be borne in mind in considering assistance for hotel improvement is that the bulk of our potential tourist market is not likely to be interested in luxurious accommodation. Simple, clean and above all, cheap facilities—such as are available in some continental countries—are more likely to bring visitors who will return. The provision of motels would meet the needs of touring motorists, particularly in the west. While the scope for motels, at any rate of American standards, may be limited by the short distances involved, any possibilities in this field should be fully explored.

Accommodation provided by Transport and other Undertakings

5. C.I.E.'s accounts show the concern's catering department, including hotels, to be operating at a profit. Working profit in 1955-56 and in 1956-57 amounted to £29,000 and £38,000, respectively, before allowing for an appropriate element of general charges (Transport Stock interest, etc.). To the six hotels at present operated (viz., at Sligo, Galway, Mulrany, Kenmare, Killarney and Parknasilla) will, presumably, be added the G.N.R. hotel at Bundoran, on completion of the merger with the part of the G.N.R. in the State. C.I.E. have been modernising their hotels and, in view of the importance of providing additional first-class accommodation for tourists, further investment in the hotels is desirable. There is also room for additional investment in the provision of new or improved catering facilities at important tourist terminal points (e.g., Cobh) and, indeed, wherever throughout the C.I.E. system advantage to the tourist trade could be expected to result.

6. In order that the C.I.E. hotels may be developed to the best advantage, consideration should be given to the establishment of a special organisation, subsidiary to the main transport undertaking, which could pursue an intensive programme of development. The existence of a separate organisation would also make it easier to watch the profitability of investment.

7. In Britain, some brewery concerns operate hotels on an extensive scale; here, one leading brewery has already interested itself in the business, and the trade generally might be induced to carry this development further.

Foreign Participation

8. Efforts might be made to attract American capital and enterprise for the purpose of hotel construction and management. It has been suggested, for instance, that the Hilton group might be induced to interest themselves in a large American-style hotel in Dublin. Hilton hotels have already been established in Istanbul and Madrid; these have been built by local capital but are operated and managed by Hilton Hotels International, Inc. It has been stated that Hiltons do not normally concern themselves with hotels of less than about 350 rooms. The terms on which Hiltons operate are understood to be as follows :—

(a) they lease the hotel for 20 years;

(b) they provide technical advice on layout and construction and provide stocks and working capital;

(c) they require a guarantee of $33\frac{1}{3}\%$ of profits *before* deduction of tax.

While construction of a large-scale, American-style hotel would be a speculative venture, the possibility of interesting the Hilton group or other foreign hotel companies ought not be ruled out and efforts might be made to secure their participation in hotel development in this country.

Taxation Relief for Hotels

9. Generally, hotels and furnishings are eligible in the same way as factory premises and plant for taxation allowances. As regards buildings, the Finance (Miscellaneous Provisions) Act, 1956, provides for the grant of an *initial* allowance for income-tax purposes of 10% of the capital expenditure incurred in the construction of any industrial buildings. As an incentive to hotel-keepers to extend their accommodation, hotel premises were included in the definition of industrial buildings. In addition, the cost of ordinary maintenance and repairs is

allowed against revenue in computing profits for tax purposes. There is no depreciation allowance as such for buildings, either factory or hotel. A relatively insignificant allowance—one-sixth of the annual valuation for Schedule A purposes—is given in respect of mills and factories in which heavy machinery is working. Factory and hotel owners alike enjoy an *initial* allowance of 20% in respect of the purchase of factory plant or hotel equipment of a permanent and durable nature. Where furnishings (other than soft furnishings) would not be eligible for the initial allowance, their replacement value is allowed when in fact they are replaced. It would be desirable that any further allowances granted for industry should, where appropriate, be made applicable to hotels. In particular, in view of the need for additional and more modern accommodation, it seems desirable that depreciation of hotel buildings over a reasonable period should be allowed as a charge against profits.

Development of Tourist Resorts

10. Generally speaking, Irish tourist resorts are lacking in amenities. Bathing facilities, promenades, parks and recreational facilities and other amenities of various kinds need to be provided or improved.

11. Under the Tourist Traffic Act, 1952, the Minister for Industry and Commerce may, on the recommendation of Bord Fáilte Éireann and with the concurrence of the Minister for Finance, guarantee loans required for the purpose of providing amenities and services at tourist resorts; in addition, he may authorise the Board to make grants towards the payment of interest on such loans. A scheme for such guarantees and grants has been in operation since October, 1953. Although development proposals have been formulated by local interests, very little real progress has been made in carrying out major improvements. Only two applications for guaranteed loans for resort development have been recommended to the Minister for Industry and Commerce by the Board, and only one has been accepted.

12. The failure of the guaranteed loan scheme is due to the fact that it can, of necessity, be applied only in the case of works which will earn revenue out of which loans can be repaid with interest. Examples of works of this kind are ballrooms, entertainment halls, amusement parks, boating lakes, pitch and putt courses and tennis courts. There are, however, many improvement works which are essential for the proper and orderly development of tourist resorts but which are not directly revenue-earning and consequently cannot normally be financed by means of loans. Works of this kind include basic site development, provision of promenades, parks, riverside walks and pathways. The past experience of Bord Fáilte

Éireann in relation to resort development works supports the view that substantial investment of this type is an essential basis for the expansion of earnings in other directions. It is clear, however, that such works will have to be financed otherwise than by way of loan if the general development of tourist resorts is to be achieved within a reasonable time.

13. Bord Fáilte Éireann receive a grant-in-aid, the maximum amount being fixed by statute at £500,000. It was contemplated that some of this grant-in-aid should be used for resort development but as the new grants towards additional bedroom accommodation have also to come out of the grant, the balance available would not make an appreciable impact on the problem of improving tourist resorts. It is, therefore, necessary to consider allocating substantial sums from other sources for the execution of non-revenue-earning works in the major holiday resorts. These works should be of a substantial nature, as small works should be looked after by Bord Fáilte Éireann from its own resources. If value is to be obtained from this expenditure the work must be of such a nature as to make a radical improvement in the facilities available. As there are 26 major tourist resorts in the country, the aggregate sum required might be about £1 million and, spread over 10 years, the annual expenditure would be about £100,000. The works to be undertaken in each resort under these State grants would constitute part of an overall development plan to be drawn up by the local authority and the local development company, in consultation with Bord Fáilte Éireann. A grant from the State should be conditional on a local contribution to development of the resort. A time limit might be placed on the commencement and execution of the works so as to ensure that works were put in hand without delay. The whole scheme might, indeed, be limited to 10 years' operation so as to encourage rapid resort development.

Improved berthing and passenger disembarkation facilities at Cobh, Dún Laoghaire, etc.

14. A deep-water pier for liners at Cobh is a suggestion which has been cropping up from time to time over the past thirty-five years. There are no recent estimates but it would be safe to assume that a suitable pier would cost at least £2 million. There would be substantial continuing maintenance costs and other facilities, such as tugs, would also have to be provided. There is, however, no prospect that such a pier would be used to any significant extent. Cobh is not a terminal port and the liner companies are interested, above all, in the speed of turn-round there; they have never indicated any interest in having such a pier. Berthing facilities of this kind would not, so far as is known, be required in conjunction with any shipbuilding proposals.

15. It follows that liners calling at Cobh will probably continue to be served by tenders, and both in this respect and in the handling of passengers' luggage there is considerable scope for improvement. The existing tenders, which were old Mersey ferry boats, were acquired by the Cork Harbour Commissioners after the war, when it was found impossible to induce commercial interests to resume the tender services which they had provided pre-war. The tenders, though seaworthy, are in urgent need of replacement. At a rough estimate, new tenders would probably cost up to £250,000 each. The Harbour Commissioners have recently placed an order for a new tender and Exchequer assistance might, if necessary, be made available for the provision of further new vessels. The tenders have been available also, to some extent, for excursion parties. It is possible that with new and more attractive boats this side of the business might be developed.

16. There are no specific proposals before the Department of Industry and Commerce at the moment for improvements in disembarkation and passenger-handling facilities at Cobh. Worthwhile improvements could probably be effected without very great outlay. The position is being examined by Bord Fáilte Éireann.

17. The position at Dún Laoghaire is even more important than at Cobh as Dún Laoghaire is the main gateway to our tourist attractions. Conditions at the pier are very congested in summer and at other periods of peak traffic, and the Department of Industry and Commerce are sponsoring plans for a complete reconstruction and enlargement of the pier. The cost of such a project might be regarded as productive in so far as it is designed to maintain and expand our important tourist revenue.

18. Improved ferry services from Britain, particularly for accompanied private cars, would also assist the tourist industry. One British company is anxious to provide a service from Preston to Dublin Port but is prevented from doing so by the attitude of the Trade Unions. (Reference is made in Chapter 16 to the Unions' attitude towards the use of container traffic at the Port). A ferry service has also been suggested for the Holyhead-Dún Laoghaire route and the Department of Industry and Commerce are in touch with British Railways about the provision of a modern passenger-ferry vessel on this route when the *Princess Maud* is being replaced. In that event, special facilities would be needed at Dún Laoghaire to enable cars to be driven ashore. Regard should be had to this possibility in connection with the examination of the reconstruction scheme envisaged for the Mail Boat pier. It is questionable whether it would be economic to incur heavy expenditure on the provision of car-loading facilities *both* at North Wall and Dún Laoghaire. An air car-ferry service may,

possibly, be provided at some time in the future. In view of the importance of the tourist industry and, in particular, of securing an expansion in income from British tourists, who are our best customers, examination of these matters and of any facilities considered desirable at other important tourist entry points should be pressed ahead as rapidly as possible.

Game Reserves

19. This country is often spoken of as a sportsman's paradise. The proposals outlined in Chapter 13 for the development of inland fisheries and sea angling are designed to attract fishing enthusiasts. Shooting facilities are, however, sadly lacking. The importance of preserving game and restocking suitable districts is obvious. In particular, large tracts of mountainous country in the West should provide suitable facilities for grouse shooting. Forest plantations might also be suitable as pheasant and woodcock reserves. Bord Fáilte have already introduced a scheme to restock certain game. There is considerable scope for development along these lines with a view particularly to the formation of large shooting estates.

CHAPTER 24

CONCLUSIONS

Employment Considerations

1. Throughout this study, while there have been some general references to employment, attention has been directed primarily towards productive development. This has been deliberate and has not been due to any lack of concern about unemployment. It is from productive development that the employment worth having from a national viewpoint, i.e., lasting employment, will arise, and the study advocates the *maximum* productive development which our financial and material resources will allow. It is possible that even this maximum development may not provide a permanent job at the wages he is prepared to accept for everyone wanting to stay in Ireland.

2. It would have been quite unreal to approach the question of development from the aspect of employment, that is by setting out the number of jobs required and then attempting to plan how these might be created. There is no sure way in which development works can be planned to produce self-sustaining jobs for a specified large number of individuals of varying capacity and skill. The number itself would be a formidable one if it were to cover not only those now idle who are able and willing to work in Ireland but also those who add to the potential labour force every year but are at present involuntary emigrants. Self-sustaining jobs, i.e., jobs producing goods or services saleable at competitive prices, cannot be created to order. The jobs that can be created, to a limited extent, by public works have no lasting basis; they add nothing to the national output of saleable goods and services and they can survive only as long as the works themselves last or other works, involving a similar redistribution of the community's income, are substituted for them. In any case, the capital available for public works of any kind is not unlimited and can be used for one purpose only at the expense of others. In a very real sense the direct provision of work on unproductive schemes prevents the provision of lasting and useful work in as much as scarce capital is used up for wasteful ends, the burden of taxation is made heavier, costs are raised and productive enterprises hindered and discouraged.

3. The fact is that neither full employment nor unlimited supplies of capital can be procured to order. Stress has been laid in this study (Chapters 2 and 4) both on the question of the *acceptability* of the

standard of living afforded by home employment—no plan could in any circumstances guarantee full employment at whatever standard of living the employees chose to name—and on the question of the capital resources likely to be available for development, of which an optimistic assessment has been made. It is reasonable to expect that additional employment of a lasting and acceptable character will be provided by following the general lines of productive development indicated in the study. There would be nothing to be gained by setting up fanciful employment targets; failure to reach such targets would only produce disillusionment. On the other hand, the comprehensive exploitation of the opportunities of development which do exist would inspire confidence in the country's future and would lead both directly and indirectly to an expansion of employment on a permanent basis.

SUMMARY OF PRINCIPLES AND SUGGESTIONS

General

4. The principles emerging from this study and the specific suggestions put forward for future development may now be summarised. A rigid five- or ten-year plan would not be suitable to our circumstances. Nevertheless, it is necessary to look outside the framework of year-to-year budgeting and effectively to coordinate financial and economic policy over longer periods. We now lag so far behind most other European countries in material progress that even a spectacular increase in efficiency and output will leave us at a relative disadvantage. If we are to catch up at all, our rate of improvement must exceed theirs. There are also important psychological reasons for having an integrated development programme. Realistic and mutually consistent aims can stimulate the interest, enthusiasm and resurgence of will which the nation's progress now demands.—(Chapter 1).

5. The outstanding features of the country's general economic position are the low income per head of the population and the related phenomena of high emigration and high unemployment, and low production and productivity. External reserves have had to be depleted in order to finance investment at a higher level than that warranted by current savings. Private investment has been small and public investment, though on a relatively large scale, has been primarily social in character and for that reason has failed to give that significant expansion in basic industries which is necessary for real and continuing development of the economy. The high rate of social investment has involved heavy charges for the service of public debt and these charges, together with the increased cost of social services and other forms of redistributive public expenditure, have entailed relatively high taxation which is a disincentive to saving and private enterprise.—(Chapter 2).

Necessity for more Productive Investment

6. From this background emerges the main general principle that, if we are to avoid economic stagnation and continual loss of population, public and private development of a productive character must be stimulated and organised so as to overshadow the non-productive development which now bulks so largely in public investment and in national capital formation as a whole. The raising of output in agriculture and industry *on a competitive basis* should, therefore, have a much higher priority than at present in the allocation of savings. The volume of current savings must not only be maintained but increased and the utmost use made of means of raising output which are sparing of capital, so as to make the savings go as far as possible. The opportunity to switch from non-productive to productive investment will occur in part automatically with the satisfaction to a major degree of social needs (e.g., housing) but it should be reinforced by a positive curtailment of non-productive outlay.—(Chapter 2—Section II).

Education, Efficiency and New Techniques

7. Increased investment in productive development cannot alone guarantee success. The conditions of economic progress are complex, including better education, efficient management, the will to work harder and more intelligently, the seeking out and adoption of improved methods and techniques and a readiness at all times to apply scientific advances. These various factors have a particular relevance to our case because we are relatively backward in agriculture and industry. —(Chapter 1 and Chapter 2—Section II).

Importance of Agriculture

8. The immediate potentialities of increased agricultural production are very great. The realisation of these potentialities in any large degree would, by increasing the purchasing power of the farming community, raise generally the demand for goods and services, leading to expansion of industry and additional employment. The provision of lasting employment turns on the concurrent development of manufacturing industry (mainly for export) and of tertiary industries, particularly tourism. All this can be set in motion by improvements in agriculture.—(Chapter 2—Section II).

Fiscal Policy

9. Fiscal policy must be in harmony with the objective of stimulating productive investment, which in our circumstances means that it should favour saving, encourage enterprise and discourage excessive consumption. High and inequitable taxation is one of the greatest impediments to economic progress. The way towards stabilisation and reduction of taxation lies in moderating the growth of net debt service charges by

reducing the proportion of non-productive and increasing the proportion of productive projects in public investment, in curbing the increase in administrative charges, in deferring further improvements in social services pending a steady growth in real national income, in keeping subsidies to a minimum, in directing expenditure generally into productive channels and in effecting every reasonable economy. The positive objective of fiscal policy should be to arrive quickly at the point at which it will be possible to give the economy the tonic of a significant reduction in taxation, particularly in direct taxation on incomes, profits and savings.—(Chapter 3).

Wages and Salaries

10. To ensure competitive costs per unit of output it may be necessary to accept for a time lower wage rates than in Britain. Economic expansion could be seriously hindered by restrictive practices by trade unions and by frequent and indiscriminate increases in wages and salaries exceeding any benefit from increases in productivity and causing a general rise in production costs. These are amongst the greatest inflationary forces and are a constant threat to the balance of payments. —(Chapter 3).

Monetary Policy

11. The Irish economy cannot be insulated against outside economic and financial influences. Our currency policy, as determined by statute, gives us a measure of latitude since it is aimed at the maintenance of parity not with a *real* standard but with a monetary standard (the pound sterling). Our aim should be to maintain a high level of productive activity without jeopardising the exchange value of our currency.—(Chapter 3).

Credit and Commercial Banking

12. Credit has an important part to play but must be kept from being inflationary. Credit creation cannot be an independent source of capital. The aim of the commercial banks should be to make credit available on the most liberal terms possible consistent with retaining the goodwill of depositors and preserving their own solvency. Fluctuations in their external reserve ratio within the range 27-33% may be regarded as normal but fluctuations outside that range will call for corrective action by way of a relaxation or of a tightening of domestic credit. Amalgamations between banks should be facilitated by legislation as they would tend to free additional resources and to lower lending rates. The banks (and insurance companies) should join the State in providing long-term capital for industry through the Industrial Credit Company and should provide the capital required for agricultural development either through the Agricultural Credit Corporation or their own branches.—(Chapter 3).

Central Banking

13. There should be the closest liaison between the Minister for Finance and the Central Bank so that effect may be given to financial policies favouring development to the utmost but avoiding any significant deficit in the balance of payments. If domestic savings prove insufficient to meet the demands for productive capital purposes and if the external accounts are in order, future increases in the Legal Tender Note issue could be backed by Irish Government securities, making about £3½ million a year available on average for productive domestic investment. The commercial banks should deposit a substantial proportion of their liquid sterling funds with the Central Bank in the form of *interest-bearing* balances, and the clearing of cheques between banks should be effected as far as possible by drawing on these balances, the Central Bank acting as a discount house by investing the balances on a short-term basis. This would increase the resources of the Central Bank for rediscounting activities, which is particularly desirable. The question whether these arrangements can facilitate maximum economic progress without balance of payments difficulties should be fully tested before any consideration is given to encroaching upon the *existing* reserves of the Legal Tender Note Fund. Generally, evolution rather than revolution should be the guiding principle.—(Chapter 3).

Development Resources and Needs

14. If the proposals in the study are put into effect it is estimated that monetary savings will rise over the next five years from £45 million per annum to £55 million per annum. Roughly speaking, this level of savings would maintain the present level of public and private investment, without any draw on external capital or any external borrowing. If more capital is required for productive projects, external reserves amounting on average to £3½ million per annum could be applied (see under Central Banking) to finance external deficits incurred to step up domestic capital formation. Available resources might be supplemented by external borrowings for specific productive projects, primarily from international institutions but also by way of direct participation of externs in new industrial enterprises. Since private development has been so limited up to the present, it is probable that for some time to come a demand for productive capital will have to be generated in the public sector to secure maximum development. It follows that policy should provide for new public, as well as private, investment of an economic kind. So that the best use may be made of resources and costs kept to a minimum, economy in the use of capital is necessary, and policy should be framed to encourage this in the many ways in which it can be done, e.g., by conservation of existing assets, avoidance of duplication in investment, and reducing peak demands for services.—(Chapter 4).

Agricultural Development—General

15. The overriding necessity of Irish agriculture is to produce in quantity at prices competitive in world markets; increased production will itself reduce unit costs.—(Chapter 5).

Grasslands

16. The key to agricultural expansion lies in a dynamic grasslands policy. Our grasslands are seriously neglected and starved of fertiliser. A rational policy of pasture rehabilitation requires that priority be given to the application of phosphates, followed by potash, at the same time increasing, where necessary, the present use of lime. Later, the use of nitrogenous fertilisers should be emphasised. A comprehensive soil survey is the necessary corollary of such a programme. The campaign to improve pasture management techniques and proper conservation of grass for winter feeding should be intensified.—(Chapter 6).

Cattle

17. It is vital to secure a substantial increase in cattle output. This involves an increase in breeding stocks, particularly in beef areas. Specialisation in those areas in the breeding of beef cattle would be of great benefit. For the present dairying areas, the question of the most suitable breed, having regard to the system of farming practised there, is all-important; because of conflicting views, further detailed and scientific investigations are urgently necessary. Better feeding, a reduction in the incidence of livestock diseases and a more rational organisation of existing rearing and marketing arrangements would reduce stock losses and increase cattle output. The most pressing requirement facing the cattle industry at the moment is the elimination of bovine tuberculosis.—(Chapter 7).

Milk

18. The general objectives must be the reduction of the cost of production of milk by every possible means and the diversion of milk from buttermaking into more remunerative outlets. Provided that progress is being made towards the achievement of these objectives, a limited and gradually declining Exchequer subsidy can be tolerated, but in the last resort any permanent subsidisation of agricultural products must come in the main from the agricultural industry as a whole. The best solution would be for farmers generally to feed surplus whole milk to calves and every encouragement should be given to them to adopt this course. Increased consumption of milk and cheese should also be fostered. It would be desirable to assist Irish producers of chocolate crumb, cheese and preserved milk to expand and improve production for any promising markets.—(Chapter 8).

211

Beef and Mutton

19. The importance of the British market to Irish producers of both live and dead meat, and the importance of the Irish supply to Britain, argues for a joint approach by both countries. A bilateral beef policy would be of mutual benefit and would accord with modern internationalism in economic affairs. An expansion in processed meat exports to other markets would be most desirable and State aid might be provided to finance technical research into the industry's problems. It would be desirable that slaughtering companies operate their own supply farms, and the possibilities of a contractual supply system with graziers and cooperative organisations should be investigated.— (Chapter 8).

Pigs and Bacon

20. Production costs are much too high for competitive marketing. Since feeding barley is a raw material in pig production, its price should be freed and left to be determined by that of the end-product (see also Chapter 10). The concentration of fattening in areas where barley is grown would reduce significantly the cost of rearing pigs and it is on this basis that the guaranteed price-structure for pigs should be established. The more extensive operation of pig farms and of central marketing based on a contractual supply system could also help to cut costs. Pig progeny testing should be pushed ahead as rapidly as possible and the comparative merits of the Irish Large White and Landrace breeds submitted to objective tests. A full-scale unit for general research into the production of pig products is desirable; this should be coordinated as far as possible with research in the beef and mutton industry. A more definite curb is required to the bacon subsidy in accordance with the principles outlined in Chapter 12. In the long run the best solution—if it could be achieved—would be a link with the British price structure.—(Chapter 9).

Wheat

21. If the "married price" arrangement for wheat proves unsatisfactory, a *flexible* guaranteed price policy might be substituted, the views of the millers' and of the farmers' organisations immediately concerned being obtained on the feasibility of a contractual system which would solve the problem of surplus wheat and ensure that, as a cash crop, barley would not be replaced by wheat. Contractual growing should in any case be encouraged as far as possible. It is desirable to raise the general level of the quality of Irish wheat, and only varieties which are suitable to Irish soil and climate should be grown. The crop should be marketed in a more orderly way and in this connection the whole question of wheat drying by farmers should be re-assessed. The examination of the technical milling and baking problems arising from

the extended use of Irish wheat should be pressed ahead vigorously.—(Chapter 10).

Agricultural Credit

22. It will be necessary to ensure that demand for additional credit to finance increased production can be met in full and without delay. This subject is being separately examined but the following points are noted for consideration:—

    (a) the rationalisation of agricultural credit schemes should be pursued, emphasis being laid on schemes to encourage production which should be operated in close association with the local agricultural advisory services;

    (b) the security conditions stipulated by the Agricultural Credit Corporation should be relaxed since there is little point in insisting on conditions which many farmers cannot satisfy;

    (c) any additional funds required by the Corporation should be made readily available from the banks and, if necessary, from the Exchequer, which should also guarantee the Corporation against financial loss;

    (d) there should be close working relationships between the Corporation and the commercial banks and the possibility of devising a system in which local bank branches would act as agents of the Corporation should be investigated;

    (e) the adequacy of present hire-purchase facilities for farmers should be examined;

    (f) it might be possible to encourage existing creamery and other cooperative societies to give additional credit to their members.
—(Chapter 10).

Agricultural Trade Relations

23. The problems raised by the marketing of increased agricultural output underline the need for satisfactory external trading relations. In the Free Trade Area negotiations, our aim must be to broaden the scope for increased agricultural exports to continental countries and to ensure that there will be no disimprovement in our existing arrangements with Britain.—(Chapter 10).

Agricultural Education and Instruction

24. Improvement of farming skills over the next five years or so must be achieved largely through the advisory services. The broadening and deepening of the educational system will take longer but no time should be lost in giving the educational system a rural bias.

(a) *Primary Education*

The teaching of nature study is the most effective means of giving a rural bias to primary education and there seems to be no good reason why this subject should not be taught in rural primary schools generally.

(b) *Vocational Education*

Rural vocational schools have an immense potential but it will not be fully realised until the educational activities of the Departments of Agriculture and Education are completely coordinated. As a first step in broadening the scope of vocational education, it might be possible, in cooperation with the advisory services, to provide a further two or three years' basic part-time education during the winter months; this would have the additional merit of bringing the agricultural instructor into close contact with the younger farmers. More rural vocational schools will have to be provided; meanwhile, with the co-operation of the national school managers, post-primary agricultural education could be spread more widely by using some primary schools for teaching rural science after normal school hours. This would involve a marked expansion in the number of rural science teachers whose terms of employment should be good enough to attract graduates of the proper calibre. Rural science should be taught to girls as well as boys.

(c) *Secondary Education*

While agricultural science cannot become part of the general secondary school curriculum, the amount of teaching in basic science subjects should be increased.

(d) *Advisory Services*

The policy of increasing the number of general advisors should be pressed ahead vigorously until the present figure of 200 is increased to at least 300. Instructors need special training, particularly in public relations and farm management. A greater degree of supervision of individual instructors is necessary; it is also important that only the most suitable persons be appointed to County Committees of Agriculture. Coordination and a degree of integration of the different services would improve their efficiency, and a final decision on the future of the Parish Plan should form part of this rationalisation. The whole system must be backed by specialist services; the nucleus of these already exists in the Department of Agriculture.

(e) *Universities*

The question of the availability of employment for all agricultural science graduates needs to be considered in view of the prospective increased output of the agricultural faculties; a further matter requiring examination is whether the available openings offer conditions of service commensurate with the important contribution such graduates can make to economic development. An immediate requirement is the raising of the standard of entry into agricultural faculties. It is of the utmost importance that the agricultural faculties should be strengthened, and that additional State aid should be provided. Apart from other considerations, it is vital that An Foras Talúntais shall be supplied with a trained staff for research and that a trained corps be made available to disseminate research results.

(f) *General*

The problem of broadening rural education is primarily one of public relations for the agricultural and educational authorities. The aid of the agricultural associations and the clergy should be enlisted in the task. The extension of a travelling library service throughout the country could give the ordinary farmer the means of self-education at home. There is need both for some form of farm apprenticeship and for making land available for letting for a term of years. Steps should be taken to force onto the market land abused under conacre and agistment lettings.—(Chapter 11).

State Aid to Agriculture

25. State aid to agriculture is now running at an annual rate of over £18 million. A strong case exists for

(i) reducing the amount devoted to subsidising final products and enlarging the provision for reduction of production costs —on the general principle that a policy of limited and diminishing subsidies can be justified if progress is being made in permanently reducing production costs;

(ii) diverting a substantial part of Land Project expenditure so as to increase the provision for more urgent and more immediately productive purposes, especially the subsidisation of phosphatic fertilisers for grasslands;

(iii) diverting much of the expenditure on miscellaneous improvements schemes (mainly road works) so as to increase the provision for farm buildings;

(iv) strengthening the educational and advisory services;

(v) increasing the amount expended on research and, in particular, on progeny testing of all livestock;

(vi) not halving the annuities in future cases of land division, since the full annuity represents a lenient assessment;

(vii) gradually transforming the Agricultural Grant (which amounts to £5.6 million in 1958-59) into forms of aid more directly serving to lower production costs, e.g., subsidisation of fertilisers, increased research, education, advisory services, etc. A beginning might be made by fixing the Agricultural Grant at £5 million, thus freeing £0.6 million per annum for sub-sidisation of phosphates.

26. The re-allocation of aid recommended at (ii) and (vii) above should make a sum of about £1 million available annually to reduce the cost of fertilisers, to which the Government might consider adding £1 million a year for ten years.

27. Since the limiting factor to the eradication of livestock diseases at present is lack of professional personnel, the first requirement is to prepare a programme showing what *must* be done and, in the light of this, to estimate manpower needs and the Exchequer subvention necessary. There does not seem to be any good ground for increasing expenditure on arterial drainage until more immediate needs are fully met.—(Chapter 12).

Fisheries and Marine Products

28 (a) *Sea Fisheries*

The size and type of boat is the key to the problem of the expansion of the fishing industry. Considerable amounts of capital would be required for even a small fleet of distant-water (140-foot) trawlers and, in the earlier stages, large-scale development of the industry must be based on boats in the 70-foot category which are suitable for fishing in any waters off the Irish coast; if this policy is to be successful, adequate harbour accommodation and training facilities will have to be provided. We should undertake our own research programmes, This would require the expansion of the existing professional staff and the provision of buildings and equipment.

(b) *Inland Fisheries and Sea Angling*

Planned development of salmon and trout fisheries is already proceeding. There is considerable scope for increased exports of eels and sea angling appears to offer excellent prospects as a tourist attraction.

(c) *Marine Products*

Increased production of sea-rod meal and of animal feeding stuffs from other types of seaweed is desirable; this may require the expansion of Arramara Teo. Exports of carrageen have distinct possibilities and the efforts to increase production might be intensified.—(Chapter 13).

Forestry and Forest Products

29. The most recent assessment of available data indicates that continuance of the State planting programme can be justified on economic as well as on social grounds. A more accurate appraisal of forestry yields is at present in progress; the results will enable firmer conclusions to be drawn. Private planting has been on a very small scale, but the payment of larger grants and intensified propaganda is expected to bring about an increase in planting.

30. The development of native industries based on forest products should have the two-fold object of meeting home requirements as far as possible and of developing exports in processed form. A committee, representative of pulp and paper manufacturers, has been examining the problem and it is possible that it will recommend that the increased supplies of thinnings expected over the next ten years would be best disposed of by the expansion of existing industries. State intervention does not appear necessary at present but the position will need to be kept under review.—(Chapter 14).

Industrial Development

31. Further industrial development, accompanied by the raising of agricultural output and purchasing power, is the best means of achieving a balanced economy. Capital is necessary but the real shortage is of ideas, and these are likely to fructify only if domestic conditions favour profit-making.—(Chapter 15).

(a) *Promotion of Industry*

For the better promotion of industry, An Foras Tionscal should have sole responsibility for the administration of industrial grants, leaving the Industrial Development Authority as the specialist promotional agency. Close liaison between the bodies concerned with the development of industry is necessary.

(b) *Industrial Credit Company*

The Industrial Credit Company should have adequate funds available to enable it to discharge its functions: a minimum of £2 million a year on average of State finance is suggested, and it is hoped that additional funds would be made available by the banks, insurance companies and, if necessary, extern institutions such as the World Bank. Although it has not hitherto proved practicable for the company to operate investment trusts or unit trust funds, recent developments indicate a more favourable climate for their initiation. The matter should be kept under close review.

(c) Decentralisation

A realistic appraisal of development prospects indicates that, apart from exceptional cases, industries must be at or near the larger centres of population. Special subsidisation of remote areas by more extensive grants for industrial development is wasteful and retards progress in areas better situated.

(d) Foreign Participation

We can no longer rely for industrial development on extensive tariff and quota protection. Foreign industrialists will bring skills and techniques we need, and continuous and widespread publicity abroad is essential to attract them. If foreign industrial investment does not rapidly increase, a more radical removal of statutory restrictions on such investment should take place.

(e) Development of Foreign and Home Markets

Córas Tráchtála should be used to the full to further exports to all parts of the world that offer possibilities, the British market receiving particular attention. Widespread and continuous advertising is essential for success. The home market also needs to be developed and prejudice against Irish goods broken down. The cooperation of distributors in this task is important.

(f) Research

The full development of industry will require considerable fundamental research; to be adequate, this will require State assistance. In the underdeveloped state of our economy it is necessary to preserve a proper balance between pure and applied research. A systematic programme should be followed. The Institute for Industrial Research and Standards has only a small technical staff and could probably expand its activities if given the necessary funds. In connection with the Scholarship Exchange Scheme financed from American Grant Counterpart funds, emphasis should be placed on research and training having a bearing on production. The work of the Geological Survey Office could be enhanced in value if additional finance were made available.

(g) Efficiency, Productivity and Technical Education

If we are to progress, the general level of efficiency and productivity In industry must be raised; the reduction in tariffs which membership of a European Free Trade Area would entail will help to achieve this. We should participate more fully in the European Productivity Agency of the O.E.E.C. The work of the Irish Management Institute deserves the fullest support, and the specialised courses for management at present being conducted in Dublin should be extended to other centres. In urban vocational schools a proper balance should be preserved between fundamental education and technical training; fees for art and hobby courses should reflect the cost of providing them. Some economy should be possible in school building through a degree of integration with the national school system and modification of the present high construction standards. The Employment Exchanges could, perhaps, provide a comprehensive placement and advisory service.

(h) *Restrictive Labour Practices*

Restrictive labour practices retard industrial progress; in future this factor will assume even greater importance. This is an appropriate field for special study. In the meantime, it should be possible to obtain an enlightened approach from workers and trade unions in the context of general measures for development of the economy. There is a definite need in industry for machinery for continuous consultation between employers and workers on matters such as these.—(Chapter 16).

Some Industries Based on Agricultural Products

32. (a) *Biscuits*

The potentialities of biscuit exports should not be jeopardised for lack of capital essential to expansion. If necessary the industry should receive assistance from the Industrial Credit Company.

(b) *Vegetables, Fruit, etc.*

The most urgent requirement is the improvement of production, marketing and distribution techniques; certain suggestions relating to production are made in Chapter 20 (paragraph 11). There is scope for the development of a processing and export trade. The experience of Comhlucht Siúicre Éireann Teo. would be valuable in developing the industry.

(c) *Sweets*

The sweet factory of the Dairy Disposal Company in Limerick, if organised to concentrate on an attractive high-grade product, could play a pilot rôle in exports.

(d) *Whiskey and Gin*

The joint efforts which are now being made by the distillers and

Córas Tráchtála to expand sales of Irish whiskey in the American market might be supported with additional finance. The question of expanding exports to Britain and the Six Counties deserves attention. If the distillers find difficulty in building up their own export organisation, it might be possible for them to arrange to avail of the Guinness organisation for sales promotion and marketing. There are possibilities for developing exports of gin.

(e) *Leather and Leather Products*

A large expansion in the leather industry could follow from increased home killings of cattle. Research into improved tanning methods should enable the production at home of better quality leather now imported and help the industry to recover the markets lost to substitutes. There is scope on the agricultural side for improving the quality of hides and skins. Further improvements in design and finish would stimulate exports of leather products. A leather development centre should be helpful; alternatively, the Institute for Industrial Research and Standards might specially investigate the position.—(Chapter 17).

Turf

33. As regards briquettes, further expansion should be deferred until the two new briquetting factories are in operation and an assessment of unsatisfied demand can be made. To increase sales of machine-won turf to the general public, persistent and widespread publicity and special attention to easing delivery, storage and handling problems will be necessary. Continuous research into the production of better turf-burning apparatus will also be necessary and a hire-purchase system may have to be introduced to encourage the provision of modern storage facilities and the installation of up-to-date stoking and burning apparatus, particularly in factories and institutions. Public institutions might, if necessary, be facilitated as regards loans for the purpose. There may be opportunities for the export of turf to the Six Counties.

34. Further investigation of the possibilities of establishing industries based on turf as a raw material should be encouraged, and Bord na Móna should undertake, or arrange for, more intensive research in these fields. The Board, or if necessary a separate public agency, should establish pilot plants for likely new lines and carry out initial development of markets. Large-scale development of promising lines could be pursued even if there should be no prospect of private participation.

35. As the fortunes of Bord na Móna are largely bound up with those of the E.S.B., the closest cooperation between the two Boards is obviously necessary. An up-grading of the existing Joint Technical Committee is suggested.—(Chapter 18).

Fertiliser Industry

36. It is desirable that the country should, as far as possible, be self-sufficient in fertilisers. The main difficulty in the establishment of an ammonium nitrate industry is the risk that demand for the product may not rise to the economic production level and that exports could not be disposed of at economic prices.—(Chapter 19).

Electricity

37. (a) *Development Policy—Rural Electrification*

The E.S.B. will for some years have substantial surplus generating capacity. Apart from the over-capitalisation resulting from the excess generating plant, a serious burden is also entailed by the losses on uneconomic rural electrification; it has been estimated that these will be of the order of £1¼ million a year by 1963, assuming completion of rural electrification by that time. The decision to transfer to the Exchequer one-half of the capital charges on rural electrification outlay from 1st April, 1958 onwards, does not remove the basic difficulty. No material increase in agricultural production can be expected from the extension of supply to the remoter areas remaining to be connected. These factors lead to the conclusion that the completion of the rural electrification programme should be tapered off so as to moderate the loss which will fall on the general electricity consumer and the tax-payer.

(b) *Stimulation of Demand for Electricity*

The growth of demand for current should be accelerated by expansion of the economy but it is a matter of urgency that special steps be taken to stimulate demand. The maintenance and intensification of sales pressure by the E.S.B. is essential; joint publicity arrangements with Bord na Móna should be advantageous. The E.S.B. should be able to win a larger share of domestic custom, particularly the custom of local authority tenants. The use of electricity for agricultural purposes could be further stimulated. The equipment of pilot farms—both general and horticultural—with electrical apparatus could well be extended. Continuous sponsoring of pilot schemes in respect of new uses for electricity in the industrial and commercial sectors is also desirable. Electrical components and accessories should be standardised by the Board in cooperation with the Industrial Development Authority and the Institute for Industrial Research and Standards.

(c) *Research and Efficiency*

Apart from maintaining efficiency by close contact with development abroad, the Board can continue to benefit from independent investigation and research.—(Chapter 20).

Steel, Shipbuilding, Telephones and Engineering

38. (a) Steel

Proposals for the extension of the steel works at Haulbowline, involving a total capital investment provisionally estimated at £2 million, have been approved in principle by the Government. The development plan is envisaged as the first phase in a programme for the expansion of a major steel industry producing pig iron from imported ore and having an increased range of finished products. The final phase, which would involve very heavy capital expenditure, would, in the opinion of Irish Steel Holdings, Ltd., be feasible only on the basis of foreign investment.

(b) Shipbuilding and Repairing

There is considerable scope for the development of Haulbowline as a ship-repairing centre. This would provide a useful basis for a ship-building industry.

(c) Telephones

An increase from £1½ million to £2 million in the yearly allocation of capital for telephone extensions would be justified. As regards the question of the scope for home manufacture and assembly of telephone equipment, there seems little likelihood that the bulk of the items at present imported could be economically produced here.

(d) Public Engineering Workshops

The railway engineering workshops at Inchicore and Dundalk could provide the nucleus for an engineering industry. The Dundalk Engineering Works, Ltd., which has taken over the Dundalk works, is about to formulate long-term plans for development, one of its proposals relating to the partial manufacture and assembly of a small motor car. The best hope of success in this line would appear to lie in the active participation of established foreign manufacturers. The question whether heavy repair work for public bodies could, with advantage, be centralised at Inchicore should be examined. This, if feasible, would create one fairly large unit which could contract for outside work. Subject to further study of the matter, there is a prospect that Aer Lingus, with an investment of £150,000, may be able to undertake aircraft engine over-haul work now done by a British company. In present conditions, opportunities for the Irish company to engage in the manufacture of aircraft components are strictly limited.—(Chapter 21).

Mineral Development

39. (a) Coal

Our needs of anthracite could be met from home sources and an export surplus developed. Under the American Grant Counterpart Agreement a sum of £80,000 has been provided for a three-year exploration scheme with a view to the expansion of output. The Geological Survey Office originally proposed a larger scheme costing £160,000. If the preliminary results of the approved scheme are not discouraging and the full cooperation of the owners of the deposits is forthcoming, the Exchequer might supplement the Counterpart funds to the extent necessary to prove deposits which would form the basis of an annual production of at least 300,000 tons.

(b) *Molybdenum, etc.*

Commercial development of molybdenite deposits should be encouraged. Enquiries by foreign companies suggest that, if favourable royalty and taxation arrangements were made, it might be possible to have an exploration made of some areas for oil and gas reserves.—(Chapter 22).

Tourism

40. (a) *Hotel Accommodation and Other Catering Facilities*

The heavy cost of new hotel accommodation in relation to the number of weeks' occupancy at seaside resorts justifies the decision to make available grants for additional bedroom accommodation in such resorts. Similar encouragement should be extended to angling districts. The scope for motels should be fully explored; generally, stress should be laid on the provision of simple, clean and cheap accommodation. Any further taxation allowances for industry—particularly in relation to depreciation of buildings—should, where appropriate, be made available to hotels. C.I.E. have been modernising their hotels, and further investment in these hotels and in improved catering facilities at main terminal and other important tourist points throughout the C.I.E. system is desirable; consideration should be given to the establishment of a special subsidiary organisation which could pursue an intensive policy on these lines. One leading brewery has already taken an interest in the Irish hotel industry and the trade generally might, perhaps, be induced to go further in this direction. Efforts should be made to attract American and other foreign capital and enterprise for hotel construction and management.

(b) *Tourist Resorts*

Bathing facilities, promenades, parks, recreation facilities and amenities of various kinds need to be provided or improved. A State grant of £1 million spread over ten years is suggested. The works to be undertaken at each resort should be substantial and should constitute part of an overall development plan to be drawn up by the local authority and the local development company in consultation with Bord Fáilte Éireann. A grant from the State should be conditional on a local contribution. A time limit should be fixed for the execution of the works and the whole scheme should be limited to, perhaps, a period of ten years. There is also considerable scope for extending shooting facilities, particularly in the formation of large shooting estates. Inland fisheries and sea angling as tourist attractions are discussed in Chapter 13.

(c) *Port Facilities*

There is considerable room for improvement of disembarkation facilities at points such as Cobh and Dún Laoghaire. The tenders used by the Cork Harbour Commissioners for servicing liners need to be replaced; the Commissioners have placed an order for a new tender and Exchequer assistance might, if necessary, be made available for the provision of further vessels. The position at Dún Laoghaire, as the main gateway to our tourist attractions, is most important, and examination of the additional facilities needed there and at other important tourist entry points should be pressed ahead rapidly.—(Chapter 23).

ESTIMATE OF COST

41. An attempt—however rough—must now be made to set out the amount of finance which would be required by the State and State agencies (such as the Industrial Credit Company) to give effect to the various proposals and suggestions put forward in this study. It will be understood that in many cases detailed plans and costings would be necessary for accuracy and that, in their absence, only very tentative figures could be used. Moreover, there is necessarily an arbitrary element in the assignment of cost to particular financial years. In view of the many qualifications to which they are subject, the estimates (which are shown in Appendix 9) should be regarded as indicative only of orders of magnitude. Subject to these remarks, the capital cost is estimated to rise from approximately £0.5 million in 1958-59 (taken as the first operative year) to over £11 million by 1962-63 and to amount to £34 million approximately over the five-year period; these figures do not include any provision for the nitrogenous fertiliser project. The expenditure for 1962-63 would be divided as follows :—

	£ million
Agriculture	3·00
Fisheries	0·70
General Industrial Development	5·75
Specific Industrial Development (Steel and telephones)	1·00
Tourism	0·85
	11·30

These figures—and those in Appendix 9—relate to costs *additional* to those for existing services financed by the State and State agencies. They are *net* figures, i.e., they exclude expenditure which it is proposed to meet by diverting existing State aid (e.g., part of the Agricultural Grant and Land Project expenditure) to new purposes. A forecast of the public capital programme for 1958-59 to 1962-63, taking account both of present policies (Appendix 5) and the suggestions of this study (Appendix 9) appears as Appendix 10. The total projected public capital investment in the period would, as shown in that Appendix, amount to £212 million approximately.

42. The proposals in this study may be said to conform, in their financial implications, to the following general scheme: —

(i) the expected level of savings will suffice to maintain the present volume of public and private investment (Chapter 4);

(ii) the estimated cost of the proposals will more than offset the decline—some £10 million gross by 1962-63 (see Appendix 5) —which would otherwise take place in social and other public investment;

(iii) if productive development requires more capital than can be obtained from current savings, suitable domestic assets might be accepted as backing for *future* issues of Legal Tender Notes, thereby freeing, on average, some £3½ million a year of external reserves.

(iv) if productive projects were to arise beyond those for which provision is made in the study, recourse for finance to the World Bank or other external lenders would be necessary; and

(v) it is envisaged that savings, economies in expenditure and expanding revenue should enable any additional non-capital expenditure to be met without jeopardising the objective of lower rates of direct taxation.

EFFECT OF PROPOSALS

43. Between 1949 and 1956 the volume of gross national product increased at an annual rate of about 1%. It is not possible to say with any degree of certainty what effect the proposals made in this study would have in accelerating this rate of increase. Not all the details of the various proposals are available at this stage and, even if they were, the absence of an input-output analysis would make it impossible to trace, and estimate, their effects on the economy. However, making all allowances for the indeterminacy of the available information, there is good reason to believe that, if the proposals were adopted, the rate of increase in the volume of gross national product could, in time, be doubled, which would double real national income in 35 years. While this figure is subject to many reservations, it is clear that, if it could be achieved, we would have made substantial progress in reducing unemployment and the flow of emigration, and in increasing employment and the living standards of our people.

44. Finally, it should again be emphasised that this study is only a contribution to the framing of a programme of national development. It is hoped that it will stimulate further ideas for the undertaking of *productive* projects, particularly in the private sector. It needs, moreover, to be supplemented by continuing arrangements to study and promote development possibilities. The body set up for this purpose might include—in addition to the Secretaries of the Departments of Finance, the Taoiseach, Agriculture, Industry and Commerce and Lands—the Governor of the Central Bank, the Chairman of the Industrial Development Authority, the Managing Director of the Agricultural Credit Corporation, the Director of the Central Statistics Office and the professional economists now serving on the Capital Investment Advisory Committee (Professor Carter, Dr. Ryan and Mr. Lynch).

Oifig an Aire Airgeadais,
16 Nollaig, 1957.

Economic Development

The Minister for Finance circulates, herewith, for the information of the Government, a copy of a minute dated 12th December, 1957, from the Secretary of his Department.

Minister,

1. This note records what I have said to you orally about the desirability of attempting to work out an integrated programme of national development for the next five or ten years, which I believe will be critical years for the country's survival as an economic entity.

2. I have not a " Plan " in mind. There would be little sense in trying to establish any rigid pattern of development for a small country so exposed to the perpetual flux of world economic forces. But I have thought for some time that it would be a useful national service to prepare a study embracing the following three elements : —

    (i) as groundwork, a brief outline of the present state of the economy, concentrating on the main deficiencies and opportunities;

    (ii) a statement of the principles to be followed in order most effectively to correct the defects and realise the opportunities; and

    (iii) indications of the specific forms of productive development which appear to offer the best prospects.

3. Various Commissions have surveyed the Irish economy most thoroughly and it would be a waste of time and effort to cover the ground again. What is urgently necessary is *not* to know that more resources should be devoted to productive rather than non-productive purposes but rather to know what are the productive purposes to which resources should be applied and what unproductive, or relatively unproductive, activities can, with the minimum social disadvantage, be curtailed to set free resources for productive development.

4. This is urgent for at least five reasons : —

    (i) the growing comment on the absence of a comprehensive and integrated programme is tending to deepen the all-too-prevalent mood of despondency about the country's future;

227

(ii) in the context of such a programme it would be easier to win acceptance for particular decisions of policy which, presented in isolation, might be strenuously opposed;

(iii) a slowing down in housing and other forms of social investment must be faced from now on because of the virtual satisfaction of needs over wide areas—and it is necessary to find productive investments which will prevent the unemployment problem from becoming very serious;

(iv) the favourable state of our balance of payments is, in part, the result of painful adjustments and could so easily be disturbed that it is most important to confine increases in national expenditure as far as possible to projects of a *productive* character;

(v) it is not enough to count on proposals being made by the World Bank Mission when it comes next May or June—we should be doing our own homework if for no other reason than to equip ourselves to make the most of the World Bank's expert assistance and advice.

5. While I deprecate planning in any rigid sense, I am convinced of the psychological value of setting up targets of national endeavour, provided they are reasonable and mutually consistent. There is probalbly a particular need in this country at present to harness the enthusiasm of the young and buttress the faith of the active members of the community in this way. But there is nothing to be gained by setting up fanciful targets. Failure to reach such targets would quickly produce disillusionment and renew the feeling of national despondency. Neither is there any use in suggesting that through some simple expedient, like reform of the banking system, rapid expansion of employment and living standards can be assured. Some improvements in the banking field are desirable but there is no solution to our difficulties in financial expedients. Greater output per head and increased saving (with corresponding restraint in consumption, both private and public) are essential conditions of economic improvement. Moreover, unless the individual members of the community have sufficient patriotism and realism to accept the standard of living produced by their own exertions here—even if it should continue for some time to be lower than the standard available abroad—the basis for economic progress simply does not exist.

6. With all this in mind and feeling that the central position of the Department of Finance gives us a special responsiibility for studying how economic progress can be promoted, I began some time ago the task of bringing together in an accessible form the information which seems most relevant to the determination of future policy in the economic sphere. I append the heads of the scheme on which, with the help of the Central Statistics Office, Mr. C. H. Murray and others, I have been working. It is intended to cover the three points indicated in paragraph 2 above.

7. This, I believe, is work that can best be done, as regards force, consistency and reasonableness, under one person's direction, provided that person has free access for information, advice and assistance to officers of the other Departments and State organisations concerned. What should be produced for consideration is a coherent and constructive document, bound by a realistic appraisal of the resources likely to be available rather than by Departmental allegiances; otherwise an official of the Department

of Finance would find rather strange the rôle of advocate rather than critic of new forms of expenditure! Departments, as such, should I suggest remain officially uncommitted until the work is referred to them for critical examination prior to its formal consideration by the Government.

8. I would willingly—and as quickly as possible—complete the work in hands, on the basis outlined above, if it is felt that it serves a need and would be of assistance to the Government.

9. At some point consideration might perhaps be given to the question of inviting a wider range of views than those of Departments only but this is still some distance off.

T. K. Whitaker.
12th December, 1957.

SCHEME OF WORK

1. Introduction.
2. Economic position—general outline.
3. Development needs and resources.
4. Finance.
5. Agriculture—general.
6. Grasslands.
7. Cattle.
8. Milk and milk products.
9. Pigs and bacon.
10. Wheat and tillage generally.
11. Agricultural education—advisory services, etc.
12. State aid to agriculture.
13. Agricultural credit.
14. Agriculture—conclusions.
15. Fisheries.
16. Forestry.
17. Industry—general.
18. ⎫
19. ⎬ Particular industrial possibilities.
20. ⎭
21. Tourism.
22. Conclusions.

Roinn an Taoisigh,
Baile Átha Cliath.
18 Nollaig, 1957.

S. 16066.
An Rúnaí Príobháideach,
An tAire Airgeadais.

I am to refer to the memorandum dated the 16th instant submitted by the Minister for Finance with a copy of a minute dated the 12th December, 1957, from the Secretary of his Department regarding the working-out of an integrated programme of national development and to inform you that, at a meeting of the Government held on the 17th instant, it was arranged: —

(1) that the Minister would approve the proposals, submitted to him in the minute, for the preparation of a study embracing: —

(a) as groundwork, a brief outline of the present state of the economy, concentrating on the main deficiencies and opportunities,

(b) a statement of the principles to be followed in order most effectively to correct the defects and realise the opportunities and

(c) indications of the specific forms of productive development which appear to offer the best prospects; and

(2) that, for the purposes of the study, the Secretary of the Department of Finance would have free access, for information, advice and assistance, to officers of the other Departments and State organizations concerned.

M. Ó Muimhneacháin.

Rúnaí an Rialtais.

APPENDIX 2

1. *Industrial Credit Company, Limited, and Trade Loan Guarantees.*

The Industrial Credit Company, Limited, a State-sponsored company specialising in the provision of permanent long-term and medium-term capital for new and established enterprises, offers the following facilities: —

(a) It advises clients on their capital requirements, on the most appropriate capital structure and on the most suitable means of obtaining new capital.

(b) It underwrites capital issues and handles the specialised work involved in capital flotation.

(c) It subscribes for shares of public and private companies usually with a view to the eventual sale of the shares.

(d) It makes long-term or medium-term loans repayable by fixed instalments over an agreed period.

The authorised capital of the company is £5 million of which £2 million has been issued and paid up. To date the company has been responsible for the provision of some £17 million of capital for Irish industries. As a result of the enactment of the Industrial Credit (Amendment) Act, 1958, facilities for access to capital by the company have been improved. This Act empowers the Minister for Finance (1) to take up directly shares in the company without the necessity for a public issue, (2) to guarantee the principal and interest of borrowings by the company up to a limit of £5 million and (3) to guarantee the payment of a minimum dividend on shares of the company held by parties other than him. Further, the Irish commercial banks have agreed to participate on a long-term basis in the financing of the company and have intimated their willingness in principle to make a contribution amounting to £1,800,000. This sum will afford the company, after discharging its overdraft indebtedness and after financing directly its liabilities under existing bank guarantees, a balance of about £400,000 for new business. In addition, a provision of £1,000,000 has been included in the 1958/59 Capital Budget which will be used to purchase shares in the company. The company will then have almost £1½ million available for new projects apart from whatever may become available to it by the turning over of its existing capital.

Arising out of the enlargement of the resources of the Industrial Credit Company, the system by which loans for industrial purposes are guaranteed under the Trade Loans (Guarantee) Acts is being replaced by an alternative system by which similar loans will be provided by the Industrial Credit Company. Under these Acts, State guarantees have been given for loans amounting to over £3.2 million. The change will reduce the legal formalities involved and will mean that applications for loans will be dealt with more expeditiously.

2. *Amendment of Control of Manufactures Acts.*

It has been represented that the Control of Manufactures Acts, 1932 and 1934, which were designed to secure that the control and ownership of Irish industry would be in Irish hands to the greatest possible extent, have tended in some instances to discourage investment and participation by external interests in Irish industry. The Acts have been amended by the Industrial Development (Encouragement of External Investment) Act, 1958, which, *inter alia,* frees from the operation of the previous Acts any company which (i) carries on business solely for export, or (ii) carries on business primarily for export and makes a *bona fide* offer to the Irish public of 50% of its voting shares.

3. *Removal of Price and Profit Control.*

During the War it was necessary to apply rigid controls over prices and profits. Under the Prices Act, 1958, these controls have been dispensed with except for such measures as are necessary to protect the public from price excesses deriving from restrictive business practices, inefficiency in protected industries and temporary shortages.

4. *Company Law Reform.*

Proposed comprehensive amendments to company law will include the removal of certain provisions in the existing law which operate to discourage investment in industry whether by nationals or non-nationals.

5. *Non-Repayable Grants.*

To encourage the establishment of industries in the less developed areas in the west and south-west special grants and other facilities (up to a maximum of £4 million) are available from State funds to firms setting up industries in those areas. An independent statutory body, An Foras Tionscal (The Undeveloped Areas Board) has been established to administer the grants. The grants, which are outright gifts of capital, can amount to the full cost of the factory site and buildings, one-half the cost of plant and machinery, and the full cost of training workers.

Under the Industrial Grants Act, 1956, there is authority in appropriate cases to afford somewhat similar facilities (up to a maximum of £2 million) for industrial projects in other parts of the country.

6. *Remission of Local Taxation.*

For the first seven years local taxation on new factory ɩbuildings is reduced to one-third of the ordinary rate. In the undeveloped areas the period of reduction may be extended to ten years.

7. *Tax relief on export profits.*

As a special incentive to encourage exports, the Finance (Miscellaneous Provisions) Act, 1956, provided for the remission, for a period of five years, of 50% of the tax on profits of companies derived from *new or increased* exports of goods manufactured and exported by them. The Finance Act, 1957, increased the rate of remission to 100%, as from April, 1958, and provided also an alternative relief of 25% of the tax on the *whole* of a company's profits from the sale of goods manufactured and exported by it. Under the Finance Act, 1958, the maximum period of remission of tax in respect of *new or increased* exports has been extended to ten years.

8. *Tax Relief for plant and machinery.*

As an encouragement to increased industrial production and modernisation, an accelerated depreciation allowance for plant and machinery has been made available as from April, 1958. The allowance takes the form of an increase of 25% in the basic rates of wear and tear for tax purposes. There is also provision for an "initial" allowance (i.e. an expedited depreciation allowance) of 20% of capital expenditure on new machinery or plant acquired since April, 1956.

9. *Tax Relief on new buildings.*

In 1956 provision was made under which, in the case of new industrial buildings, including hotels, 10% of the capital expenditure incurred after September, 1956, is allowed as a deduction in computing profits for tax purposes.

10. *Tax Relief for mineral development.*

Profits arising from the operation of certain *new* mining enterprises are exempt from income tax and corporation profits tax for four years from the date on which production commences; for each of the following four years 50% of the profits are so exempted. In the case of *existing* mines, relief may be claimed for such period as remained, on the 6th April, 1956, out of eight years from the date on which production commenced. The relief applies only to non-bedded mineral deposits, including deposits of copper, lead, zinc, pyrites, barytes, gold and silver.

In the case of *new* coal mines, 50% of the profits are exempt from income tax and corporation profits tax for ten years. The relief applies also, in the case of *existing* mines, to profits arising from increases in the volume of coal production over that achieved in the years ended September, 1955, or September, 1956.

Relief is granted in respect of capital expenditure on searching for deposits or developing underground mines. In addition, depreciation allowances may be granted on a favourable basis to operators of mines, quarries or ore smelters.

11. *Taxation remission on dividends and interest from Irish industrial companies.*

Section 7 of the Finance Act, 1932, as amended, provides for a 20% tax remission on dividends and interest from certain investments by Irish residents in Irish industry. The Finance Act, 1957, extended this tax abatement, as from April, 1958, to all securities issued to the public subsequent to 1932 by Irish manufacturing concerns.

12. *Tax concession for shipping.*

The "initial" allowance of 20% (see para. 8) is granted in respect of expenditure on second-hand, as well as new, ships. As from April, 1958, an alternative "investment" allowance of 40% is, however, available in respect of expenditure on new ships. The "investment" allowance is not deductible from the capital expenditure in ascertaining the amounts of annual wear and tear allowances, i.e., it does not operate to reduce the amount of such allowances which, in addition, are increased by 25% from April, 1958 (para. 8).

13. *Assistance to Exporters.*

In addition to facilities normally available to industrialists through the diplomatic and consular services a special company, Córas Tráchtála Teoranta, has been set up by the Government to assist exporters. The company, whose services are free, puts exporters in touch with prospective customers abroad, conducts market research and provides advice and assistance generally in connection with exports. There is a State-sponsored scheme of political risk insurance in respect of exports to certain countries.

14. *Freedom to take out profits.*

Dividends, interest and profits on all investments may be freely transferred to the foreign investor's country in the appropriate currency. Capital may be freely repatriated at any time in the currency in which it was originally invested and this right also extends to appreciation of such capital.

APPENDIX 3

State Expenditure 1957/58 compared with 1950/51
(Non-Capital)
£000s

	1950–51	1957–58 (provisional)	Increase	Decrease
Service of Debt	7,198	22,902	15,704	—
Social Services	11,591	24,352	12,761	—
Remuneration	22,401	32,764	10,363	—
Health	3,124	7,869	4,745	—
Agricultural Price Supports ...	—	4,139	4,139	—
Payments to Road Fund on foot of Motor Taxation receipts ...	2,814	5,683	2,869	—
Pensions	2,855	4,975	2,120	—
Railways	980	3,089	2,109	—
Agricultural Grant	3,934	5,506	1,572	—
Education	1,334	2,337	1,003	—
Defence	1,943	2,630	687	—
Grants to Industry	—	360	360	—
Special Employment Schemes Office	520	802	282	—
Post Office	984	1,140	156	—
Gardaí	143	321	178	—
Wireless Broadcasting	110	115	5	—
Consumer Food Subsidies ...	13,089	2,238	—	10,851
Other Items (Net)	4,050	5,088	1,038	—
Total	77,070	126,310	60,091	10,851

Net Increase: £49,240,000

Notes:

(1) Civil service, teachers', army, garda, etc., pay is aggregated under " Remuneration " and such headings as social services, health, education, etc., do not, therefore, include remuneration.

(2) The figures for " Railways " and " Post Office " are exclusive, respectively, of repayments to the Central Fund of advances to meet interest payments on Transport Stocks and Telephone Capital Repayments both of which items are included under " Service of Debt."

APPENDIX 4

TREND IN CERTAIN CATEGORIES OF MONETARY SAVINGS
£000s

Change of Deposits in

Year	Post Office Savings Bank (1)	Trustee Savings Banks (2)	Savings Certificates (3)	British P.O. Savings Bank and Savings Certificates (4)	Commercial Banks Deposit Accounts (5)	Building Societies (6)	Life Assurance (7)	New Irish Public Authority Issues† (8)	Total (1) to (8) (9)
1947	+ 508	+ 48	+ 416	− 688	+ 8,479	+ 2,230	+ 1,155	—	12,148
1948	+ 2,116	+ 281	+ 573	− 540	− 4,995	+ 2,075	+ 1,801	13,400	14,711
1949	+ 4,939	+ 883	+ 654	− 492	+ 5,900	+ 1,226	+ 2,179	6,700	21,989
1950	+ 4,213	+ 675	+ 415	− 524	− 241	+ 896	+ 2,448	8,600	16,482
1951	+ 5,226	+ 949	+ 660	− 537	+ 2,400	+ 867	+ 2,782	600	12,947
1952	+ 3,711	+ 561	+ 2,086	− 560	+ 797	+ 728	+ 3,264	17,000	27,587
1953	+ 4,697	+ 744	+ 1,428	− 552	+ 11,212	+ 952	+ 3,614	20,300	42,395
1954	+ 4,972	+ 1,020	+ 1,018	− 475	+ 5,695	+ 1,246	+ 4,052	13,400	30,928
1955	+ 4,446	+ 687	+ 523	− 502	− 2,341	+ 1,060	+ 4,126	15,900	23,899
1956	+ 2,358	+ 524	+ 2,292	− 539	− 613	+ 1,200‡	+ 4,300‡	16,900	26,422
1957	+ 2,600	+ 360	+ 750	− 540	+ 6,270	+ 1,300‡	+ 4,700‡	20,190*	35,630

† Excludes subscriptions by banks.
‡ Estimated.
* Including Prize Bonds and public Exchequer Bill issues.

FORECAST OF CAPITAL PROGRAMME OF PUBLIC AUTHORITIES 1958–59 TO 1962–63
ON BASIS OF PRESENT POLICIES.

£ million

	1958-59	1959-60	1960-61	1961-62	1962-63	Total
1. Building and Construction (other than 2)						
(i) Housing (a) ...	9·72	9·87	9·67	8·67	8·17	46·10
(ii) Sanitary and miscellaneous services	2·56	2·30	2·30	2·25	2·00	11·41
(iii) National and vocational schools	1·45	1·50	1·50	1·50	1·50	7·45
(iv) Other building and construction	1·08	1·55	1·55	1·55	1··0	7·13
Total ...	14·81	15·22	15·02	13·97	13·07	72·09
2. Ports, harbours and airports	0·84	1·30	1·15	1·00	1·00	5·29
3. Transport (b) ...	6·07	1·57	0·83	1·08	1·02	10·57
4. Telephones ...	1·45	1·45	1·45	1·45	1·45	7·25
5. Agriculture (c) ...	4·91	5·96	6·65	7·35	5·95	30·82
6. Agricultural Credit	0·25	0·40	0·40	0·40	0·40	1·85
7. Forestry	1·22	1·00	1·00	1·00	1·00	5·22
8. Fisheries	0·19	0·25	0·25	0·25	0·25	1·19
9. Fuel and Power ...	7·00	6·74	6·88	7·11	5·69	33·42
10. Industrial Credit ...	2·80(d)	0·50	0·50	0·50	0·50	4·80
11. Industrial Grants ...	0·65	0·65	0·65	0·65	0·65	3·25
12. National Development Fund	0·55	0·50	0·46	—	—	1·51
Total Capital Investment by Public Authorities	40·74	35·54	35·24	34·76	30·98	177·26
Deduct—Capital expected to be provided by public bodies from internal sources	4·29	3·24	3·23	3·64	3·54	17·94
Net amount to be financed from Exchequer and non-Exchequer sources	36·45	32·30	32·01	31·12	27·44	159·32

(a) These figures include tentative estimates of increased expenditure arising from a decision to finance the purchase of secondhand houses under the Small Dwellings (Acquisition) Acts and new legislation providing for increased grant and loan facilities for housing.

(b) Railways, shipping and air services.

(c) Voted capital provision for agriculture and arterial drainage.

(d) Includes £1·4m. for funding of existing bank overdrafts and £0·5m. brought forward from 1957/58 pending passing of legislation.

APPENDIX 6

Primary Schools.

1. Rural science was a compulsory subject in national schools until 1934, when it was dropped to permit of increased attention to Irish. Since then it has been an optional subject, and in 1955 was taught in only 173 schools (out of a total of some 4,900) to less than 4,000 pupils (out of a total of 486,000).

Rural Vocational Schools.

2. These provide continuation education for pupils between 14 and 17 years of age. About 20,000 boys and girls attend whole-time vocational courses; of these about 11,000 are in rural areas and towns of less than 5,000 population. In the case of the majority of the latter group the boys are taught rural science and the girls domestic science. Rural science is not agriculture; it is a selection of the elements of the basic sciences—physics, chemistry, botany, geology, bacteriology—taught in a manner that relates them to practical agricultural problems. The object of the two-year course is to provide a basic scientific education on which the agricultural instructor can later build. In addition to day classes, weekly evening classes in rural science for adults are conducted at the schools; the average attendance is 1,700. While the aim is the same as that for the day classes—the study of the basic scientific principles underlying agriculture—the classes are conducted on discussion group lines. Approximately 100 rural vocational schools (out of a total of some 260, rural and urban) have rural science teachers. To put the matter in another perspective, there are about 1,500 whole-time vocational teachers in the country, of whom some 400 are in urban areas, so that one teacher in every eleven outside those areas is a rural science teacher. It is estimated that up to 80 more day schools, mostly rural, are required to extend the present service to the whole country, and a further 60 or so rural science teachers will be necessary for this purpose. Between 100 and 200 one-roomed buildings for evening classes in remote areas may also be necessary.

3. In addition to formal teaching in rural science, the vocational schools conduct a number of practical educational schemes. Chief among these is the Practical Projects Scheme inaugurated in 1952, which is expanding rapidly. Under this, each pupil carries out some project relating to his home environment. The projects may range from papering a room to rearing a caif but all have the same aim—to stimulate thought and continued interest in problems which will develop initiative and experiment. This scheme is generally run in cooperation with the local branch of Macra na Tuaithe. Another of these schemes is a system of simple soil testing carried out by the pupils on local land under the supervision of the teacher. This is a growing activity in the rural science programme and is carried out in about 20 schools at present. For some years these schools have also tested seeds grown by local farmers, but the growing practice of using certified seed is curtailing this activity.

4. The rural vocational schools have the greatest numbers of pupils of any of the institutions giving agricultural education, yet even these cover only a fraction of the potential audience. At the 1951 Census of Population there were some 50,000 boys and 46,000 girls aged from 13 to 15, inclusive, living in rural areas and towns under 5,000 population. In the 1954-55 school year less than 11,000 of this group attended vocational schools and of these only 5,000 or so were boys (only boys are taught rural science). In other words only one boy in every ten in those areas followed a rural science course. The number of pupils is increasing each year, although slowly.

Winter Agricultural Classes.
5. These run from October to March each year and are given by the County Committee agricultural instructors at various centres within their areas. The classes are held two or three times a week. Attendance at these classes, which is on the increase, averages more than 5,000. In addition, the instructors give lectures which draw attendances of about 25,000 a year. Lectures on horticulture, bee-keeping, poultry-keeping, and buttermaking by the relevant instructors account for a further 20,000 or so. The average attendance at all these lectures is about 25, and those attending, are, as a rule, all engaged in farming.

Agricultural Schools and Colleges.
6. There are three residential agricultural schools administered by the Department, at Athenry, Ballyhaise and Clonakilty. These were established early in the present century to fill an intermediate position between the winter agricultural classes run by agricultural instructors and the short courses given at the Albert College. The total accommodation at these schools is only 90, but in latter years the numbers seeking admission have exceeded this figure. To meet this demand the school at Athenry has, since 1953, been reserved for short courses of one to four weeks. The number of students attending these schools in any year is about 250, of whom about 65 would be taking an eleven-month course, the remainder attending short courses.

7. The Munster Institute, Cork, confines its activities to training girls in poultry science and butter-making; in future years it will also carry out large-scale poultry breeding and research. It offers two courses: one of two years' duration which qualifies girls for posts as poultry instructors or as teachers of these subjects in schools, the other of about five months for farmers' daughters who intend to return to the farm. A year's training at a recognised school of rural domestic economy is required before entrance, which is approximately of matriculation standard. About 14 qualify each year from the diploma (two-year) course, while the shorter certificate course is taken by about 30 students each year. The total student body numbers about 90 in any year. Short summer courses of wider application have been provided in recent years for women members of Macra na Feirme and Muintir na Tíre but these are unlikely to affect the main stream of the Institute's curriculum, which is highly specialised.

8. The only other facilities for agricultural education provided in residential schools are the private agricultural colleges and rural domestic economy schools. There are six of the former, one co-educational, and thirteen of the latter. There are also five residential secondary schools which include agriculture as part of their regular curriculum. All are aided by State grants towards teachers' salaries, capital and current expenditure. The boys' agricultural schools cater for 15-year-olds and upwards, giving a

10-month course. While many of the students use these schools as a stepping-stone to admission to University degree courses, the majority return to their home farm. Accommodation at these schools is at present stretched to the utmost by the 350 or so pupils in attendance, but it is expected to become freer when a recently opened school at Multyfarnham, Co. Westmeath, becomes fully operative. About 800 pupils each year attend the rural domestic economy schools, where courses are expressely designed for farmers' daughters who will return to their homes.

Secondary Schools.

9. The amount of agricultural education given in secondary schools is negligible. In 1957 only 97 pupils took agricultural science as a subject for the Intermediate Certificate examination and only 159 for the Leaving Certificate. The total number of pupils being taught agricultural science in that year was only 694 out of a total of over 60,000.

University Colleges.

10. Finally, there are the Universities. U.C.D. provides a 4-year course leading to the degree of B.Agr.Sc. Formerly one-year courses in agriculture and horticulture were also provided, but since March, 1957, these have been discontinued to make room for the numbers taking the degree course, which have increased from 202 in 1954 to 314 in 1957. Up to the latter year, the output of graduates averaged 35 a year, including 3 or 4 from T.C.D., which by an arrangement with U.C.D., avails of the facilities of that college. In 1957, however, 47 graduated, and for the next few years at least, the annual crop of graduates will number 70 to 80. University College, Cork, provides a four-year course leading to the degree of B. Sc. (Dairying) and a two-year diploma course for intending creamery managers. The total student body averages 140, of whom 80 would be pursuing the diploma course. About three or four degrees and some twenty-five diplomas are conferred each year. In addition, students both at U.C.C. and U.C.G. may pursue the first two years of the B.Agr.Sc. degree course at those colleges. The remaining two years must, however, be taken at U.C.D.

Agricultural Instructors.

11. It is on the agricultural instructors employed by the County Committees that the brunt of the work of raising the standard of the community's agricultural knowledge and expertise falls. The growth in their numbers in recent years, particularly in the number of general instructors, is illustrated by the following table: —

NUMBERS OF COUNTY COMMITTEE INSTRUCTORS

At 31st March	Horticulture and Beekeeping	Poultry, Butter and Cheesemaking	General Agriculture	Total
1939	42	58	43	143
1946	46	62	68	176
1951	51	80	88	219
1952	46	79	105	230
1953	50	79	118	247
1954	51	81	129	261
1955	50	81	142	273
1956	55	80	152	287
1957	56	79	160	295
1958	58	76	180	314

In addition to organising winter classes and lectures, writing articles for local papers, conducting field trials and demonstrations (about 2,000 of these are staged annually or about 13 per agricultural instructor), their chief function is to visit farmers in their areas to advise them on their problems. Farm visits in 1957 numbered 235,000 or about 750 per instructor. All these instructors are graduates.

12. In addition to the facilities provided by the County Committees, the Department of Agriculture itself conducts schemes of instruction. These are: —

Parish Plan.

13. This dates from 1950, when the Department proposed that the advisory services be placed on a parish basis and come under the direct control of the Department. The plan envisaged the appointment of an instructor for every three parishes, or roughly 1,000 farmers. The instructors are Junior Agricultural Inspectors of the Department, are graduates, and are paid on much the same scale as County Committee instructors. Their efforts are supplementary to those of the latter, but are organised on a purely parish basis. They were appointed at the request of local rural groups such as Macra na Feirme, Muintir na Tíre, etc. There are at present 24 Parish Agents. There are altogether forty posts for such officers in the Department, but it is understood that the appointment of further numbers is not contemplated save in special cases where a poor county committee could not afford the same intensity of advisory service as a wealthier authority.

Congested Districts.

14. The Department operates a general advisory system in the Congested Districts which is supplementary to the County Committee system. This is administered locally by a staff of 111 non-graduate advisory agents each of whom is assigned a number of parishes and is required to live locally. Their advisory activities are very limited: most of their time is spent administering the Congested Districts schemes of the Department. They also conduct some field demonstrations and trials.

15. These are the only general schemes of instruction operated by the Department. The following specialist facilities are also available:—

Dairy Produce.

16. Regular visits, both for inspection and instruction purposes, are made by the Department's inspectors to creameries. Samples are taken, analyses made, and the results communicated to the creamery. Free courses in buttermaking and cheesemaking and bursary assistance towards the creamery managers' course in U.C.C. are provided. In addition, courses are given from time to time in egg-testing, grading and packing.

Cow Testing.

17. The Department's Instructors in Cow Testing inspect and supervise the operation of local cow-testing associations. In addition, these associations are aided by grants, and their local supervisors are granted allowances and attend courses of instruction run by the Department.

Potatoes.

18. A staff of thirty-five, with seasonal assistance, provides general advice on the growth and marketing of potatoes. Their functions, however, are inspectorial rather than advisory.

Veterinary.

19. The veterinary officers of the Department give a number of lectures at local centres on special topics, generally at the instance of the County Committees. Seventy-one such lectures were given in 1956/57.

Research.

20. At U.C.D., agricultural research incidental to teaching is carried out, but limitations of staffing and equipment severely curtail this. Fundamental research is on an extremely limited scale, but specific problems are investigated, with the aid of grants, on behalf of the Department. These grants will amount to some £4,000 in the current year. Research work carried out by the Department is necessarily more specialised and more closely directed towards the solution of particular policy problems. The main centres of research are Backweston and Ballinacurra, for plant breeding and seed propagation, Johnstown Castle for soil testing and general grassland and crop research, Glenamoy for blanket bog research, Abbotstown for veterinary research, the pig progeny testing stations at the Munster Institute and Ballyhaise for pig breeding and some miscellaneous experiments mainly connected with cutaway bog research at Derrybrennan, Co. Offaly. The farms at Clonakilty, Ballyhaise, Athenry, the Munster Institute and Abbotstown are also being used for crop (including grassland) and animal research.

Annual Exchequer Expenditure on Education and Research.

21. Annual expenditure on education and research is difficult to assess: it is not possible, for instance, to put a figure on the amount involved in the teaching of rural science in Vocational Schools. The following table, however, gives an indication of the amounts spent from voted moneys (figures are *net* 1958-59 provisions):—

	£
* Departmental research work	246,000
* Agricultural education	373,000
County Committee grants and Departmental advisory services	324,500
Departmental technical staff	147,000
Congested Districts schemes	139,000
	£1,229,500

* For details see Appendix 7.

This does not show the total expenditure of County Committees of Agriculture—the State grants only represent about half their income. It does, however, include the cost of the Department's technical staff, most of whom are not engaged on either educational or advisory work.

242

APPENDIX 7

State Aid to Agriculture, 1958/59

Note : Voted provisions are those shown in the 1958-59 Estimates volume, *less* any relevant appropriations-in-aid; non-voted provisions represent Departmental estimates at 31 March, 1958.

Department of Agriculture.

	£
Land Project	2,482,000
Butter export subsidy	1,400,000
Bovine tuberculosis eradication scheme	909,000
Wheat subsidy	800,000
Farm buildings and water supplies schemes	714,000
Bacon export subsidy	650,000
Ground limestone subsidy	448,000

Agricultural education :

Agricultural schools ..	161,000	
Private schools ..	109,000	
Veterinary College ..	61,000	
University grants ..	88,000	
Botanic Gardens ..	30,000	
	449,000	
less appropriations-in-aid	76,000	373,000

	£
Grants for pasteurisation plant	300,000*
Grants to county committees of agriculture	287,500

Research :

Backweston	84,000	
Johnstown Castle ..	106,000	
Glenamoy	42,000	
Abbotstown	82,000	
U.C.D.	4,000	
Pig progeny testing ..	10,000	
Miscellaneous	7,000	
	335,000	
less appropriations-in-aid	89,000	246,000

	£
Superphosphate subsidy	200,000
Administration of Acts and Statutory Orders	192,000
Departmental technical staff	147,000
Special agricultural schemes (Congested Districts)	139,000
Improvement of milk production	48,000
Improvement of poultry and egg production	47,000
Departmental advisory services (including Parish Plan) ..	37,000
Improvement of livestock	21,000
Grants to rural organisations	12,000*
Grant to Irish Agricultural Organisation Society	11,000
Grant to Irish Countrywomen's Association	2,600
	£9,466,100

* Expenditure from these grants will be recouped in full from American Grant Counterpart funds.

243

Department of Local Government.

	£
Agricultural Grant	5,620,000
Works under Local Authorities (Works) Act	50,000
	5,670,000

Department of Lands.

Deficiency in Land Bond Fund	720,500
Improvement of Land Commission estates	594,000
Interest and Sinking Fund on Land Bonds issued for bonus to vendors and Costs Fund	117,200
	1,431,700

Office of Public Works.

Arterial drainage (including machinery)	695,000
Capital expenditure on Department of Agriculture land and buildings	84,000
	779,000

Special Employment Schemes Office.

	£	
Minor employment schemes ..	130,000	
Development work on bogs ..	160,000	
Rural improvement schemes ..	200,000	
	490,000	
less appropriations-in-aid	29,000	461,000

Department of the Gaeltacht.

Improvement schemes	90,000

Revenue Commissioners.

Rebate on petrol used for agricultural purposes	40,000
Total:	£17,937,800

Note : Figures in brackets represent total allocations.

	£
Bovine tuberculosis eradication scheme (£423,000)	152,000
Supplementary byre grants (£230,000)	6,000
A.I. scheme in north-west (£40,000)	8,000
Peatland experimental station, Glenamoy (£65,000) ..	25,000
Orchard planting, Dungarvan (£32,500)	4,400
Pig progeny testing station (£80,000)	—
Backweston farm (£181,000)	—
Drainage schemes (£287,000)	57,000
Department of Agriculture schools and farms (£150,000)	5,500
	£257,900

NOTE:
The allocations for bovine tuberculosis eradication and supplementary byre grants are approaching exhaustion; one pig progeny station has been completed; development works at Backweston and other Departmental schools and farms are still in the planning stages.

TOTAL ESTIMATED STATE EXPENDITURE ON AGRICULTURE, 1958/59

	£
Voted and non-voted	17,937,800
National Development Fund	257,900
	£18,195,700

INDUSTRIAL PRODUCTION: GROSS OUTPUT, NET OUTPUT AND AVERAGE NUMBER OF PERSONS ENGAGED IN INDUSTRIES COVERED BY THE CENSUS OF INDUSTRIAL PRODUCTION

	All Industries			Transportable Goods		
	(a)	(b)	(c)	(d)	(e)	(f)
	Gross Output	Net Output	Average numbers engaged	Gross Output	Net Output	Average numbers engaged
Year	£m.	£m.	Thousands	£m.	£m.	Thousands
1926	59·5	23·1	103	50·3	17·1	62
1938	90·0	36·0	167	73·1	25·3	103
1943	110·0	41·6	144	97·9	32·6	99
1945	136·2	48·3	153	120·1	37·8	107
1947	185·3	66·8	186	156·9	49·8	124
1950	285·6	97·5	222	235·5	68·6	144
1954	398·3	129·5	233	331·7	91·9	154
1955	411·2	135·3	235	341·5	97·1	157
1956	n.a.	132 *	227*	n.a.	93 *	152*
1957	n.a.	132 *	220*	n.a.	92 *	149*

* Provisional

NOTE:

Gross Output measures the selling value of all goods produced and covers the cost of materials, wages and salaries, etc.

Net Output represents the gross output less the cost of materials used.

Transportable Goods Industries cover mining, quarrying and turf, and manufacturing industries.

All Industries include transportable goods industries, building and construction, railways, electricity and gas works undertakings, etc.

VOLUME INDICES OF INDUSTRIAL PRODUCTION

BASE 1953 = 100

Year	All Industries and Services covered by Census of Industrial Production	Transportable Goods (Mining, Quarrying and Turf and Manufacturing)
1926	33·6	35·2
1938	54·7	53·6
1943	39·9	44·1
1945	47·5	53·5
1947	62·1	65·2
1950	92·4	91·4
1954	105·0	103·3
1955	107·8	107·5
1956	104·0*	102·0*
1957	104·0*	101·7*

* Provisional

NOTE:

The figures in the above tables are not strictly comparable throughout. Thus the Census of Industrial Production taken in 1926 excluded the Shannon Scheme and the construction of railway vehicles. Such changes of definition would not, however, materially affect the conclusions derived.

	Gross Output	Net Output	Average number engaged	Net Output per person engaged
Transportable Goods	£m.	£m.	Thousands	£
Mining, quarrying and turf production	7·4	5·2	8·7	597
Manufacturing Industries				
—Food	134·2	23·2	34·8	668
—Drink	18·5	10·7	7·9	1,359
—Tobacco	31·5	2·5	2·7	922
—Other manufactures	150·0	55·5	102·5	542
Total Manufacturing Industries	334·1	91·9	147·8	622
Total Transportable Goods Industries	341·5	97·1	156·5	621
Building, Construction and Service-type Industries :—				
Laundry, dyeing and cleaning	2·3	1·7	4·3	398
Building and construction	27·3	13·2	26·7	495
Utilities (gas, water and electricity)	21·0	11·3	12·9	877
Transport	3·0	1·9	4·7	416
Local authorities and government departments	16·1	10·0	30·1	333
Total Building and Services	69·7	38·1	78·5	485
Grand Total	411·2	135·3	235·1	575

Estimated Net Capital Cost of Development Proposals

£ million

Nature of Development	1958-59	1959-60	1960-61	1961-62	1962-63	Total
1. Agriculture						
(a) Credit provided through Agricultural Credit Corporation ...	—	0·50	1·00	1·50	2·00	5·00
(b) Special subsidisation of fertilisers ...	—	1·00	1·00	1·00	1·00	4·00
2. Fisheries						
Additional boats, harbour development, processing establishments, etc. ...	0·10	0·40	0·50	0·60	0·70	2·30
3. Industrial Development (General)						
(a) Industrial Credit Company ...	—	2·00	3·00	4·00	4·50	13·50
(b) Research, efficiency, productivity, technical education, etc. ...	—	0·10	0·20	0·30	0·50	1·10
(c) Extension of activities of various State-sponsored concerns (including mineral development) ...	—	0·10	0·25	0·50	0·75	1·60
4. Irish Steel Holdings, Ltd. ...	—	—	0·50	0·50	0·50	1·50
5. Telephones ...	0·25	0·50	0·50	0·50	0·50	2·25
6. Tourism						
(a) Hotel accommodation and other catering ...	0·05	0·20	0·25	0·35	0·50	1·35
(b) Resort development ...	0·05	0·10	0·10	0·10	0·10	0·45
(c) Port facilties ...	—	0·10	0·15	0·25	0·25	0·75
Totals ...	0·45	5·00	7·45	9·60	11·30	33·80

NOTES

1. The above figures are subject to the qualifications mentioned in Chapter 24, paragraph 41.

2. *Agriculture* :

   (i) *Agricultural Credit Corporation* : In addition, repayments of advances, roughly estimated to amount to £0·70 m. over the five-year period, are expected to be available for reissue.

   (ii) *Fertilisers* : The special Exchequer subsidy of £1 million a year for ten years suggested in Chapter 12 (paragraph 6) is treated as capital above. It is also recommended (in Chapter 12, paragraph 6) that a sum, which is estimated at about £1 million, be made available annually by diversion from the Agricultural Grant and other existing aids and applied to fertilisers. Total additional subsidisation of fertilisers would therefore amount to £2 million annually.

   (iii) *Education, Advisory and Veterinary Services, Research, Marketing, etc.* (*Chapters* 8, 9, 11 *and* 12) : It is assumed that the cost of improving and extending these services as recommended will be met by diversion of moneys from existing aids for other purposes and no additional cost is, therefore, included above.

3. *Industrial Development* : In the estimate for the increased requirements of the Industrial Credit Company it is assumed that the banks and insurance companies will contribute substantial funds in addition to the average of £2 million a year of State aid.

4. *General* : In all cases the figures above cover only *additional* capital costs estimated to arise from the proposals and suggestions made in the study ; they do not include requirements on the basis of existing policies which are estimated in Appendix 5.

248

APPENDIX 10

PUBLIC CAPITAL PROGRAMME 1958-59 TO 1962-63 ON BASIS OF APPENDICES 5 AND 9 COMBINED

£ million

	1958-59	1959-60	1960-61	1961-62	1962-63	Total
1. Building and construction (other than 2 and 3)	14·81	15·22	15·02	13·97	13·07	72·09
2. Ports, harbours and airports	0·89	1·65	1·55	1·60	1·65	7·34
3. Tourism (Hotels, resorts, etc. ; port facilities included at 2)	0·10	0·30	0·35	0·45	0·60	1·80
4. Transport	6·07	1·57	0·83	1·08	1·02	10·57
5. Telephones	1·70	1·95	1·95	1·95	1·95	9·50
6. Agriculture	4·91	6·96	7·65	8·35	6·95	34·82
7. Agricultural Credit	0·25	0·90	1·45	2·10	2·85	7·55
8. Forestry	1·22	1·00	1·00	1·00	1·00	5·22
9. Fisheries (Harbour development included at 2)	0·24	0·40	0·50	0·50	0·55	2·19
10. Fuel and Power	7·00	6·74	6·88	7·16	5·74	33·52
11. Industry	0·65	0·85	1·60	1·90	2·35	7·35
12. Industrial Credit	2·80	2·50	3·50	4·50	5·00	18·30
13. National Development Fund	0·55	0·50	0·46	—	—	1·51
TOTAL CAPITAL INVESTMENT BY PUBLIC AUTHORITIES	41·19	40·54	42·74	44·56	42·73	211·76
Deduct : Capital expected to be provided by public bodies from internal sources	4·29	3·24	3·28	3·84	3·99	18·64
Net amount to be financed from Exchequer and non-Exchequer sources	36·90	37·30	39·46	40·72	38·74	193·12

249